CliffsNotes®

Firefighter Exam

CRAM PLAN™

CliffsNotes®

Firefighter Exam

CRAM PLAN™

Northeast Editing, Inc.

WILEY

John Wiley & Sons, Inc.

About the Authors

Northeast Editing, Inc., has been developing electronic and print products for educational publishers since 1992. Founded by Tracey Vasil Biscontini, the company works with clients to create high-quality, socially sensitive test-preparation and library-reference products, textbooks, teacher guides, and trade books for students of all ages. Located in a former rectory in Jenkins Township, nestled between Wilkes-Barre and Scranton in northeastern Pennsylvania, the company employs 14 full-time editors, several part-time employees, and a large pool of local freelance authors and editors. The staff enjoys a relaxed work environment that feels like a home away from home. When they're not hard at work, the editors and writers at Northeast Editing enjoy breaks in a large backyard and take time to scratch the bellies of the three rescued cats that live at the office.

Authors' Acknowledgments

Northeast Editing would like to extend special thanks to Greg Tubach, our acquisitions editor, and Elizabeth Kuball, our project editor, for their advice and patience during every step of this project.

Editorial

Acquisitions Editor: Greg Tubach

Project Editor: Elizabeth Kuball

Copy Editor: Catherine Schwenk

Technical Editor: Stacy Bell

Composition

Proofreader: Shannon Ramsey

John Wiley & Sons, Inc., Composition Services

Table of Contents

Introduction

The desire to become a firefighter is a calling. Many career firefighters will tell you that they didn't choose their profession—it chose them. Firefighters work around the clock, seven days a week extinguishing fires and assisting in emergencies, often saving lives. These brave individuals frequently face danger from flames, smoke, collapsing buildings, and hazardous materials. Most will tell you, however, that the satisfaction they get from helping people far outweighs the risks of the job.

To stay safe and keep others safe, firefighters must be able to think quickly, make decisions, and maintain their composure in stressful and dangerous situations. They must work well with others, as their lives often depend on their ability to think and act as a team.

Because their job is such an important one, firefighters must meet specific eligibility requirements: They must pass a rigorous written exam and physical ability test; undergo a background check as well as medical and psychological examinations; and participate in an oral interview.

If you're holding this book, you know that a prospective firefighter must be organized and diligent to meet the high standards required for the job. Think of this book as a tool that will help you become a firefighter. This book will prepare you for the written exam in an organized and timely manner, and provide you with additional information about the physical ability test, application requirements, and oral interview.

Firefighter Career Opportunities

If you're thinking about becoming a firefighter, there are a wide range of career opportunities available to you. Once you gain some experience, you'll have many opportunities for advancement. The following will provide you with a brief description of some of the possible career opportunities for a firefighter, which may vary from location to location.

Firefighter

Firefighters are called first responders because they are often first to respond to an emergency. When an alarm sounds, they respond to house and wilderness fires. They also respond to other emergencies, such as traffic accidents and water rescues. Performing their job effectively requires that they master many tasks: they connect hoses to fire hydrants, maneuver ladders, and perform salvage duties and inspections.

Firefighters work both in the public and private sectors, and they can be either paid firefighters or volunteers. Most paid firefighters work in the public sector and respond to the general public. Firefighters in the private sector typically work for large companies that have their own fire departments to respond to emergencies. These companies might deal in hazardous chemicals or oil. They employ only a small group of firefighters who are specially prepared to deal with disasters involving these types of materials. While volunteer firefighters are required to undergo training and demonstrate skills, they are usually not required to take the written exams that firefighters applying for paid positions must take and pass.

When firefighters are not responding to emergencies, they clean and maintain equipment, perform drills, and exercise to stay in peak physical condition.

Firefighter Engineer

Don't confuse a firefighter engineer with the type of engineer who has earned a specialized college degree. A firefighter engineer fights fires and responds to emergencies just as a regular firefighter does, but is often more concerned with equipment and drives the fire truck. A firefighter engineer might inspect fire equipment, including fire hydrants, and oversee fire drills at businesses and schools.

Fire Lieutenant

A fire lieutenant is a step above a firefighter. Fire lieutenants oversee the fire company and may also be responsible for maintaining equipment, such as hoses, as well as hiring, training, and scheduling staff. Fire lieutenants respond to fire alarms just as firefighters do. Fire lieutenants are compensated for their extra responsibilities with a higher salary.

Fire Captain

Fire captains are fairly high up on the firefighting career ladder. While they still fight fires, fire captains are responsible for the entire fire station. A fire captain oversees personnel, inspects fire equipment, such as hoses and ladders, and inspects fire trucks. When responding to a call, the fire captain typically determines the nature of the fire, the condition of the structure, and the source of the water supply. Fire captains also inspect commercial buildings for fire hazards and report such hazards to fire inspectors.

Battalion Chief

The battalion chief is above the fire captain and the third in command within a fire station. The battalion chief reports directly to the assistant fire chief and the fire chief. He or she frequently supervises firefighters at the scene of a fire or emergency. The battalion chief must be an emergency medical technician (EMT), and in larger cities, he or she may be a paramedic. Battalion chiefs are often shift commanders and assist in the preparation of budgets.

Assistant Fire Chief

The assistant fire chief reports directly to and assists the fire chief. The duties of the assistant fire chief include overseeing the staff, maintaining schedules, and creating and overseeing fire-prevention programs within the community. The assistant fire chief oversees all policies and procedures related to the department.

Fire Chief

The fire chief is the head honcho of a fire station. He or she is in command at all emergencies. The fire chief has the final say in disciplinary matters, budgets, and safety policies. Fire chiefs frequently communicate with other fire departments and ensure that local businesses comply with fire regulations. Fire chiefs issue licenses and permits, and compile reports after a fire has been extinguished. Fire chiefs typically work long hours that include nights and weekends. They are paid a high salary to compensate for their hard work, knowledge, and years of experience.

Other Positions

In addition to an assistant fire chief, larger departments might also have a deputy fire chief, who shares some responsibilities with the assistant fire chief. The deputy chief may perform administrative tasks and be in charge of disciplining staff.

Large fire departments might also have one or more fire inspectors. A fire inspector's main duty is to inspect structures to ensure that they meet fire-safety standards. Fire inspectors issue citations to building owners who do not comply with fire-safety regulations.

Becoming a Firefighter

To become a firefighter, you must pass a strict screening process. This process determines whether you are truly qualified for a career in firefighting. The following provides a brief overview of the various steps in the selection process. The order of the steps may vary.

Find an Announcement

Fire departments post an announcement on their website when they have a vacancy. These announcements usually list the exam that applicants must take to be considered for the position. Most applicants for firefighter positions must take a written exam, a physical ability test, undergo a background check as well as medical and psychological evaluations, and participate in an oral interview.

Fill Out an Application

The selection process begins when you fill out an application. Depending on the size and finances of the department you wish to join, applications may be distributed at regular intervals or when new positions become available. Applicants must satisfy a number of important requirements before they can fill out an application:

- Education: A college degree is not usually required to become a firefighter, but you must have a high school diploma or proof that you passed the General Education Development (GED) test.
- Age: Most fire departments require applicants to be at least 18 years old; some departments require applicants to be 21. Fire departments may also have maximum-age requirements for applicants.
- Residency: Most fire departments require you to live in the area in which you're applying. For example, if you're applying for a firefighter position in Philadelphia, you may have to live in Philadelphia. However, don't panic if you don't live in an area where a job is posted. Most fire departments give you six months to move there after you're hired for the job.
- Citizenship: You must be a U.S. citizen.
- Language: You must speak English.
- Driver's license: You must have a valid driver's license and an acceptable driving record.
- Criminal record: You cannot have any felony convictions or dishonorable discharges from the military.
- Vision: You must have natural or corrected 20/20 vision and normal color vision.
- Substance abuse: You cannot have a history of drug or alcohol abuse.

These requirements may vary from department to department. Check with your local department to learn about its specific requirements before you fill out an application.

Pass a Written Exam

Because you're already reading this book, you probably know that you will have to pass a written exam to become a firefighter. The firefighter written exam is a general aptitude test designed to assess your critical-thinking abilities. For more on the written exam, turn to the "About the Written Exam" section of this Introduction.

Pass a Physical Ability Test

Because firefighting can be physically demanding, you will need to pass a physical ability test, which is designed to assess your stamina and overall physical fitness. The various components of the physical ability test demonstrate your muscular strength, flexibility, endurance, and aerobic conditioning. The following describes some of the activities that you may be asked to complete during this test:

- Carry victim (simulated with a dummy)
- Drag hoses
- Complete obstacle course
- Perform stair climbing
- Raise and climb a ladder
- Use firefighting tools to perform actions such as forcible entry and search and rescue

Submit to a Background Investigation

Fire departments routinely research candidates' personal backgrounds to ensure that the information in their applications and personal history statements are accurate. If you reach this stage of the selection process, a detective or other qualified investigator will conduct a thorough background check. The detective will investigate your past by reviewing personal information such as your educational accomplishments, employment history, criminal record, driving record, and military service, if applicable. In many cases, the detective will also interview people who know you, including acquaintances, neighbors, teachers, and co-workers. This investigation helps the department construct a clear picture of your character.

For some departments, you may also be required to take a polygraph or "lie detector" test as a part of this investigation. A qualified polygraph operator will administer the test, asking you a series of basic questions about your background. The results of this test will then be forwarded to investigators and utilized as part of your background investigation. During this test, it is very important to answer all questions truthfully. Don't attempt to cover up any previous indiscretions. Many past mistakes can be easily overlooked but lies cannot. Remember that truthfulness is a key factor throughout the selection process and any dishonesty on your part will only hurt your chances of becoming a firefighter.

Undergo Medical and Psychological Evaluations

Clearly, a firefighter needs to be healthy, both mentally and physically. As part of the selection process, you will have to submit to medical and psychological examinations that evaluate your overall health:

- Medical evaluation: The medical evaluation is designed to both assess your physical health and to determine whether you have any preexisting conditions that may inhibit your ability to perform the duties of a firefighter.

- Psychological evaluation: The psychological evaluation is designed to evaluate your mental health. This assessment helps the department assess your judgment and common sense, qualities that are of vital importance to a firefighter. It can also help to demonstrate any mental health conditions that may affect your ability to work as a firefighter. The psychological evaluation may be performed by a professional psychologist, or it may be given as a written assessment.

The medical and psychological evaluations are critical because, due to the dangers involved in firefighting, it is extremely important that all firefighters are physically and mentally fit. Firefighters with any physical or mental deficiencies may present a danger to themselves and their co-workers.

Undergo an Oral Interview

When a fire department is hiring new firefighters, those candidates who score the highest on the various qualifying exams are often asked to undergo an oral interview in which a panel of reviewers asks the applicant questions about his or her background. The reviewers may ask about information on your application or about anything that was discovered during the background investigation.

About the Written Exam

One of most important steps in becoming a firefighter is passing the firefighter exam. This written exam is specially designed to test your competency in several critical subject areas.

Although the length and time limit of the firefighter exam may vary according to standards set by individual states or departments, most of these exams require candidates to answer approximately 100 multiple-choice questions along with a personality attributes section in about two-and-a-half to three hours.

The following are the basic question types you are likely to find on the firefighter exam.

Verbal Comprehension

Verbal-comprehension questions on the firefighter exam test your ability to understand written language, including individual words as well as sentences and phrases. On the test, you are given descriptions of events and asked questions about them. For example, you might read an incident report about a traffic accident and then answer questions about details in the incident report, such as the make and color of one of the vehicles involved. You are allowed to look back at the passage to find this information. Some firefighter exams refer to these questions as reading-comprehension questions.

Verbal Expression

Verbal-expression questions on the firefighter exam test your knowledge of vocabulary and grammar as well as the way in which words are ordered. One type of verbal-expression question has a sentence with a blank in it. You have to choose the word that correctly fills in the blank. Another type of question has a sentence with five words underlined. You have to choose the underlined word that is spelled incorrectly.

Writing Skills

Writing-skills questions on a firefighter exam ask you to read several sentences and identify the error in each sentence based on rules stated before the question. For example, you might have to determine whether a sentence contains a grammar error, punctuation error, capitalization error, or spelling error.

Problem Sensitivity

To answer problem-sensitivity questions, you have to identify the existence of a problem as well as elements of the problem. You read a short passage, usually containing three or four paragraphs, and then identify what the main problem in the passage is. For example, you might read a passage about a fire that injured several residents of an apartment building. You might be asked a question about which resident suffered the most serious injuries based on the information in the passage. Once again, you can look back at the passage to help you answer the question.

Situational Questions

These questions test your ability to use good judgment and ask you to choose the best action in a given situation. For example, you might have to choose the best action to take if your landlord refuses to comply with housing regulations.

Deductive Reasoning

When you use deductive reasoning, you apply general rules to specific information or a specific situation. You may be asked questions requiring you to use deductive reasoning on the firefighter exam. For example, you might read a list about common tools that firefighters use—this is the general information. You will then answer questions about these tools, such as which you should use in a given situation.

Inductive Reasoning

Inductive reasoning is the opposite of deductive reasoning. To answer questions on the firefighter exam asking you to use inductive reasoning, you are given the situation first—the specific information—and then asked to find a rule that applies to it. These types of questions often include a passage containing several paragraphs or a table or chart. For example, you might read a passage and have to choose the title that is best for the passage.

Information Ordering

Information-ordering questions might ask you to place statements in chronological order. For example, you might be given a list of patient conditions and then be asked to determine the order in which you should treat their injuries.

Mathematical Reasoning

Mathematical-reasoning questions on the firefighter exam ask you to use mathematical operations to solve a problem. You will often be asked to find a relationship between two things—such as the length of a hose and the number of firefighters needed to carry it. Then you choose the choice that makes a correct statement based on this information.

Number Facility

Number-facility questions ask you to use mathematical operations to determine the answer to a question. For example, a question might tell you that the average height of each story in a business office is 15 feet. Then it might ask what size ladder you need to reach the fourth floor.

Mathematical Skills

Some firefighter exams contain mathematical-skills questions. To answer these types of questions, you may have to determine the decimal equivalent of a fraction or how many square feet are in a diagram.

Observation and Memory

Observation-and-memory questions might ask you to observe an image or a diagram for a period of time, such as five minutes. Then you will be asked to turn the page so that you can no longer see the image or diagram and answer questions about it.

Spatial Orientation

Because it's important for firefighters to have a good sense of direction, some exams include spatial-orientation question. You might be asked questions about floor plans and diagrams.

Mechanical Aptitude

Mechanical-aptitude questions are about tools. For example, you might look at several pictures of tools and be asked to determine which tool you should use for forcible entry.

Personality Attributes

Some firefighter exams ask you to complete personality attribute assessments. There is no right or wrong answer to these questions. You will be asked to rate a series of statements using this scale:

1 Strongly agree
2 Agree
3 Neither agree nor disagree

4 Disagree
5 Strongly disagree

For example, you might have to use this scale to evaluate the following statement: "I am the kind of person who remains calm under pressure." It is extremely important to honestly evaluate statements on a personality attribute assessment. Many of these tests have built-in "lie scales" designed to identify candidates who are lying to try to get a good evaluation.

About This Book

As you begin to prepare for the firefighter exam, your first step should be to choose the appropriate cram plan. Depending on how much time you have to study for the exam, you may select the two-month plan, the one-month plan, or the one-week plan. Each plan includes a study schedule for you to follow and describes how much time you'll need to complete each task.

You should get started by taking the Diagnostic Test. Your errors on this test will pinpoint your weaknesses and help you discover the areas that require additional attention. In each chapter you will find practice exercises that will help sharpen your skills in different subject areas. Taking the Practice Test at the end of the book will provide you with an opportunity to preview your possible performance on the firefighter exam.

I. Diagnostic Test

Answer Sheet

Section 1

1 Ⓐ Ⓑ Ⓒ Ⓓ	6 Ⓐ Ⓑ Ⓒ Ⓓ	11 Ⓐ Ⓑ Ⓒ Ⓓ	16 Ⓐ Ⓑ Ⓒ Ⓓ
2 Ⓐ Ⓑ Ⓒ Ⓓ	7 Ⓐ Ⓑ Ⓒ Ⓓ	12 Ⓐ Ⓑ Ⓒ Ⓓ	17 Ⓐ Ⓑ Ⓒ Ⓓ
3 Ⓐ Ⓑ Ⓒ Ⓓ	8 Ⓐ Ⓑ Ⓒ Ⓓ	13 Ⓐ Ⓑ Ⓒ Ⓓ	18 Ⓐ Ⓑ Ⓒ Ⓓ
4 Ⓐ Ⓑ Ⓒ Ⓓ	9 Ⓐ Ⓑ Ⓒ Ⓓ	14 Ⓐ Ⓑ Ⓒ Ⓓ	19 Ⓐ Ⓑ Ⓒ Ⓓ
5 Ⓐ Ⓑ Ⓒ Ⓓ	10 Ⓐ Ⓑ Ⓒ Ⓓ	15 Ⓐ Ⓑ Ⓒ Ⓓ	20 Ⓐ Ⓑ Ⓒ Ⓓ

Section 2

1 Ⓐ Ⓑ Ⓒ Ⓓ	6 Ⓐ Ⓑ Ⓒ Ⓓ	11 Ⓐ Ⓑ Ⓒ Ⓓ	16 Ⓐ Ⓑ Ⓒ Ⓓ
2 Ⓐ Ⓑ Ⓒ Ⓓ	7 Ⓐ Ⓑ Ⓒ Ⓓ	12 Ⓐ Ⓑ Ⓒ Ⓓ	17 Ⓐ Ⓑ Ⓒ Ⓓ
3 Ⓐ Ⓑ Ⓒ Ⓓ	8 Ⓐ Ⓑ Ⓒ Ⓓ	13 Ⓐ Ⓑ Ⓒ Ⓓ	18 Ⓐ Ⓑ Ⓒ Ⓓ
4 Ⓐ Ⓑ Ⓒ Ⓓ	9 Ⓐ Ⓑ Ⓒ Ⓓ	14 Ⓐ Ⓑ Ⓒ Ⓓ	19 Ⓐ Ⓑ Ⓒ Ⓓ
5 Ⓐ Ⓑ Ⓒ Ⓓ	10 Ⓐ Ⓑ Ⓒ Ⓓ	15 Ⓐ Ⓑ Ⓒ Ⓓ	20 Ⓐ Ⓑ Ⓒ Ⓓ

Section 3

1 Ⓐ Ⓑ Ⓒ Ⓓ	6 Ⓐ Ⓑ Ⓒ Ⓓ	11 Ⓐ Ⓑ Ⓒ Ⓓ	16 Ⓐ Ⓑ Ⓒ Ⓓ
2 Ⓐ Ⓑ Ⓒ Ⓓ	7 Ⓐ Ⓑ Ⓒ Ⓓ	12 Ⓐ Ⓑ Ⓒ Ⓓ	17 Ⓐ Ⓑ Ⓒ Ⓓ
3 Ⓐ Ⓑ Ⓒ Ⓓ	8 Ⓐ Ⓑ Ⓒ Ⓓ	13 Ⓐ Ⓑ Ⓒ Ⓓ	18 Ⓐ Ⓑ Ⓒ Ⓓ
4 Ⓐ Ⓑ Ⓒ Ⓓ	9 Ⓐ Ⓑ Ⓒ Ⓓ	14 Ⓐ Ⓑ Ⓒ Ⓓ	19 Ⓐ Ⓑ Ⓒ Ⓓ
5 Ⓐ Ⓑ Ⓒ Ⓓ	10 Ⓐ Ⓑ Ⓒ Ⓓ	15 Ⓐ Ⓑ Ⓒ Ⓓ	20 Ⓐ Ⓑ Ⓒ Ⓓ

Section 4

1 Ⓐ Ⓑ Ⓒ Ⓓ	6 Ⓐ Ⓑ Ⓒ Ⓓ	11 Ⓐ Ⓑ Ⓒ Ⓓ	16 Ⓐ Ⓑ Ⓒ Ⓓ
2 Ⓐ Ⓑ Ⓒ Ⓓ	7 Ⓐ Ⓑ Ⓒ Ⓓ	12 Ⓐ Ⓑ Ⓒ Ⓓ	17 Ⓐ Ⓑ Ⓒ Ⓓ
3 Ⓐ Ⓑ Ⓒ Ⓓ	8 Ⓐ Ⓑ Ⓒ Ⓓ	13 Ⓐ Ⓑ Ⓒ Ⓓ	18 Ⓐ Ⓑ Ⓒ Ⓓ
4 Ⓐ Ⓑ Ⓒ Ⓓ	9 Ⓐ Ⓑ Ⓒ Ⓓ	14 Ⓐ Ⓑ Ⓒ Ⓓ	19 Ⓐ Ⓑ Ⓒ Ⓓ
5 Ⓐ Ⓑ Ⓒ Ⓓ	10 Ⓐ Ⓑ Ⓒ Ⓓ	15 Ⓐ Ⓑ Ⓒ Ⓓ	20 Ⓐ Ⓑ Ⓒ Ⓓ

Section 5

1 Ⓐ Ⓑ Ⓒ Ⓓ	6 Ⓐ Ⓑ Ⓒ Ⓓ	11 Ⓐ Ⓑ Ⓒ Ⓓ	16 Ⓐ Ⓑ Ⓒ Ⓓ
2 Ⓐ Ⓑ Ⓒ Ⓓ	7 Ⓐ Ⓑ Ⓒ Ⓓ	12 Ⓐ Ⓑ Ⓒ Ⓓ	17 Ⓐ Ⓑ Ⓒ Ⓓ
3 Ⓐ Ⓑ Ⓒ Ⓓ	8 Ⓐ Ⓑ Ⓒ Ⓓ	13 Ⓐ Ⓑ Ⓒ Ⓓ	18 Ⓐ Ⓑ Ⓒ Ⓓ
4 Ⓐ Ⓑ Ⓒ Ⓓ	9 Ⓐ Ⓑ Ⓒ Ⓓ	14 Ⓐ Ⓑ Ⓒ Ⓓ	19 Ⓐ Ⓑ Ⓒ Ⓓ
5 Ⓐ Ⓑ Ⓒ Ⓓ	10 Ⓐ Ⓑ Ⓒ Ⓓ	15 Ⓐ Ⓑ Ⓒ Ⓓ	20 Ⓐ Ⓑ Ⓒ Ⓓ

CUT HERE

Section 6

1 Ⓐ Ⓑ Ⓒ Ⓓ	6 Ⓐ Ⓑ Ⓒ Ⓓ	11 Ⓐ Ⓑ Ⓒ Ⓓ	16 Ⓐ Ⓑ Ⓒ Ⓓ
2 Ⓐ Ⓑ Ⓒ Ⓓ	7 Ⓐ Ⓑ Ⓒ Ⓓ	12 Ⓐ Ⓑ Ⓒ Ⓓ	17 Ⓐ Ⓑ Ⓒ Ⓓ
3 Ⓐ Ⓑ Ⓒ Ⓓ	8 Ⓐ Ⓑ Ⓒ Ⓓ	13 Ⓐ Ⓑ Ⓒ Ⓓ	18 Ⓐ Ⓑ Ⓒ Ⓓ
4 Ⓐ Ⓑ Ⓒ Ⓓ	9 Ⓐ Ⓑ Ⓒ Ⓓ	14 Ⓐ Ⓑ Ⓒ Ⓓ	19 Ⓐ Ⓑ Ⓒ Ⓓ
5 Ⓐ Ⓑ Ⓒ Ⓓ	10 Ⓐ Ⓑ Ⓒ Ⓓ	15 Ⓐ Ⓑ Ⓒ Ⓓ	20 Ⓐ Ⓑ Ⓒ Ⓓ

Section 7

1 Ⓐ Ⓑ Ⓒ Ⓓ	6 Ⓐ Ⓑ Ⓒ Ⓓ	11 Ⓐ Ⓑ Ⓒ Ⓓ	16 Ⓐ Ⓑ Ⓒ Ⓓ
2 Ⓐ Ⓑ Ⓒ Ⓓ	7 Ⓐ Ⓑ Ⓒ Ⓓ	12 Ⓐ Ⓑ Ⓒ Ⓓ	17 Ⓐ Ⓑ Ⓒ Ⓓ
3 Ⓐ Ⓑ Ⓒ Ⓓ	8 Ⓐ Ⓑ Ⓒ Ⓓ	13 Ⓐ Ⓑ Ⓒ Ⓓ	18 Ⓐ Ⓑ Ⓒ Ⓓ
4 Ⓐ Ⓑ Ⓒ Ⓓ	9 Ⓐ Ⓑ Ⓒ Ⓓ	14 Ⓐ Ⓑ Ⓒ Ⓓ	19 Ⓐ Ⓑ Ⓒ Ⓓ
5 Ⓐ Ⓑ Ⓒ Ⓓ	10 Ⓐ Ⓑ Ⓒ Ⓓ	15 Ⓐ Ⓑ Ⓒ Ⓓ	20 Ⓐ Ⓑ Ⓒ Ⓓ

Section 8

1 Ⓐ Ⓑ Ⓒ Ⓓ	6 Ⓐ Ⓑ Ⓒ Ⓓ	11 Ⓐ Ⓑ Ⓒ Ⓓ	16 Ⓐ Ⓑ Ⓒ Ⓓ
2 Ⓐ Ⓑ Ⓒ Ⓓ	7 Ⓐ Ⓑ Ⓒ Ⓓ	12 Ⓐ Ⓑ Ⓒ Ⓓ	17 Ⓐ Ⓑ Ⓒ Ⓓ
3 Ⓐ Ⓑ Ⓒ Ⓓ	8 Ⓐ Ⓑ Ⓒ Ⓓ	13 Ⓐ Ⓑ Ⓒ Ⓓ	18 Ⓐ Ⓑ Ⓒ Ⓓ
4 Ⓐ Ⓑ Ⓒ Ⓓ	9 Ⓐ Ⓑ Ⓒ Ⓓ	14 Ⓐ Ⓑ Ⓒ Ⓓ	19 Ⓐ Ⓑ Ⓒ Ⓓ
5 Ⓐ Ⓑ Ⓒ Ⓓ	10 Ⓐ Ⓑ Ⓒ Ⓓ	15 Ⓐ Ⓑ Ⓒ Ⓓ	20 Ⓐ Ⓑ Ⓒ Ⓓ

Section 9

1 Ⓐ Ⓑ Ⓒ Ⓓ	6 Ⓐ Ⓑ Ⓒ Ⓓ	11 Ⓐ Ⓑ Ⓒ Ⓓ	16 Ⓐ Ⓑ Ⓒ Ⓓ
2 Ⓐ Ⓑ Ⓒ Ⓓ	7 Ⓐ Ⓑ Ⓒ Ⓓ	12 Ⓐ Ⓑ Ⓒ Ⓓ	17 Ⓐ Ⓑ Ⓒ Ⓓ
3 Ⓐ Ⓑ Ⓒ Ⓓ	8 Ⓐ Ⓑ Ⓒ Ⓓ	13 Ⓐ Ⓑ Ⓒ Ⓓ	18 Ⓐ Ⓑ Ⓒ Ⓓ
4 Ⓐ Ⓑ Ⓒ Ⓓ	9 Ⓐ Ⓑ Ⓒ Ⓓ	14 Ⓐ Ⓑ Ⓒ Ⓓ	19 Ⓐ Ⓑ Ⓒ Ⓓ
5 Ⓐ Ⓑ Ⓒ Ⓓ	10 Ⓐ Ⓑ Ⓒ Ⓓ	15 Ⓐ Ⓑ Ⓒ Ⓓ	20 Ⓐ Ⓑ Ⓒ Ⓓ

Section 10

1 Ⓐ Ⓑ Ⓒ Ⓓ	6 Ⓐ Ⓑ Ⓒ Ⓓ	11 Ⓐ Ⓑ Ⓒ Ⓓ	16 Ⓐ Ⓑ Ⓒ Ⓓ
2 Ⓐ Ⓑ Ⓒ Ⓓ	7 Ⓐ Ⓑ Ⓒ Ⓓ	12 Ⓐ Ⓑ Ⓒ Ⓓ	17 Ⓐ Ⓑ Ⓒ Ⓓ
3 Ⓐ Ⓑ Ⓒ Ⓓ	8 Ⓐ Ⓑ Ⓒ Ⓓ	13 Ⓐ Ⓑ Ⓒ Ⓓ	18 Ⓐ Ⓑ Ⓒ Ⓓ
4 Ⓐ Ⓑ Ⓒ Ⓓ	9 Ⓐ Ⓑ Ⓒ Ⓓ	14 Ⓐ Ⓑ Ⓒ Ⓓ	19 Ⓐ Ⓑ Ⓒ Ⓓ
5 Ⓐ Ⓑ Ⓒ Ⓓ	10 Ⓐ Ⓑ Ⓒ Ⓓ	15 Ⓐ Ⓑ Ⓒ Ⓓ	20 Ⓐ Ⓑ Ⓒ Ⓓ

CUT HERE

Section 1: Observation

Time: 25 minutes

20 questions

Directions (1–20): Answer the following questions solely on the basis of the information provided.

Questions 1–4 refer to the following figure and passage.

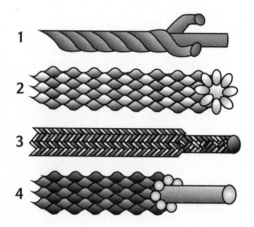

One of the most common tools firefighters use is rope. They may use rope in rescue attempts, rappelling, hauling, and raising and lowering heavy loads. Because certain types of rope are stronger than others, firefighters should know which type of rope would work best for particular tasks. The four most common types of rope are as follows (see the figure for an illustration):

- **Braided ropes** can be made of either natural or synthetic fibers. They're made by intertwining (braiding) strands of rope together. Braided ropes are favored by some firefighters because they will not twist, as laid ropes will. However, because the load-bearing fibers of braided ropes are exposed, they're subjected to abrasion and may be damaged easily.

- **Braid-on-braid** ropes are known as jacketed ropes because both the core and the sheath are braided. The sheath is typically braided using a herringbone pattern. Braid-on-braid ropes are often very strong and can support a large amount of weight because their strength is equally divided between the sheath and the core. Although it's resistant to some abrasion, firefighters may struggle with this rope because the sheath can slide along the inner core.

- **Kernmantle ropes** are another kind of jacketed rope. This rope is similar to braid-on-braid ropes because it's composed of two parts: a braided covering (known as a sheath or mantle) and load-bearing strands (called kerns). The kern is made of high-strength fibers and accounts for almost all of the rope's strength. The mantle covers the kern and provides the kern protection from abrasion. This type of rope is most commonly used as rescue rope.

- **Laid ropes** are made by twisting three types of yarn together. Laid ropes can be tight or lose and can be made from just about any yarn-like material. The type of material used to make the rope depends on how the rope will be used. Of the common ropes, laid rope is the most susceptible to damage and abrasion because at every point, each of the three yarns is exposed to the elements. Although these ropes break easily, firefighters know when a laid rope is damaged because they can see every part of the yarn at all times, making inspection easy.

1. Using information from the passage and figure, you can conclude that Rope 3 is a

   A. laid rope.
   B. braided rope.
   C. kernmantle rope.
   D. braid-on-braid rope.

2. Which two ropes have sheaths that cover their cores?

   A. Rope 1 and Rope 2
   B. Rope 2 and Rope 3
   C. Rope 3 and Rope 4
   D. Rope 2 and Rope 4

3. You're examining the department's ropes for damages when you find a rather loose rope that appears to be fraying. Upon closer inspection, you notice that all three pieces of the rope are worn down. You remove the rope from the wall so your fellow firefighters will not respond to the next emergency with a damaged tool. Which type of rope did you most likely inspect?

   A. laid rope
   B. braided rope
   C. kernmantle rope
   D. braid-on-braid rope

4. What is another name for a laid rope?

   A. abrasive rope
   B. twisted rope
   C. rescue rope
   D. resistant rope

Questions 5–9 refer to the following figure.

5. How many trophies are in the trophy case?

   A. 5
   B. 6
   C. 7
   D. 8

6. Which tripping hazard is located in front of the emergency exit door?

   A. papers
   B. garbage
   C. pencils
   D. trophy

7. The fire alarm is located directly to the

   A. right of the trophy case.
   B. left of the newspaper stand.
   C. right of the garbage can.
   D. left of the emergency exit.

8. If you entered this hallway from the left side of this image, in which order would you pass these items?

   A. trophy case, garbage can, newspaper stand, lockers, fire alarm, emergency exit
   B. garbage can, newspaper stand, trophy case, lockers, emergency exit, fire alarm
   C. lockers, garbage can, newspaper stand, trophy case, fire alarm, emergency exit
   D. newspaper stand, trophy case, lockers, garbage can, emergency exit, fire alarm

9. Which of the following is true regarding this illustration?

   A. The newspaper stand is empty.
   B. Only two of the three lockers on the top row have locks.
   C. There are two plaques, a medal, and four trophies in the trophy case.
   D. The fire extinguisher is obstructed by the garbage can and the newspaper stand.

Questions 10–14 refer to the following figure and passage.

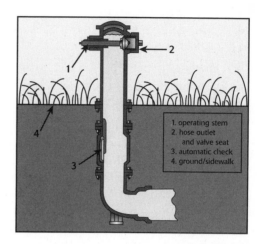

1. operating stem
2. hose outlet and valve seat
3. automatic check
4. ground/sidewalk

Two main types of fire hydrants exist: wet barrel and dry barrel. The figure pictures a wet barrel hydrant. Wet barrel hydrants are those that are filled with water year-round. They don't have main valves or drain holes, and their operating stem runs horizontally through the top of the hydrant, rather than vertically down the barrel. The operating stem is connected to the hydrant's hose outlet and valve seat. You won't find wet barrel hydrants in areas of the country that experience winter months with consistent temperatures of 32°F or lower.

Whether a hydrant is a wet barrel or a dry barrel, its bonnets, barrels, and footpieces are typically made of cast iron. Working parts are made of bronze and valve facings can be made of materials such as rubber or leather. This ensures that the valve facings will not rust if the hydrant is exposed to such conditions. The number of hydrants in a particular area depends on the types of construction and occupancy in the area, as well as the size of the water mains, pumping capacities, and area congestion. Typically, you'll find a hydrant near each street intersection and then spaced 350 to 400 feet apart, depending on the value of the property in the area.

10. Where does water exit a wet barrel hydrant?

 A. 1
 B. 2
 C. 3
 D. 4

11. Of the following areas, where would wet barrel hydrants *least likely* appear?

 A. Honolulu, Hawaii
 B. Dallas, Texas
 C. New York, New York
 D. San Francisco, California

12. According to the passage, what is one difference between a dry barrel hydrant and a wet barrel hydrant?

 A. Wet barrel hydrants have a drain hole and dry barrel hydrants do not.
 B. Dry barrel hydrants have an operating stem that runs vertically down the barrel.
 C. Wet barrel hydrants have to be placed 350 to 400 feet apart and dry barrel hydrants do not.
 D. Dry barrel hydrants have rubber valve facings and wet barrel hydrants have bronze valve facings.

13. In a wet barrel hydrant, you should always expect to find water

 A. below the operating stem.
 B. above ground level.
 C. below ground level.
 D. all of the above

14. All the following predict the number of hydrants in a particular area, EXCEPT the

 A. number of water mains.
 B. types of construction.
 C. climate of the area.
 D. congestion of the area.

Questions 15–17 refer to the following figure and passage.

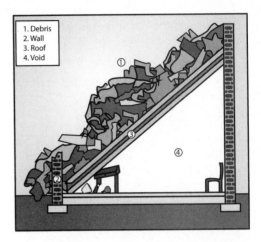

Firefighters understand that most structures collapse in predictable ways. Identifying the type of collapse and understanding what happened to the structure to cause such a collapse helps firefighters know whether victims may be alive under the rubble. The four most common types of structural collapses are cantilever, lean-to, pancake, and *v*-shaped. In the figure, debris gathered on the roof and became too heavy for the roof to support. The collapse created a void between the walls and beneath the roof.

15. What type of structural collapse appears in the figure?

 A. cantilever
 B. lean-to
 C. pancake
 D. *v*-shaped

16. Which part of the figure suffered significant damage and ultimately caused the collapse?

 A. 1
 B. 2
 C. 3
 D. 4

17. If a person was seated on the chair when this structural collapse occurred, firefighters may assume the victim

    A. is alive, not seriously injured, and waiting to be rescued.
    B. is injured, but can dig himself out of the rubble.
    C. has been crushed and needs medical assistance.
    D. has not survived the structural collapse.

Questions 18–20 refer to the following figure.

The arc indicates the path the ladder will travel if it is raised perpendicular to the building.

18. Which of the following may happen if the ladder travels along the indicated path?

    A. The firefighters may drop the ladder and injure themselves.
    B. The utility pole may fall and the neighborhood will lose power.
    C. The firefighters may be able to reach victims trapped on the third floor.
    D. The ladder may hit the power lines and the firefighters may be electrocuted.

19. After examining the details in this image, which of the following is true?

    A. The fire started on the third floor.
    B. The ladder is too short to reach the third floor.
    C. The power lines are not live and are nonthreatening.
    D. The path the ladder will travel if it is raised perpendicular can cause injury.

20. How can firefighters raise the ladder in this image so they can reach the third floor of the building?

    A. Collapse the ladder to 15 feet and then raise it.
    B. Avoid the overhead wires by using a parallel raise.
    C. Request additional assistance by a ladder company truck.
    D. Extend the ladder to 30 feet and pivot toward the building.

IF YOU FINISH BEFORE TIME IS CALLED, CHECK YOUR WORK ON THIS SECTION ONLY. DO NOT WORK ON ANY OTHER SECTION IN THE TEST.

Section 2: Memory

Time: 45 minutes

20 questions

Directions (1–20): Study the information provided for 10 minutes. Then turn the page and answer the questions. Don't look back.

Questions 1–10 refer to the following figure.

1. Where did the fire start?

   A. attic
   B. bedroom
   C. living room
   D. basement

2. How many flowers are in the image?

   A. 4
   B. 5
   C. 6
   D. 7

3. How many portraits are on the walls of the house?

   A. 1
   B. 2
   C. 3
   D. 4

4. Which of the following is true about the fire scene?

   A. The tree grows apples.
   B. The basement door is padlocked.
   C. The bedroom has two closet doors.
   D. A bird's nest is located on the roof of the porch.

5. If the windows on the leeward side of the house were closed, where would the smoke most likely travel first?

   A. up into the attic
   B. out the front door
   C. down to the first floor
   D. out the windward side of the house

6. What is the number of the house?

   A. 1
   B. 3
   C. 13
   D. 33

7. In what direction is the wind blowing?

   A. north
   B. south
   C. east
   D. west

8. How would you describe the weather conditions?

   A. sunny
   B. rainy
   C. snowy
   D. mild

9. How many lamps are in this home?

   A. 1
   B. 2
   C. 3
   D. 4

10. Where is the bird in this image?

    A. on the roof of the porch
    B. in the tree in the backyard
    C. on the windward side of the roof
    D. on the leeward side of the roof

Questions 11–15 refer to the following passage.

In July, firefighters from Department 448 receive a report of a residential fire at 4:37 p.m. The fire is located at a single-family dwelling at 339 Curtis Lane. The firefighters put on their gear and load their equipment in Engine 9 and Engine 11. On the way to the location, Engine 9 gets a flat tire and the driver pulls over to change it.

Engine 11 reaches the scene of the fire at 4:49 p.m. and sees flames shooting from the rear of the structure. Two firefighters lay a supply line from a hydrant located one street over from the fire on Maple Lane, while the remaining six firefighters initiate incident command. It is unclear if any victims are trapped inside. A neighbor tells the firefighters that two middle-aged women live in the home with two dogs and a cat, but she is unsure if they are home. Three firefighters proceed into the burning single-story home and keep in contact with the other firefighters outside the home via radio.

In the meantime, Engine 9 contacts the unit from Engine 11 to tell them they are en route and are four minutes out. The three firefighters emerge from inside the house with the animals in their arms, and report there are no victims inside. They rush back inside to fight the fire, which is contained to the walls of a small sunroom located at the rear of the house.

Engine 9 arrives on scene at 5:01 p.m. and the firefighters on board give some of the firefighters from Engine 11 a break. Two firefighters lay an additional line and begin to attack the fire as a third firefighter goes inside the structure to help the other three firefighters already inside.

By 5:10 p.m. the fire has been extinguished and Engine 9 begins to pack up both engines' equipment, while firefighters from Engine 11 perform salvage duties and investigators determine the cause of the fire to be unknown. Both engines arrive back at the firehouse at 6:45 p.m.

11. What held up Engine 9 from getting to the fire?

    A.   a stuck vehicle
    B.   a train
    C.   a flat tire
    D.   an accident

12. How many victims were trapped in the fire?

    A.   two dogs and a cat
    B.   two middle-aged men, three dogs and two cats
    C.   three cats and a dog
    D.   two middle-aged women, two dogs, and a cat

13. What was the location of the fire?

    A.   645 Maple Lane
    B.   437 Curtis Street
    C.   501 Maple Street
    D.   339 Curtis Lane

14. What time did Engine 9 arrive at the scene of the fire?

    A.   4:49 p.m.
    B.   4:57 p.m.
    C.   5:01 p.m.
    D.   6:45 p.m.

15. What was the cause of the fire?

    A.   an electrical malfunction
    B.   undetermined
    C.   a lit cigarette
    D.   arson

Questions 16–20 refer to the following passage.

A group of firefighter trainees are attending a seminar on hose lays. Veteran firefighter Jim Langley is conducting the seminar. He is teaching the prospective firefighters about the two most important and commonly used hose lay techniques: the forward lay and the reverse lay.

The most commonly used hose lay technique, Langley remarks, is the forward lay. He tells the trainees that, in the forward lay, the hose is laid from the hydrant to the fire scene. According to Langley, when performing a forward lay, the fire engine pulls up to the hydrant and the hydrant person pulls off enough hose to reach from the truck to the hydrant, plus a little extra to surround the hydrant. The end of the hose is then wrapped around the hydrant. Once the hose has been secured, the fire engine can then slowly drive toward the fire scene as the hydrant person ensures that there are no kinks in the line. Langley adds that the forward lay is used when there is sufficient water pressure available from the source.

The main alternative to the forward lay, Langley points out, is the reverse lay. He says that the reverse lay is the exact opposite of the forward lay, meaning that the hose line is laid from the fire scene to the hydrant. Langley explains that a reverse lay is used when the fire engine proceeds directly to the fire scene and all critical equipment is removed because the truck will be removed from the scene. The end of the hose is then attached to a sturdy object and the engine slowly pulls away toward the hydrant. This method, Langley adds, is most useful when the water pressure from the source is not high enough and the engine pump must be used to increase it.

16. Firefighter Langley says that the reverse lay is commonly used when

   A. there is sufficient water pressure available from the source.
   B. no hydrants are located near the scene of the fire.
   C. the water pressure from the source is not high enough.
   D. multiple trucks need to use water from one hydrant.

17. In the forward lay, once the hose is wrapped around the hydrant,

   A. all critical equipment is removed from the truck.
   B. the engine moves from the hydrant to the fire scene.
   C. the hydrant person pulls more hose off the truck.
   D. the hose is connected to the hydrant.

18. According to Langley, all critical equipment is removed from the truck before a reverse lay is performed because

   A. this makes it easier to retrieve items.
   B. the truck needs to be as light as possible.
   C. the truck will be left unattended.
   D. the truck will be removed from the scene.

19. What is the next step in the reverse lay after the equipment is removed?

   A. The truck proceeds to the hydrant.
   B. The hose is removed and wrapped around the hydrant.
   C. The hose is removed and attached to a sturdy object.
   D. The hydrant person ensures that there are no kinks in the line.

20. Langley indicates that the forward lay is only used when

   A. there will only be one hose line used from source to scene.
   B. there is sufficient water pressure available from the source.
   C. there is no working engine pump available.
   D. the scene is too dangerous for a reverse lay to be performed.

IF YOU FINISH BEFORE TIME IS CALLED, CHECK YOUR WORK ON THIS SECTION ONLY. DO NOT WORK ON ANY OTHER SECTION IN THE TEST.

Section 3: Spatial Orientation

Time: 25 minutes

20 questions

Directions (1–20): Answer the following questions solely on the basis of the figure provided. For maps of streets, remember to follow the legal direction of the flow of traffic.

Questions 1–5 refer to the following map.

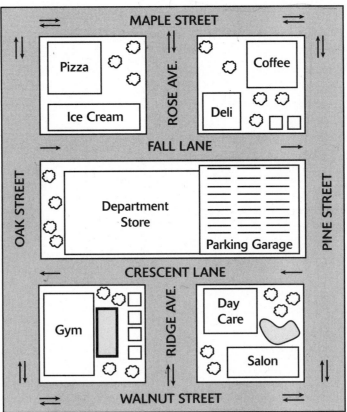

1. Starting at the intersection of Maple and Pine streets, if you are walking and were to travel south, turn right, turn right, turn left, and then make a final left, you would be closest to the

   A. gym.
   B. day care.
   C. deli.
   D. ice cream shop.

2. If you're at the coffee shop, what direction would you travel to get to the gym?

   A. northeast
   B. southwest
   C. northwest
   D. southeast

3. On your break, you head to the pizza place on the corner of Oak and Maple streets. If you parked your car in the parking garage and came out of the garage on Crescent Lane, which of the following routes would get you to the pizza place in the least amount of time?

   A. west on Crescent Lane and north on Oak Street
   B. east on Crescent Lane, north on Pine Street, west on Maple Street
   C. west on Crescent Lane, south on Ridge Avenue, west on Walnut Street, north on Oak Street
   D. east on Crescent Lane, north on Pine Street, west on Fall Lane, and north on Oak Street

4. What is the quickest route to drive from the salon to the deli?

   A. north on Pine Street, west on Fall Lane, north on Rose Avenue
   B. west on Walnut Street, north on Oak Street, east on Fall Lane, north on Rose Avenue
   C. west on Walnut Street, north on Oak Street, east on Maple Street, south on Pine Street, west on Fall Lane, north on Rose Avenue
   D. north on Pine Street, west on Crescent Lane, north on Oak Street, east on Fall Lane, north on Rose Avenue

5. Starting at the intersection of Ridge Avenue and Crescent Lane, if you were walking and were to travel west, turn right, turn right, turn left, and then make a final right, you would be closest to the

   A. salon.
   B. gym.
   C. coffee shop.
   D. department store.

Questions 6–10 refer to the following map.

6. You respond to an activated fire alarm. You ascend the fire stairs and proceed down the hallway, entering the first door on your left. Once inside, you proceed through the first opening on your right. Where are you?

   A. kitchen of Apartment 1
   B. bath of Apartment 2
   C. bedroom 2 of Apartment 1
   D. living room of Apartment 2

7. During a fire, you're sent to search for victims in Apartment 2. At this point, you are standing at the end of the hallway between bedroom 1 and bedroom 2, facing toward the kitchen. Placing your right hand on the wall right next to you, you proceed down the hallway, through the opening, and out the main door of the apartment. How many doors will you touch with your right hand before you reach the main exit?

   A. 1
   B. 2
   C. 3
   D. 4

8. Upon arriving at the scene of a fire, you learn that a fire in Apartment 1 has traveled from the kitchen into the living room, blocking the main entrance to the apartment, and that two victims are in bedroom 2. Which of the following would be the *safest* way to rescue the victims in bedroom 2?

   A. Instruct the victims to leave bedroom 2 and proceed to bedroom 1, where they can access the fire escape.

   B. Instruct the victims to leave bedroom 2 and proceed to the main entrance of the apartment, where they can proceed down the hallway to the fire stairs.

   C. Instruct the victims to come to the window of bedroom 2, where firefighters will conduct a ladder rescue.

   D. Instruct the victims to remain in bedroom 2 and wait for firefighters to extinguish the fire before coming out.

9. A fire in bedroom 1 of Apartment 1 has blocked the fire escape. Which of the following would be the most direct route for a person in bath 1 to exit the apartment?

   A. through the dining room, into the kitchen, and out a kitchen window via a ladder

   B. into the dining room, through the living room, and out the main entrance of apartment 1

   C. into the dining room, through the living room, into bedroom 2, and out the window via a ladder

   D. into the dining room, through the living room toward the office, into the office, and out the window via a ladder

10. During a search-and-rescue operation, you enter Apartment 2 through the main entrance. Placing your left hand on the wall directly to your left, you begin your search. Eventually you come to an opening in the wall and you continue left. You come to a door and proceed inside. At this point you are in the

    A. kitchen.
    B. bath 1.
    C. bedroom 3.
    D. bedroom 2.

Questions 11–15 refer to the following map.

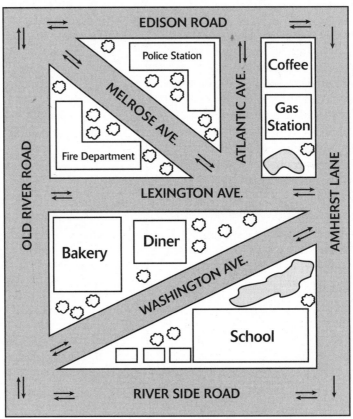

11. Your fire department is giving a presentation at the school when you receive a report of a car accident at the corner of Edison Road and Atlantic Ave. The fire engine is parked facing west on River Side Road. The most direct route for you to get to the accident is

    A. east on River Side Road, north on Amherst Lane, and west on Edison Road.
    B. west on River Side Road, northeast on Washington Ave., west on Lexington Ave., north on Old River Road, southeast on Melrose Ave., and north on Atlantic Ave.
    C. east on River Side Road, north on Amherst Lane, west on Lexington Ave., and north on Atlantic Ave.
    D. west on River Side Road, north on Old River Road, and east on Edison Road.

12. You start out traveling west on Edison Road. You make a left and travel southeast on Melrose Ave. You make a right and travel west on Lexington Ave. You turn left onto Old River Road and stop. Where are you?

    A. bakery
    B. fire department
    C. school
    D. police station

13. You ride with the fire inspector to check hydrants throughout your town. You start out at the northwestern corner of the fire department and travel south on Old River Road. You turn left on Lexington, right onto Amherst, right onto River Side Road, and right onto Washington Ave. What direction are you now traveling?

    A. southeast
    B. southwest
    C. northeast
    D. southwest

14. You decide to pick up coffee for the firefighters on your shift. After leaving the coffee shop, you just start traveling west on Edison Road when you realize that you forgot your wallet at the coffee shop. What is the most direct route to return to the coffee shop, retrieve your wallet, and make it back to the fire department in time for the start of your shift?

    A. Travel southeast on Melrose Ave., east on Lexington Ave., north on Amherst Lane, west on Edison Road, and south on Old River Road.
    B. Travel southeast on Melrose Ave., north on Atlantic Ave., east on Edison Road, south on Amherst Lane, and west on Lexington Ave.
    C. Travel south on Atlantic Ave., northwest on Melrose Ave., east on Edison Road, south on Amherst Lane, west on Lexington Ave., northwest on Melrose Ave., and south on Old River Road.
    D. Travel south on Atlantic Ave., west on Lexington Ave., north on Old River Road, east on Edison Road, south on Amherst Ave., east on River Side Road, and north on Old River Road.

15. If you're at the Gas Station facing south on Amherst and you turn right on Lexington Ave., right on Atlantic Ave., left on Edison Road, and left on Melrose Ave., you'll end up between the

    A. school and the diner.
    B. fire department and the police station.
    C. police station and the coffee shop.
    D. fire department and the bakery.

Questions 16–20 refer to the following floor plan.

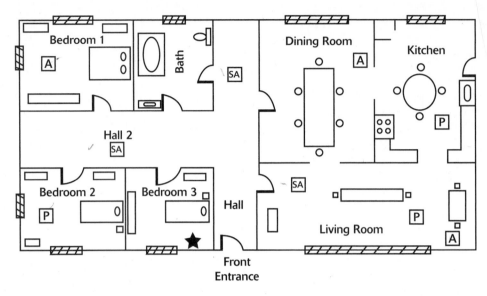

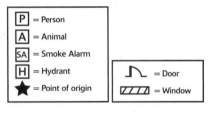

16. Given the point of origin, the fire was most likely caused by

    A. a pan left on the stove.
    B. gas ignited by a discarded cigarette.
    C. an electric fan malfunction.
    D. a candle that set fire to a shower curtain.

17. How many smoke alarms are installed in the house?

    A. 1
    B. 2
    C. 3
    D. 4

18. A firefighter enters through a window at the northwest corner of the house. How many people and animals can be rescued from this room?

    A. 1 person
    B. 1 animal
    C. 1 person and 1 animal
    D. 2 people

19. The person in Bedroom 2 has escaped with the animal in Bedroom 1 through the window in that room. The fire quickly spreads into Hall 1 and blocks the front entrance. Which lives are now most in danger?

    A. the animal in the dining room
    B. the person in the kitchen
    C. the person in the kitchen and the animal in the living room
    D. the person in the living room and the two remaining animals

20. Including both people and animals, how many lives are in danger in the burning house?

    A. 3
    B. 4
    C. 5
    D. 6

IF YOU FINISH BEFORE TIME IS CALLED, CHECK YOUR WORK ON THIS SECTION ONLY. DO NOT WORK ON ANY OTHER SECTION IN THE TEST.

Section 4: Reading Comprehension

Time: 25 minutes

20 questions

Directions (1–20): Answer the following questions solely on the basis of the information provided.

Questions 1–4 refer to the following passage.

Your fire department is dispatched to a reported fire at a private residence located at 43 Sussex Road, Middleton. According to the dispatcher, a witness called 911 and reported seeing heavy smoke emanating from the roof at the rear of his neighbor's home.

You arrive on the scene at 4:02 p.m. Bystander Kevin Peters says he called 911 after noticing the smoke. He also says that the owner of the residence is not at home. From the outside, he could not tell what the source of the fire was. At the rear of the home, thick, black smoke is pouring out of a hole in the roof and flames are now visible.

After extinguishing the flames from the exterior, firefighters enter the home to confirm that there are no victims and to determine the cause of the fire. The pattern of damage inside the home leads firefighters to the attic. Upon entering the attic, firefighters find extensive damage and a sparking wire. The fire is confirmed to be fully extinguished at 4:17 p.m.

Firefighter Richard Franklin spoke to Peters and the homeowner, who arrived on scene a short time later. The homeowner indicated that he had been doing electrical work in his attic the day before and may have made a wiring mistake. With thanks from the homeowner and Mr. Peters, the firefighters left the scene are returned to the station at 4:43 p.m.

1. The witness reported seeing smoke emanating from which part of his neighbor's home?

   A. chimney
   B. windows
   C. roof
   D. basement

2. How many persons were inside the home at the time of the fire?

   A. none
   B. 1
   C. 2
   D. 3

3. At was time was the fire officially extinguished?

   A. 4:02 p.m.
   B. 4:17 p.m.
   C. 4:29 p.m.
   D. 4:43 p.m.

4. Which of the following was the most likely cause of the fire?

   A. kitchen accident
   B. arson
   C. electrical failure
   D. unattended flame

Questions 5–6 refer to the following chart.

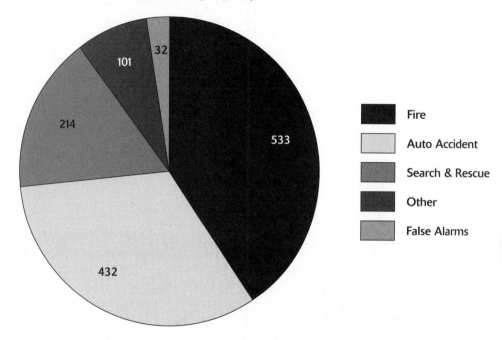

Bridgeville Fire Department 2010 Emergency Response Breakdown

5. Which month had the highest number of reported fires in 2010?

    A. June
    B. July
    C. August
    D. September

6. During which month was the number of reported fires the same in both 2009 and 2010?

    A. December
    B. February
    C. May
    D. November

Questions 7–9 refer to the following passage.

The following fires were reported in the town of Port Griffith. The following descriptions of each fire are based on its determined cause.

- **Kitchen accident (March 23):** A homeowner reported a kitchen fire that resulted from a cooking accident. Bacon grease in a frying pan ignited and the flames quickly spread across the countertop. The kitchen sustained moderate damage before the homeowner was able to locate a fire extinguisher just prior to firefighters' arrival on scene.
- **Arson (March 25):** Witnesses reported a fire in a vacant residence. The home sustained significant damage. Upon inspection, firefighters located a gas can and charred rags scattered throughout the residence. Based on this, the fire was ruled an arson.
- **Negligence (March 30):** A wildfire was reported in a forested area. Witnesses stated that several hikers lit a small fire and then left it unattended. The fire was successfully contained after approximately 45 minutes.
- **Electrical failure (April 2):** A security guard at a department store reported a fire in the store's maintenance room. After arriving on the scene, firefighters extinguished the flames and determined that an electrical component in the room overheated and ignited. The maintenance room sustained heavy damage and the surrounding areas of the store sustained moderate smoke and water damage.

7. How long did it take for firefighters to contain the wildfire?

   A. 30 minutes
   B. 35 minutes
   C. 40 minutes
   D. 45 minutes

8. On which day did firefighters respond to a grease fire?

   A. March 23
   B. March 25
   C. March 30
   D. April 2

9. What evidence led firefighters to believe that the March 25 fire was arson?

   A. a melted electrical component
   B. structural damage
   C. a gas can and rags
   D. eyewitness accounts

Questions 10–12 refer to the following table.

Fire Classifications	
Classification	**Description**
Class A	Involves normal combustible materials like wood, fabric, paper, rubber, solid plastic
Class B	Involves flammable/combustible liquids like oil, grease, gasoline
Class C	Involves active electrical equipment
Class D	Involves combustible metals like sodium, uranium, magnesium
Class K	Involves combustible cooking oils/fats in nonprivate kitchens

10. A house fire sparked by faulty wiring would most likely be classified as

    A. Class A.
    B. Class B.
    C. Class C.
    D. Class D.

11. Which of the following would most likely be considered a Class D fire?

    A. an out-of-control garbage fire
    B. a chemical fire at a laboratory
    C. a grease fire at a cafeteria
    D. a car fire caused by burning oil

12. A restaurant fire caused by spilled peanut oil would most likely be classified as

    A. Class A.
    B. Class B.
    C. Class D.
    D. Class K.

Question 13 refers to the following chart.

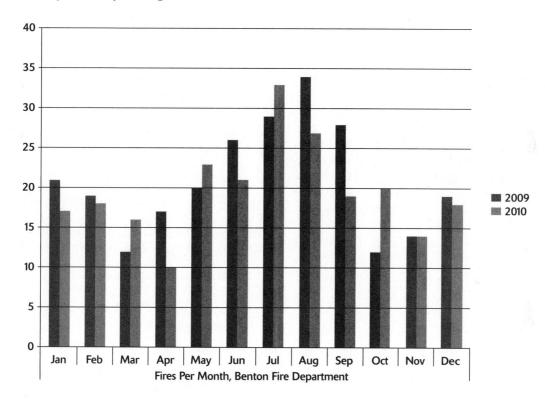

Fires Per Month, Benton Fire Department

13. Based on the chart, in 2010, the Benton Fire Department responded to the fewest number of

    A. fires.
    B. search and rescues.
    C. false alarms.
    D. auto accidents.

Questions 14–17 refer to the following passage.

Your fire department has been dispatched to the scene of a traffic accident on a busy interstate highway. A tractor trailer, driven by Scott Nash, jackknifed on the highway and struck two other vehicles in the process. When the truck lost control, a black 2008 Mercedes Benz, driven by Ana Torres, collided with the side of the tractor trailer. Moments later, a silver 2002 Honda Civic, driven by Benjamin Giordano, was forced off the road into the guardrail where it was pinned by the tractor trailer's cab.

Mr. Nash, who was wearing his seatbelt at the time of the accident, received only minor cuts and scratches and required only minimal medical attention.

Ms. Torres, who was wearing her seatbelt at the time of the accident, was unconscious at the time paramedics arrived on the scene. She had lacerations on her face, torso, and extremities. Her left arm appeared to be broken and she exhibited abnormal breathing sounds.

Mr. Giordano, who was wearing his seatbelt at the time of the accident, was conscious and pinned inside his vehicle. He had numerous lacerations and abrasions. He complained of severe pain in his right leg, though it was not initially visible when paramedics first arrived. Firefighters were forced to extricate Mr. Giordano from his vehicle using the Jaws of Life.

14. According to the passage, Ms. Torres

   A. required minimal medical attention.
   B. was pinned inside her car.
   C. suffered a broken neck.
   D. was found unconscious.

15. Which of the individuals were wearing seatbelts at the time of the accident?

   A. all three
   B. Nash only
   C. Torres and Giordano only
   D. none of them

16. The word *extricate* most nearly means

   A. examine.
   B. remove.
   C. entangle.
   D. transport.

17. Mr. Giordano was driving a

   A. tractor trailer.
   B. Honda Civic.
   C. Mercury Milan.
   D. Mercedes Benz.

Questions 18–20 refer to the following passage.

In the normal course of fighting fires, firefighters use a wide variety of tools, including:

- **Air chisel:** Compressed air device used to cut sheet metal
- **Booster lines:** Mounted rubber hose used for initial attack on fire
- **Chocks:** Wood, metal, or plastic blocks used to hold a door open
- **Life gun:** Fires a projectile attached to a cord to people trapped in burning structures
- **Pike pole:** Steel hooked tool attached to a long pole used for pulling, probing, or dragging

18. Which tool would firefighters be most likely to use first upon arriving on the scene of a fire?

   A. pike pole
   B. chocks
   C. booster line
   D. air chisel

19. Which tool would firefighters be most likely to free an injured victim who is trapped in a car?

    A. pike pole

    B. chocks

    C. life gun

    D. air chisel

20. Chocks would most likely be used to

    A. cut into the side of a car.

    B. secure the entrance to a burning building.

    C. rescue a person in an inaccessible area.

    D. safely pull down a structure in danger of collapse.

IF YOU FINISH BEFORE TIME IS CALLED, CHECK YOUR WORK ON THIS SECTION ONLY. DO NOT WORK ON ANY OTHER SECTION IN THE TEST.

Section 5: Verbal Expression

Time: 25 minutes

20 questions

Directions (1–4): Choose the word that best completes the sentence.

1. Last Wednesday, firefighters _____ 11 people from a burning apartment building.

   A. rescue
   B. rescued
   C. have rescued
   D. will have rescued

2. Firefighter Frank Johnson accidentally left _____ helmet at the station.

   A. our
   B. his
   C. their
   D. its

3. Several firefighters agreed that chemical fires are the _____ type of fire to extinguish.

   A. difficult
   B. difficultest
   C. more difficult
   D. most difficult

4. The rescue team found that the accident victim was trapped _____ her vehicle.

   A. across
   B. among
   C. inside
   D. beyond

Directions (5–6): Select the misspelled word in each sentence.

5. While his partners worked to contain the fire, Firefighter Kelly monitored the water pressure gages on the truck.

   A. contain
   B. monitored
   C. pressure
   D. gages

6. Smoke detectors must be regularly maintained if they are to serve as relliable fire safety devices.

   A. detectors
   B. maintained
   C. relliable
   D. devices

Directions (7–10): Choose the word that best completes the sentence.

7. _____ leadership skills on the scene were impressive; he swiftly took command and coordinated all activities.

   A. His
   B. Him
   C. He
   D. Her

8. The fire squad immediately _____ into action whenever a call comes in.

   A. jump
   B. jumps
   C. jumped
   D. jumping

9. _____ the growing danger, Firefighter Chang entered the burning home to rescue the unconscious occupant.

   A. Despite
   B. Except
   C. Against
   D. Between

10. In a forest fire, containment is the _____ part of the whole firefighting process.

    A. difficult
    B. more difficult
    C. difficulter
    D. most difficult

Directions (11–12): Select the misspelled word in each sentence.

11. Firefighter Morales cautiously assented the ladder to the fourth floor ledge where the trapped child awaited rescue.

    A. cautiously
    B. assented
    C. ledge
    D. awaited

12. Before they can earn certification, prospective firefighters must demonstrate their practical skills and judgement and reasoning abilities.

    A. certification
    B. prospective
    C. judgement
    D. abilities

Directions (13–20): Choose the word that best completes the sentence.

13. The best method for protecting _____ in the event that your clothing catches fire is to stop, drop, and roll.

    A. ourselves
    B. yourself
    C. himself
    D. herself

14. The fire marshal walked _____ the entire building while trying to determine the cause of the fire.

    A. before
    B. toward
    C. through
    D. without

15. In her report, Firefighter Lowell indicated that the squad _____ the fire by 11:38 p.m.

   A. extinguish
   B. extinguishes
   C. had extinguished
   D. have extinguished

16. Fire extinguishers provide a _____ means of putting out a fire before much damage is done.

   A. speedy
   B. speedier
   C. speediest
   D. more speedy

17. The back draft phenomenon can result in _____ explosion that can cause serious injury.

   A. an abrupt
   B. an abrupter
   C. a more abrupt
   D. a most abrupt

18. The captain returned the glove to the firefighter from _____ he borrowed it.

   A. who
   B. whom
   C. what
   D. whose

19. Investigators were able to determine that the fire _____ because of a discarded cigarette.

   A. begins
   B. have begun
   C. had began
   D. began

20. Knowing that water would only worsen a grease fire, Kate threw a moistened towel _____ the flaming pan.

   A. within
   B. underneath
   C. onto
   D. after

IF YOU FINISH BEFORE TIME IS CALLED, CHECK YOUR WORK ON THIS SECTION ONLY. DO NOT WORK ON ANY OTHER SECTION IN THE TEST.

Section 6: Deductive, Inductive, and Logical Reasoning

Time: 25 minutes

20 questions

Directions (1–20): Answer the following questions solely on the basis of the information provided.

Questions 1–4 refer to the following passage.

Firefighters use the following four general methods to extinguish the flames of a fire:

- **Reducing the temperature:** Fires need heat to continue burning, and one of the main ways firefighters extinguish fires is by cooling them with water. To put out a fire by reducing the temperature, firefighters must apply enough water to absorb the heat produced by combustion. Water, however, is generally used only when dealing with ordinary combustibles; it is not used to fight fires involving flammable liquids, energized electrical equipment, or flammable metals.

- **Removing the fuel:** Without fuel, a fire cannot burn. To put out a fire by removing the fuel, firefighters may cut off a fuel supply, or they may remove fuel from a fire's path. Fuel removal is often used to extinguish fires involving flammable liquids.

- **Removing the oxygen:** A fire needs oxygen to burn. By cutting off a fire's supply of oxygen—for example, by smothering the flames with a foam that creates a barrier between the fire and its oxygen supply or by spraying an inert gas such as carbon dioxide on the flames, which displaces the oxygen in the surrounding air, firefighters can stop the combustion process. Foams and carbon dioxide extinguishers are often used on fires involving flammable liquids; carbon dioxide extinguishers may be used on energized electrical equipment, too.

- **Inhibiting the chain reaction:** Combustion requires an ongoing chemical reaction to continue burning. Firefighters can interrupt this chemical reaction by using specialized extinguishing agents, such as dry chemicals, halogenated agents (halons), or dry powder, which interrupt the chain reaction. Specialized dry chemicals may be used on fires involving flammable liquids; halons or dry chemicals may be used on energized electrical equipment; dry powder may be used on flammable metals.

1. A woman is cooking dinner and leaves a pan on the stove while she checks on her toddler in the next room. When she returns, flames are shooting out of the pan. She grabs a lid and drops it onto the pan, and the fire quickly goes out. What firefighting method best describes how the woman extinguished the fire?

   A. reducing the temperature
   B. removing the fuel
   C. removing the oxygen
   D. inhibiting the chain reaction

2. Firefighters respond to a factory for a fire involving magnesium shavings. Which method will firefighters most likely use to extinguish this fire?

   A. reducing the temperature
   B. removing the fuel
   C. removing the oxygen
   D. inhibiting the chain reaction

3. Firefighters respond to a residential fire. Upon their arrival, they discover that a gas stove is the source of the flames. Based on this information, which of the following methods will firefighters least likely use to extinguish the fire?

   A. reducing the temperature
   B. removing the fuel
   C. removing the oxygen
   D. inhibiting the chain reaction

4. A man is watching television when his screen goes black, and he begins to smell smoke. During his investigation, he discovers a bundle of electrical cords that have caught fire. Based on this information, which of the following extinguishing agents would firefighters most likely use to put out the fire?

   A. water
   B. carbon dioxide
   C. foam
   D. dry powder

Questions 5–8 refer to the following passage.

The driver of a motorcycle is traveling at a high rate of speed and runs a stop sign. The driver of a car tries to swerve to miss hitting the motorcycle, but her car clips the motorcycle's back tire. The motorcyclist is thrown from his motorcycle and lands in a nearby field. The woman momentarily loses control of her car and strikes a nearby tree.

Firefighters arrive on the scene and proceed to assess the situation. The driver of the car is a 27-year-old woman who appears pale and is trembling. She has a small laceration where she struck her head on the side window during the accident. She also has a large bruise across her left shoulder and is complaining of pain in her right side, just above where her seatbelt latched. Her passenger, a toddler securely latched in a car seat in the backseat, is crying but appears unharmed. Firefighters help the woman and her child out of the car and send them to the hospital in an ambulance.

The motorcyclist is lying in a grassy field near a large rock. Firefighters suspect that he has a brain injury. His helmet appears to be cracked, and he is unconscious. His left foot is twisted at an awkward angle. His left index finger appears to be broken, and he has numerous scrapes, cuts, and bruises on his arms. Firefighters also determine that he has dislocated his left shoulder. Firefighters dispatch a local air ambulance to transport the motorcyclist to the nearest hospital for evaluation.

5. What symptom of the driver of the car most likely indicates broken ribs?

   A. She appears pale.
   B. She can't stop trembling.
   C. She has pain in her right side.
   D. She has a large bruise across her shoulder.

6. Why do firefighters most likely suspect that the motorcyclist has a brain injury?

   A. He is lying near a large rock.
   B. His motorcycle helmet is cracked.
   C. His shoulder appears to be dislocated.
   D. He is unconscious.

7. The motorcyclist most likely landed

   A. on his back.
   B. on his right side.
   C. on his stomach.
   D. on his left side.

8. An appropriate title for this passage is

   A. "Evaluating Accident Victims."
   B. "The Dangers of Motorcycle Riding."
   C. "Air Ambulance Procedures."
   D. "The Importance of Wearing a Helmet."

Question 9 refers to the following passage.

Wildfires caused by lightning burned more than 2 million acres of land in 2010.

In 2010, human activities caused nine times as many wildfires as lightning.

Wildfires burned more than 3 million acres of land in 2010.

In 2010, wildfires caused by human activities burned more than 1 million acres of land.

9. According to the information provided, which of the following is most accurate?

A.   In 2010, human-caused wildfires were responsible for the destruction of nine times more land than lightning-caused wildfires were.

B.   In 2010, although human activities resulted in more wildfires than lightning did, the wildfires caused by lightning were more destructive.

C.   In 2010, lightning was nine times more likely to cause a wildfire than human activities were.

D.   In 2010, though lightning results in more wildfires than human activities did, the human-caused wildfires were more destructive.

Question 10 refers to the following passage.

Firefighters often use gasoline-powered chain saws to cut wood, such as trees or branches that have fallen during severe weather.

Gasoline-powered ventilation saws are often used when firefighters need to cut an opening in a rooftop to vent trapped smoke and gases from a structure.

Firefighters may opt to use a gasoline-powered rotary saw, or circular saw, for various operations on the fire ground, as the blades for this saw can be changed based on the material that needs to be cut.

The blade of an electrically powered reciprocating saw moves back and forth as it cuts through materials.

10. According to the information provided, which of the following is most accurate?

A.   Firefighters use many different types of gasoline-powered saws.

B.   Power saws are common cutting tools used by firefighters.

C.   Gasoline-powered saws are easier to use than electric saws.

D.   All power saws used by firefighters can complete the same tasks.

Questions 11–13 refer to the following passage.

Many businesses, apartment buildings, hospitals, schools, and even homes utilize automatic sprinkler systems to protect people and property from fire. The most common type of automatic sprinkler system is known as a wet pipe system. Such systems include pipes that run throughout a structure. These pipes are attached to a water supply line that feeds water under pressure to the pipes. During a fire, heat activates the sprinkler heads attached to the pipes. The sprinkler heads spray water in a certain pattern to extinguish the flames.

Sprinkler heads may be attached to the water pipes in various positions. The following are the most common types of sprinklers:

- **Sidewall sprinkler:** Sidewall sprinklers protrude from the side of the water pipe. This type of sprinkler has two deflectors, which cause the water to fan out into the room and spray back toward the wall. Often found in small rooms, sidewall sprinklers are used when a water pipe cannot be located in the ceiling.

- **Pendant sprinkler:** Pendant sprinklers protrude downward from the bottom of the water pipes, which are usually located along the ceiling. They are the most common type of sprinkler. The deflector of a pendant sprinkler looks like a little sunburst. Its shape breaks apart the stream of water, thereby creating a hemispherical spray of water. Some pendant sprinklers are concealed within the ceiling and covered with a decorative cap. In the presence of high heat, their caps fall off, and they drop below ceiling level to dispense water.

■ **Upright sprinkler:** Upright sprinklers, as their name suggests, protrude upward from the top of the water pipes, which are usually located along the ceiling. The deflector of an upright sprinkler looks a bit like a bottle cap. Upon activation, the water sprays upward into the deflector. Like the deflector in a pendant sprinkler, the deflector in an upright sprinkler breaks apart the stream of water into a hemispherical spray of water, which it directs back toward the floor.

■ **Special-purpose sprinkler:** Special-purpose sprinklers are designed for specific uses or for use in specific conditions. Sprinklers with a special coating designed to prevent corrosion are used in corrosive atmospheres, such as those with a high concentration of chemicals, corrosive gases, or salt in the air or those that often experience cool temperatures with high humidity, such as cellars and basements.

11. A new factory is being constructed one block from the ocean. Based on this information, which type of sprinkler would firefighters most likely recommend for use in the factory?

    A. sidewall
    B. pendant
    C. upright
    D. special-purpose

12. During the planning stages for a new college dormitory, builders determine that it will be impossible to place water pipes in the ceilings of the rooms. Based on this information, which type of sprinkler will they most likely install in each dorm room?

    A. sidewall
    B. pendant
    C. upright
    D. special-purpose

13. In April, firefighters inspected the sprinkler systems in an apartment building, a hospital, three schools, and four local businesses. The sprinklers they most often encountered during their inspections were probably

    A. sidewall.
    B. pendant.
    C. upright.
    D. special-purpose.

Questions 14–16 refer to the following passage.

At 1:47 p.m., firefighters were dispatched to a brush fire in the woods behind a rural dwelling. Upon arriving at the scene, firefighters found the homeowner, a 57-year-old man, trying to contain the spread of the flames with a garden hose. A light wind was blowing the smoke from the fire directly into the man's face. The man was coughing and experiencing shortness of breath. Firefighters asked the control center to dispatch paramedics and an ambulance to the residence. In the meantime, they pulled the man away from the fire and set to work containing and extinguishing the fire. When the ambulance arrived, the man told the medics that he had started to develop a headache.

As firefighters doused the flames, they noticed a burn barrel, which still contained some smoldering ashes, at the edge of the man's property line. After the fire was completely extinguished, firefighters asked the man if he knew how the fire had started. The man stated that he had burned some trash in the burn barrel that morning and everything had been fine. Later, however, he smelled smoke, and when he looked out his window, he saw the fire and called 911.

14. Based on his symptoms, the homeowner is most likely suffering from the effects of

    A. a stroke.
    B. a heart attack.
    C. smoke inhalation.
    D. shock.

15. Which of the following most likely caused the brush fire?

    A. The homeowner intentionally set some dried brush on fire.
    B. An ember from the homeowner's burn barrel set some dried brush on fire.
    C. A neighbor set some dried brush on fire while burning trash in a burn barrel.
    D. Dry conditions and a light wind spontaneously ignited the fire.

16. Firefighters most likely called for paramedics and an ambulance because they

    A. wanted medical personnel on standby in case anyone got hurt.
    B. needed additional personnel to help them contain the blaze.
    C. feared that the fire was going to quickly grow out of control.
    D. suspected that the homeowner was in need of medical assistance.

17. Consider the following sequence of numbers:

    1, 4, 7, 10, _____, 16

    Which number correctly completes the sequence?

    A. 11
    B. 12
    C. 13
    D. 15

18. Consider the following series of images:

    Which of the following images correctly completes the series?

    A.

    B.

    C.

    D.

19. Consider the following sequence of numbers:

    1, 7, 19, 43, _____, 187

    Which number correctly completes the sequence?

    A. 68
    B. 73
    C. 84
    D. 91

20. Consider the following series of images:

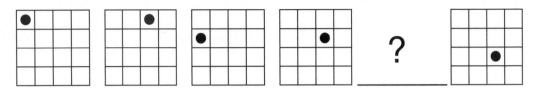

Which of the following images correctly completes the series?

A.

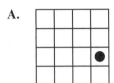

B.

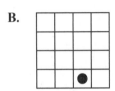

C.

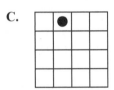

D.

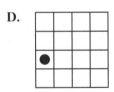

IF YOU FINISH BEFORE TIME IS CALLED, CHECK YOUR WORK ON THIS SECTION ONLY. DO NOT WORK ON ANY OTHER SECTION IN THE TEST.

Section 7: Information Ordering

Time: 25 minutes

20 questions

Directions (1–20): Answer the following questions solely on the basis of the information provided.

Questions 1–4 refer to the following passage.

Firefighters use a number of prying tools during forcible entry operations, but the Halligan bar is especially useful, especially when trying to pry open doors. The Halligan bar has a claw, or fork, on one end. On the opposite end, it has a combination of a blade (also called an adze or a wedge) and a tapered pick. The following are the steps that should be followed when using a Halligan bar to pry open an outward-swinging door using the blade end of the bar, in no particular order. (*Note:* This procedure requires two firefighters.)

■ Firefighter B uses a small sledgehammer to strike the area behind the blade of the Halligan tool to force the blade into the space between the door jamb and the door.

■ Firefighter A positions the blade end of the Halligan bar right above or below the lock. If the door has multiple locks, the blade should be placed between them.

■ Firefighter A pushes down and out on the forked end of the Halligan bar to force the door open.

■ Firefighter A ensures that the blade is wedged securely between the door and the jamb before applying pressure to the forked end of the Halligan bar.

1. What is the logical order of the steps given in the passage?

   A. 2, 1, 4, 3
   B. 1, 2, 3, 4
   C. 4, 3, 1, 2
   D. 3, 4, 2, 1

2. According to the above statements, what step should you perform *after* Firefighter B uses a sledgehammer to force the blade of the Halligan bar into the space between the door jamb and the door?

   A. Position the Halligan bar's blade above or below the lock (or between two locks).
   B. Ensure that the Halligan bar's blade is wedged securely between the door jamb and the door.
   C. Apply pressure to the forked end of the Halligan bar.
   D. Push down and out on the forked end of the Halligan bar to force the door open.

3. Of the steps listed below, which one should be performed *last?*

   A. Firefighter B should force the blade of the Halligan tool between the door jamb and the door by striking behind it with a sledgehammer.
   B. Firefighter A should ensure that the blade of the Halligan tool is wedged securely between the door jamb and the door.
   C. Firefighter A should push down and out on the forked end of the Halligan bar.
   D. Firefighter A should position the blade of the Halligan bar above or below the lock.

4. According to the passage, Firefighter B is involved only in the

    A. first step.
    B. second step.
    C. third step.
    D. fourth step.

Questions 5–8 refer to the following passage.

Firefighters work with many types of ladders in their day-to-day activities, but one of the most common is the wall ladder, which is also known as the single ladder. Working with a simple wall ladder may seem easy, but to ensure their safety, firefighters follow very specific procedures when they raise these, and all other, types of ladders. The following are the steps firefighters follow when raising wall ladders that are more than 14 ft long, in no particular order:

- Using a hand-over-hand motion, raise the ladder until it is standing in a vertical position against the structure.
- Pull the heel end of the ladder toward yourself (away from the structure) until the ladder is at an appropriate angle for climbing.
- Before climbing the ladder, double-check the climbing angle and make sure that the ladder is resting securely both on the ground and against the structure.
- Place the heel end, or feet, of the ladder against the structure to help securely heel the ladder as it is raised.

5. What is the logical order of the steps given in the passage?

    A. 3, 2, 4, 1
    B. 4, 1, 2, 3
    C. 1, 4, 3, 2
    D. 2, 3, 1, 4

6. According to the above statement, which step should you perform *first*?

    A. Raise the ladder until it is positioned vertically against the structure.
    B. Pull the heel end of the ladder toward yourself.
    C. Place the heel end of the ladder against the structure.
    D. Check the climbing angle and the security of the ladder's placement.

7. According to the passage, raising the ladder to a vertical position is part of the

    A. first step.
    B. second step.
    C. third step.
    D. fourth step.

8. Which of the following should be performed during the *last* step?

    A. heeling the ladder against the structure
    B. pulling the heel of the ladder until an appropriate climbing angle is reached
    C. using a hand-over-hand motion to raise the ladder
    D. checking the security of the ladder on the ground and against the structure

Questions 9–12 refer to the following passage.

Firefighters take excellent care of their fire hoses. After all, fire hoses carry the water that firefighters use to extinguish fires. They want them to be in top-notch condition at all times. Depending on their intended purposes, fire hoses can be rolled in a number of different ways. A few common hose rolls are the straight roll, the donut roll, and the twin donut roll.

When preparing fire hoses for storage, firefighters often roll hoses using the straight roll method. Before completing the straight roll, the firefighter should lay the entire length of hose on a clean, dry, flat surface. To complete the straight roll, the firefighter begins at the male hose coupling. He or she rolls the male coupling onto the hose to start the roll and then continues rolling the hose until he or she reaches the female hose coupling. As the firefighter rolls, he or she should try to keep the coils in line with each other. When the roll is complete, the firefighter lays the roll flat on the ground and taps any coils that extend beyond the rest of the roll into place with his or her hands or feet. When the firefighter has finished the straight roll, he or she should place the fire hose in the proper storage area.

9. According to the passage, what is the *first* thing a firefighter should do when conducting a straight roll?

   A. Roll the male coupling onto the hose to start the roll.
   B. Lay the entire length of hose on a clean, dry, flat surface.
   C. Keep the coils of the hose roll in line with each other.
   D. Place the fire hose in the proper storage area.

10. According to the passage, when should the firefighter tap any coils that extend beyond the rest of the roll into place?

   A. directly after laying the length of the hose on a clean, dry, flat surface
   B. right before rolling the male hose coupling onto to the hose
   C. directly after the laying the completed roll flat on the ground
   D. right before reaching the female end of the hose coupling

11. Which of the following correctly summarizes the steps for performing the straight hose roll in order?

   A. Lay the entire hose on a flat, dry surface. Starting at the male end, roll the hose toward the female end. Lay the roll flat on the ground. Tap any protruding coils into place.
   B. Starting at the male end, roll the hose toward the female end. Lay the roll flat on the ground. Lay the entire hose on a flat, dry surface. Tap any protruding coils into place.
   C. Lay the roll flat on the ground. Starting at the male end, roll the hose toward the female end. Tap any protruding coils into place. Lay the entire hose on a flat, dry surface.
   D. Tap any protruding coils into place. Lay the entire hose on a flat, dry surface. Starting at the male end, roll the hose toward the female end. Lay the roll flat on the ground.

12. According to the passage, after the firefighter taps any coils that extend beyond the rest of the roll into place, the firefighter should

   A. lay the entire length of hose on a clean, dry, flat surface.
   B. continue rolling the hose until reaching the female hose coupling.
   C. lay the completed roll flat on the ground.
   D. place the fire hose in the proper storage area.

Questions 13–16 refer to the following passage.

Firefighters at Smithfield Fire Department are trained to treat injuries of various degrees of seriousness upon their arrival at the scene of a motor vehicle accident. Victims in need of cardiopulmonary resuscitation (CPR)—that is, those who are not breathing or for whom no pulse is detected—are treated first. Next, firefighters treat bleeding wounds, such as deep lacerations. They then treat victims suffering from shock, followed by victims with broken bones. Other scrapes and bruises are treated last.

On a particular day, Smithfield firefighters respond to a three-car motor vehicle accident involving five victims. Melanie James is a 27-year-old female with a deep laceration on her forehead that is oozing blood. Her husband, Carl James, is a 29-year-old male with a broken arm. Gerald Thomas is a 65-year-old male who went into cardiac arrest, at which point he lost control of his car and caused the wreck. Janice Floyd is a 38-year-old woman suffering from shock. Her son, Kevin Floyd, is a 13-year-old boy with a large contusion on his right shoulder.

13. Based on the passage, which of the following people should be treated *last*?

   A. Melanie James
   B. Carl James
   C. Gerald Thomas
   D. Kevin Floyd

14. Based on the passage, which of the following people should be treated *right after* Janice Floyd?

   A. Gerald Thomas
   B. Kevin Floyd
   C. Melanie James
   D. Carl James

15. Based on the passage, Melanie James should be treated *directly after*

   A. Gerald Thomas.
   B. Carl James.
   C. Kevin Floyd.
   D. Janice Floyd.

16. The conditions/injuries sustained by the five victims of this accident are listed below, in no particular order. Based on Smithfield Fire Department's protocol, determine the order in which the conditions/injuries should be treated.

   1. large contusion
   2. deep bleeding laceration
   3. cardiac arrest
   4. broken arm
   5. shock

   A. 2, 3, 5, 1, 4
   B. 4, 5, 1, 2, 3
   C. 3, 2, 5, 4, 1
   D. 5, 4, 3, 2, 1

Questions 17–20 refer to the following passage.

Firefighters must often fight fires that begin in the basement of structures such as homes, office buildings, or high-rises. These fires are difficult because firefighters cannot attack the flames until they are close to them, which means they must enter the underground space. Because heat, smoke, and embers rise through open spaces, the staircases leading to the basement of structures typically act as a chimney. The staircases allow the fire and smoke to spread to higher floors and make it difficult for firefighters to descend the stairs into the basement to fight the fire. The following are steps firefighters normally follow to safely fight basement fires:

1. Identify heavy objects that may be positioned above the team when they are attacking the fire in the basement. Remove, if possible.

2. Search for a point on the ground floor where ventilation can occur. This spot should be far away from the stairs firefighters will use to enter the basement.

3. Properly ventilate the basement by cutting holes in the ground floor and setting up fans, if available.

4. Adjust the nozzle of the hose to shoot a wide fog pattern.

5. Descend the stairs.

   Note: At any time, additional teams may choose to ventilate the higher floors and attics when a basement fire is occurring. Oftentimes, heat and fire gases travel through the building and accumulate in these areas. Flashover may occur if the area is not vented.

17. When should firefighters ventilate the basement via the ground floor?

    A. Before a team descends the basement stairs

    B. After spraying the basement using a wide fog pattern

    C. Before locating an area to cut away from the basement stairs

    D. Before identifying and removing heavy objects above the fire

18. If firefighters wish to prevent flashover fires, what must they do when they arrive on the scene?

    A. Ventilate higher floors and attics

    B. Remove heavy objects from the higher floors

    C. Attack the flames in the basement immediately

    D. Adjust their nozzles so they can use a wide fog pattern

19. Firefighter Andrews is part of a team that responds to a structural fire. When the team arrives on the scene, they learn that the fire began in the basement and the entire house is filled with thick smoke. Andrews and his team enter the building, locate the basement stairs and the position of the flames below, and then move filing cabinets and a large couch to the other side of the room. They then split into two teams: one descends the basement stairs, the other moves to the attic to ventilate via the roof. Which step did Andrews and his crew forget to complete before parting ways?

    A. Identify the fire's location

    B. Determine the possibility for flashover

    C. Ventilate the basement via the ground floor

    D. Remove the furniture from the house entirely

20. According to information provided in the passage, which of the following is true?

    A. Flashover is possible only when flames begin in the basement.

    B. Closing the door at the top of the stairs will prevent the spread of smoke and embers.

    C. Ventilation should always occur directly above the bottom of the basement stairs.

    D. Firefighters move or remove heavy objects so they don't fall through weakened floorboards.

IF YOU FINISH BEFORE TIME IS CALLED, CHECK YOUR WORK ON THIS SECTION ONLY. DO NOT WORK ON ANY OTHER SECTION IN THE TEST.

Section 8: Problem Sensitivity

Time: 25 minutes

20 questions

Directions (1–20): Answer the following questions solely on the basis of the information provided

---

Questions 1–3 refer to the following passage.

Personnel from your fire department were dispatched to the scene of a three-car motor vehicle accident. Several individuals involved in the accident were injured. According to the testimony of those involved and eyewitness reports, a white 2003 Ford Mustang, driven by Anthony Murray, ignored a red traffic light and was struck by a red 2007 Dodge Ram, driven by Gerald Hines, as it passed through the intersection. Subsequently, the Dodge Ram was rear-ended by a silver 2001 Volkswagen Passat, driven by Danielle Wallace.

Mr. Murray, who was driving alone and not wearing a seatbelt at the time of the accident, complained of severe pain in his left shoulder and leg. His shoulder appeared slightly deformed. He had a laceration on the left side of his head that was bleeding profusely. Though he appeared to be aware of his surroundings, Mr. Murray showed some signs of disorientation and occasionally exhibited garbled, incoherent speech.

Mr. Hines, who was wearing his seatbelt at the time of the accident, complained of persistent neck pain. He suffered numerous cuts and bruises. He also suffered some minor facial lacerations as a result of his impact with his airbag, the force of which broke his glasses. He was traveling with a single passenger, his wife, Roberta Hines. She suffered only minor injuries and had no specific complaints.

Ms. Wallace, who was wearing her seatbelt at the time of the accident, was traveling with her three children: Matthew, Rebecca, and Michael Wallace. Ms. Wallace had a severe laceration on her forehead that was bleeding profusely. She also complained of lower chest pain on the right side that increased when she attempted to breathe. The area appeared tender and sensitive. Matthew Wallace, seated in the front passenger seat and not wearing a seatbelt, suffered numerous cuts and bruises and severe right arm pain. He appeared to be holding the appendage at an unnatural angle. Rebecca and Michael Wallace, both seated in the rear of the vehicle with their seatbelts on, were uninjured.

1. Based on the information in the passage, which of the following individuals would appear to be the *most* seriously injured?

   A. Danielle Wallace
   B. Anthony Murray
   C. Matthew Wallace
   D. Gerald Hines

2. Based on the information in the passage, which of the following individuals would appear to be the *least* seriously injured?

   A. Gerald Hines
   B. Danielle Wallace
   C. Matthew Wallace
   D. Roberta Hines

3. Based on the information in the passage, which of the occupants of the 2001 Volkswagen Passat was the *most* seriously injured?

   A. Rebecca Wallace
   B. Matthew Wallace
   C. Danielle Wallace
   D. Michael Wallace

Question 4 refers to the following passage.

Firefighter Richards has been observing the behavior of Firefighter Murphy, who has been one of the fire department's most reliable and well-liked members for the past 10 years. Previously, Firefighter Murphy had always been easygoing and relaxed, but over the last few months, he has appeared to become increasingly stressed and distant. He has been working an unusually high number of shifts, seemingly taking every available shift he can get. He has also been eating only whatever he can find around the firehouse and no longer orders out with his fellow firefighters. He has seemed exceedingly burnt-out and tired, but refuses to acknowledge his condition and continues to sign himself up for additional shifts.

4. Based on the information in the passage, if Murphy were having a problem, it would most likely be

A. financial.
B. health related.
C. alcohol.
D. family related.

Question 5 refers to the following passage.

Firefighter Rodriguez has been observing the behavior of Firefighter Willis, who has been working for the fire department for the last 25 years. Over the years, Willis earned a reputation for being one of the station's most capable and athletic firefighters. In recent months, Willis has not seemed himself, however. He seems to be a little slower on scene than he used to be and has started to become fatigued more easily. Rodriguez has also noted that Willis often appears frustrated with his performance and has become increasingly dependent on others to assist him with tasks he once easily completed on his own. When asked about the issue, Willis denies anything is wrong, but his behavior indicates that something is upsetting him.

5. Based on the information in the passage, if Willis were having a problem, it would most likely be

A. marital.
B. job stress.
C. drug related.
D. health related.

6. Your fire department receives all of the following notifications in one day. Of these notifications, which should be considered the *most* urgent?

A. an EMS call involving a motorcyclist who may have suffered a broken leg
B. a report of a house fire in a suburban residential area
C. a request to conduct a fire drill at a local elementary school
D. a call about a brush fire in a rural field

Question 7 refers to the following passage.

Firefighter Weathers has been observing the behavior of Firefighter Valenti, who is a rookie firefighter still in his first year with the fire department. When Valenti first joined the department, he was enthusiastic and anxious to prove himself in the field. Over the eight months he has now been a part of the team, Valenti has become noticeably less enthusiastic about his job. He seems nervous and uncomfortable, especially when on the scene of a call. At the station, he seems depressed and edgy. Although polite, he does not seem to enjoy socializing with his co-workers, appearing introverted and preferring to be alone.

7. Based on the information in the passage, if Valenti were having a problem, it would most likely be

A. health related.
B. drugs or alcohol.
C. work-related stress.
D. marital.

Questions 8–10 refer to the following passage.

Personnel from your fire department were dispatched to a traffic accident involving two cars and a motorcycle. According to eyewitness accounts, a 2004 Hyundai Sonata, driven by Marisol Hernandez, attempted to merge into the passing lane of a highway and collided with a 2006 Pontiac Grand Prix, driven by Joseph Davidson. The force of the impact caused both drivers to spin out of control. Subsequent to this, a 2010 Honda Interceptor motorcycle traveling at high speeds and driven by Jeffery Burke struck the driver's door of Mr. Davidson's vehicle, which had come to rest in the middle of the roadway. Ms. Hernandez's vehicle, meanwhile, struck the guardrail head-on and was resting on the shoulder.

Ms. Hernandez, who had been wearing her seatbelt at the time of the accident, suffered numerous cuts and bruises and complained of severe pain in her right shoulder and clavicle. She was very distraught and seemed extremely shaken.

Mr. Davidson, who had been wearing his seatbelt at the time of the accident, had sustained a number of serious soft-tissue wounds and complained of severe pain in his left side from his hip to his ankle. His left arm also appeared to be broken. Due to the extensive damage to his car, rescuers were forced to remove the driver's door so as to safely extract the patient. There were also three other passengers in this vehicle. Davidson's wife Cynthia, seated in the front passenger seat, sustained several lacerations and complained of neck pain. His son Peter, who was seated in the rear driver's side seat, also suffered lacerations. His daughter Samantha, who was seated in the rear passenger's side seat and was not wearing her seatbelt, suffered a broken right arm from having been thrown into the back of the seat in front of her.

Mr. Burke was ejected from his motorcycle and landed on the ground on the other side of the Grand Prix. When paramedics arrived on the scene, Burke was unconscious. His helmet was broken and blood was flowing from underneath it. His right arm and shoulder appeared to be situated at an unnatural angle and a severe avulsion was found on his right leg, which also appeared to be broken. The patient was largely unresponsive and exhibited notably diminished vital signs.

8. Based on the information in the passage, which of the following individuals would appear to be the *most* seriously injured?

   A. Joseph Davidson
   B. Marisol Hernandez
   C. Cynthia Davidson
   D. Jeffery Burke

9. Based on the information in the passage, which of the following individuals would appear to be the *least* seriously injured?

   A. Marisol Hernandez
   B. Joseph Davidson
   C. Peter Davidson
   D. Jeffery Burke

10. Based on the information in the passage, which of the occupants of the Davidson's vehicle was the *most* seriously injured?

    A. Joseph Davidson
    B. Samantha Davidson
    C. Cynthia Davidson
    D. Peter Davidson

Question 11 refers to the following passage.

Firefighter Danielson has been observing the behavior of Firefighter Jackson, who has been working with the fire department for the last seven years. Two months ago, Jackson had knee surgery and was off on medical leave for two weeks. After his return, Jackson's behavior became increasingly erratic. He has become shaky and tense both in the field and at the station. He has been experiencing frequent bouts of paranoia, often easily losing his temper with his co-workers. He also looks worn out and tired, though he claims it's just because he hasn't gotten enough sleep lately. Danielson has also noticed that Jackson has been taking some sort of medication at least several times a day.

11. Based on the information in the passage, if Jackson were having a problem, it would most likely be related to

    A.   job stress.
    B.   drugs.
    C.   family.
    D.   finances.

Question 12 refers to the following passage.

Firefighter Hughes has been observing the behavior of Firefighter Roberts, who has been working with the fire department for more than 10 years. In recent months, Roberts has displayed some questionable behavior that has been disturbing to some of his co-workers. On multiple occasions, Roberts has shown up for work disheveled and disoriented. He is often irascible and hostile toward the other firefighters, berating them if they ask about his personal life. In addition, he has progressively gotten more and more out of shape and tends to struggle to work efficiently. Hughes has also noticed that, after finishing his shifts, Roberts frequently heads straight to a nearby pub down the street and doesn't emerge for hours.

12. Based on the information in the passage, if Roberts were having a problem, it would most likely be related to

    A.   health issues.
    B.   alcohol issues.
    C.   marital issues.
    D.   drug issues.

13. Your fire department receives all of the following notifications in one day. Of these notifications, which should be considered the *most* urgent?

    A.   a report of an overheated car that has caught fire
    B.   an EMS call regarding an elderly fall victim with a broken hip
    C.   a call to rescue a pet cat that is stuck in a tree
    D.   a request to check the smoke detectors at a nursing home

Question 14 refers to the following passage.

Firefighter Ling has been observing the behavior of Firefighter Kaufman, who has been working with the fire department for the last 15 years. For a few months now, Kaufman has been exhibiting severe mood swings, often ranging from depression and withdrawal to anger and disdain. During most shifts, he speaks endlessly about his wife, telling anyone who will listen how he happens to feel about her at the moment. A number of times, Ling has overheard Kaufman talking to his wife on the phone and having loud, angry arguments. Lately, Kaufman has, from time to time, been sleeping at the station instead of going home at night.

14. Based on the information in the passage, if Kaufman were having a problem, it would most likely be

    A.   job stress.
    B.   health related.
    C.   drugs.
    D.   marital.

Questions 15–17 refer to the following passage.

Personnel from your fire department responded to a traffic accident involving four separate vehicles. The driver of the first vehicle, Harold Reed, reported that he dozed off at the wheel and accidently swerved his 2001 Ford Focus into oncoming traffic. Reed's car struck a 1993 Chrysler LeBaron driven by Jennifer Collins. The impact of this collision caused the Focus to swing back into its original lane, at which point it was broadsided by a 2005 Nissan Maxima driven by Lawrence Jones. Simultaneously, the LeBaron was rear-ended by a vehicle that had been traveling behind it, a 1998 Toyota Camry, driven by Martin Kowalski.

Mr. Reed, who was traveling with his wife, sustained extensive soft-tissue damage and complained of severe pain in his right knee, which he said had struck the dashboard during the impact. It appeared swollen and inflamed. He also had a deep cut above his right eyebrow that was bleeding profusely. His wife Susan, who had been sitting in the front passenger seat, also suffered numerous cuts and bruises and complained of neck pain. Both had been wearing their seatbelts.

Ms. Collins, who had not been wearing her seatbelt, was ejected from her seat and found on the hood of her car. When paramedics arrived, she was unconscious and bleeding heavily from a wound in her head. Her cranial features appeared distorted and her neck was positioned at an unnatural angle. Two passengers were also found inside the vehicle. Maxine Samuels, who had been seated in the front passenger seat with her seatbelt fastened, suffered a number of severe cuts and was bleeding profusely. She also complained of severe abdominal pain. Visual examination revealed distention and discoloration. A passenger in the rear of the car, Michelle Spencer, was found lying on the floor of the car. She was disoriented and did not have any complaints.

Lawrence Jones and his son Rodger, who had both been wearing their seat belts, were standing outside their car when paramedics arrived. Lawrence had sustained a head wound and complained of mild dizziness. Rodger was holding his left wrist, which he said had been struck by his airbag.

Mr. Kowalski, who had been traveling alone with his seatbelt on, was found disoriented and coughing up blood. He complained of severe chest pain, though he did not present with any other signs of cardiac distress. He was also having difficulty breathing.

15. Based on the information in the passage, which of the drivers would appear to be *most* in need of immediate medical attention?

   A. Martin Kowalski
   B. Harold Reed
   C. Jennifer Collins
   D. Lawrence Jones

16. Based on the information in the passage, which of the drivers would appear to be the *least* in need of immediate medical attention?

   A. Martin Kowalski
   B. Harold Reed
   C. Jennifer Collins
   D. Lawrence Jones

17. Based on the information in the passage, which of the following passengers was the *most* seriously injured?

   A. Maxine Samuels
   B. Rodger Jones
   C. Susan Reed
   D. Michelle Spencer

18. Your fire department receives all of the following notifications in one day. Of these notifications, which should be considered the *most* urgent?

    A. an EMS call regarding a single car accident
    B. a request to participate in a local parade
    C. a dispatch to a tenth-floor fire at an office building
    D. a call regarding a residential kitchen fire

Question 19 refers to the following passage.

Firefighter Paulson has been observing the behavior of Firefighter Dawson, who has been working with the fire department for five years. A few weeks ago, Dawson confided in Paulson that she had recently started dating a new boyfriend and was very excited about him. Since that time, the normally outgoing and cheerful Dawson has become noticeably quieter and more timid. A few days ago, she showed up to work with a black eye and a large bruise on the side of her face. When Paulson asked her what happened, she simply blurted out that she had accidentally fallen at home and then quickly tried to change the subject.

19. Based on the information in the passage, if Dawson were having a problem, it would most likely be

    A. drugs.
    B. domestic violence.
    C. job stress.
    D. health related.

Question 20 refers to the following passage.

Firefighter Nichols has been observing the behavior of Firefighter Mitchell, who has been working with the fire department for three years. During his first two years with the department, Mitchell was an energetic, hardworking young man who got along very well with his co-workers and was a valuable member of the team. Over the last year, however, his behavior has become erratic and his job performance has been inconsistent at best. He frequently appears jittery and on edge. He has also been losing weight, becoming thinner and frailer at an alarming rate. His relationship with the other firefighters has become strained and marked with numerous angry outbursts. He habitually shows up late. Two days ago, Nichols saw a small bag that looked as though it contained white powder fall out of Mitchell's lockers as he was gathering his things.

20. Based on the information in the passage, if Mitchell were having a problem, it would most likely be

    A. health related.
    B. drugs.
    C. domestic violence.
    D. financial.

IF YOU FINISH BEFORE TIME IS CALLED, CHECK YOUR WORK ON THIS SECTION ONLY. DO NOT WORK ON ANY OTHER SECTION IN THE TEST.

Section 9: Mathematics

Time: 25 minutes

20 questions

Directions (1–20): Select the best answer for each question.

1. You are sent abroad to attend a training camp with four fellow firefighters. You've been told the average temperature at your destination is 42.5°C. What is the temperature in degrees Fahrenheit (°F)?

   A. 78
   B. 83.5
   C. 98
   D. 108.5

2. $0.998 + 4.223 + 6.50 \div 0.25 = ?$ Round to the nearest tenth.

   A. 9.9
   B. 16.5
   C. 31.2
   D. 42.3

Question 3 refers to the following figure.

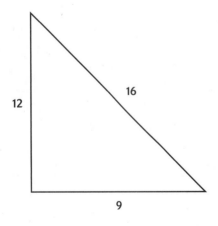

3. Find the perimeter of the triangle.

   A. 16
   B. 25
   C. 37
   D. 42

4. $\dfrac{14}{5} + \dfrac{21}{4} - \dfrac{6}{2} + \dfrac{9}{10} =$

   A. 5.95
   B. 7.78
   C. 8.36
   D. 11.26

5. $(4x + 9)(3x - 6) =$

   A. $12x^2 + 3x - 54$
   B. $7x^2 + 51x - 54$
   C. $-12x^2 + 51x - 54$
   D. $-7x^2 + 3x + 54$

6. $(x^{15})(4x^{15}) =$

   A. $4x$
   B. $4x225$
   C. $4x^{-1}$
   D. $4x^{30}$

7. Your fire department responds to an activated fire alarm at an apartment building that is 7.5 miles from the station. If the fire department arrives at the apartment building in 9 minutes, what was the average speed the fire engine traveled on the way to the location of the fire?

   A. 50 miles per hour
   B. 55 miles per hour
   C. 60 miles per hour
   D. 75 miles per hour

8. Each year, firefighters at your local department receive a holiday bonus. Firefighters who have been with the company less than 5 years typically receive a bonus that is 2 percent of their yearly salary. Firefighters who have been with the company for 5 to 10 years receive a bonus that is 3 percent of their salary. Firefighters who have dedicated 10 to 15 years with the same company receive a bonus that is 4 percent of their yearly salary. Based on this information, if the trend continues, what percentage of their yearly salary would firefighters with 25 to 30 years of experience with the same company receive as their holiday bonus?

   A. 5.0 percent
   B. 5.5 percent
   C. 6.5 percent
   D. 7.0 percent

9. $649.99 – $29.77 + $8.35 × $56.23 =

   A. $989.62
   B. $1,089.74
   C. $1,258.92
   D. $1,649.03

Question 10 refers to the following figure.

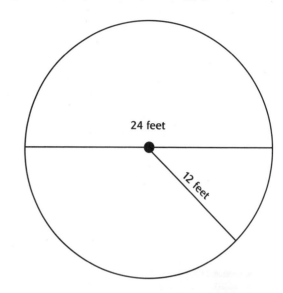

10. Find the circumference of the circle. *Remember:* π = 3.14.

    A. 55 ft
    B. 75 ft
    C. 120 ft
    D. 150 ft

11. $\frac{2}{3} \times 0.78 + 4\frac{1}{4} - \frac{6}{8} =$

    A. 0.26
    B. 1.98
    C. 4.02
    D. 6.25

12. Simplify: $\frac{1}{8^{-4}}$

    A. $-\frac{1}{8}$
    B. $\frac{1^4}{8}$
    C. −4,096
    D. 4,096

13. Solve for x: $\dfrac{9x+3}{3} = 37$

 A. 9
 B. 12
 C. 18
 D. 24

14. What is 42 percent of 575?

 A. 0.241
 B. 2.415
 C. 41.25
 D. 241.5

15. A firefighter must climb 12 flights of stairs during a fitness test. Each flight of stairs has 9 steps. How many total steps must the firefighter climb during the fitness test?

 A. 99
 B. 108
 C. 113
 D. 122

16. If you can complete 12 training exercises in 5 days, how many training exercises can you complete in 7 days? Round to the nearest whole number.

 A. 14
 B. 17
 C. 19
 D. 22

17. Solve for x: $16x + 11 = 9(9 - 14)$

 A. −3.5
 B. −1.6
 C. 4.6
 D. 7.8

18. If a fire extinguisher costs $49.99 and is on sale for 38 percent off, how much would it cost on sale?

 A. $19.00
 B. $25.99
 C. $30.99
 D. $40.00

19. If Sergeant Alexander can run 5.5 miles in 30 minutes, how many miles can he run in 18 minutes?

 A. 1.8
 B. 2.5
 C. 3.3
 D. 4.0

Question 20 refers to the following table.

Yearly Cost of Equipment		
Quarter	Months	Cost of Equipment
1	January–March	$7,550.63
2	April–June	$562.99
3	July–September	$225.00
4	October–December	$4,761.02

20. Based on the information provided in the table, how much more did the fire department spend in the first two quarters than in the last two quarters?

 A. $3,127.60
 B. $3,352.00
 C. $3,690.59
 D. $4,138.02

IF YOU FINISH BEFORE TIME IS CALLED, CHECK YOUR WORK ON THIS SECTION ONLY. DO NOT WORK ON ANY OTHER SECTION IN THE TEST.

Section 10: Mechanical Aptitude

Time: 25 minutes
20 questions

Directions (1–20): Answer the following questions solely on the basis of the information provided.

Question 1 refers to the following figure.

1. The image shows three gears of different sizes. If Gear B rotates in a clockwise direction, which other gear(s) will rotate in the same direction?

   A. Gear C only
   B. Gear A only
   C. Gears A and C
   D. none of the gears

Question 2 refers to the following figure.

2. Which gear will make the most revolutions per minute?

   A. Gear A
   B. Gear B
   C. Gear C
   D. Gear D

3. Which of these tools has a long handle and a metal head with a point and hook?

   A. Clemens hook
   B. drywall hook
   C. San Francisco hook
   D. pike pole

4. What do a hydraulic spreader, a Kelly tool, and a Halligan bar have in common?

   A. They are used to cut through light materials.
   B. They are used to break up materials.
   C. They are used to pry open objects.
   D. They are used to help remove trapped accident victims.

5. Which of these tools would most likely be used to deliver a soft blow to an object?

   A.

   B.

   C.

   D.

Questions 6–7 refer to the following figure.

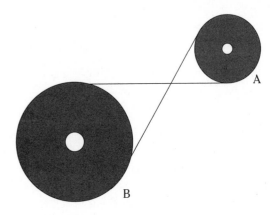

6. Wheel B is twice the size of Wheel A. If Wheel B makes 75 revolutions per minute, how many revolutions per minute does Wheel A make?

   A. 30
   B. 45
   C. 75
   D. 150

7. Which of the following statements about the pulley setup is true?

   A. If Wheel A spins clockwise, Wheel B spins counterclockwise.
   B. Wheel A spins slower than Wheel B.
   C. Neither wheel can spin in the pulley setup.
   D. If Wheel A spins clockwise, Wheel B spins clockwise.

Question 8 refers to the following figure.

8. This tool would most likely be used to

   A. break up materials.
   B. move heavy objects.
   C. carry or move materials.
   D. remove plaster or siding.

Question 9 refers to the following figure.

9. During forcible entry operations, this tool would most likely be used for

   A. prying.
   B. pulling.
   C. pushing.
   D. cutting.

Questions 10–11 refer to the following figure.

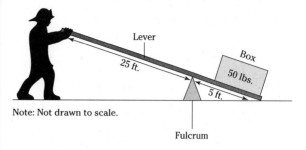

Note: Not drawn to scale.

10. How many pounds of force must the firefighter apply to the lever to lift the box?

    A. 10
    B. 20
    C. 25
    D. 50

11. If the weight of the box was increased to 150 pounds and if the firefighter moved the fulcrum 5 feet farther from the box, how much force would he have to apply to lift the box?

    A. 20
    B. 35
    C. 70
    D. 100

Question 12 refers to the following figure.

12. What is the name of this tool?

    A. bolt cutter
    B. chisel
    C. utility knife
    D. punch

Question 13 refers to the following figure.

13. During forcible-entry operations, this tool would most likely be used for

   A.   prying.
   B.   striking.
   C.   cutting.
   D.   pulling.

Question 14 refers to the following figure.

14. What is the name of this tool?

   A.   pick
   B.   multipurpose hook
   C.   screwdriver
   D.   Hux bar

15. A firefighter would most likely use a New York hook for

   A.   prying or pulling an object.
   B.   removing drywell.
   C.   removing plaster.
   D.   ventilating and turning off a gas line.

16. What will happen if you turn a nut on a standard-thread screw counterclockwise?

   A.   It will move down the screw.
   B.   It will not turn on a standard-thread screw.
   C.   It will move up the screw.
   D.   It will be difficult to turn.

17. If a spring stretches 15 inches under a pull of 30 pounds, how many inches will the spring stretch under a pull of 150 pounds?

   A.   25
   B.   50
   C.   75
   D.   100

18. Which of these saws has teeth similar to a chainsaw?

   A.   ventilation saw
   B.   rotary saw
   C.   reciprocating saw
   D.   hacksaw

19. A shovel would most likely be used to

   A.   hoist or secure objects.
   B.   carry or move materials.
   C.   grip objects.
   D.   turn off a gas line.

Question 20 refers to the following figure.

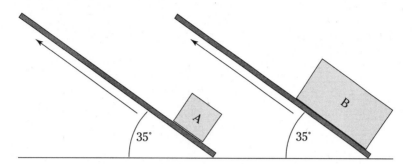

20. Boxes A and B are made of the same material and weigh the same. Based on the image above, which box will require more effort to push it up the inclined plane?

   A. The boxes will require no effort to be pushed up the inclined plane.
   B. The boxes will require the same amount of effort to be pushed up the inclined plane.
   C. Box A will require more effort to push it up the inclined plane.
   D. Box B will require more effort to push it up the inclined plane.

IF YOU FINISH BEFORE TIME IS CALLED, CHECK YOUR WORK ON THIS SECTION ONLY. DO NOT WORK ON ANY OTHER SECTION IN THE TEST.

Answer Key

Section 1: Observation

1. D	6. C	11. C	16. B
2. C	7. D	12. B	17. A
3. A	8. A	13. D	18. D
4. B	9. D	14. C	19. D
5. B	10. B	15. B	20. B

Section 2: Memory

1. B	6. C	11. C	16. C
2. D	7. C	12. A	17. B
3. C	8. B	13. D	18. D
4. B	9. C	14. C	19. C
5. A	10. C	15. B	20. B

Section 3: Spatial Orientation

1. D	6. A	11. D	16. C
2. B	7. B	12. A	17. C
3. A	8. C	13. C	18. B
4. B	9. B	14. B	19. D
5. C	10. C	15. B	20. D

Section 4: Reading Comprehension

1. C	6. D	11. B	16. B
2. A	7. D	12. D	17. B
3. B	8. A	13. C	18. C
4. C	9. C	14. D	19. D
5. B	10. C	15. A	20. B

Section 5: Verbal Expression

1. B	6. C	11. B	16. A
2. B	7. A	12. C	17. A
3. D	8. B	13. B	18. B
4. C	9. A	14. C	19. D
5. D	10. D	15. C	20. C

Section 6: Deductive, Inductive, and Logical Reasoning

1. C	6. D	11. D	16. D
2. D	7. D	12. A	17. C
3. A	8. A	13. B	18. C
4. B	9. B	14. C	19. D
5. C	10. B	15. B	20. D

Section 7: Information Ordering

1. A	6. C	11. A	16. C
2. B	7. B	12. D	17. A
3. C	8. D	13. D	18. A
4. B	9. B	14. D	19. C
5. B	10. C	15. A	20. D

Section 8: Problem Sensitivity

1. B	6. B	11. B	16. D
2. D	7. C	12. B	17. A
3. C	8. D	13. A	18. C
4. A	9. C	14. D	19. B
5. D	10. A	15. C	20. B

Section 9: Mathematics

1. D	6. D	11. C	16. B
2. C	7. A	12. D	17. A
3. C	8. D	13. B	18. C
4. A	9. B	14. D	19. C
5. A	10. B	15. B	20. A

Section 10: Mechanical Aptitude

1. D	6. D	11. C	16. A
2. C	7. A	12. C	17. C
3. D	8. A	13. B	18. A
4. C	9. D	14. A	19. B
5. B	10. A	15. A	20. D

Answer Explanations

Section 1: Observation

1. **D** You know that Rope 3 is a braid-on-braid rope because of its herringbone pattern and the appearance of both its sheath and its core. While these braids are resistant to some abrasion, firefighters may encounter issues with braid-on-braid ropes because the sheath tends to slide along the core, exposing it and making it difficult to use. *(See Chapter V, Section A.)*

2. **C** Ropes 3 and 4 both have sheaths that cover their cores. Rope 3 is a braid-on-braid rope, which is made using a herringbone pattern. It is somewhat resistant to abrasion. Rope 4 is a kernmantle rope, which is made of a braided covering (the mantle) and a load-bearing core (the kern). The mantle of a kernmantle rope absorbs most of the rope's damage, thus protecting the strongest part of the rope, the kern, from abrasion. *(See Chapter V, Section A.)*

3. **A** You most likely inspected a laid rope. Laid ropes can be tightly or loosely twisted. They're made of three separate pieces of yarn; each piece of yarn is frequently exposed to the environment. Because of this exposure, and the lack of protection of a sheath, these ropes break easily. Due to the missing protective covering sheaths provide, firefighters can easily see if a laid rope is damaged from abrasion. *(See Chapter V, Section A.)*

4. **B** Laid ropes are also known as twisted ropes. This alternative name comes from the way they're constructed. To make a laid rope, three pieces of yarn are twisted together. The way they're twisted—tight or loose—and the materials they're made from depend on the task they'll be expected to perform once constructed. *(See Chapter V, Section A.)*

5. **B** There are six trophies in the trophy case: three on the top row and three on the bottom row. In the middle row sits a plaque and a winning medal. *(See Chapter V, Section A.)*

6. **C** Pencils are located in front of the emergency exit door. Pencils in the middle of the hallway are a tripping hazard, especially when they are located in front of an exit that people will run to in the event of an emergency. The papers on the floor in front of the trophy case are also a tripping hazard, but they are not in front of the exit. *(See Chapter V, Section A.)*

7. **D** The fire alarm is located directly to the left of the emergency exit. This also makes it located directly to the right of the lockers, but this is not an answer option available for you to choose. *(See Chapter V, Section A.)*

8. **A** If you entered this hallway from the left side of this image, you would pass the trophy case, garbage can, newspaper stand, lockers, fire alarm, emergency exit. You would also pass the fire extinguisher, which is hidden behind the garbage can and the newspaper stand. *(See Chapter V, Section A.)*

9. **D** In this illustration, the fire extinguisher is obstructed by the garbage can and the newspaper stand. The other choices are incorrect because all of the lockers have locks; the trophy case holds one medal, one plaque, and six trophies; and the newspaper stand is full. *(See Chapter V, Section A.)*

10. **B** Water exits a wet barrel hydrant when a hose is connected to the hose outlet and valve seat, which is indicated by the number 2 on the figure. Choices A, C, and D are incorrect because you cannot connect a hose to the operating stem, automatic check, or into the ground surrounding a wet barrel hydrant. *(See Chapter V, Section A.)*

11. **C** Wet barrel hydrants would be least likely to appear in New York, New York, because of the northeastern United States' cold winters. New York receives quite a bit of snow and ice in the winter months; the temperature drops below 32°F frequently. With these temperatures and conditions, the ground consistently freezes. If a wet barrel hydrant were to be placed in a city like New York, the water inside the barrel would freeze. The hydrant would then become unusable in the event of an emergency. Choices A, B, and D are incorrect because these locations rarely see below-freezing temperatures. *(See Chapter V, Section A.)*

12. **B** The passage states that wet barrel hydrants "don't have main valves or drain holes and their operating stem runs horizontally through the top of the hydrant, rather than vertically down the barrel." This would indicate that dry barrel hydrants have an operating stem that runs vertically down the barrel. The position of the operating stem in a wet barrel hydrant is indicated by the number 1 in the figure. *(See Chapter V, Section A.)*

13. **D** In a wet barrel hydrant, you should always expect to find water throughout the entire barrel, which means that it is located below the operating stem and above and below ground level. The barrel of a wet barrel hydrant is always filled with water, which is why this type of hydrant cannot be placed in an area where water freezes frequently. *(See Chapter V, Section A.)*

14. **C** The climate of the area does not predict the number of fire hydrants placed in a particular neighborhood. This factor will certainly determine the type of hydrant placed in an area, but it will not affect the number of hydrants on a particular street or in a specific city. Factors such as the number of available water mains in an area, area congestion, types of construction, and even the area's estimated property value will determine the total number of wet or dry hydrants in one area. *(See Chapter V, Section A.)*

15. **B** The figure shows a lean-to collapse. These types of structural collapses occur when one wall fails and the opposite wall remains upright and intact. The side of the roof that was supported by the collapsed wall dropped to the floor, thus creating a void shaped like a triangle. *(See Chapter V, Section A.)*

16. **B** As indicated by the figure's labels, the wall is represented by the number 2. The wall pictured on the left side of the image could not support the weight of the debris on the roof and buckled under the pressure, thus causing the collapse. *(See Chapter V, Section A.)*

17. **A** If a person was seated on the chair against the wall pictured on the right side of the figure, firefighters may assume the victim is alive, not seriously injured, and waiting to be rescued. The void is large enough that the victim would have room to breathe and move. Had the void been smaller or had the wall collapsed where the victim was seated, he or she may have been seriously injured or killed by the collapse. *(See Chapter V, Section A.)*

18. **D** If the ladder travels along the indicated path, the ladder may hit the power lines and the firefighters may be electrocuted. Bumping the utility pole with the ladder won't make the pole fall to the ground and kill power in the entire neighborhood, and the arc of this path is not so complicated that the ladder should fall on the firefighters while they are raising it. Choice C is incorrect because even though the ladder is the perfect height to reach the third floor, firefighters will not be able to set it against the building because it will first be entangled in the power lines, which are in the path of the arc. *(See Chapter V, Section A.)*

19. **D** The path the ladder will travel if it is raised perpendicular can cause injury. The figure shows that the path the ladder will travel will lead it straight into the utility pole. If the pole is live, the firefighters guiding the ladder may be injured. As there is no evidence in the image to indicate that the power has

been shut off, you should assume that the utility pole is functioning properly. Choice A is incorrect because there is no evidence to support the claim that the fire started on the third floor. Choice B is also incorrect because it appears the ladder is, in fact, tall enough to reach the third floor of the building. *(See Chapter V, Section A.)*

20. **B** To successfully raise the ladder without causing harm to themselves, firefighters should avoid the overhead wires by using a parallel raise. This raise has a much smaller arc than a perpendicular raise and will ensure that the firefighters don't hit the utility pole. Extending the ladder to 30 feet or collapsing it to 15 feet and trying a perpendicular raise will still cause the ladder to hit the wires, as the pole is 15 feet tall. The question asks how firefighters can raise "this" ladder and not another one not included in the figure, so they cannot request assistance from a ladder truck, which would contain its own ladder. Choice C is therefore incorrect. *(See Chapter V, Section A.)*

Section 2: Memory

1. **B** The flames on the bed indicate that the fire in this illustration began in the bedroom. *(See Chapter V, Section B1.)*

2. **D** This illustration contains seven flowers: three near the front porch, two in a vase in the living room, and two at the base of the tree in the backyard. *(See Chapter V, Section B1.)*

3. **C** This illustration contains three portraits hanging on the wall. They're all located on the wall behind the staircase running from the first floor to the second. *(See Chapter V, Section B1.)*

4. **B** In this image, the basement door is padlocked. Choices A, C, and D are incorrect because the tree is not growing apples, there does not appear to be closets in the bedroom, and there isn't a bird's nest on the roof of the porch. *(See Chapter V, Section B1.)*

5. **A** If the windows on the leeward side of the house were closed, the smoke from the fire would most likely travel up into the attic before it went down to the first floor (Choice C) or out the front door of the house (Choice B). The figure indicates that a bit of smoke is already making its way up through the trap door in the floor of the attic, which is located in the bedroom. The smoke would not be able to escape the house via the windward windows because wind is coming in through those windows (Choice D). *(See Chapter V, Section B.)*

6. **C** The number 13 is printed on the mailbox in front of the house. *(See Chapter V, Section B1.)*

7. **C** The wind in this picture is blowing east. You know this because the wind direction is indicated by a right-facing arrow. *(See Chapter V, Section B1.)*

8. **B** Rain is falling from clouds positioned over the house; therefore, you would describe the weather as rainy. Choices A and D are incorrect because the sun doesn't appear in this picture, so you cannot confirm that the conditions are sunny or mild. Also, raindrops indicate rain; snowflakes do not appear in this image, making Choice C incorrect. *(See Chapter V, Section B1.)*

9. **C** There are three lamps in this figure: one on either side of the bed on the second floor and one to the left of the armchair in the living room. *(See Chapter V, Section B1.)*

10. **C** The bird in this image is perched on the windward side of the roof. *(See Chapter V, Section B1.)*

11. **C** Engine 9 was held up from getting to the fire at the same time as Engine 11 because of a flat tire. *(See Chapter V, Section B2.)*

12. **A** A neighbor tells the firefighters that two middle-aged women live in the home with two dogs and a cat, but she is unsure if they are home. Three firefighters proceed into the burning structure and rescue two dogs and a cat. They report that no other victims were inside the home. *(See Chapter V, Section B2.)*

13. **D** The location of the fire is at 339 Curtis Lane. This is not to be confused with Maple Lane, which is located one street over from the fire, and is the location of the fire hydrant from which the firefighters laid a supply line. *(See Chapter V, Section B2.)*

14. **C** Although both Engine 11 and Engine 9 left the firehouse at the same time, Engine 9 got a flat tire and had to pull over to change it. Engine 11 arrived at the scene of the fire at 4:49 p.m., while Engine 9 arrived a short time later at 5:01 p.m. *(See Chapter V, Section B2.)*

15. **B** The investigators determine the cause of the fire to be unknown, so the cause was undetermined. There was no mention of any other cause of the fire. *(See Chapter V, Section B2.)*

16. **C** In the passage, Langley says that the reverse lay is commonly used when the water pressure from the source is not high enough. *(See Chapter V, Section B2.)*

17. **B** Once the hose has been wrapped around the hydrant in the forward lay procedure, the engine moves from the hydrant to the fire scene. *(See Chapter V, Section B2.)*

18. **D** All critical firefighting equipment is removed from the truck before the reverse lay procedure starts because the truck will be removed from the scene and positioned near the hydrant. The truck must be positioned near the hydrant so it can attain a secure connection between the hydrant and its hoses. *(See Chapter V, Section B2.)*

19. **C** In the reverse lay, once all the critical equipment has been removed from the truck, the hose is removed and attached to a sturdy object before the truck proceeds to the hydrant. *(See Chapter V, Section B2.)*

20. **B** According to Langley, the forward lay is used only when there is sufficient water pressure available from the source. *(See Chapter V, Section B2.)*

Section 3: Spatial Orientation

1. **D** If you started at the intersection of Maple and Pine streets and traveled south, you would turn right onto Fall Lane, right onto Rose Avenue, left onto Maple Street, and left onto Oak Street and you would be closest to the ice cream shop. *(See Chapter V, Section C.)*

2. **B** The gym is located at the intersection of Oak and Walnut streets, so you would have to travel southwest from the coffee shop to get to the gym. *(See Chapter V, Section C.)*

3. **A** If you come out of the parking garage on Crescent Lane, the fastest route to take would be west on Crescent Lane and north on Oak Street. *(See Chapter V, Section C.)*

4. **B** The quickest route to drive from the salon to the deli is west on Walnut Street, north on Oak Street, east on Fall Lane, and north on Rose Avenue. The routes stated in Choices A and D are incorrect because they require you to make illegal turns onto one-way streets. The route stated in Choice C is incorrect because it is much longer than the route in Choice B. *(See Chapter V, Section C.)*

5. **C** If you started at the intersection of Ridge Avenue and Crescent Lane and traveled west, you would turn right onto Oak Street, turn right onto Fall Lane, turn left onto Rose Avenue, and turn right onto Maple Street, you would be closest to the coffee shop. *(See Chapter V, Section C.)*

6. **A** If you proceed down the hallway from the fire stairs and enter the first door on your left, you'll be in Apartment 1, so you can eliminate Choices B and D. Once inside, if you enter the first opening on your right, you'll be in the kitchen, not bedroom 2 (Choice C). *(See Chapter V, Section C.)*

7. **B** From the end of the hallway between bedrooms 1 and 2, your right hand will pass over the doors for bedrooms 2 and 3. You'll then proceed through the opening that leads to the main exit, but the question does not ask about openings; it specifically asks about doors. Therefore, the correct answer is 2. *(See Chapter V, Section C.)*

8. **C** If the fire has traveled from the kitchen into the living room and has blocked the main entrance, instructing the victims to leave bedroom 2 would be quite dangerous, so you can eliminate Choices A and B. Choice D is also dangerous, as it would require the victims to remain in the room for the duration of the fire. Choice C, having the victims come to the window of bedroom 2 where firefighters will conduct a ladder rescue, is the safest option. *(See Chapter V, Section C.)*

9. **B** You can eliminate Choices C and D, as these would take the person closer to the fire rather than away from it. Choice A requires entering various rooms and exiting through a window. The most direct route from bath 1 is into the dining room, through the living room, and out the main entry door. It's almost a straight line. *(See Chapter V, Section C.)*

10. **C** If you enter the apartment through the main door and place your left hand on the wall to the left, the first opening you encounter will be the opening into the kitchen/living room area. If you continue down that hall with your left hand on the wall, the next door you encounter will be the door to bedroom 3 on your left. If you proceed through this door, you'll be in bedroom 3. *(See Chapter V, Section C.)*

11. **D** The routes in Choices A and C require traveling the wrong direction on Amherst Lane, so you can eliminate those answer choices. Choice B is a very roundabout way of reaching the car accident quickly. Therefore, Choice D is the best route. It is also the easiest since the fire truck is already parked facing west. *(See Chapter V, Section C.)*

12. **A** According the information given, you finish your journey on Old River Road. The only two buildings located on this road are the Fire Department and the Bakery. The question states that you turn left onto Old River Road from Lexington Ave., which would put you very close to the Bakery. *(See Chapter V, Section C.)*

13. **C** According to the information given, you are traveling on Washington Ave., which runs from southwest to northeast across the map. You turn right onto Washington Ave. from River Side Road, which means you must be traveling northeast. *(See Chapter V, Section C.)*

14. **B** You can eliminate Choice A, because it requires traveling the wrong direction on Amherst Lane. Choice C makes an unnecessary turn up Melrose Ave. to Old River Road, when it would be much more direct to continue traveling west on Lexington. Choice D involves traveling far out of the way to return to the Fire Department. Therefore, Choice B is the most direct route. *(See Chapter V, Section C.)*

15. **B** The only part of the directions that matters is the last sentence, which states that you are on Melrose Ave. According to the map, Melrose Ave. runs between the fire department and the police station. *(See Chapter V, Section C.)*

16. **C** Because the point of origin can be found in bedroom 3, it can be inferred that the most likely cause of the fire was an electric fan malfunction. *(See Chapter V, Section C.)*

17. **C** The floor plan indicates that there are three smoke alarms in the house. The smoke alarms are located in the main hall, hall 2, and the living room. *(See Chapter V, Section C.)*

18. **B** Entering through a window at the northwest corner of the house, a firefighter could rescue one animal. *(See Chapter V, Section C.)*

19. **D** Because the person in the kitchen can easily escape through the door to the outside in that room, the person in the living room and the two remaining animals are now the lives most in danger. *(See Chapter V, Section C.)*

20. **D** Counting both people and animals, there are six lives in danger in the burning house. *(See Chapter V, Section C.)*

Section 4: Reading Comprehension

1. **C** According to the passage, the witness reported seeing smoke coming from his neighbor's roof. *(See Chapter VI, Section A.)*

2. **A** The witness reported that there was no one home at the fire, so the correct answer is none. *(See Chapter VI, Section A.)*

3. **B** According to the passage, firefighters confirmed that the fire was extinguished at 4:17 p.m. *(See Chapter VI, Section A.)*

4. **C** Based on the firefighters' discovery of a sparking wire and the homeowner's admission that he had recently been doing electrical work in the attic, it can be concluded that an electrical failure was the most likely cause of the fire. *(See Chapter VI, Section A.)*

5. **B** According to the chart, the highest number of reported fires in 2010 was recorded in July. *(See Chapter VI, Section A.)*

6. **D** According to the chart, November was the only month in which the number of reported fires was the same in both 2009 and 2010. *(See Chapter VI, Section A.)*

7. **D** The passage indicates that it took firefighters approximately 45 minutes to contain the wildfire. *(See Chapter VI, Section A.)*

8. **A** Firefighters responded to a grease fire on March 23. *(See Chapter VI, Section A.)*

9. **C** According to the paragraph, firefighters ruled that the March 25 fire was an arson after a gas can and rags were found at the scene. *(See Chapter VI, Section A.)*

10. **C** A fire that is sparked by faulty wiring would most likely be classified as Class C because it involves active electrical equipment. *(See Chapter VI, Section A.)*

11. **B** A chemical fire at a laboratory would most likely be considered a Class D fire because it probably involves combustible metals. *(See Chapter VI, Section A.)*

12. **D** Because the fire in question was caused by cooking oil and occurred in a nonprivate kitchen, this fire would most likely be considered Class K. *(See Chapter VI, Section A.)*

13. **C** The pie chart indicates that the Benton Fire Department responded to the fewest number of false alarms. *(See Chapter VI, Section A.)*

14. **D** According to the passage, Ms. Torres was found unconscious when paramedics first arrived on scene. *(See Chapter VI, Section A.)*

15. **A** The passage indicates that all three individuals were wearing their seat belts at the time of the accident. *(See Chapter VI, Section A.)*

16. **B** The word *extricate* means to free or remove. *(See Chapter VI, Section A.)*

17. **B** According to the passage, Mr. Giordano was driving a Honda Civic. *(See Chapter VI, Section A.)*

18. **C** Firefighters would be most likely to use a booster line first upon arriving on the scene of a fire because the passage states that booster lines are used for the initial attack on a fire. *(See Chapter VI, Section A.)*

19. **D** Firefighters would likely use an air chisel to rescue an injured victim trapped in a car because air chisels are capable of cutting through sheet metal. *(See Chapter VI, Section A.)*

20. **B** Based on information in the passage, chocks would most likely be used to secure the entrance to burning building. *(See Chapter VI, Section A.)*

Section 5: Verbal Expression

1. **B** Because the sentence begins with the phrase *last Wednesday,* it can be determined that it describes an event that occurred in the past and would, therefore, require a verb set in the past tense (*rescued*). *(See Chapter VI, Section B4.)*

2. **B** This sentence needs a possessive pronoun to be completed correctly. Because the subject can be identified as a singular male, the pronoun *his* would be the most appropriate possessive pronoun for use in this sentence. *(See Chapter VI, Section B3.)*

3. **D** Because this sentence compares chemical fires to all other types of fires, a superlative adjective is required. Because *difficultest* is not a word, the phrase *most difficult* is the correct choice. *(See Chapter VI, Section B2.)*

4. **C** The sentence makes the most sense if you insert the preposition *inside,* which establishes the relationship between the verb *trapped* and the object of the preposition *vehicle.* *(See Chapter VI, Section B5.)*

5. **D** The correct spelling of "gages" is *gauges.* *(See Chapter VI, Section B1.)*

6. **C** The correct spelling of "relliable" is *reliable.* *(See Chapter VI, Section B1.)*

7. **A** Because the pronoun in this sentence modifies the noun *leadership* and a male subject is indicated, the possessive pronoun *His* must be used. *(See Chapter VI, Section B3.)*

8. **B** The singular verb *jumps* should be used with the collective pronoun *squad.* *(See Chapter VI, Section B4.)*

9. **A** The sentence makes the most sense if you insert the preposition *Despite,* which establishes the relationship between the verb *growing* and the object of the preposition *danger.* *(See Chapter VI, Section B5.)*

10. **D** Because this sentence compares more than two ideas (the whole firefighting process), the superlative adjective *most difficult* should be used. *(See Chapter VI, Section B2.)*

11. **B** The correct spelling of "assented" in this sentence is *ascended*. The word *ascended* is correct in this sentence because this word means to climb or go up. The word *assented* is incorrect because this word means to approve or agree. *(See Chapter VI, Section B1.)*

12. **C** The correct spelling of "judgement" is *judgment*. *(See Chapter VI, Section B1.)*

13. **B** In this instance, the missing pronoun refers to the subject *you,* so the reflexive pronoun *yourself* would best be used to complete the sentence. *(See Chapter VI, Section B3.)*

14. **C** The sentence makes the most sense if you insert the preposition *through,* which establishes the relationship between the verb *walked* and the object of the preposition *building. (See Chapter VI, Section B5.)*

15. **C** Because this sentence describes an action that began and ended in the past, the past-perfect tense of the word *extinguish,* which is *had extinguished,* is required to complete it correctly. *(See Chapter VI, Section B4.)*

16. **A** Because this sentence contains only one object, *fire extinguishers,* the positive adjective *speedy* should be used. *(See Chapter VI, Section B2.)*

17. **A** Because this sentence contains only one object, *phenomenon,* the positive adjective *abrupt* should be used. *(See Chapter VI, Section B2.)*

18. **B** Because the missing pronoun is intended to substitute for the object of the sentence *firefighter,* the object pronoun *whom* should be used. *(See Chapter VI, Section B3.)*

19. **D** This sentence describes an event that occurred in the past, so the past-tense form of the verb *begin,* which would be *began,* should be used. *(See Chapter VI, Section B4.)*

20. **C** The sentence makes the most sense if you insert the preposition *onto,* which establishes the relationship between the verb *threw* and the object of the preposition *pan. (See Chapter VI, Section B5.)*

Section 6: Deductive, Inductive, and Logical Reasoning

1. **C** By placing the lid of the pan over the flames, the woman effectively smothered the fire. She placed a barrier between the fire and its oxygen supply. Therefore, according to the general rules for extinguishing fires, she removed the oxygen. *(See Chapter VII, Section B.)*

2. **D** According to the general rules for extinguishing fires, firefighters typically use dry powder to extinguish fires involving flammable metals. Because magnesium is a type of metal, a fire involving magnesium shavings would most likely be extinguished by inhibiting the chain reaction with dry powder. *(See Chapter VII, Section B.)*

3. **A** According to the general methods for extinguishing fires, water is not used to fight fires involving flammable liquids, energized electrical equipment, or flammable metals. Therefore, firefighters will not likely use water to fight a fire involving a gas stove. They may try to remove the fuel by shutting off the gas, remove the oxygen by smothering the flames with foam, or inhibit the chain reaction by applying a special dry chemical. *(See Chapter VII, Section B.)*

4. **B** According to the general methods for extinguishing fires, water is not used to fight fires involving energized electrical equipment, such as a television or electrical cords. Foam is used on flammable liquids, and dry powder is used on flammable metals. Energized electrical fires may be extinguished using halons, carbon dioxide, or dry chemicals. *(See Chapter VII, Section B.)*

5. **C** When using inductive reasoning, you must draw a general conclusion based on specific information. According to the passage, the woman complained of pain in her right side, just above where her seatbelt latched. Because people have ribs on both the left and right sides of their bodies, the pain in the woman's right side is a good indicator that she has broken ribs. *(See Chapter VII, Section B.)*

6. **D** Using inductive reasoning, you can draw the conclusion that the motorcyclist likely struck his head on the rock, which both cracked his helmet and knocked him out. However, the fact that the motorcycle driver is unconscious is the best indicator that he has a brain injury. *(See Chapter VII, Section B.)*

7. **D** When using inductive reasoning, you must draw a general conclusion based on specific information. The passage states that the motorcyclist sustained injuries to his left foot, his left index finger, and his left shoulder. Because the majority of the motorcyclist's injuries are on his left side, there's a good possibility that he landed on his left side. *(See Chapter VII, Section B.)*

8. **A** This question, while similar to reading-comprehension questions, asks you to use the specific details of the passage to find a title that applies to the passage as a whole—that is, to give a general idea of what the passage is about. While motorcycle riding, helmets, and air ambulances are mentioned, the passage as a whole is about evaluating different victims of an accident. Therefore, "Evaluating Accident Victims" is the best title for the passage. *(See Chapter VII, Section B.)*

9. **B** In 2010, although human activities resulted in more wildfires than lightning did, the wildfires caused by lightning were more destructive. You can determine this through logic. Based on the information, human activities caused nine times more wildfires than lightning did. However, lightning-caused wildfires destroyed more than 2 million acres of land, while human-caused wildfires destroyed more than 1 million. Therefore, the lightning-caused fires destroyed more land. *(See Chapter VII, Section B.)*

10. **B** Choice A is somewhat accurate, but it does not mention anything about electrically powered saws, such as the reciprocating saw. The sentences do not suggest how easy or difficult it is to use any of the saws, so Choice C can be eliminated. Each statement about the saws suggests a different use, so Choice D can also be eliminated. Only Choice B accurately describes each of the statements. *(See Chapter VII, Section B.)*

11. **D** Two clues are provided in the given information. The building being constructed is a factory, which suggests an industrial setting. In addition, the building is being constructed one block from the ocean, which suggests an atmosphere with a high salt concentration. Therefore, firefighters would most likely recommend special-purpose sprinklers with a coating to prevent corrosion. *(See Chapter VII, Section B.)*

12. **A** College dormitories generally contain small rooms. In addition, the information states that the water pipes cannot be located in the ceilings of the rooms. The information in the passage states that sidewall sprinklers are often found in small rooms when a water pipe cannot be located in the ceiling. Therefore, the builders will likely use sidewall sprinklers. *(See Chapter VII, Section B.)*

13. **B** The passage states that pendant sprinklers are the most common type of sprinklers. Therefore, during their inspections of various structures, firefighters probably most often encountered pendant sprinklers. *(See Chapter VII, Section B.)*

14. **C** When firefighters arrive on scene, they notice smoke blowing into the man's face. In addition, the man is coughing and experiencing shortness of breath and later develops a headache. These are all clues that the man has inhaled a lot of smoke and is suffering from smoke inhalation. *(See Chapter VII, Section B.)*

15. **B** As firefighters doused the flames, they noticed a burn barrel, which still contained some smoldering ashes, at the edge of the man's property line. The man stated that he had burned some trash in the barrel that morning. These clues suggest that an ember from the man's burn barrel sparked a fire in the dried brush. *(See Chapter VII, Section B.)*

16. **D** Firefighters called the ambulance when they noticed that the man was coughing and short of breath as a result of the smoke blowing into his face. This suggests that they called the ambulance because they suspected that the homeowner was in need of medical assistance. *(See Chapter VII, Section B.)*

17. **C** The first number in this sequence is 1. The second number is 4, which is 1 + 3. The third number is 7, which is 4 + 3. The fourth number is 10, which is 7 + 3. The fifth number is missing, but the sixth number is 16. The pattern seems to be adding 3 to each number. If you add 3 to the fourth number, you'll get 13 (10 + 3 = 13). This makes sense as 13 + 3 = 16, which fits into the sequence. *(See Chapter VII, Section B.)*

18. **C** This series starts with a star in which the bottom right point is white. In the second image, the bottom left point is white. The third image shows the middle left point white. The white point seems to be moving in a clockwise direction from one point to the next. Therefore, the fourth image should show a star with a white point on top, which fits into the sequence because the last image shows that the white point has moved to the middle right point on the star. *(See Chapter VII, Section B.)*

19. **D** The pattern in this sequence is to multiply by 2 and add 5 to each number: $1 \times 2 = 2$ and $2 + 5 = 7$; $7 \times 2 = 14$ and $14 + 5 = 19$; $19 \times 2 = 38 + 5 = 43$. Therefore, to determine the next number, multiply 43 by 2 and add: $43 \times 2 = 86$ and $86 + 5 = 91$. To check to see if 91 is the correct answer, multiply 91 by 2 and add 5: $91 \times 2 = 182 + 5 = 187$. The correct answer is 91. *(See Chapter VII, Section B.)*

20. **D** This series begins with a 4×4 square with a black dot in the first column of the first row. The second image shows the same square with a black dot in the third column of the first row. The third image shows the same square with a black dot in the first column of the second row. The fourth image shows the same square with a black dot in the third column of the second row. The last image shows the same square with a black dot in the third column of the third row. Therefore, to correctly complete the series, the missing square should show a black dot in the first column of the third row. *(See Chapter VII, Section B.)*

Section 7: Information Ordering

1. **A** The blade of the Halligan must be positioned in the space between the door and the jamb (2) before a second firefighter can strike it with a sledgehammer to force it farther into the space (1). The first firefighter should ensure that the blade is wedged securely between the door and the jamb (4) before pushing down and out on the forked end of the Halligan bar (3). Therefore, the correct order is 2, 1, 4, 3. *(See Chapter VII, Section C.)*

2. **B** After Firefighter B uses a sledgehammer to drive the wedge of the Halligan bar farther into the space between the door and the jamb, Firefighter A should ensure that blade is wedged securely in the space before applying pressure to the forked end. *(See Chapter VII, Section C.)*

3. **C** The best clue about the last step is that it is the point at which the door opens. This occurs when Firefighter A pushes down and out on the forked end of the Halligan bar. *(See Chapter VII, Section C.)*

4. **B** Firefighter B is involved in only one step of the process. After Firefighter A positions the blade of the Halligan bar between the door and the door jamb, Firefighter B uses a sledgehammer to force the

wedge farther into this space. Therefore, Firefighter B is involved in the second step. *(See Chapter VII, Section C.)*

5. **B** The first step is to heel the ladder against the structure (4). Next, the firefighter should raise the entire ladder to a vertical position against the structure (1). After that, the firefighter should pull the heel end away from the structure to an appropriate angle for climbing (2). Finally, the firefighter should check the climbing angle and ensure that the ladder is firmly against the ground and the structure (3). Therefore, the correct order is 4, 1, 2, 3. *(See Chapter VII, Section C.)*

6. **C** The first step is to place the heel end of the ladder against the structure. This must be performed before you raise the ladder into a vertical position against the building. In addition, it's performed before you start pulling the heel end away from the structure. *(See Chapter VII, Section C.)*

7. **B** Raising the ladder to a vertical position against the structure is the second step in the process. This is performed after the ladder is heeled against the structure, but before the heel of the ladder is pulled away from the structure to a proper climbing angle. Checking the climbing angle and security of the ladder's placement is the last step. *(See Chapter VII, Section C.)*

8. **D** Once the ladder is in position, you can climb it, but you should perform one other activity before you start climbing. The last step should be checking the security of the ladder on the ground and against the structure. The last step also includes checking the climbing angle. *(See Chapter VII, Section C.)*

9. **B** The passage explains the procedure for creating a straight roll, but then it states, "Before completing the straight roll, the firefighter should lay the entire length of hose on a clean, dry, flat surface." Therefore, this is the first step. *(See Chapter VII, Section C.)*

10. **C** The firefighter cannot tap the protruding coils into place until the roll is complete. Therefore, this step would be completed directly after laying the completed roll flat on the ground. *(See Chapter VII, Section C.)*

11. **A** To create the straight roll, the firefighter should lay the entire hose on a flat, dry surface. Then, starting at the male end, the firefighter should roll the hose toward the female end. When the roll is complete, the firefighter should lay the roll flat on the ground. Finally, the firefighter should tap any protruding coils into place. *(See Chapter VII, Section C.)*

12. **D** The last step in creating the straight roll is tapping the protruding coils into place. However, the passage states that after this, the firefighter should place the fire hose in the proper storage area. *(See Chapter VII, Section C.)*

13. **D** According to the passage, Smithfield Fire Department's protocol is to treat patients in the following order: 1) victims who need CPR, 2) victims with bleeding wounds, 3) victims suffering from shock, 4) victims with broken bones, 5) victims with other injuries such as scrapes and bruises. Kevin Floyd has a bruised shoulder, which means that he has the least serious injuries of the people listed. Therefore, he should be treated last. *(See Chapter VII, Section C.)*

14. **D** According to the passage, Smithfield Fire Department's protocol is to treat patients in the following order: 1) victims who need CPR, 2) victims with bleeding wounds, 3) victims suffering from shock, 4) victims with broken bones, 5) victims with other injuries such as scrapes and bruises. Janice Floyd is suffering from shock; victims with broken bones are treated after victims suffering from shock. The only victim with a broken bone is Carl James, who has a broken arm, so he should be treated directly after Janice Floyd. *(See Chapter VII, Section C.)*

15. **A** According to the passage, Smithfield Fire Department's protocol is to treat patients in the following order: 1) victims who need CPR, 2) victims with bleeding wounds, 3) victims suffering from shock, 4) victims with broken bones, 5) victims with other injuries such as scrapes and bruises. Melanie James has a bleeding laceration on her head, which means that she should be treated second only to a victim who needs CPR. The only victim who needs CPR is Gerald Thomas, so Melanie James should be treated after Gerald Thomas. *(See Chapter VII, Section C.)*

16. **C** According to the passage, Smithfield Fire Department's protocol is to treat patients in the following order: 1) victims who need CPR, 2) victims with bleeding wounds, 3) victims suffering from shock, 4) victims with broken bones, 5) victims with other injuries such as scrapes and bruises. Therefore, the firefighters should treat the injuries sustained by the victims of this car accident in the following order: cardiac arrest (3), deep bleeding wound (2), shock (5), broken arm (4), and large contusion (1). *(See Chapter VII, Section C.)*

17. **A** Firefighters should ventilate the basement via the ground floor *before a team descends the basement stairs.* This will ensure that the smoke is no longer trapped in the basement, making it more difficult for firefighters to see and attack the flames. Ventilation should occur before spraying the basement and after locating an area to cut and identifying heavy objects above the main fire; therefore, choices B, C, and D are incorrect. *(See Chapter VII, Section C.)*

18. **A** To prevent flashover fires, firefighters must ventilate higher floors and attics. This will ensure that smoke and embers that move up the basement stairs (and all other staircases throughout the structure) will move out of the structure via those holes. If ventilation does not occur, the smoke and embers will accumulate in these areas and may start a new fire and cause excessive damage. Choices B, C, and D will certainly aid the firefighters in fighting the entire fire, but if they wish to specifically avoid flashover fires, they need to ventilate the higher levels of the structure. *(See Chapter VII, Section C.)*

19. **C** Firefighter Andrews and his crew entered the basement before ventilating through the ground floor. Although they made an effort to move heavy furniture that may fall through the floor and injure firefighters below if the structure gave way, they did not create an opening to guide the smoke from the basement. Since they sent half the crew to the attic to ventilate, Choice B is incorrect because they did determine the possibility for flashover. Choice A is also incorrect because they immediately identified the location of the fire when they entered the building. Choice D is incorrect because they are not required to remove the furniture; they simply need to get it out of the way so it doesn't cause injury or make fighting the flames more difficult. *(See Chapter VII, Section C.)*

20. **D** Although the passage doesn't directly state this information, one may use a combination of common sense and the information provided to determine that *firefighters move or remove heavy objects so they don't fall through weakened floorboards.* The first step in the list states, "Identify heavy objects that may be positioned above the team when they are attacking the fire in the basement. Remove, if possible." Common sense tells you that fire can burn through and warp materials; therefore, if you're standing below a heavy object and the material beneath it is on fire, you are in great danger of being injured. Evidence that flashover is possible only when flames begin in the basement, closing the door at the top of the stairs prevents the spread of smoke and embers, and ventilation should always occur directly above the bottom of the basement stairs does not exist in this passage; therefore, Choices A, B, and C are incorrect. *(See Chapter VII, Section C.)*

Section 8: Problem Sensitivity

1. **B** Based on passage information, it can be inferred that Anthony Murray is likely the most seriously injured individual. He appears to have suffered a broken or dislocated shoulder and a possible leg injury. More important, he also sustained a head injury and shows signs of a possible concussion or other neurological problem. *(See Chapter VII, Section D.)*

2. **D** Based on passage information, it can be inferred that Roberta Hines is likely the least seriously injured individual. According to the report, she endured only minor injuries and did not have any complaints. The others all had more serious injuries and specific complaints. *(See Chapter VII, Section D.)*

3. **C** Based on passage information, it can be inferred that Danielle Wallace is the most seriously injured of the occupants of the 2001 Volkswagen Passat. In addition to a severe soft-tissue wound, Ms. Wallace also complains of pain that would likely indicate a broken rib that may or may not have damaged a lung. *(See Chapter VII, Section D.)*

4. **A** Murphy's behavior would most likely indicate that his problem is a financial one. His desire to work as many shifts as possible, which is clearly impacting his physical and mental health, may be a sign that he is in dire need of money. This hypothesis is supported by the fact that Murphy has been either unwilling or unable to pay for meals with his co-workers. *(See Chapter VII, Section D.)*

5. **D** Willis's behavior would most likely indicate that his problem is health related. The passage states that Willis has been with the fire department for 25 years and has recently shown signs of physical deterioration. Considering the length of Willis's career, it can be inferred that his present physical and mental condition is likely related to his age. *(See Chapter VII, Section D.)*

6. **B** A report of a house fire in a suburban residential area would likely be the most urgent of the given notifications. Such a fire would present the most significant threat to public welfare and would require immediate attention. *(See Chapter VII, Section D.)*

7. **C** Valenti's behavior would most likely indicate that his problem is related to job stress. The passage indicates that Valenti was in good spirits when he was first hired and implies that his demeanor worsened as he spent more time on the job. His present behavior would suggest that the pressures of being a firefighter are taking a toll on Valenti's mental health. *(See Chapter VII, Section D.)*

8. **D** Based on passage information, it can be inferred that Jeffery Burke is likely the most seriously injured individual. He appears to have sustained a serious head injury and is unconscious and unresponsive. Along with diminished vital signs, Burke's condition clearly indicates that his injuries are considerably more serious than those of the other individuals involved in the accident. *(See Chapter VII, Section D.)*

9. **C** Based on passage information, it can be inferred that Peter Davidson is likely the least seriously injured individual. According to the passage, he only sustained lacerations. The other victims all suffered more serious injuries. *(See Chapter VII, Section D.)*

10. **A** Based on passage information, it can be inferred that Joseph Davidson is likely the most seriously injured person in the vehicle in which he and his family were traveling. In addition to tissue damage and a broken left arm, the pain he is experiencing in his left side may be an indication of multiple orthopedic injuries to his lower extremities on that side. *(See Chapter VII, Section D.)*

11. **B** Jackson's behavior would most likely indicate that his problem is related to drugs. The passage indicates that he recently had knee surgery, which would likely have required him to take some kind of prescription painkiller. His erratic behavior is also similar to that exhibited by individuals who are addicted to painkillers. *(See Chapter VII, Section D.)*

12. **B** Roberts's behavior would most likely indicate that his problem is related to alcohol issues. The passage indicates that he has been displaying behavior consistent with that of someone with a drinking problem. The fact that he has also been observed frequenting a local bar would also support this conclusion. *(See Chapter VII, Section D.)*

13. **A** A report of an overheated car that has caught fire would likely be the most urgent of the given notifications. If not contained quickly, a car fire could lead to a potentially lethal explosion and would require immediate action. *(See Chapter VII, Section D.)*

14. **D** Kaufman's behavior would most likely indicate that his problem is marital. The passage indicates that Kaufman has recently been very emotional and obsessed with his wife. This information, along with arguments Ling has overheard and the fact that Kaufman has been sleeping at the station suggests the he and his wife are experiencing marital problems. *(See Chapter VII, Section D.)*

15. **C** Based on passage information, it can be inferred that Jennifer Collins is the driver most in need of immediate medical attention. The passage indicates that she has likely sustained serious head and neck injuries and she appears to be in the worst physical condition of any of the accident victims. *(See Chapter VII, Section D.)*

16. **D** Based on passage information, it can be inferred that Lawrence Jones is the driver least in need of immediate medical attention. According to the passage, he has only sustained a single notable head wound and complains only of minor dizziness. *(See Chapter VII, Section D.)*

17. **A** Based on passage information, it can be inferred that Maxine Samuels is the passenger most in need of immediate medical attention. The passage indicates that Maxine, in addition to severe, bleeding cuts, is suffering from severe abdominal pain. This complaint, together with an examination revealing distention and discoloration, would suggest she may have sustained some form of internal injury. *(See Chapter VII, Section D.)*

18. **C** A dispatch to a tenth-floor fire at an office building would likely be the most urgent of the given notifications. A widespread fire in a high-rise office building has the potential to result in serious damage and injuries, so this notification would take priority over the others. *(See Chapter VII. Section D.)*

19. **B** Dawson's behavior would most likely indicate that her problem is domestic violence. The passage indicates that Dawson has recently begun dating a new boyfriend. It also implies that her attitude and demeanor have changed since she became involved in this relationship. Finally, the black eye and bruise she displays, in addition to the change in her behavior, suggests that she may be suffering from abuse at the hands of her new boyfriend. *(See Chapter VII, Section D.)*

20. **B** Mitchell's behavior would most likely indicate that his problem is related to drugs. The passage indicates that Mitchell's attitude and appearance have changed significantly since he joined the fire department. His change in behavior, noticeable weight loss, and the bag of white powder Nichols observed falling out of his locker all suggest that Mitchell is suffering from a serious drug problem. *(See Chapter VII, Section D.)*

Section 9: Mathematics

1. **D** To solve this problem, use the temperature equation: $F = \frac{9}{5}C + 32$ and plug the numbers you know into the equation:

$$F = \frac{9}{5}C + 32$$

$$F = \frac{9}{5}(42.5) + 32$$

$$F = \frac{9 \times 42.5}{5 \times 1} + 32$$

$$F = \frac{382.5}{5} + 32$$

$$F = 76.5 + 32$$

$$F = 108.5$$

The temperature in degrees Fahrenheit is 108.5. *(See Chapter VIII, Section B.)*

2. **C** To solve this problem, use the order of operations and divide first: $6.50 \div 0.25 = 26$. Then add this number to the rest of the numbers: $0.998 + 4.223 + 26 = 31.221$. Last, round to the nearest tenth: $31.221 = 31.2$. *(See Chapter VIII, Section A.)*

3. **C** To find the perimeter of the triangle, add all three sides together, using the formula $P = a + b + c$:

$$P = 12 + 16 + 9 = 37$$

The perimeter of the triangle is 37. *(See Chapter VIII, Section E.)*

4. **A** To solve this problem, first find the common denominator, which is 20. Next, multiply each fraction to achieve the common denominator. Then add the first two fractions. Then subtract the third fraction from the sum of the first two fractions. Next, add the product of this fraction to the last fraction as shown here:

$$\frac{14}{5} + \frac{21}{4} - \frac{6}{2} + \frac{9}{10} =$$

$$\frac{56}{20} + \frac{105}{20} - \frac{60}{20} + \frac{18}{20} =$$

$$\frac{161}{20} - \frac{60}{20} + \frac{18}{20} =$$

$$\frac{101}{20} + \frac{18}{20} = \frac{119}{20}$$

Last, divide 119 by 20 to get 5.95. *(See Chapter VIII, Section B.)*

5. **A** To solve this problem, use the foil method: First: $4x \times 3x = 12\,x^2$; Outer: $4x \times -6 = -24x$; Inner: $9 \times 3x = 27x$; Last: $9 \times -6 = -54$. Then combine the like terms: $-24x + 27x = 3x$; and the result is $12x^2 + 3x - 54$. *(See Chapter VIII, Section A.)*

6. **D** When multiplying exponents with the same base, add the exponents:

$$(x^{15})(4x^{15})$$

$$4x^{15+15}$$

$$4x^{30}$$

(See Chapter VIII, Section A.)

7. **A** To solve this problem, use the formula: $d = rt$ and solve for r as shown:

$$d = rt$$
$$7.5 \text{ miles} = r \times 9 \text{ minutes}$$
$$\frac{7.5}{9} = \frac{9r}{9}$$
$$\frac{7.5}{9} = r$$

The result is $\frac{7.5}{9}$ of a mile per minute. To convert this to miles per hour, multiply the answer by 60 because 1 hour = 60 minutes:

$$\frac{7.5}{9} \times \frac{60}{1} =$$
$$\frac{450}{9} = 50 \text{ miles per hour}$$

(See Chapter VIII, Section B.)

8. **D** For every five years of service, a firefighter's holiday bonus increases by 1 percent. If a firefighter has been with the same company for 15 to 20 years, his or her bonus would be 5.0 percent of his or her salary. If he or she was with the company for 20 to 25 years, his or her bonus would be 6 percent of his or her salary. If he or she is with the company for 25 to 30 years, however, his or her bonus would be 7 percent of his or her salary. *(See Chapter VIII, Section G.)*

9. **B** To solve this problem, use the order of operations and multiply first: $8.35 \times \$56.23 = \$469.5205$. Then subtract: $\$649.99 - \$29.77 = \$620.22$. Next, add: $\$620.22 + \$469.5205 = \$1,089.7405$. Last, round to the nearest hundredth: $\$1,089.7405 = \$1,089.74$. *(See Chapter VIII, Section A.)*

10. **B** To find the circumference of the circle, use the formula $C = 2\pi r$:

$$C = 2(3.14)(12 \text{ ft})$$
$$C = 6.28 \times 12 \text{ ft}$$
$$C = 75.36 \text{ ft}$$

Now, round 75.36 feet to the nearest whole number. The circumference of the circle is 75 feet. *(See Chapter VIII, Section E.)*

11. **C** The easiest way to solve this problem is to covert the fractions to decimals by dividing the numerator by the denominator: $\frac{2}{3} = 0.67$; $4\frac{1}{4} = 4.25$; $\frac{6}{8} = 0.75$, which would be $0.67 \times 0.78 + 4.25 - 0.75$. Next, follow the order of operations and multiply first: $0.67 \times 0.78 = 0.5226$; Now, add and then subtract: $0.5226 + 4.25 - 0.75 = 4.7726 - 0.75 = 4.0226$, which would round to 4.02. *(See Chapter VIII, Section B.)*

12. **D** When working with negative exponents, the negative exponent equals the base's reciprocal with a positive exponent. In this case, $\frac{1}{8^{-4}}$ would become $\frac{8^4}{1} = 8^4 = 8 \times 8 \times 8 \times 8 = 4,096$. *(See Chapter VIII, Section B.)*

13. **B** To solve this equation, first multiply each side by 3. Then subtract 3 from each side. Then divide each side by 9 as shown here:

$$\frac{9x+3}{3} = 37$$

$$(3)\frac{9x+3}{3} = 37(3)$$

$$9x+3 = 111$$

$$9x+3-3 = 111-3$$

$$9x = 108$$

$$\frac{9x}{9} = \frac{108}{9}$$

$$x = 12$$

(See Chapter VIII, Section D.)

14. **D** You can solve this problem either by multiplying the decimals or by using cross-multiplication. To solve by multiplying the decimals: first, turn the percentage into a decimal by moving the decimal two places to the left: 42 percent = 0.42. Next, multiply this number by the number in the problem: $0.42 \times 575 = 241.5$. To solve by cross-multiplication, first, turn the percentage into a fraction by putting it over 100: $\frac{42}{100}$. Next, set up a proportion and solve:

$$\frac{42}{100} = \frac{x}{575}$$

$$24{,}150 = 100x$$

$$\frac{24{,}150}{100} = \frac{100x}{100}$$

$$241.5 = x$$

(See Chapter VIII, Section D.)

15. **B** To solve this problem, multiply the number of flights of stairs by the number of steps in each flight of stairs: $12 \times 9 = 108$. A firefighter must climb 108 total steps during the fitness test. *(See Chapter VIII, Section H.)*

16. **B** To solve this problem, set up a proportion and cross-multiply as shown:

$$\frac{12 \text{ training exercises}}{5 \text{ days}} = \frac{x}{7 \text{ days}}$$

$$84 = 5x$$

$$\frac{84}{5} = \frac{5x}{5}$$

$$16.8 \text{ training exercises} = x$$

The answer choice nearest to 16.8 is **B,** 17. *(See Chapter VIII, Section C.)*

17. A To solve this equation, first, solve the portion in parentheses; then subtract 11 from each side; next, divide each side by 16 as shown here:

$$16x + 11 = 9(9 - 14)$$
$$16x + 11 = 81 - 126$$
$$16x + 11 = -45$$
$$16x + 11 - 11 = -45 - 11$$
$$16x = -56$$
$$\frac{16x}{16} = \frac{-56}{16}$$
$$x = -3.5$$

(See Chapter VIII, Section C.)

18. C You can solve this problem either by multiplying the decimals or by using cross-multiplication and subtracting this number from the original cost. To solve by multiplying the decimals: first, turn the percentage into a decimal by moving the decimal two places to the left: Next, multiply this number by the number in the problem: 38% = 0.38: 0.38 × $49.99 = $19.00. Last, subtract this number from the original price: $49.99 – $19.00 = $30.99. To solve this problem using cross-multiplication, first, turn the percentage into a fraction by putting it over 100: $\frac{38}{100}$. Next, set up a proportion and solve:

$$\frac{38}{100} = \frac{x}{49.99}$$
$$1,899.62 = 100x$$
$$\frac{1,899.62}{100} = \frac{100x}{100}$$
$$19 = x$$

(See Chapter VIII, Section B.)

19. C To solve this problem, set up a proportion and cross multiply as shown:

$$\frac{5.5 \text{ miles}}{30 \text{ minutes}} = \frac{x}{18 \text{ minutes}}$$
$$99 = 30x$$
$$\frac{99}{30} = \frac{30x}{30}$$
$$3.3 \text{ miles} = x$$

(See Chapter VIII, Section C.)

20. A To solve this problem, add together the cost of equipment for the first two quarters: $7,550.63 + $562.99 = $8,113.62. Now, add together the cost of equipment for the last two quarters: $225.00 + $4,761.02 = $4,986.02. Last, subtract the total of the cost of equipment for the last two quarters from the total of the cost of equipment for the first two quarters: $8,113.62 – $4,986.02 = $3,127.60. *(See Chapter VIII, Section B.)*

Section 10: Mechanical Aptitude

1. **D** If Gear B rotates in a clockwise direction, then the two gears its teeth are interlocked with (Gears A and C) must rotate in the opposite direction, so Gears A and C must rotate counterclockwise. Therefore, none of the gears will rotate in the same direction as Gear B. *(See Chapter IX, Section B.)*

2. **C** Based on the image, you know that Gear C is the smallest gear and smaller gears rotate faster and at more revolutions than larger gears, so Gear C will make the most revolutions per minute. *(See Chapter IX, Section B.)*

3. **D** A pike pole has a long handle and a metal head with a point and hook that is used to create a hole in a ceiling and pull it down. A drywall hook has a long handle and a wide hook featuring teeth that looks like a small rake; a Clemens hook has a long handle with a curved groove at the end; a San Francisco hook has a long handle with a built-in gas shut-off and directional slot. *(See Chapter IX, Section A.)*

4. **C** A hydraulic spreader, a Kelly tool, and a Halligan bar are all used to pry open objects. *(See Chapter IX, Section A.)*

5. **B** A mallet would most likely be used to deliver a soft blow to an object. The other tools are a reciprocating saw, a wrench, and a hammer. *(See Chapter IX, Section A.)*

6. **D** Because Wheel A is half the size of Wheel B, it rotates twice as fast as Wheel B. If Wheel B rotates 75 revolutions per minute, then Wheel A makes twice as many revolutions, so 75 multiplied by 2 is 150. Wheel A rotates 150 revolutions per minute. *(See Chapter IX, Section B.)*

7. **A** All wheels in a belt-drive pulley setup rotate in the same direction regardless of size, unless the belt is crossed. Because the belt in the image is crossed, Wheel A and Wheel B would spin in opposite directions, so if Wheel A spins clockwise, Wheel B spins counterclockwise. *(See Chapter IX, Section B.)*

8. **A** The tool pictured is a rake, which would most likely be used to break up materials. A crowbar would most likely be used as a lever to move heavy objects; a shovel would most likely be used to carry or remove materials; and a Clemens hook would most likely be used to remove plaster or siding. *(See Chapter IX, Section A.)*

9. **D** The tool pictured is a flat-head axe, which is used to cut through floors, roofs, or ceilings. It would most likely be used for cutting in forcible-entry operations. *(See Chapter IX, Section A.)*

10. **A** To answer this question, use the formula $w \times d_1 = f \times d_2$ and plug in the information you know into the formula. The weight of the object is 50 pounds, so $w = 50$. The distance from the box to the fulcrum is 5 feet, so $d_1 = 5$. The distance from the firefighter to the fulcrum is 25 feet, so $d_2 = 25$. Solve for force (f):

$$w \times d_1 = f \times d_2$$
$$50 \times 5 = f \times 25$$
$$\frac{250}{25} = \frac{25f}{25}$$
$$10 = f$$

(See Chapter IX, Section B.)

11. **C** To answer this question, use the formula $w \times d_1 = f \times d_2$ and plug in the information you know into the formula. The weight of the object is 150 pounds, so $w = 150$. The distance from the box to the fulcrum is 10 feet, so $d_1 = 10$. The distance from the firefighter to the fulcrum is 20 feet, so $d_2 = 20$. Solve for force (f):

$$w \times d_1 = f \times d_2$$
$$150 \times 10 = f \times 20$$
$$\frac{1,500}{20} = \frac{20f}{20}$$
$$75 = f$$

(See Chapter IX, Section B.)

12. **C** The tool pictured is a utility knife, which is a lightweight cutting tool with a retractable blade that is used to cut through light materials such as paper, fabric, or cardboard. *(See Chapter IX, Section A.)*

13. **B** The tool pictured is a sledgehammer, which is a long-handled tool with a large metal head used for heavy-duty pounding or breaking. It would most likely be used for striking in forcible-entry operations. *(See Chapter IX, Section A.)*

14. **A** The tool pictured is a pick, which is a heavy-duty tool with a long handle and a metal head with one or two points used to break up earth or stone. *(See Chapter IX, Section A.)*

15. **A** A firefighter would most likely use a New York hook for prying or pulling an object or for obtaining leverage. A drywall hook is most often used to remove drywall, and a Clemens hook is most often used to remove plaster. To ventilate and turn off a gas line, a firefighter would most often use a San Francisco hook. *(See Chapter IX, Section B.)*

16. **A** When a nut on a standard-thread screw is turned counterclockwise, it will loosen, so this means the nut will move down the screw. *(See Chapter IX, Section B.)*

17. **C** To solve this problem, first determine how many times heavier the new weight is than the old weight. To do this, divide the new weight by the old weight: $150 \div 30 = 5$. Next, multiply this number by the number of inches the spring stretches under the old weight: $5 \times 15 = 75$. If you increase the weight by five times, the spring would stretch 75 inches. *(See Chapter IX, Section B.)*

18. **A** A ventilation saw, which is used to make quick cuts in roofs or walls, is a power-operated saw that has teeth similar to a chainsaw. Choice B is incorrect because a rotary saw is a power-operated saw with circular removable blades used to cut through materials such as wood, plastic, metal, or concrete. Choice C is incorrect because a reciprocating saw is a power-operated saw with a short blade that uses a push-and-pull motion to cut through a variety of materials. Finally, Choice D is incorrect because a hack saw is a handheld tool with a variety of handles and blades used to cut through wood or metal. *(See Chapter IX, Section A.)*

19. **B** A shovel would most likely be used to carry or move materials. A rope would most likely be used to hoist or secure objects; pliers would most likely be used to grip objects; and a San Francisco hook would most likely be used to turn off a gas line. *(See Chapter IX, Section A.)*

20. **D** The only difference between the two boxes is the size. They weigh the same, are made of the same material, and are positioned at the same angle on the inclined planes. Box A is smaller than Box B and therefore, has a smaller surface-to-surface contact area with the inclined plane. This means less friction exists between the surface of Box A; therefore, Box B will require more effort to push it up the inclined plane. *(See Chapter IX, Section B.)*

II. Two-Month Cram Plan

	Observation, Memory, and Spatial Orientation (Chapter V)	Reading Comprehension and Verbal Expression (Chapter VI)	Deductive, Inductive, and Logical Reasoning; Information Ordering; and Problem Sensitivity (Chapter VII)	Mathematics (Chapter VIII)	Mechanical Aptitude (Chapter IX)
8 weeks before the test	**Study Time:** 4½ hours ❑ Take the **Diagnostic Test** (Chapter I) and review the answer explanations. 　❑ Based on your errors on the **Diagnostic Test,** identify difficult topics and their corresponding chapters. These are your targeted areas.				
7 weeks before the test	**Study Time:** 2 hours ❑ Read sections A–B. ❑ Do practice questions 1–2 in Section A and practice questions 1–3 in Section B. ❑ If Section A is a targeted area, do practice questions 1–5. ❑ If Section B is a targeted area, do practice questions 1–7. ❑ Review the answer explanations for any questions you answered incorrectly.	**Study Time:** 2 hours ❑ Read Section A. ❑ Do practice questions 1–3. ❑ If Section A is a targeted area, do practice questions 1–8.	**Study Time:** 2 hours ❑ Read sections A and C. ❑ Do practice questions 1–5 in Section C. ❑ If Section C is a targeted area, do practice questions 1–7.	**Study Time:** 2 hours ❑ Read sections A and F. ❑ Do example questions 1–3 in each part of sections A and F. ❑ Make a list of the questions that you answered incorrectly in each section.	**Study Time:** 2 hours ❑ Read Section A. ❑ Do practice questions 1–7 in this section. ❑ If Section A is a targeted area, do practice questions 1–10.

(continued)

	Observation, Memory, and Spatial Orientation (Chapter V)	Reading Comprehension and Verbal Expression (Chapter VI)	Deductive, Inductive, and Logical Reasoning; Information Ordering; and Problem Sensitivity (Chapter VII)	Mathematics (Chapter VIII)	Mechanical Aptitude (Chapter IX)
6 weeks before the test	**Study Time:** 1 hour ❏ Review sections A–B. ❏ Do practice questions 3–8 in Section A. ❏ Do practice questions 4–7 in Section B. ❏ Review the answer explanations for any questions you answered incorrectly.	**Study Time:** 1 hour ❏ Review Section A. ❏ Do practice questions 4–10.	**Study Time:** 1 hour ❏ Review sections A and C. ❏ Do practice questions 6–10 in Section C.	**Study Time:** 2 hours ❏ Read sections B–C. ❏ Do example questions 1–3 in each part of sections B–C. ❏ Make a list of the questions that you answered incorrectly in each section.	**Study Time:** 1 hour ❏ Review Section A. ❏ Do practice questions 8–15 in this section. ❏ Make a list of the questions that you answered incorrectly in each section.
5 weeks before the test	**Study Time:** 2 hours ❏ Read Section C. ❏ Do practice questions 1–3. ❏ If Section C is a targeted area, do practice questions 1–6.	**Study Time:** 2 hours ❏ Read Section B. ❏ Do practice questions 1–4. ❏ If Section B is a targeted area, do practice questions 1–6.	**Study Time:** 2 hours ❏ Read sections B and D. ❏ Do practice questions 1–5 in each section. ❏ For targeted areas, do practice questions 1–8 in both sections.	**Study Time:** 2 hours ❏ Read sections D–E. ❏ Do example questions 1–3 in each part of sections D–E. ❏ Make a list of the questions that you answered incorrectly in each section.	**Study Time:** 2 hours ❏ Read Section B. ❏ Do practice questions 1–7 in this section. ❏ If Section B is a targeted area, do practice questions 1–11.
4 weeks before the test	**Study Time:** 1 hour ❏ Review Section C. ❏ Do practice questions 4–9. ❏ Review the answer explanations for any questions you answered incorrectly.	**Study Time:** 1 hour ❏ Review parts 2–5 of Section B. ❏ Do practice questions 5–10.	**Study Time:** 1 hour ❏ Review sections A and C. ❏ Redo practice questions 1–5 in Section C. ❏ Review the answer explanations for any questions you answered incorrectly.	**Study Time:** 1 hour ❏ Review sections A–C. ❏ Do practice questions 1–10. ❏ Add the questions that you answered incorrectly to the list you created. ❏ Review the list of questions that you answered incorrectly.	**Study Time:** 1 hour ❏ Review Section B. ❏ Do practice questions 8–15 in this section. ❏ Make a list of the questions that you answered incorrectly in each section.

	Observation, Memory, and Spatial Orientation (Chapter V)	Reading Comprehension and Verbal Expression (Chapter VI)	Deductive, Inductive, and Logical Reasoning; Information Ordering; and Problem Sensitivity (Chapter VII)	Mathematics (Chapter VIII)	Mechanical Aptitude (Chapter IX)
3 weeks before the test	**Study Time:** 1 hour ❏ Review sections A–C. ❏ Do practice questions 9–10 in Section A. ❏ Do practice questions 8–10 in Section B. ❏ Do practice questions 10–12 in Section C. ❏ Continue reviewing the answer explanations for any questions you answered incorrectly.	**Study Time:** 1 hour ❏ Review part 1 of Section B. ❏ Highlight any words that are unfamiliar and difficult to spell.	**Study Time:** 1 hour ❏ Redo the practice questions in sections B–D. ❏ Make a list of any questions you answered incorrectly in each section.	**Study Time:** 1 hour ❏ Review sections D–F. ❏ Do practice questions 11–20. ❏ Add the questions that you answered incorrectly to the list you created. ❏ Review the list of questions that you answered incorrectly.	**Study Time:** 1 hour ❏ Review sections A–B. ❏ Redo 5 practice questions from each section. ❏ Review any questions you answered incorrectly in each section.
2 weeks before the test	**Study Time:** 4½ hours ❏ Take the **Practice Test** (Chapter X) and review the answer explanations. ❏ Based on your errors on the **Practice Test,** identify difficult topics and their corresponding chapters. These are your targeted areas.				
	Study Time: 1 hour ❏ Review any sections in Chapter V that remain problematic. ❏ Redo 2 practice questions in each section of Chapter V.	**Study Time:** 1 hour ❏ Review any sections in Chapter VI that remain problematic. ❏ Redo any practice questions in Section A of Chapter VI. ❏ Review the highlighted words from part 1 of Section B.	**Study Time:** 1 hour ❏ Review any Deductive, Inductive, and Logical Reasoning; Information Ordering; and Problem Sensitivity questions that you answered incorrectly on the Practice Test. ❏ Determine which sections require the most attention in Chapter VII.	**Study Time:** 1 hour ❏ Review sections A and F. ❏ Redo 1 example question from each part in sections A and F. ❏ Review the list of questions that you answered incorrectly.	**Study Time:** 1 hour ❏ Review any sections in Chapter IX that remain problematic. ❏ Review any Mechanical Aptitude questions that you answered incorrectly on the Practice Test.

(continued)

	Observation, Memory, and Spatial Orientation (Chapter V)	Reading Comprehension and Verbal Expression (Chapter VI)	Deductive, Inductive, and Logical Reasoning; Information Ordering; and Problem Sensitivity (Chapter VII)	Mathematics (Chapter VIII)	Mechanical Aptitude (Chapter IX)
7 days before the test	**Study Time:** 30 minutes ❏ Review Section A. ❏ Redo practice questions 6–10.	**Study Time:** 30 minutes ❏ Review Section A. ❏ Redo practice questions 5–10. ❏ Review the highlighted words from part 1 of Section B.	**Study Time:** 30 minutes ❏ Review sections A–B. ❏ Redo practice questions 6–10 in Section B. ❏ Redo any questions you answered incorrectly in Section B. ❏ Review the list you created of questions you answered incorrectly.	**Study Time:** 30 minutes ❏ Review sections B–C. ❏ Redo 1 example question from each part in sections B–C. ❏ Review the list of questions that you answered incorrectly.	**Study Time:** 30 minutes ❏ Review Section A. ❏ Redo practice questions 1–15 in this section. ❏ Continue reviewing any questions you answered incorrectly in this section.
6 days before the test	**Study Time:** 30 minutes ❏ Review Section B. ❏ Redo practice questions 1–3.	**Study Time:** 30 minutes ❏ Review parts 2–5 of Section B. ❏ Redo practice questions 1–4 and 7–10. ❏ Review the highlighted words from part 1 of Section B.	**Study Time:** 30 minutes ❏ Review sections C–D. ❏ Redo practice questions 6–10 in each section. ❏ Redo any questions you answered incorrectly in each section. ❏ Review the list you created of questions you answered incorrectly.	**Study Time:** 30 minutes ❏ Review sections D–E. ❏ Redo 1 example question from each part in sections D–E. ❏ Review the list of questions that you answered incorrectly.	**Study Time:** 30 minutes ❏ Review Section B. ❏ Redo practice questions 1–15 in this section. ❏ Continue reviewing any questions you answered incorrectly in this section.

	Observation, Memory, and Spatial Orientation (Chapter V)	Reading Comprehension and Verbal Expression (Chapter VI)	Deductive, Inductive, and Logical Reasoning; Information Ordering; and Problem Sensitivity (Chapter VII)	Mathematics (Chapter VIII)	Mechanical Aptitude (Chapter IX)
5 days before the test	**Study Time:** 30 minutes ❑ Continue reviewing sections A–B. ❑ Redo practice questions 1–5 in Section A. ❑ Redo practice questions 1–7 in Section B.	**Study Time:** 30 minutes ❑ Review Section A. ❑ Redo practice questions 1–3 and 9–10. ❑ Read through the highlighted words from part 1 of Section B.	**Study Time:** 30 minutes ❑ Continue reviewing sections A–B. ❑ Redo practice questions 3–5 in Section B. ❑ Review the list you created of questions you answered incorrectly.	**Study Time:** 30 minutes ❑ Continue reviewing sections A–C. ❑ Redo practice questions 1–10. ❑ Add any questions you answered incorrectly to the list you created.	**Study Time:** 30 minutes ❑ Continue reviewing sections A–B. ❑ Redo practice questions 1–5. ❑ Review any questions you answered incorrectly.
4 days before the test	**Study Time:** 30 minutes ❑ Review Section C. ❑ Redo practice questions 7–9.	**Study Time:** 30 minutes ❑ Review Section B. ❑ Redo practice questions 1–6. ❑ Ask a friend or study partner to read the highlighted words from part 1 of Section B aloud. Write the words on a separate piece of paper and review your answers. Based on your errors, continue reviewing words that still present difficulties.	**Study Time:** 30 minutes ❑ Continue reviewing sections C–D. ❑ Redo practice questions 8–10 in Section C and practice questions 6–8 in Section D. ❑ Review the list you created of questions you answered incorrectly.	**Study Time:** 30 minutes ❑ Continue reviewing sections D–F. ❑ Redo practice questions 11–20. ❑ Add any questions you answered incorrectly to the list you created.	**Study Time:** 30 minutes ❑ Continue reviewing sections A–B. ❑ Redo all practice questions from each section.

(continued)

	Observation, Memory, and Spatial Orientation (Chapter V)	Reading Comprehension and Verbal Expression (Chapter VI)	Deductive, Inductive, and Logical Reasoning; Information Ordering; and Problem Sensitivity (Chapter VII)	Mathematics (Chapter VIII)	Mechanical Aptitude (Chapter IX)
3 days before the test	**Study Time:** 30 minutes ❏ Continue reviewing Section C. ❏ Redo practice questions 10–12.	**Study Time:** 30 minutes ❏ Review Section A. ❏ Redo practice questions 4–8. ❏ Read through the highlighted words from part 1 of Section B that still present a problem.	**Study Time:** 30 minutes ❏ Briefly read through sections A–D. ❏ Continue to review the list you created of questions you answered incorrectly.	**Study Time:** 30 minutes ❏ Redo 1 example question in sections A–F. ❏ Continue to review the list of questions that are problematic.	**Study Time:** 30 minutes ❏ Continue reviewing sections A–B. ❏ Continue reviewing the list of questions that are problematic.
2 days before the test	**Study Time:** 30 minutes ❏ Briefly read through sections A–C. ❏ Carefully review any practice questions that you answered incorrectly during your previous study sessions.	**Study Time:** 30 minutes ❏ Briefly read through sections A–B. ❏ Do 3 practice questions from each section.	**Study Time:** 30 minutes ❏ Continue reviewing sections A–D. ❏ Redo any Deductive, Inductive, and Logical Reasoning; Information Ordering; and Problem Sensitivity questions you answered incorrectly on the Practice Test.	**Study Time:** 30 minutes ❏ Redo any example questions and practice questions that you answered incorrectly. ❏ Continue to review the list of questions that are problematic.	**Study Time:** 30 minutes ❏ Briefly read through sections A–B. ❏ Do 5 practice questions from each section. ❏ Review the list of questions that are problematic.
1 day before the test	❏ Relax. You're well prepared for the test. ❏ Get a good night's rest.				

Morning of the test	**Reminders:**
	❏ Have a good breakfast.
	❏ Take the following items with you to the testing facility:
	    ❏ Two forms of identification, including photo ID.
	    ❏ Any documentation or other items that are required by the testing facility.
	❏ Arrive at the testing facility early and take a few minutes to walk around before the test.
	❏ Stay calm and remember to take deep breaths if you begin to feel nervous.				

III. One-Month Cram Plan

	Observation, Memory, and Spatial Orientation (Chapter V)	**Reading Comprehension and Verbal Expression (Chapter VI)**	**Deductive, Inductive, and Logical Reasoning; Information Ordering; and Problem Sensitivity (Chapter VII)**	**Mathematics (Chapter VIII)**	**Mechanical Aptitude (Chapter IX)**
4 weeks before the test	**Study Time:** 4½ hours ❏ Take the **Diagnostic Test** and review the answer explanations. 　　❏ Based on your errors on the **Diagnostic Test,** identify difficult topics and their corresponding chapters. These are your targeted areas.				
	Study Time: 2 hours ❏ Read sections A–C. ❏ Do practice questions 1–2 in Section A. ❏ If Section A is a targeted area, do practice questions 1–5. ❏ Do practice questions 1–3 in Section B. ❏ If Section B is a targeted area, do practice questions 1–7. ❏ Do practice questions 1–3 in Section C. ❏ If Section C is a targeted area, do practice questions 1–6.	**Study Time:** 2 hours ❏ Read sections A–B. ❏ Do practice questions 1–4 in Section A. ❏ If Section A is a targeted area, do practice questions 1–8. ❏ Do practice questions 1–4 in Section B. ❏ If Section B is a targeted area, do practice questions 1–6.	**Study Time:** 2 hours ❏ Read sections A and C. ❏ Do practice questions 1–5 in Section C. ❏ If Section C is a targeted area, do practice questions 1–7. ❏ Make a list of any questions you answered incorrectly.	**Study Time:** 2 hours ❏ Read sections A, E, and F. ❏ Do example questions 1–3 in each part of each section. ❏ Make a list of the questions that you answered incorrectly in each section.	**Study Time:** 2 hours ❏ Read Section A. ❏ Do practice questions 1–7 in this section. ❏ If Section A is a targeted area, do practice questions 1–10.

(continued)

	Observation, Memory, and Spatial Orientation (Chapter V)	Reading Comprehension and Verbal Expression (Chapter VI)	Deductive, Inductive, and Logical Reasoning; Information Ordering; and Problem Sensitivity (Chapter VII)	Mathematics (Chapter VIII)	Mechanical Aptitude (Chapter IX)
3 weeks before the test	**Study Time:** 1 hour ❏ Review sections A–C. ❏ Do practice questions 3–10 in Section A. ❏ Do practice questions 4–10 in Section B. ❏ Do practice questions 4–12 in Section C. ❏ Make note of any practice questions that you answered incorrectly.	**Study Time:** 1 hour ❏ Review sections A–B. ❏ Do practice questions 5–8 in Section A. ❏ Do practice questions 5–6 in Section B.	**Study Time:** 2 hours ❏ Read sections B and D. ❏ Do practice questions 1–5 in each section. ❏ For targeted areas, do practice questions 1–8 in each section. ❏ Keep track of any questions you answered incorrectly.	**Study Time:** 2 hours ❏ Read sections B–D. ❏ Do example questions 1–3 in each part of each section. ❏ Make a list of the questions that you answered incorrectly in each section.	**Study Time:** 2 hours ❏ Read Section B. ❏ Do practice questions 1–7 in this section. ❏ If Section B is a targeted area, do practice questions 1–11.
2 weeks before the test	**Study Time:** 1 hour ❏ Continue reviewing sections A–C. ❏ Redo any practice questions that you answered incorrectly in your previous study sessions.	**Study Time:** 1 hour ❏ Continue reviewing sections A–B. ❏ Do practice questions 9–10 in Section A. ❏ Do practice questions 7–10 in Section B. ❏ Highlight any words that are unfamiliar or difficult to spell in part 1 of Section B. ❏ Review these words over the next few study sessions.	**Study Time:** 1 hour ❏ Review sections A–C. ❏ Do practice questions 6–10 in Section C. ❏ Continue to note any questions that you missed.	**Study Time:** 1 hour ❏ Review sections A–F. ❏ Do practice questions 1–20. ❏ Add any questions that are problematic to the list of the questions that you answered incorrectly in each section.	**Study Time:** 2 hours ❏ Review sections A–B. ❏ Do practice questions 11–15 in Section A. ❏ Do practice questions 12–15 in Section B.
7 days before the test	**Study Time:** 4½ hours ❏ Take the **Practice Test** (Chapter X) and review the answer explanations. ❏ Based on your errors on the **Practice Test,** identify difficult topics and their corresponding chapters. These are your targeted areas.				

	Observation, Memory, and Spatial Orientation (Chapter V)	Reading Comprehension and Verbal Expression (Chapter VI)	Deductive, Inductive, and Logical Reasoning; Information Ordering; and Problem Sensitivity (Chapter VII)	Mathematics (Chapter VIII)	Mechanical Aptitude (Chapter IX)
6 days before the test	**Study Time:** 1 hour ❑ Redo any Observation, Memory, and Spatial Orientation questions that you answered incorrectly on the Practice Test. ❑ Review any sections of Chapter V that still require your attention.	**Study Time:** 1 hour ❑ Based on your errors on the Practice Test, review the sections in Chapter VI that remain problematic. ❑ Ask a friend or study partner to read the highlighted words from part 1 of Section B aloud. Write the words on a separate piece of paper and review your answers. Based on your errors, continue reviewing words that still present difficulties.	**Study Time:** 1 hour ❑ Redo any Deductive, Inductive, and Logical Reasoning; Information Ordering; and Problem Sensitivity questions that you answered incorrectly on the Practice Test. ❑ Review sections B and D. ❑ Redo practice questions 1–5 in each section.	**Study Time:** 1 hour ❑ Redo any Mathematics questions that you answered incorrectly on the Practice Test. ❑ Review sections A, E, and F. ❑ Redo 1 example question in each part of each section.	**Study Time:** 1 hour ❑ Redo any Mechanical Aptitude questions that you answered incorrectly on the Practice Test. ❑ Review sections A–B. ❑ Redo practice questions 1–7 in each section. ❑ Review any questions that you answered incorrectly.
5 days before the test	**Study Time:** 1 hour ❑ Review sections A–B. ❑ Redo practice questions 1–5 in Section A. ❑ Redo practice questions 1–7 in Section B.	**Study Time:** 1 hour ❑ Review Section A. ❑ Redo practice questions 5–10. ❑ Review the highlighted words from part 1 of Section B.	**Study Time:** 1 hour ❑ Review sections A and C. ❑ Redo practice questions 1–5 in Section C.	**Study Time:** 1 hour ❑ Review sections B–D. ❑ Redo 1 example question in each part of each section.	**Study Time:** 1 hour ❑ Review Section A. ❑ Redo practice questions 8–15. ❑ Review any questions that you answered incorrectly.
4 days before the test	**Study Time:** 1 hour ❑ Continue reviewing sections A–B. ❑ Redo practice questions 6–10 in Section A. ❑ Redo practice questions 8–10 in Section B.	**Study Time:** 1 hour ❑ Review Section B. ❑ Redo practice questions 5–10. ❑ Review the highlighted words from part 1 of Section B.	**Study Time:** 1 hour ❑ Continue reviewing sections B and D. ❑ Redo practice questions 6–10 in each section.	**Study Time:** 1 hour ❑ Continue reviewing sections A–C. ❑ Redo practice questions 1–10.	**Study Time:** 1 hour ❑ Review Section B. ❑ Redo practice questions 8–15. ❑ Review any questions that you answered incorrectly.

(continued)

	Observation, Memory, and Spatial Orientation (Chapter V)	Reading Comprehension and Verbal Expression (Chapter VI)	Deductive, Inductive, and Logical Reasoning; Information Ordering; and Problem Sensitivity (Chapter VII)	Mathematics (Chapter VIII)	Mechanical Aptitude (Chapter IX)
3 days before the test	**Study Time:** 30 minutes ❏ Review Section C. ❏ Redo practice questions 1–6 in this section.	**Study Time:** 30 minutes ❏ Continue reviewing sections A–B. ❏ Redo 3 practice questions from each section. ❏ Read through the highlighted words from part 1 of Section B.	**Study Time:** 30 minutes ❏ Continue reviewing sections A and C. ❏ Redo practice questions 6–10 in Section C. ❏ Review the list you created before the test.	**Study Time:** 30 minutes ❏ Continue reviewing sections D–F. ❏ Redo practice questions 1–10. ❏ Review the list of questions that are problematic.	**Study Time:** 30 minutes ❏ Continue reviewing sections A–B. ❏ Review any questions that you answered incorrectly.
2 days before the test	**Study Time:** 30 minutes ❏ Continue reviewing Section C. ❏ Redo practice questions 7–12. ❏ Redo any practice questions that you answered incorrectly in your previous study sessions.	**Study Time:** 30 minutes ❏ Briefly review sections A–B. ❏ Quiz yourself on any highlighted words from part 1 of Section B that present any difficulties.	**Study Time:** 30 minutes ❏ Briefly review sections A–D. ❏ Redo any practice questions that you answered incorrectly in each section. ❏ Review the list you created before the test.	**Study Time:** 30 minutes ❏ Continue reviewing sections A–F. ❏ Redo all the practice questions. ❏ Continue to review the list of questions that are problematic.	**Study Time:** 30 minutes ❏ Continue reviewing sections A–B. ❏ Redo all practice questions from each section.
1 day before the test	❏ Relax. You're well prepared for the test. ❏ Get a good night's rest.				
Morning of the test	**Reminders:** ❏ Have a good breakfast. ❏ Take the following items with you to the testing facility: ❏ Two forms of identification, including photo ID. ❏ Any documentation or other items that are required by the testing facility. ❏ Arrive at the testing facility early and take a few minutes to walk around before the test. ❏ Stay calm and remember to take deep breaths if you begin to feel nervous.				

IV. One-Week Cram Plan

	Observation, Memory, and Spatial Orientation (Chapter V)	Reading Comprehension and Verbal Expression (Chapter VI)	Deductive, Inductive, and Logical Reasoning; Information Ordering; and Problem Sensitivity (Chapter VII)	Mathematics (Chapter VIII)	Mechanical Aptitude (Chapter IX)
7 days before the test	**Study Time:** 4½ hours ❏ Take the **Diagnostic Test** and review the answer explanations. ❏ Based on your errors on the **Diagnostic Test,** identify difficult topics and their corresponding chapters. These are your targeted areas.				
6 days before the test	**Study Time:** 2 hours ❏ Read sections A–B. ❏ Do practice questions 1–5 in Section A. ❏ If Section A is a targeted area, do practice questions 1–8. ❏ Do practice questions 1–3 in Section B. ❏ If Section B is a targeted area, do practice questions 1–7. ❏ Make note of any practice questions that you answered incorrectly.	**Study Time:** 2 hours ❏ Read Section A. ❏ Do practice questions 1–4 in Section A. ❏ If Section A is a targeted area, do practice questions 4–8.	**Study Time:** 2 hours ❏ Read sections A and C. ❏ Do practice questions 1–3 in Section C. ❏ If Section C is a targeted area, do practice questions 1–5. ❏ Keep track of any questions you answered incorrectly.	**Study Time:** 2 hours ❏ Read sections A, E, and F. ❏ Do example questions 1–3 in each part of each section. ❏ Make a list of the questions that you answered incorrectly in each section.	**Study Time:** 2 hours ❏ Read Section A. ❏ Do practice questions 1–10 in this section. ❏ Make a list of the questions that you answered incorrectly in each section.

(continued)

	Observation, Memory, and Spatial Orientation (Chapter V)	Reading Comprehension and Verbal Expression (Chapter VI)	Deductive, Inductive, and Logical Reasoning; Information Ordering; and Problem Sensitivity (Chapter VII)	Mathematics (Chapter VIII)	Mechanical Aptitude (Chapter IX)
5 days before the test	**Study Time:** 2 hours ❏ Read Section C. ❏ Do practice questions 1–6. ❏ If Section C is a targeted area, do practice questions 1–9. ❏ Make note of any practice questions that you answered incorrectly.	**Study Time:** 2 hours ❏ Read Section B. ❏ Do practice questions 1–4 in Section B. ❏ If Section B is a targeted area, do practice questions 1–6. ❏ Highlight any words that are unfamiliar or difficult to spell in part 1 of Section B.	**Study Time:** 2 hours ❏ Read sections B and D. ❏ Do practice questions 1–5 in each section. ❏ If Section B is a targeted area, do practice questions 1–8. ❏ If Section C is a targeted area, do practice questions 1–8. ❏ Keep track of any questions you answered incorrectly.	**Study Time:** 2 hours ❏ Read sections B–D. ❏ Do example questions 1–3 in each part of each section. ❏ Make a list of the questions that you answered incorrectly in each section.	**Study Time:** 2 hours ❏ Read Section B. ❏ Do practice questions 1–7 in this section. ❏ Make a list of the questions that you answered incorrectly in each section.
4 days before the test	**Study Time:** 1 hour ❏ Review sections A–C. ❏ Do practice questions 6–10 in Section A. ❏ Do practice questions 4–10 in Section B. ❏ Do practice questions 7–12 in Section C. ❏ Make note of any practice questions that you answered incorrectly.	**Study Time:** 1 hour ❏ Review sections A–B. ❏ Do practice questions 5–10 in Section A. ❏ Do practice questions 5–10 in Section B. ❏ Review the highlighted words from part 1 of Section B.	**Study Time:** 2 hours ❏ Review sections A–D. ❏ Do practice questions 4–10 in Section A. ❏ Do practice questions 5–10 in Section B. ❏ Do practice questions 5–12 in Section C. ❏ Continue to note any questions that you missed.	**Study Time:** 2 hours ❏ Review sections A–F. ❏ Do practice questions 1–20. ❏ Review any practice questions that you answered incorrectly.	**Study Time:** 2 hours ❏ Review sections A–B. ❏ Do practice questions 11–15 in Section A. ❏ Do practice questions 8–15 in Section B. ❏ Review any questions that you answered incorrectly.
3 days before the test	**Study Time:** 4½ hours ❏ Take the **Practice Test** (Chapter X) and review the answer explanations. ❏ Based on your errors on the **Practice Test,** identify difficult topics and their corresponding chapters. These are your targeted areas.				

	Observation, Memory, and Spatial Orientation (Chapter V)	Reading Comprehension and Verbal Expression (Chapter VI)	Deductive, Inductive, and Logical Reasoning; Information Ordering; and Problem Sensitivity (Chapter VII)	Mathematics (Chapter VIII)	Mechanical Aptitude (Chapter IX)
2 days before the test	**Study Time:** 1 hour ❑ Redo any Observations, Memorization, and Spatial Orientation questions that you answered incorrectly on the Practice Test. ❑ Review any sections of Chapter V that still require your attention.	**Study Time:** 1 hour ❑ Based on your errors on the Practice Test, review the sections in Chapter VI that remain problematic. ❑ Ask a friend or study partner to read the highlighted words from part 1 of Section B aloud. Write the words on a separate piece of paper and review your answers. Based on your errors, continue reviewing words that still present difficulties.	**Study Time:** 1 hour ❑ Redo any Deductive, Inductive, and Logical Reasoning; Information Ordering; and Problem Sensitivity questions that you answered incorrectly on the Practice Test. ❑ Review sections A–D. ❑ Redo 3 practice questions from each section.	**Study Time:** 1 hour ❑ Redo any Mathematics questions that you answered incorrectly on the Practice Test. ❑ Review sections A–F. ❑ Redo practice questions 1–10.	**Study Time:** 1 hour ❑ Redo any Mechanical Aptitude questions that you answered incorrectly on the Practice Test. ❑ Review sections A–B. ❑ Redo 5 practice questions from each section. ❑ Review any questions that you answered incorrectly.
1 day before the test	**Study Time:** 1 hour ❑ Briefly review sections A–C. ❑ Redo any practice questions that you answered incorrectly in each section.	**Study Time:** 1 hour ❑ Briefly review sections A–B. ❑ Redo any practice questions that you answered incorrectly in each section. ❑ Review the highlighted words from part 1 of Section B.	**Study Time:** 1 hour ❑ Briefly review sections A–D. ❑ Redo any practice questions that you answered incorrectly.	**Study Time:** 1 hour ❑ Briefly review sections A–F. ❑ Redo practice questions 11–20. ❑ Redo any practice questions that you answered incorrectly.	**Study Time:** 1 hour ❑ Briefly review sections A–B. ❑ Redo any practice questions that you answered incorrectly.

Morning of the test	**Reminders:**
	❑ Have a good breakfast.
	❑ Take the following items with you to the testing facility:
	  ❑ Two forms of identification, including photo ID.
	  ❑ Any documentation or other items that are required by the testing facility.
	❑ Arrive at the testing facility early and take a few minutes to walk around before the test.
	❑ Stay calm and remember to take deep breaths if you begin to feel nervous.				

V. Observation, Memory, and Spatial Orientation

When responding to fires or other emergencies, firefighters must be alert in every way. They have to be attentive to the victims, their fellow firefighters, and the fire itself. They need to know if bystanders are in danger and how fast the fire is spreading. The best firefighters have the ability to briefly look at a scene, yet notice everything—the number of men and women fighting the fire, the name of the store across the street, and even the color of the neighboring houses.

Firefighters need to be aware of their surroundings at all times. They need to know where they are in relation to buildings such as the courthouse, the police station, or the hospital. They must understand how long it will take them to get from one point to another and they must know the quickest, yet safest, route. This is why the written firefighter exam includes questions about observation, memory, and spatial orientation. As a firefighter, you'll need to know how to read a map or floor plan, recall vital directions or images from your memory, and make crucial observations.

Many people think that having a good memory and being observant are innate abilities, which means people are simply born with these talents. While this may be true for some, we all know a few people who always lose their keys, forget their mother's birthdays, or get lost when leaving the city. If you're one who struggles in these areas, don't panic—there's always room for improvement. In this chapter, we'll teach you a few tips that will help your observational skills and memory (not to mention, your test scores) improve.

A. Observation

Before you can memorize what something looks like, you need to see it and understand what it is. When you're a firefighter, just seeing something isn't good enough; you need to do more than glance or look at it. You need to *observe* it—to study it and absorb all the information it's giving you. Giving an event or person this kind of attention, even if it's only for 30 seconds, will allow you to understand what's going on around you and help you decide how to respond.

Observations allow you to figure out how things work. They also help you remember things later. One of the most important sets of observations you'll make as a firefighter is called the *scene size-up*. This process should take place even before you step foot on the scene. As you approach the scene of the emergency, you should take notice of the environment. You should pay attention to the scents in the air and the weather conditions. Notice if traffic is backed up or detoured. As you approach, note how many other emergency responders are on the scene. While unloading your equipment, be aware of where the fire is, how fast it's growing, and where any victims are located.

You cannot expect to arrive at the scene of an emergency and get to work without knowing all the details. While you'll receive bits and pieces of information on the way to the scene, you really won't know what you're dealing with until you actually arrive. This is why sizing up the scene is so important—the visual and aural information you receive at this time will help you fill in any gaps the original briefing left in your mind. Understanding what's going on will help you know what you need to do to save lives and prevent property damage.

Questions on the written firefighter exam that test your observational skills often provide you with diagrams or illustrations of firefighter-related objects such as fire hydrants, firetrucks, or pieces of equipment. You may also need to examine an illustration of an accident or house fire. These diagrams and illustrations may have labels, keys, or captions that you'll need to read to attain extra information about what you're examining. In the next few sections, we'll teach you a few tricks you can use to help you choose the correct answer when you're dealing with observational questions on the exam.

1. Using Memory Devices

You may not know it, but if you've ever employed small tricks to remember things, you've used mnemonic devices. These devices may be sounds, words, or even images that help you remember details about particular topics. Firefighters, especially those who are new to the profession, use mnemonic devices daily. These devices typically include words and phrases that represent longer, detailed ideas. Think back to any math courses you took in high school. Do you remember using the phrase, "Please Excuse My Dear Aunt Sally"? This phrase may have helped you remember the order of operations: *p*arentheses, *e*xponents, *m*ultiplication, *d*ivision, *a*ddition, and *s*ubtraction. Some of the most common mnemonic devices firefighters use are:

BELOW

- Building
- Extent
- Location
- Occupancy
- Water supply

ENAMES

- Environment
- Number of patients
- Additional resources
- Mechanism of injury/illness (MOI)
- Extrication
- Special consideration

IDEAL

- Identify arriving units
- Describe what you see
- Explain what you intend to do
- Assume command
- Let incoming units know what you want them to do

Another common, yet odd phrase that firefighters use helps them look for 13 specific things when they size up the scene. Examine the following list to see why this phrase is employed by so many firefighters across the nation.

COAL WAS WEALTH

- **Construction:** What are the materials used to build the house, barn, apartment building, or office building? Firefighters should always be aware of what comprises the structure that's on fire, so they know how quickly the fire will spread and which methods they should use to fight it.

- **Occupancy:** Who uses the building? What do they use it for? Firefighters should know whether the building is a factory, warehouse, or storage facility. They should know if it's a store or a deli and if apartments are located above it. Knowing what the building is used for will help them envision what kind of property is inside, from highly flammable chemical agents to fire-resistant safes and lockboxes.

- **Area:** How much space does the fire occupy? Firefighters should not only know how big the fire is when they arrive on the scene, but also how big it might get. To determine this, firefighters should know the size of the entire structure.

- **Life:** How many people are in danger? Firefighters' first priority when they arrive on the scene is to save lives. These could be the lives of victims trapped inside a burning building, a car, or an elevator, but they may also be the lives of their fellow firefighters, emergency responders, or bystanders.

- **Weather:** How are the weather conditions? Firefighters know that weather conditions affect the way they fight fires. High winds may create a higher sense of urgency when fighting a fire while snow or rain may make it easier to put out flames. The temperature may also play a part in how quickly they can respond, as icy roads and frozen pipes may make for slower driving and difficulty achieving a water flow.

- **Apparatus and equipment:** What tools and people are available to fight the fire? These tools may include everything from fire hoses and ladder trucks to hydraulic saws and oxygen tanks. Firefighters should also know how many emergency responders are on the scene, including police officers, paramedics, and EMT-Basics.

- **Street conditions:** Will the position of anything on the street make fighting a fire difficult? Firefighters should be aware of icy or wet streets, the location of fire hydrants and utility poles, and the possibility of traffic. If they're in a residential neighborhood, they should know where stop signs, street lights, and one-way streets appear.

- **Water:** What's the available water supply? Before they arrive on the scene, firefighters should know if hydrants are near the burning structure or if they'll need to use a portable water tank. When they arrive, they should locate the hydrants and make sure they're accessible.

- **Exposures:** Will anything be damaged if the fire spreads? If the wind picks up or firefighters are unable to contain the blaze, they must consider what will be damaged when the fire spreads. These may be additional rooms or floors in houses, neighboring buildings, or even bystanders.

- **Auxiliary appliances:** What are the devices on scene that may help firefighters put out flames? These may include a building's own sprinkler system, fire extinguishers, or standpipe system.

- **Location:** What's the position of the fire? Firefighters need to know where the fire is taking place, so they know how to attack it. Firefighters use different methods when attacking basement fires than they do when fighting attic fires or fires within a building's walls.

- **Time:** What time of day is the fire? Time is important to consider when fighting a fire because it often determines how many people are in danger. For example, a fire in a residential neighborhood in the middle of the night may injure heavy sleepers while a fire during the day at a local grocery store would endanger hundreds of shoppers.

- **Height:** How tall does the building stand? Knowing the height of a building allows firefighters to know if they need to use ladder trucks to fight the fire or rescue trapped victims.

You can definitely use COAL WAS WEALTH in the field, but you can also use it while studying for the written firefighter exam. Throughout this book, you'll find numerous illustrations of emergency scenes. Flip through the pages, find a scene, and apply COAL WAS WEALTH. See if there's enough information in the pictures for every bullet. Practicing using COAL WAS WEALTH will help you remember what you need to know when you size up a scene in the future.

Tip: If you just can't seem to remember the phrase COAL WAS WEALTH, try rearranging the letters to form other words or phrases such as WALLACE WAS HOT. The way you remember these 13 things isn't nearly as important as the act of actually recalling them. Invent your own devices—they may be fun to create and easier to remember than ours!

2. Using Patterns

Successfully rescuing a victim may depend on your ability to detect structural damage, collapsing ceilings, or narrow passageways within seconds. If you simply rush into a burning building without taking a few seconds to examine your surroundings, you may cause harm to both the victim and yourself. One of the best ways to better your observational skills is to train yourself to look for details in every situation. Using patterns during scene size-up will help you find these crucial details.

Patterns can also help you determine the correct answers to questions on the written firefighter exam. Rather than staring at random parts of a diagram or an image, using a pattern forces you to look closer at smaller areas. This makes the observational process more manageable and allows you to see smaller details that you may miss if you were to skim the page.

To examine a photograph, an illustration, a map, or a diagram using a pattern, try the following steps:

1. **Examine the entire image.** The first thing you should do when you come across an image on the exam is look at the entire picture to determine its main event. What is this image about? A car accident? A house fire? Maybe a toxic spill? Once you figure it out, look outside of the image to see if there's a key, legend, or caption. You'll most likely need information from these later.

2. **Create a pattern.** The pattern you use to examine these images is completely up to you. You can move your eyes from the left side of the page to the right and then move down a line and go right to left. You could start at the top, scan to the bottom, and then return your eyes to the top again. You can even go in circles or squares, starting from the outermost border and working your way to the middle of the image. The way you approach these images should be comfortable for you; make sure you choose a method that won't confuse you.

3. **Scan the image.** Use your pattern to scan the whole image. We suggest you skim slowly, so you can read any words you encounter. If something catches your eye, give it some attention—it's there for a reason.

4. **Notice the details.** As you're scanning the image, look for the important details, such as those listed in the COAL WAS WEALTH list. You may also consider examining the image for the following:
   - **Layout:** Where is the building located? How many floors does it have? How tall is it? Are hydrants located nearby? How close is the building in question to its neighboring structures? You should also gather information about the interior layout. How many rooms are on each floor? Is there a sprinkler or standpipe system? How many windows do you see?

- **People:** Who are the owners of the house? Did their family or friends make it outside? Are people trapped inside? How old are they? Where were they last seen? Are they males or females? Who is in the most danger? What's the fastest, but safest, route to their location?

- **Words and labels:** Read everything related to the image, whether it's a sign above a door stating the hours of operation or a caption below the image describing what's happening in the picture. Also be sure to look for keys or legends. Check out the next section, "Reading Accompanying Words and Passages," for more information on working with words and images.

- **Hazards:** Are there additional issues on the scene? Do you see damaged or downed power lines? Are there any liquids on the ground other than water? Is the flow of traffic creating any difficulties or challenges?

5. **Examine the entire picture again.** Think about all the little things you noticed as you used your pattern to scan the image. Now, as you glance over the entire image, put these new pieces of information together to form a story. Do you see anything new?

Now, look at the following figure, which shows a cross-section of a house on fire. Evaluate it using a pattern you create. Important details in the diagram are labeled with numbers that correspond with the list beside the image. You may study the diagram piece by piece in numerical order of the labels, or you may choose to work from left to right, looking at a label and then matching it with its description.

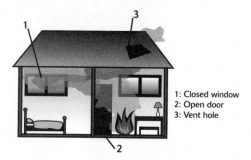

1: Closed window
2: Open door
3: Vent hole

3. Reading Accompanying Words and Passages

As we've previously discussed, images on the firefighter exam may contain words, sentences, or even entire passages. When you're scanning an image, whether using your pattern or mnemonic devices, you should read every word you come across. These words may appear as labels, descriptive captions, informative passages or lists, and in legends or keys.

a. Labels

You'll most often see words that act as labels on images on the firefighter exam. These labels will provide you with crucial information such as street names, types of buildings, dates, or measurements. They may also tell you whether a street runs only one way, a door leads to an emergency exit, or where the fire alarms are located.

Consider for a moment the importance of labels. If you're presented with a floor plan that doesn't contain a single label and are told that a victim is trapped beneath rubble in Apartment 3C, how are you supposed to know where to go? Which room is 3C? Are you even on the third floor? Without accompanying words, this floor plan may be useless to you. This idea works with maps, diagrams, and even illustrators of emergency scenes.

Spend a few minutes studying the following figure.

If the creator of the image didn't include the names of the stores, would you know which building was the pizza shop? Or the coffee house? How would you know which street the image depicts if you couldn't read the street sign? Illustrators place labels and words in these images for a reason: to make choosing the correct answer easier for you. When you're examining an image, it's important to read (not just look at) every word you see.

Tip: Don't let events in the image distract you from reading the words. While these events are important, they cannot steal the spotlight. You need to spend an equal amount of time studying every part of the image. When you close your eyes, you should be able to picture the street sign reading Main St., as well as the car that's on fire in the parking lot to the right of the pizza shop. You should know that the apartment building is named Main St. Apartments, and you should recall a dark puddle leaking from the torched car. Together, these images and words tell a story.

b. Captions

Aside from labels, you may also see a few captions with images on the written firefighter exam. Captions are typically located beneath the image they accompany. They contain extra information about the image. Sometimes this information describes what is happening in the image. Captions may also provide related facts about the event or circumstance depicted in the image, or they may draw your attention to a part of the image that the artist feels is more important than the rest. Captions are usually one to two sentences long.

c. Passages

Most maps and floor plans you'll encounter on the written firefighter exam will stand alone; other than the labels on the map, for example, you won't have much to read. Many of the illustrations and diagrams you see, however, will be paired with informational passages of varying lengths.

These passages may further describe the action or event taking place in the image. If they accompany diagrams, they may provide you with examples of when the piece of equipment in the diagram may be used. Sometimes, the question set is based mainly on the passage, but the illustration or diagram is used to clarify the information you've read. Regardless of how many questions are about information in the passage and how many are based on the image, you should still spend ample time examining both the passage and the image. It's important to determine how they're related and why they're both important to the question set.

While many of the passages you see with images on the firefighter exam will be one to two paragraphs long, others may contain lists. These lists may be directions on how to use a piece of equipment in a diagram or they may contain steps a firefighter would follow to help the victim shown in the illustration. Be sure to thoroughly read every list you see, as some of the questions on the exam will ask you to apply what you've read to the accompanying image.

d. Keys/Legends

In addition to words within images on the written firefighter exam, you'll also encounter many symbols. These symbols will most likely appear on maps and floor plans, not within illustrations or even in diagrams. However, you should always be on the lookout for them.

The creators of these maps and floor plans won't expect you to automatically know what each symbol means. Instead, they'll provide the meanings for these symbols in keys or legends near the image. Normally, these keys are marked *Key* and contain a short list of the symbols found in the image. A key for a map may look like this:

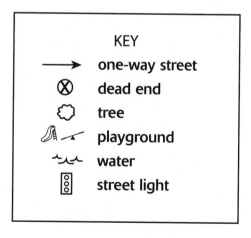

Some of the most common symbols on maps and floor plans are shown in the following chart. As you answer the practice items and take the practice tests in this book, you'll most likely become familiar with these symbols and their meanings. However, this doesn't mean that you shouldn't glance over the key on every map and floor plan you encounter when taking the exam. Sometimes, a symbol you may know to represent one thing may be used for something else. For example, a small tree may be used to represent an entire forested area on one map, while on another it may simply represent an old oak in someone's backyard. Make sure you're certain of what every symbol means before you begin interpreting the data from the image.

COMMON MAP AND FLOOR PLAN SYMBOLS

Symbol	Meaning	Symbol	Meaning
→	one-way street		route/highway
⇄	two-way street		door
	tree		window
	park/playground	- -	open doorway
	house/residential area		bed
▽	yield		chair/sofa
	stop		chair
	street light		sliding door
⊕	intersection		stairs
⊗	railroad crossing		stove
	pool		standpipe system
	pond		sprinkler system
		E	elevator

Practice

Directions (1–10): Answer the following questions solely on the basis of the information provided.

Questions 1–2 refer to the following figure and passage.

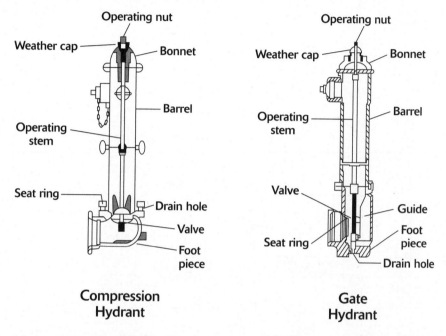

Compression
Hydrant

Gate
Hydrant

The most common type of fire hydrant used today is called a dry barrel hydrant. These hydrants restrict the flow of water through the barrel of the hydrant when it is turned off. The water used for the hydrant sits well below the frost line, which means there is little chance that the water will be frozen when firefighters need to use it.

Two common types of dry barrel hydrants are the compression hydrant and the gate hydrant. Of the two, compression hydrants are the most common and are easier to close. The main valve seals tightly, which reduces the risk of leakage. In both the compression hydrant and the gate hydrant, threads at the end of the operating stems aid in opening the operating nut and closing the main valve. Gate hydrants differ from compression hydrants because they feature a gate valve that slides up and down in the base of the hydrant to open and close the waterway.

1. Which hydrant part appears on the gate hydrant, but not on the compression hydrant?

   A. guide
   B. barrel
   C. drain hole
   D. operating nut

2. Which of the following is true?

   A. Firefighters encounter more gate hydrants than compression hydrants.

   B. Compression hydrants seal main valves by moving threads up and down the barrel.

   C. The water in both compression hydrants and gate hydrants is at risk of freezing in the winter.

   D. Both compression hydrants and gate hydrants contain threads located at the end of operating stem systems.

Questions 3–5 refer to the following figure.

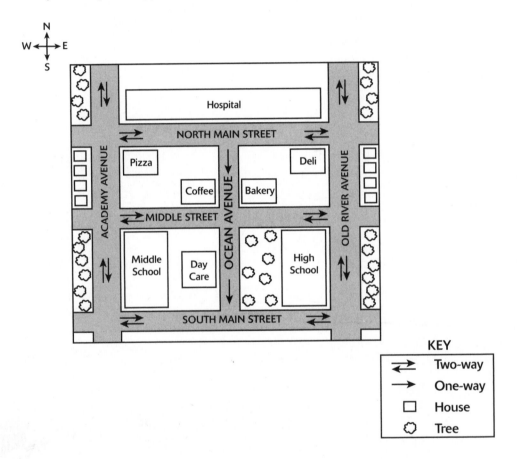

3. Which of the following is located at the northeast corner of North Main Street and Old River Avenue?

   A. house

   B. tree

   C. deli

   D. bakery

4. The coffee shop is located at the intersection of which two streets?

    A. North Main Street and Middle Street
    B. Ocean Avenue and Academy Avenue
    C. South Main Street and Old River Avenue
    D. Middle Street and Ocean Avenue

5. According to the map, Academy Avenue is

    A. a street that runs east to west.
    B. a one-way street.
    C. lined with both houses and trees.
    D. perpendicular to Old River Avenue.

Questions 6–8 refer to the following figure.

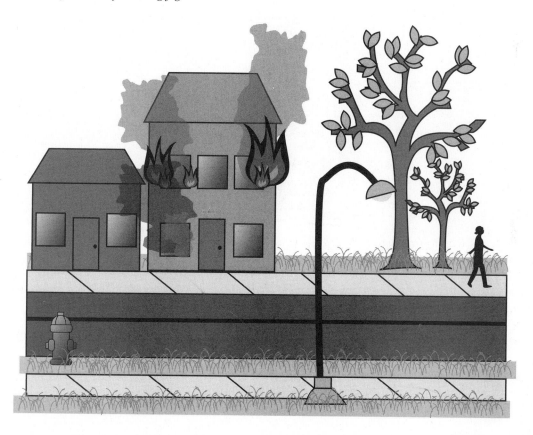

6. Which of the following is in the most danger of being damaged or injured by the house fire?

    A. trees
    B. bystander
    C. street light
    D. house next door

7. After examining the location of the flames, a firefighter may assume that the point of origin was in

    A. the basement.
    B. the front yard.
    C. a first-floor room.
    D. a second-floor room.

8. The fire hydrant in this image is located directly

    A. beside the street light.
    B. to the right of the bystander.
    C. in front of the neighboring house.
    D. to the left of the house that is on fire.

Questions 9–10 refer to the following figure and passage.

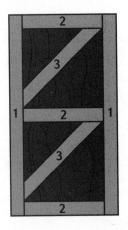

1. Frame
2. Ledge
3. Brace

    Three of the most common types of ledge doors are the frame-and-ledge door, the ledge door, and the frame-and-brace door. The diagram shows a frame-and-brace door. These doors are normally made of thin wood such as plywood sheeting or particleboard and are easy to break down. Many times, these doors are secured with locks, hasps, padlocks, bolts, or bars. Ledge doors, which are also called batten doors, are most popular on warehouses, storerooms, barns, and sheds.

9. The frame on a frame-and-brace door is found on the door's

    A. top.
    B. side.
    C. bottom.
    D. middle.

10. Which of the following is NOT true of ledge doors?

    A. They're also known as batten doors.
    B. They're made of a combination of thin wood.
    C. They're often found on barns, sheds, and warehouses.
    D. They're difficult to break down, especially when locked.

Answers

1. **A** According to the diagram, the gate hydrant contains a guide, while the compression hydrant does not. The guide is located behind the valve and seat ring in the base of the barrel. Choices B, C, and D are incorrect because both the compression hydrant and the gate hydrant contain barrels, drain holes, and operating nuts.

2. **D** According to the passage, both compression hydrants and gate hydrants contain threads located at the end of operating-stem systems. These threads make it easier to open the operating nut and close the main valve. When the valve is sealed tightly, the chance of water leaking from the hydrant decreases drastically. Choice A is incorrect because firefighters are more likely to use compression hydrants than gate hydrants because compression hydrants are more popular. Choice B is incorrect because gate hydrants feature a gate valve that moves up and down inside the barrel—compression hydrants don't have a part that moves this way. Finally, Choice C is incorrect because compression hydrants and gate hydrants are dry barrel hydrants, which means the water in them is stored below the frost line and should not freeze.

3. **B** A tree is located on the northeast corner of North Main Street and Old River Avenue. You can determine this by locating the intersection of these two streets and then, using the compass rose, find the direction of northeast. Choices A, C, and D are incorrect because the house is located on the southeast corner of this intersection, the deli is located on the southwest corner, and the bakery isn't located on this intersection at all.

4. **D** The coffee shop is located at the intersection of Middle Street and Ocean Avenue. Specifically, it's on the northwest corner of the intersection. Choices A, B, and C are incorrect because North Main Street and Middle Street do not intersect, nor do Ocean Avenue and Academy Avenue; the high school is located at the corner of South Main Street and Old River Avenue.

5. **C** According to the map, Academy Avenue is lined with both houses and trees. The pizza shop and middle school are also located on Academy Avenue. Choices A, B, and D are incorrect because Academy Avenue is a two-way street that runs north to south, not east to west; it is also parallel to Old River Avenue, not perpendicular to it.

6. **D** Because the house next door is so close to the house that is on fire, it is in danger of suffering property damage. The image shows that the smoke from the fire is already moving toward the neighboring house. Choices A, B, and C are incorrect because the tree, bystander, and street lights are not close enough to the fire to be damaged or injured at this time.

7. **D** After examining the location of the flames, a firefighter may assume that the point of origin was in a second-floor room. Because both windows on the second floor are filled with flames, one would assume that the fire started in one of these rooms. Choice C is invalid because the first floor is filled with smoke, but no flames yet. Had the fire started on the first floor, flames would be in the first-floor windows, as well. The image does not provide evidence that would lead a firefighter to assume that the fire first began on the lawn or in the basement, so Choices A and B are incorrect as well.

8. **C** The fire hydrant in this image is located directly in front of the neighboring house. Choices A, B, and D are incorrect because the hydrant is located down the street from the bystander and the street light and to the left—though not *directly* to the left—of the house that's on fire. The neighboring house is located *directly* to the left of the house that's on fire.

9. **B** The frame on a frame-and-brace door is found on the door's side. Frames run up and down the side of the doors, while ledges cross the top, bottom, and middle, making Choices A, C, and D incorrect. Braces run diagonally between the top and middle ledges and the middle and bottom ledges.

10. **D** The passage states that ledge doors are easy to break down because they're made of thin wooden materials; therefore, the following statement is NOT true of ledge doors: They're difficult to break down, especially when locked. Choices A, B, and C are incorrect because these statements are true: ledge doors are also known as batten doors, they're made of a combination of thin wood, and they're found on barns, sheds, and warehouses.

B. Memory

Now that you've become familiar with the process of observing, which goes beyond simply seeing, it will be easier for you to answer other questions on the written firefighter exam, such as those that require you to use your memory. As we mentioned before, some people are simply born with good memories. Others need to train themselves to notice things and recall them later.

Memorization is tested on the firefighter exam because firefighters often have little time to absorb and study materials. Instead, they must listen to instructions or examine a floor plan and almost immediately transfer this knowledge to their short-term memory so they can recall blocked routes, the location of fire escapes, and information about emergency victims later. When responding to an emergency, firefighters have little time to prepare—especially when lives are at stake.

This urgency is represented on the exam in the form of question sets that require you to study an illustration, read a passage, or both, for a certain amount of time. (The length of time you get to memorize this information depends on the test you take.) During this period, you'll have to pay close attention to the information in front of you. You'll have to make observations, use patterns to find small details, and maybe even use mnemonic devices to remember the information you do acquire. At this time, you'll want to clear your head of all other matters and focus only on the information you're provided.

> **Tip:** To improve your focus on the written firefighter exam, get at least eight hours of sleep the night before the exam. Also, eat a hearty breakfast so you'll have enough energy to stay alert. Try to schedule the exam during a time when you have very little going on. This includes social events such as weddings, birthday parties, anniversaries, or even exams if you're enrolled in school. The less you have to worry or think about, the easier it will be to focus on the firefighter exam. The easier it is to focus, the more you'll remember.

After you've studied the image, you'll be asked to turn the page and seal the booklet. At this point, you may or may not be allowed to jot down notes about the image. You must then read the questions pertaining to the image and select the correct answers without looking back at the illustration or accompanying passage. This process may sound intimidating, but don't let it get to you. In this section, we'll give you some tips that will help you recall both visual and written information on the firefighter exam.

1. Recalling Visual Information

One of the best pieces of advice we can give you on recalling visual information is to try to visualize the image the second after you've turned the page. Close your eyes and recall the image you've just evaluated.

If you used a pattern to assess the image, go over the pattern in your mind. If your pattern had you moving left to right, visualize the way the image appeared from the left side of the page to the right.

As the picture becomes clear in your mind, think about the important details: Where were the windows and doors located? Where was the fire or car accident? Is anyone hurt? Where are the bystanders and the victims? Are there any additional hazardous conditions you noticed? If you're allowed to make notes on your booklet or on scratch paper, make lists using COAL WAS WEALTH or other devices such as BELOW or ENAMES.

Now, read each question one at a time. Try not to peek ahead, as seeing extra words and details may confuse you and alter the accurate picture you already have in your mind. If you encounter a question that doesn't bring to mind a specific area of the image, close your eyes and go through COAL WAS WEALTH again, scanning the picture in your mind for exact details.

Study the following figure for a few minutes. When you're certain you know everything about the image, close the book and try to sketch the image on a piece of blank paper. When you're finished, compare your sketch with our illustration and see how many things you remembered. While you're sketching, don't be afraid to use patterns and mnemonic devices to remember areas of the picture.

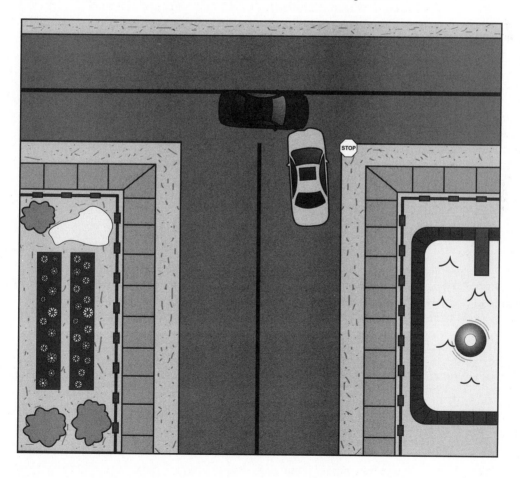

Did you remember it all? Which car had the stop sign? How many rafts were in the swimming pool? Did the sidewalks have handicap-accessible corners? How many plants were in the garden and what types were they? What was the weather like?

Remember: You should take notice of every single detail in an image, from the number of flowers in a garden to the phone number on a billboard in the background. Even those details that don't seem related to the event occurring in the image may appear in questions and answer choices on the exam. Everything is fair game, so be prepared to scour every inch of the images presented to you.

2. Recalling Written Information

If you have a stellar photographic memory, recalling written information may be as easy for you as recalling visual information. Think about it: Because you see written information, it's technically visual information. Remembering details in a passage may be more difficult than recalling details from an image, however, because you don't just look at a bunch of words and automatically understand them. You need to read the sentences word for word and comprehend what this information is telling you. You need to multi-task—especially if you're planning on recalling your information from a mental image of the passage. This requires you to memorize the information you received from the page as well as the position of the words on the page. This is difficult, but not impossible.

If you don't want to memorize what the passage looks like (and we don't blame you if you don't!), there are other strategies you can use to recall written information on the firefighter exam. These include taking notes and making lists. If you're given a few minutes to jot down what you remember about the passage after you've examined it—but before you're allowed to read the questions—take this time to make notes of important details in the passage. Answer the following questions:

- Who?
- What?
- When?
- Where?
- How/why?

After you answer these questions, you can also make a list of the other details you remember from the passage. Write down times and weather conditions, names, and measurements. If you remember colors, directions, or street names, write them down, as well. It's more likely that you'll be asked about specific details than general ones.

Written information you may have to recall will include sets of directions, lists of equipment and their uses, reports of car accidents or house fires, arson reports, and passages that describe events happening in accompanying images.

Practice

Directions (1–10): Study the information provided for 10 minutes. Then turn the page and answer the questions. Don't look back.

Questions 1–3 refer to the following figure.

1. The fire in this image started

   A. in the middle of the couch.
   B. at the site of an electrical outlet.
   C. in the tree outside and spread inside.
   D. after the cord of the lamp fell into the fish bowl.

2. The letters on the toy blocks on the floor are:

   A. A, B, C
   B. M, V, D
   C. N, Q, R
   D. M, P, Z

3. Which of the following is true about the figure?

   A. There are three pillows on the couch.
   B. The sprinkler system has been activated.
   C. One of the birds outside is perched in its nest.
   D. The fire started in the outlet to the left of the couch.

Questions 4–7 refer to the following figure and passage.

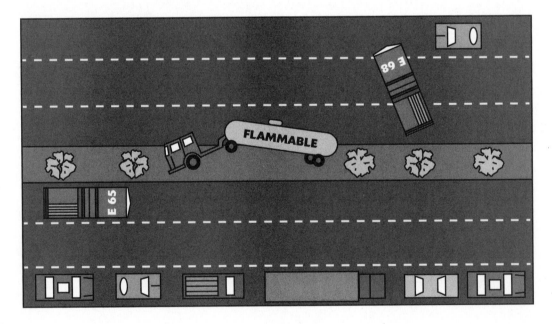

Firefighters must tend to fires in vehicles transporting flammable fuels with extreme caution. When a vehicle overturns or crashes, firefighters must first determine what type of cargo the vehicle is carrying. If the driver of the vehicle is unresponsive, firefighters may slowly approach the vehicle to read the manifests or placards that describe the solutions, chemicals, and containers the vehicle holds. Once firefighters have this information, they can attack any flames in the safest and most efficient way possible.

When a truck has turned over on a busy highway, as seen in the figure above, firefighters are tasked with the duties of rescuing victims, controlling traffic, and attacking the flames. Firefighters must always be alert when responding to a traffic accident, as their chances of being struck by a vehicle driving by are great. To decrease this risk, the first firefighters on the scene are instructed to use their trucks to keep traffic out of the incident lane as well as an additional lane on either side of the incident. If police officers are not present on the scene, firefighters may direct a steady flow of traffic around the department vehicles and away from the incident.

Firefighters must never approach the ends of an overturned or damaged vehicle that is on fire; these vehicles—especially those containing flammable shipments—frequently explode. These explosions rip the storage vessels, and their pieces become projectiles that shoot from the ends of the containers. Instead, firefighters should approach these vehicles at a right angle. Although the first priority is always to save lives, firefighters responding to these incidents must also attempt to prevent property damage and environmental pollution.

4. A firefighter is LEAST likely to perform which of the following duties when responding to an emergency involving an overturned vehicle?

   A.   directing traffic
   B.   rescuing victims
   C.   interviewing witnesses
   D.   attacking flames

5. If the driver of the vehicle in the image was unresponsive, how would firefighters on the scene of the accident know if the vessel contains flammable liquids?

   A.   ask bystanders
   B.   read the vessel's label
   C.   open the vehicle and search it
   D.   call the company that owns the truck

6. How should firefighters approach an overturned or damaged vehicle that is on fire?

   A.   from the front
   B.   at a right angle
   C.   at a diagonal
   D.   from the back

7. Why are the fire trucks in this image parked across the highway's lanes?

   A.   They are not yet in the correct position to fight the fire.
   B.   They keep cars traveling in either direction out of the incident lane.
   C.   They need to park at a 90° angle to keep their equipment safe in case of explosion.
   D.   They create traffic jams so firefighters can attack the flames without worrying about being struck by passing vehicles.

Questions 8–10 refer to the following passage.

In December, firefighters from Department 222 receive a report of a fire in a residential neighborhood at 1:30 a.m. They dress quickly and load their gear into Engine 14 and Engine 17. On the way to the location, Engine 14 is forced to find another route when the minivan traveling in front of it on Ashbury Avenue gets stuck in the snow. Engine 17 arrives at 2 Beaker Lane at 1:43 a.m.

Half of the firefighters with Company 17 lay a supply line from a hydrant located at the end of the house's driveway while the other half initiates incident command. Two firefighters proceed into the burning two-story home, having received word that a 15-year-old male victim is trapped inside. The firefighters outside of the house contact dispatch via the radio to let them know the exact location of the fire, the conditions of the fire, and that they shouldn't need additional resources.

Engine 14 arrives on the scene at 1:49 a.m. Firefighters from Company 17 emerge with the rescued victim at 1:50 a.m. Men and women with Engine 14 lay an additional line and assist Company 17 in attacking the fire. Firefighters determine that the fire started in the kitchen, located on the first floor, and smoke and flames quickly traveled up a staircase in the kitchen and filled the second floor.

By 2:15 a.m., police and paramedics have arrived, and the blaze is under control. Firefighters from both companies perform salvage duties and department investigators determine the fire was not arson. At 3:30 a.m., Engine 14 and Engine 17 pull into Department 222's garage. Firefighters hang and store their equipment, and the department chief begins his paperwork.

8. What was the location of the fire?

    A. 2 Beaker Lane
    B. 14 Ashbury Lane
    C. 17 Beaker Avenue
    D. 222 Ashbury Avenue

9. What is the first thing members of Engine Company 14 do when they arrive on the scene?

    A. initiate incident command
    B. rescue a 15-year-old male victim
    C. lay an additional supply line
    D. determine that the fire started in the kitchen

10. In all, how much time passed between the time the department received the report and the time the engines returned to the department's garage?

    A. 30 minutes
    B. 1 hour
    C. 2 hours
    D. 3 hours

Answers

1. **B** The fire in this image started at the site of an electrical outlet. The outlet is located beneath the window on the right-hand side of the page. Flames are shooting from the top outlet and smoke is gathering. A window has been broken so the smoke can escape.

2. **D** The letters on the toy blocks on the floor are *M, P, Z.* Blocks P and M are on the bottom of the small tower and Block Z is on the top.

3. **B** In this image, the sprinkler system has been activated. You know this because water droplets have begun to fall from the ceiling. Choice A is incorrect because there are only two pillows on the couch, Choice C is incorrect because the birds in the tree are not resting in the nest, and Choice D is incorrect because the fire started in the outlet to the right of the couch, not the left.

4. **C** When responding to an emergency involving an overturned vehicle, a firefighter is least likely to spend time interviewing witnesses at the scene. This is the job of a police officer or investigator. Firefighters may have to speak to the driver of the vehicle about the contents of the vessel, but they shouldn't conduct an in-depth interview with the driver about the accident. Although police officers are typically in charge of directing traffic at the scene, sometimes firefighters may need to perform this duty if they arrive before police officers. Firefighters are also in charge of rescuing victims and attacking the fire.

5. **B** If the driver of the vehicle in the image was unresponsive, firefighters on the scene of the accident would know whether the vessel contains flammable liquids if they read the vessel's label. You can see that the vessel is marked "flammable," indicating that it does contain flammable liquids. Firefighters should never search an overturned vehicle that is on fire, making Choice C incorrect. The passage doesn't mention anything about asking bystanders or calling the company that owns the truck, so Choices A and D are also incorrect.

6. **B** Firefighters should approach an overturned or damaged vehicle that is on fire at a right angle. This reduces the risk of being injured by projectiles if the vessel were to explode and rip apart. Choices A, C, and D are incorrect because explosions will most likely shoot out the ends of the overturned vehicle; therefore, it's safest to avoid the ends and approach at a 90°, or right, angle.

7. **B** The fire trucks in the image are parked across the lanes of the highways because these vehicles keep cars traveling in either direction out of the incident lane. They also block off one more lane so drivers don't get too close to the scene. Firefighters do not wish to create traffic jams on busy highways; if possible, they allow drivers to pass the scene at slow speeds. The trucks do not need to be parked at 90° angles; however, firefighters do need to approach the vehicle on foot in this way.

8. **A** The fire took place at 2 Beaker Lane. Engine 17 arrived at the location of the fire at 1:43 a.m. Engine 14 was delayed because it needed to find a new route when the minivan traveling in front of it became stuck in the snow on Ashbury Avenue.

9. **C** When Engine 14 arrives on the scene at 1:49 a.m., members of Company 17 have previously initiated incident command, laid the first supply line, and entered the house in search of the 15-year-old male victim. As Engine 14 pulls up, two firefighters from Engine Company 17 emerge with the rescued victim. The first thing members of Engine Company 14 do is lay an additional supply line. They then assist Engine Company 17 in attacking the fire.

10. **C** In all, 2 hours passed between the time the department received the report and the time the engines returned to the department's garage. The passage stated that the department received the call at 1:30 a.m. They fought the fire and pulled their engines into the department's garage at 3:30 a.m. Between 1:30 a.m. and 3:30 a.m., two hours passed.

C. Spatial Orientation

Many of the questions you'll encounter on the written firefighter exam will require you to be spatially oriented. This means that you must be able to read maps and floor plans, follow directions, and plan safe routes. *Spatial orientation* is our innate ability to sustain our body orientation in relation to our physical surroundings. This orientation takes place while we're in motion and when we're at rest.

Spatial orientation is a vital skill for firefighters to have—at times, knowing where you are can be the difference between life and death. It sounds serious, and it is. Firefighters enter new and unfamiliar environments every day. Due to smoke, fire, and the loss of power, they're often caught in conditions where they can barely see. These factors make entering a burning building difficult—and transporting a victim from the building to a safe place even more challenging.

Firefighters should always know where they are, where they need to be, and how to get there. This is especially important when they enter a burning structure and must find a quick and safe way out. This is why floor plans appear on the exam; they test candidates' abilities to read and interpret the plan and then choose a path despite obstacles such as smoke, fire, or blocked entrances.

Maps also appear on these exams because firefighters must know how to make it from one point to another in record time—without breaking any laws or causing damages or injuries. Of course, they can turn their lights and sirens on and pick up the pace, but they cannot travel the wrong way down one-way streets or avoid lights by cutting through parking lots. These actions may endanger other drivers.

Tip: As with memorization questions, spatial orientation questions are easier to answer if you improve your observational skills. Read every part of the map or floor plan and make sure you know what each symbol listed in the key represents. Examine the entire map or floor plan using a pattern or mnemonic device.

Spatial orientation skills are important whether you're finding your way through a dark corridor in a deserted high school or traveling through a residential neighborhood dotted with one-way streets in the snow. You should always know where you are and where you're going. You should be on the look out for things that may make travel and exploration difficult, such as roadblocks, bystanders, weather conditions, or the loss of electricity. Although newer fire engines and trucks may have global positioning systems (GPS units), you won't have a device such as this when you're scouring warehouses filled with smoke, flames, or hot embers. For this reason, it's important that you improve your spatial orientation skills. In this section, we'll give you some tips that will help you do just that.

1. Details

Maps and floor plans on the written firefighter exam will contain many details that will help you answer questions correctly. These details may come in the form of symbols or words. As we discussed in the "Reading Accompanying Words and Passages" section earlier, information found in labels, captions, accompanying descriptions, and keys/legends can help you interpret diagrams, such as maps and floor plans.

In addition to the common symbols found on page 102, you will also gain most directional cues from the compass rose that accompanies your image. As we've discussed, a compass rose indicates which direction is north, south, east, and west. You may see different variations of compass roses. Some are shown here.

2. Tracing the Route

The first thing you should do when confronted with a question set that requires you to interpret a map or floor plan is study the image, of course. Then, read the first question. Don't let your eyes wander to the answer choices just yet, though. Reading these choices may confuse you or influence you to choose the incorrect answer. Instead, after you've read the first question, return to your map or floor plan. Now it's time for you to trace the route.

Consider the following map. It should look familiar to you, as we used a larger version of it in the set of practice questions for the "Observations" section earlier.

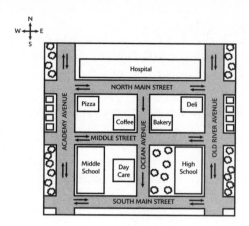

On the written firefighter exam, you may be presented with a question similar to the following:

> If you're standing outside the coffee shop on the corner of Ocean Avenue and Middle Street and you travel west, make two left-hand turns, and stop at the second intersection you pass, which building is on your left?

After reading this question, you should then return your gaze to the map provided and attempt to trace this route using the information provided. If you're allowed to, trace the route on the map with your pencil so you can keep track of where you are, where you're going, and where you've been.

Your map should look like this when you're finished tracing:

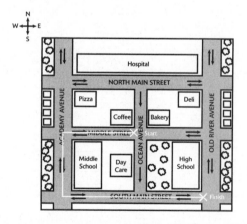

If you followed directions, you'll find that if you were to stand at the corner of Ocean Avenue and Middle Street and then travel west, make two left-hand turns, and stop at the second intersection you encounter, the high school would be on your left. Now that you know the right answer, you can examine the answer choices that accompany the question and choose the answer that reads *high school*.

> **Remember:** If you're traveling south and you're asked to make a right-hand turn, you're now traveling west—not east. When traveling north, right-hand turns take you east and left-hand turns take you west. However, when you're traveling south, you're moving down the page in the opposite direction of north; therefore, your right-hand turns will take you west and your left-hand turns will take you east.

3. Examining Answer Choices

Sometimes you'll find questions that require you to read every answer choice. These questions typically ask you to choose the shortest, quickest, or safest route among the four routes or paths listed. How are you supposed to know which one is correct? It's simple—try them all!

Trace each of the routes until you find the one that leads you to your destination. As you trace, make a mental note of which route takes you the longest or which path takes you past your destination entirely. When working with a map, pay attention to directional cues that may indicate that the route takes you down a one-way street the wrong way. While tracing the path on a floor plan, take notice of any obstructions that may fall in the path, such as closed doors, holes in the floor, or broken staircases.

Practice

Directions (1–12): Answer the following questions solely on the basis of the information provided.

Questions 1–3 refer to the following figure.

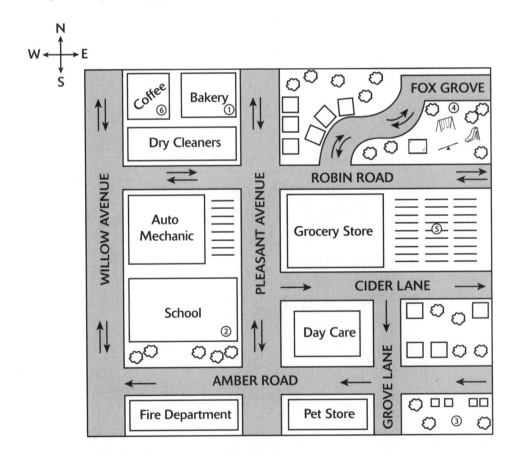

1. You're traveling east on Cider Lane. You turn right on Grove Lane, left on Amber Road, right on Pleasant Avenue, and then left on Robin Road. What direction are you now traveling?

   A. north
   B. south
   C. east
   D. west

2. Starting at the intersection of Fox Grove and Robin Road, you travel west down Robin Road and then make a left on Pleasant Avenue and travel two blocks. On the intersection of the second block, you make a right-hand turn, another right-hand turn, and then stop at the first intersection. Which of the following is on your right-hand side?

   A. dry cleaners
   B. bakery
   C. auto mechanic
   D. pet store

3. You're at the fire department when you receive a call that there is a fire at point 3. Which of the following routes will get you to point 3 while abiding by all traffic laws?

   A. east on Amber Road, north on Pleasant Avenue, east on Cider Lane, south on Grove Lane
   B. north on Willow Avenue, east on Robin Road, south on Pleasant Avenue, east on Cider Lane, south on Grove Lane
   C. west on Amber Road, north on Willow Avenue, south on Pleasant Avenue, east on Amber Road, south on Grove Lane
   D. north on Willow Avenue, west on Robin Road, south on Pleasant Avenue, west on Cider Lane, south on Grove Lane

Questions 4–6 refer to the following figure, which is the third floor of a five-story building.

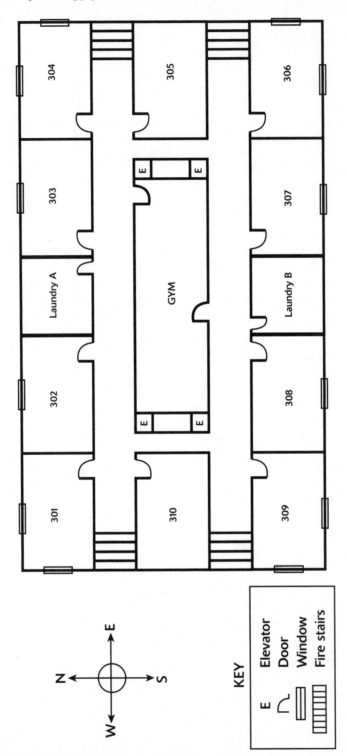

4. If a fire started in Apartment 310, which emergency staircase should the residents of Apartment 301 use to exit the building?

   A.   elevator across from Apartment 310
   B.   staircase between apartments 309 and 310
   C.   elevator across from Apartment 305
   D.   staircase between apartments 304 and 305

5. A fire has started in Apartment 306. The residents of Apartment 306 escape safely. Residents in which apartments are now in the most danger?

   A.   Apartment 305
   B.   Apartment 307
   C.   Apartment 307 and Apartment 406
   D.   Apartment 307 and Apartment 407

6. You enter the floor using the emergency stairs located between apartments 309 and 310. You make a left, a right, and then continue down the hallway and down the stairs at the end of the hall. Following this route, you passed all the following EXCEPT

   A.   the gym.
   B.   Laundry A.
   C.   Laundry B.
   D.   Apartment 304.

Questions 7–9 refer to the following figure.

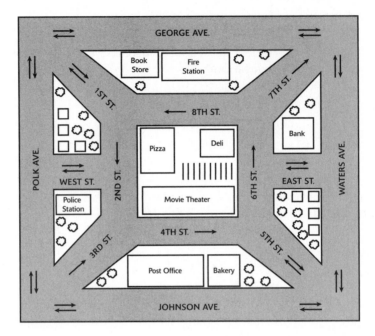

7. You're outside the George Avenue entrance to the fire station when a woman approaches you and asks you to help her get into her car. She's locked her keys inside and the engine is running. She tells you the car is parked in the lot behind the movie theater. If you were to walk, which of the following routes would get you to her car in the LEAST amount of time?

    A. east on George Avenue, south on Waters Avenue, west on East Street

    B. east on George Avenue, southwest on 7th Street, and south on 6th Street

    C. west on George Avenue, southeast on 1st Street, west on 8th Street, south on 8th Street

    D. west on George Avenue, southwest on 1st Street, south on 2nd Street, east on 4th Street, and north on 6th Street

8. Starting at the intersection of 5th Street, Johnson Avenue, and Waters Avenue, if you were to travel northwest and then turn right, turn left, and then make a final left, you would be closest to the

   A. bank.
   B. book store.
   C. police station.
   D. movie theater.

9. You exit the house on the corner of East Street and Waters Avenue and get into your car, which is parked facing south on Waters Avenue. You make a right onto Johnson Avenue and pass the bakery and the post office. At the first intersection, you contemplate your route to the pizza shop. Which route would be the fastest?

   A. northeast on 3rd Street, north on 2nd Street, and east on 8th Street
   B. north on Polk Avenue, east on West Street, north on 2nd Street, and west on 8th Street
   C. northeast on 3rd Street, east on 4th Street, north on 6th Street, and west on 8th Street
   D. north on Polk Avenue, east on George Avenue, southeast on 1st Street, and east on 8th Street

Questions 10–12 refer to the following figure.

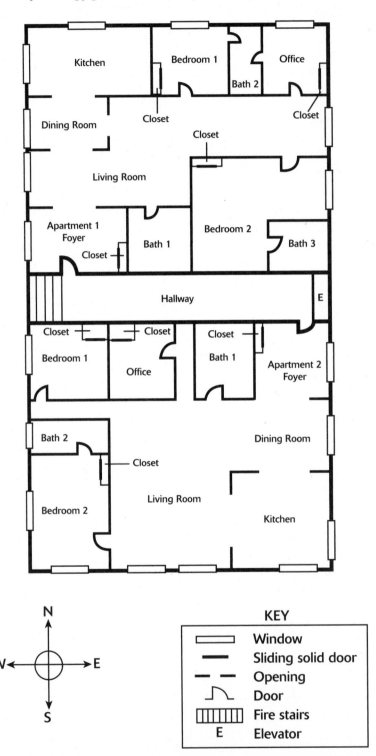

10. If a fire starts in the living room of Apartment 2, which rooms are immediately exposed to the fire?

    A. bedroom 2 and kitchen
    B. kitchen and dining room
    C. dining room and bath 1
    D. bedroom 2, kitchen, and dining room

11. If a fire starts in the office of Apartment 1, what is the quickest route out of the apartment building for occupants of the office?

    A. Step into the hallway. Continue down the hallway, enter the dining room and then continue through the living room and the foyer. Exit the apartment and continue down the hallway to exit the building using the elevator.
    B. Cross through bathroom 2 and into bedroom 1. Step into the hallway. Continue through the living room and the foyer and then exit the apartment. Continue down the hallway and exit the building via the elevator.
    C. Step out of the office. Continue through the living room and foyer and then exit the apartment. Leave the building via the stairs.
    D. Cross through bathroom 2 and into bedroom 1. Step into the hallway, enter the dining room and then continue through the living room and the foyer. Exit the apartment and then use the stairs to exit the building.

12. Based on the floor plan of the apartments, which of the following images represents what the apartment building would look like from the west?

    A.
    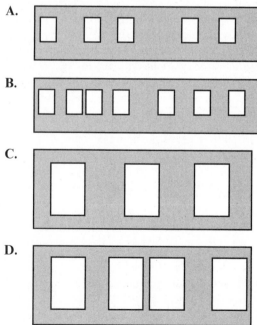
    B.

    C.

    D.

Answers

1. **D** After traveling east on Cider Lane, you turn right on Grove Lane. You're now traveling south. Then, you turn left on Amber Road and begin traveling west. A right on Pleasant Avenue allows you to travel north and a final left on Robin Road changes your course to head west.

2. **C** You are facing south at the corner of Fox Grove and Robin Road. After traveling west down Robin Road, you approach the intersection of Robin Road and Pleasant Avenue. You turn left, which takes you south down Pleasant Avenue for two blocks. At the intersection of Pleasant Avenue and Amber Road, you turn right. Now you're traveling west on Amber Road. You make another right and travel north on Willow Avenue. You stop at the first intersection, where Willow Avenue and Robin Road meet. On your right-hand side is the auto mechanic.

3. **B** If you're at the fire department when a fire starts at point 3, you would need to travel north on Willow Avenue, east on Robin Road, south on Pleasant Avenue, east on Cider Lane, and south on Grove Lane to arrive at point 3 without breaking any traffic laws. Choices A, C, and D are incorrect because each of these choices has you traveling the wrong way down a one-way street. On this map, Amber Road, Cider Lane, and Grove Lane are all one-way streets.

4. **D** If a fire began in Apartment 310, the residents of Apartment 301 should use the staircase between Apartments 304 and 305 to exit the building. In the event of a fire, elevators should never be used to flee the scene. If the fire spreads, it may damage cords or kill the power, thus leaving residents of the building trapped in the metal elevator car. Choice B is incorrect because this staircase is located right next to the origin of the fire. Instead, residents of Apartment 301 should use the exit on the opposite side of the building, running away from the fire, not toward it.

5. **C** If a fire started in Apartment 306 and the apartment's residents had safely escaped, the residents in Apartment 307 and Apartment 406 would then be in the most danger. Apartments 306 and 307 share a wall; therefore, they're connected and the fire can spread quickly to Apartment 307. Apartment 305 is also in danger of smoke and fire damage, but the flames must first cross the hall, making choice A incorrect. One can assume that Apartment 406 is located directly above Apartment 306, which means the flames can weaken the floor of Apartment 406. Although Apartment 407 may also be in danger of damage from smoke and flames, the fire must first spread to Apartments 406 and 307 (which share a wall and a floor/ceiling, respectively) before Apartment 407 catches fire.

6. **C** You enter the floor using the emergency stairs located between Apartments 309 and 310. You make a left and pass two elevators. Then you make a right and pass Apartment 302, Laundry A, Apartment 303, and the gym. As you continue down the hallway, you'll pass Apartments 304 and 305. This route does not allow you to pass Laundry B.

7. **B** From the station's entrance on George Avenue, you would reach the woman's car in the least amount of time if you were to travel east on George Avenue, southwest on 7th Street, and south on 6th Street. Because you're traveling by foot, you do not need to follow the one-way directional cues on 6th and 7th Streets.

8. **C** Starting at the intersection of 5th Street, Johnson Avenue, and Waters Avenue, if you were to travel northwest on 5th Street and then turn right onto 6th Street, turn left onto 8th Street, and then make a final turn left onto Second Street, you would be closest to the police station, which is located on the corner of Polk Avenue and West Street.

9. **C** From the intersection of Johnson Avenue and 3rd Street, the shortest route to the pizza shop would be northeast on 3rd Street, east on 4th Street, north on 6th Street, and west on 8th Street. The routes stated in choices A, B, and D require you to make illegal turns onto one-way streets and are therefore incorrect answers.

10. **B** If a fire starts in the living room of Apartment 2, the rooms immediately exposed to the fire are the kitchen and the dining room. These rooms don't have any doors or walls to shield them from smoke, embers, or flames. Although bedroom 2 is near the living room, it is not in as much danger, making Choices A and D incorrect. Choice C is not correct because Bath 1 is farther from the living room, where the fire started, and has an exterior wall and a door to block most of the smoke and fire damage.

11. **C** If a fire starts in the office of Apartment 1, the quickest route out of the apartment building for occupants of the office is to step into the hallway. They should continue through the living room and foyer and then exit the apartment. They should leave the building via the stairs. Elevators should not be in use during a fire, making Choices A and B incorrect. Choice D suggested a longer route than Choice C.

12. **B** This image represents the west side of the apartment building. Choice A shows the east, Choice C shows the north, and Choice D shows the south.

VI. Reading Comprehension and Verbal Expression

Reading and writing are important parts of everyday life. Think about everything you read each day from newspapers, magazines, and books to simple directions before assembling something such as a bookshelf. Now think about how much you actually comprehend, or absorb, after reading. Do you remember which headlines were important in today's newspaper? What step is next after you connect part A to part B? Comprehending what you read is just as important as being able to read.

One way to understand what you just read is by mastering the art of verbal expression. Verbal expression is how you convey information to others, which includes grammar, spelling, and vocabulary skills. If you don't know the meaning of certain words in a passage or if something is misspelled, you might not be able to fully comprehend what you read—that's why those grammar skills you learned in high school will come in handy today.

Before you can actually become a firefighter, you must pass a written test that may include reading comprehension and verbal expression questions. Don't stress out about this section of the exam. We'll review the basic grammar rules and provide you with examples of the different passages, reading comprehension questions, and verbal expression questions that you may see on the firefighter exam.

A. Reading Comprehension

On the reading comprehension section of the firefighter exam, you'll be asked to read a passage or look at a chart or table and then answer questions based on what you just read. The passages can be as short as a few sentences or as long as a few paragraphs, and they usually include details related to the work of a firefighter. The tables might include information such as types of tools or equipment. This doesn't mean that you'll have to know the ins and outs of what firefighters do or learn procedures and terminology. The answers to the questions can be found directly in the passages, and you can refer back to them as needed.

Tip: When reading a passage, concentrate on important details, taking notes as needed.

One way to help you comprehend the information in the passages is to answer the following questions while reading:

- **Who** is the passage about? Take note of the different people mentioned throughout the passage.
- **What** happened in the passage? Identify what is going on in the passage.
- **When** did the event happen? Take note of the time and date mentioned throughout the passage.
- **Where** did the event take place? Identify the location of the event.
- **Why** or **How** did the event happen? Identify what caused the event to happen.

Asking yourself these types of questions while you read can help determine the main idea of the passage. Every passage contains a main idea, which explains what the passage is about, and supporting details that help you determine the meaning of the passage.

1. Types of Passages

You will encounter three types of passages on the firefighter exam. Short passages are typically a few sentences long and contain few details, while long passages contain multiple paragraphs with more details. The other type of passage is a chart, which is an image, a graph, or a diagram along with titles and keys used to convey information, or a table, which contains neatly organized rows and columns of information along with headers and titles to further explain this information.

a. Short Passages

Short passages can be arranged as one or two short paragraphs containing a few sentences or a bulleted list.

The following is an example of a short passage that might be seen on the firefighter exam:

Firefighter Wilford included the following information on a fire prevention pamphlet:

- Never leave cooking food unattended.
- Do not leave a portable heater running while unattended.
- Replace worn or damaged electrical cords.
- Never smoke in bed.
- Do not leave candles lit while unattended.

b. Long Passages

Long passages typically describe situations or events, using numerous details, and usually contain multiple paragraphs.

The following is an example of a long passage that might be seen on the firefighter exam:

Engine Company 14 was dispatched to the scene of a fire at 4:32 p.m. at Hot Cross Breads, located at the corner of May and Spring streets. Jim Nichols, an employee from a neighboring business (Little One's Day Care Center), smelled smoke and called 911. He said he went outside to see where the smoke was coming from and saw flames shooting out from the roof. He, along with two daycare workers and seven children, evacuated the building as a safety precaution.

The bakery was closed for the day, so no one was inside the building at the time. Engine Company 14 arrived at the scene about 4:41 p.m. and firefighters saw smoke coming from the roof near the back of the bakery. After extinguishing the flames, the firefighters proceeded into the building to make sure no victims were inside and to look for the source of the fire. After determining the building was clear, they found a small fire inside one of the ovens at the back of the bakery. The firefighters carefully opened the oven to reveal two flaming loaves of bread and were able extinguish the fire using a handheld fire extinguisher found in the rear of the bakery. The fire was out by 4:50 p.m.

Firefighter Ramsey spoke to Nichols, who called 911 to report the fire, as well as Naomi Rajev, the owner of the bakery, whom Nichols called after calling 911. Rajev explained that she had left the bakery two hours earlier to run errands and must have forgotten to take the last batch of bread out of the oven. She was thankful no one was hurt and the firefighters were able to save her business. Engine Company 14 left the scene of the fire and returned to the station at 5:26 p.m.

c. Charts and Tables

Just like a passage, charts and tables contain information that is used to answer questions. The difference between a chart and a table is how the information is presented to the reader. The information in a chart can be arranged as a line graph, pie chart, or bar chart, etc. The information in a table is arranged in rows and columns. Note that the title of the chart or table is the main idea, or what the table or chart is about.

The following is an example of a chart that might be seen on the firefighter exam:

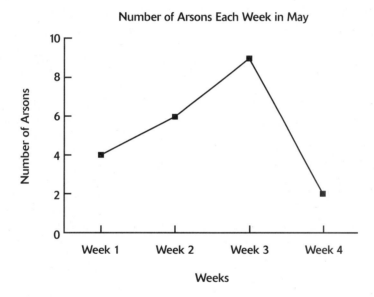

The following is an example of a table that might be seen on the firefighter exam:

Types of Knots Firefighters Use	
Type of Knot	**Use**
Bowline	To hoist items
Clove Hitch	To secure a rope to an object
Figure-Eight Follow Through	To join two pieces of rope of equal diameters together; to tie a rope around an object
Fisherman's Knot	To secure two pieces of rope together
Half Hitch	To stabilize tall objects

2. Types of Questions

A piece of advice—before you even begin reading the passages on the reading comprehension section of the written firefighter exam, take a look at the questions that follow each passage. If you have the time, read them carefully. This way, you'll know what to look for when you read the passage.

You'll encounter three styles of questions on the exam: multiple choice, true and false, and fill in the blank. Each time, you'll choose your answer from a list of two to five options. Although some questions may seem tricky, don't be intimidated—the correct answer is always there. You just have to find it.

After examining the questions, you'll be able to look for key words in the passage, which will make answering the questions easier. If you're allowed to write on your test, underline words in the passage that match words in the questions you've previously read. If your test center doesn't allow you to write in the test booklet, use a piece of scrap paper to jot down notes.

> **Tip: After reading the questions carefully, go to the beginning and quickly scan the passage once or twice, looking for words that might help you answer the questions later. Once you've underlined these words or phrases, return to the beginning of the passage and read it from top to bottom carefully and slowly, making sure to concentrate on the words around the keywords you've marked.**

You'll encounter many different types of questions in the reading comprehension section of your firefighter exam.

a. Finding Essential Details

Many of the questions you'll have to answer after reading passages on the firefighter exam will ask you about specific details in the passage. You'll encounter two different types of details in the passages you read: supporting details and minor details. *Supporting details* are essential to understanding the passage. They also *support* the main idea of the passage by providing evidence that explains the passage's message. *Minor details* aren't nearly as important to the passage. They provide you with additional information, but without them you would still understand the passage as having the same meaning.

Questions that ask you to find essential details in the passage may be similar to those listed here.

- Who was the victim?
- Which department responded to the call?
- How many firefighters were on the scene?
- What was the cause of the traffic accident?
- What most likely caused the fire?
- When did the accident occur?
- What time of day did the fire begin?
- Where did the fire begin in the building?
- What was the address of the building?

- Why did the fire start?
- Why did the gas leak?
- Why did the driver lose control of his car?

Because you'll have the passage in front of you while you answer these questions, you'll be able to refer back to the passage to locate the correct answer whenever you need to. Most of the time, the answer you're looking for is stated directly in the passage. You shouldn't need to draw conclusions or rely on prior experience or knowledge to answer these detail questions.

> **Tip: To answer these questions at a faster pace (thus leaving time for more challenging questions in later sections of the test), you should consider taking notes on the important details you come across while reading the passage. To figure out which details are most important, try pretending that you're an investigative journalist instead of a firefighter. Which questions would a journalist need to ask before he or she could print a story? Remember the five Ws: Who? What? When? Where? Why? (or How?).**

b. Determining the Main Idea

Some questions in the reading comprehension section of the firefighter exam will ask you to figure out what the entire passage is about. Oftentimes, the main idea is stated directly in the passage and may appear as a topic sentence—all you have to do is find it. (Hint: It's most likely at the beginning or end of the passage.) Other times, you'll have to piece together details in the passage to determine the main idea.

Questions about the main idea of a passage may look similar to the following:

- What is the main idea of the passage?
- What is the passage mainly about?
- Which of the following is the best title for this passage?
- Which statement best summarizes the passage?

Remember the correct answers to these questions will state what the *whole* passage is about. If the answer options seem too specific, they're most likely details from the passage and are incorrect answers to the question at hand.

To help you find the main idea of a passage, write down notes about the most important details as you read the passage. These details are most likely supporting details. When you've finished reading, review the notes you've taken and look for a common thread, or a relationship. What the details have in common, or the way they're related to one another, is most likely the main idea of the passage.

c. Drawing Conclusions

Questions that ask you to draw conclusions about what you've read in the passage can be difficult, but are definitely not impossible. These questions are harder than most because the answer isn't directly stated in the passage; instead, you have to piece together details in the passage until the conclusion becomes clear to you.

To answer these questions, try thinking of them in terms of a simple math problem: $A + B = C$. Your details are A and B while C is your conclusion. When you put A and B together, the answer you come up with is most likely going to be the conclusion you're searching for.

Sometimes when you're answering questions that ask you to draw a conclusion, you may feel like you're being asked to predict the future. Although this sounds complicated, it's not. Simply think about what would happen when you put two things together (such as a spark and jet fuel, or an icy road and a speeding car) and you'll come up with the answer quickly.

d. Charts and Tables

Charts and tables are stapled all over fire department message boards, as department officials use them to keep track of everything from equipment to house chores and even department budgets. Because you'll most likely see multiple tables and charts hanging on the walls of your firehouse when you're a firefighter, you should probably know how to read and interpret them. This is why questions about tables and charts appear in the reading comprehension section of the firefighter exam.

The best tables and charts are neatly organized and easy to read. To better understand the information presented to you so that you can quickly and correctly answer questions about it, do the following when you see either one on the test:

1. **Scan the questions first.** This will save you time later, as you'll know which keywords to look for when you're examining the chart itself.
2. **Read the title.** The title of the chart or table contains a hidden gem: the main idea. From the title, you'll be able to determine exactly what the information in the rest of the chart or table is about.
3. **Read the column and row headings.** You'll be able to interpret the information in the tables and charts you see if you read the headings on top of the columns and to the left of the rows. In these spots, you'll find out exactly what the numbers or words in the charts or tables represent. Sometimes, labels in these areas let you know which units of measurements you're dealing with.
4. **Inspect the key/legend on charts.** When you encounter a chart, look for its key or legend. Typically, this box includes information about the colors or symbols used to represent facts on the chart.
5. **Watch for footnotes.** Sometimes you may see an asterisk (*) in a table. This normally tells you to look below the table where a line of text will further explain an idea to you. Just because an asterisk isn't present doesn't mean a table won't have a footnote, however. Sometimes these footnotes give you information about when or where the data in the table was gathered.
6. **Look for exact information.** To answer some questions about charts or tables on the firefighter exam, you may have to do some basic math. Other questions, however, will ask you for details that you may find directly in the table or chart itself. Read the table or chart carefully, looking for key words that will help you answer the question.

e. Defining or Identifying Unfamiliar Words

One of the tougher types of questions in the reading comprehension section of the written firefighter exam is the type that asks you to define words that may be unfamiliar to you. You may think you know what the majority of these words mean, but others may be words you've never seen before. These questions are included on the exam because the ability to define vocabulary words is a key part of comprehending what you read. If you're unfamiliar with a word and can't figure out its meaning, you run the risk of misunderstanding the passage as a whole.

To answer some questions, you may not need to work too hard at determining a word's definition because the meaning of the word is stated directly in the passage. Other questions may require a bit of detective work, which means you'll have to use context clues to find the answer. *Context clues* are pieces of information located in the sentences surrounding the unfamiliar or new word.

Context clues may be whole definitions, synonyms, or antonyms.

- **Definition:** As we previously discussed, sometimes the meaning of the unfamiliar word is stated in the passage, and you simply have to find it. All you have to do is find it. Occasionally, writers will work these definitions into their passages because they may assume readers need help determining the meaning of the word they wish to use. Definitions within a sentence may look similar to this: "When Bill received his award during dinner, he gave a speech in which he acknowledged, or expressed thanks to, his wife and co-workers who supported him in his research." The definition in this sentence shows that *acknowledge* means to *express thanks or gratitude through recognition.*

- **Synonym:** In an attempt to add variety to their writing, many authors use synonyms, or words with similar meanings, instead of using the same word again and again. Many times, synonyms are adjectives, or describing words. When you get to an unfamiliar word, study the words around it to see if any of them may be a synonym for the new word. For example, consider the following sentence: "The rain hampered Anna's work; the large droplets prevented her from digging in her garden and planting her tomato seeds." The words *hampered* and *prevented* are synonyms, and although *hampered* may be new for you, you can assume it means *stopped* or *disrupted* based on the word *prevented.*

- **Antonym:** To show that two ideas differ, authors often use antonyms, or words with opposite meanings, in their writing. Chances are strong that if you know the meaning of an unfamiliar word's antonym, you'll be able to figure out the definition of the unfamiliar word. For example, "With a warning from their mother not to dawdle in the candy aisle, the Stevenson triplets each grabbed a pack of gum and rushed to the side of their mother's shopping cart." From this sentence, you can tell that *dawdle* and *rushed* are opposites; because you know that *to rush* means to move quickly, you can assume that *dawdle* means to move slowly.

If you're still having a hard time determining a word's meaning, try looking directly at the word you're struggling with instead of at the words surrounding it. Attempt to break down the word into parts. If you can figure out the meaning of the smaller parts, you should be able to combine them to determine the meaning of the entire word. Word parts that contain meaning are:

- **Roots:** A root is the part of the word that serves as its base and attributes the most meaning to the word itself. Examples of roots include *path* (in pathology) and *press* (in repress). The following table contains a list of some of the most common root words and their meanings.

Common Root Words

Root	Meaning	Root	Meaning
alter	other	hemo	blood
amphi	both ends	hydro	water
ann	year	junct	join
anthro	relating to humans	liber	free
aqua	water	log	word
arch	chief	lum	light
arthro	joint	magn	large
aud	sound	mater	mother
bell	bad, war	min	small
bibli	relating to books	morph	form
bio	life	mut	change
brev	short	neuro	nerve
cap	seize	nom	name
carn	meat	oper	work
cede, ceed	go, yield	pac	peace
chrom	color	pater	father
chron	time	path	suffer
circum	around	pneum	lung
cogn	know	pod	feet
corp	body	port	carry
crat	ruler	press	squeeze
cred	believe	psych	mind
cruc	cross	scrib	write
crypt	hidden	sed	sit
culp	guilt	sequ	follow
demo	people	simil	same
derm	skin	son	sound
dic	speak	spec	see
domin	rule	spir	breathe
dynam	power	tang, tact	touch
ego	self	temp	time
equ	equal	terr	earth
flux	flow	therm	heat
form	shape	tract	pull
frac, frag	break	vac	empty
frater	brother	vit	life
graph	writing	zoo	animal

- **Prefixes:** Prefixes are word parts found at the beginning of words. When added to a root word, a prefix can entirely change the meaning of the word. Examples of prefixes include *dec-* (in decade) and *mal-* (in malignant). The following table includes many of the prefixes you will see on the firefighter exam.

Common Prefixes

Prefix	Meaning	Prefix	Meaning
a-	no, not	mal-, male-	wrong, bad
ab-, abs-	away, from	multi-	many
anti-	against	nom-	name
bi-	two	omni-	all
com-, con-	with, together	ped-	foot
contra-, counter-	against	que-, quer-, ques-	ask
de-	away from	re-	back, again
dec-	ten	semi-	half
extra-	outside, beyond	super-	over, more
fore-	in front of	tele-	far
geo-	earth	trans-	across
hyper-	excess, over	un-	not
il-	not		

- **Suffixes:** Suffixes are similar to prefixes, except these word parts are found at the end of root words. They, too, can change the meaning of the word. Examples of suffixes include *-ic* (in chocoholic) and *-less* (in mindless). Additional examples of suffixes you may see while preparing for the written portion of the firefighter exam are listed in the following table.

Common Suffixes

Suffix	Meaning	Suffix	Meaning
-able, -ible	capable of	-ism	act, practice
-age	action, result	-ist	characteristic of
-al	characterized by	-ity	quality of
-ance	instance of an action	-less	not having
-ation	action, process	-let	small one
-en	made of	-ment	action, process
-ful	full of	-ness	possessing a quality
-ic	consisting of	-or	one who performs a task
-ical	possessing a quality of	-ous	having
-ion	result of act or process	-y	quality of
-ish	relating to		

Tip: You don't have to memorize these charts, especially because they don't contain anywhere close to all the common roots, prefixes, or suffixes used in the English language. Instead, study them and use other books such as dictionaries and thesauruses to look up additional word parts before you sit down to take your exam.

f. NOT or EXCEPT

Most test takers select incorrect answers on these exams because they don't understand what the questions are asking them to do or find. The best way to avoid this misunderstanding is to read the question thoroughly. Some questions you'll see have the words *not* or *except* in them. This should signal that you're looking for a detail that isn't mentioned in the passage. If the detail is mentioned in the passage, however, it may not be related to the topic discussed in the question you're working on. Read the passage carefully to determine whether this detail is relevant.

It's hard to miss questions containing the words *not* or *except* because these words are typically italicized or boldfaced letters. When you see these questions, read them carefully and be sure you understand what you're being asked to find before you refer back to the passage for the answer.

Practice

Directions (1–3): Answer the following questions solely on the basis of this passage.

A large number of fires has been reported in the town of Rockville. The following are descriptions of each fire.

Restaurant: (June 7)—The cause of the fire was determined to be negligence. An employee left a towel saturated with oil on the grill and it caught fire. The kitchen sustained minor damage because the sprinkler system put out the fire before firefighters arrived at the scene.

Office building: (June 12)—The cause of the fire was determined to be soot buildup in the chimney. Damage was limited to the rear of the building closest to the chimney because firefighters were able to contain the fire.

School: (June 19)—The cause of the fire has not yet been determined. Much of the school, including furniture and computer equipment, was destroyed, but the building structure remains intact.

Multifamily dwelling: (June 24)—The cause of the fire was determined to be arson and is under investigation. Three of the five apartment units in the dwelling sustained major fire damage and were destroyed, while the other two apartments suffered minor smoke and water damage.

1. How many units were destroyed in the multifamily dwelling fire?

   A. Two
   B. Three
   C. Four
   D. Five

2. The cause of the fire has been determined for all of the following fires, EXCEPT the:

   A. office building.
   B. restaurant.
   C. multifamily dwelling.
   D. school.

3. According to the passage, what day did the restaurant fire occur?

   A. June 4
   B. June 7
   C. June 19
   D. June 24

Directions (4): Answer the following question solely on the basis of this chart.

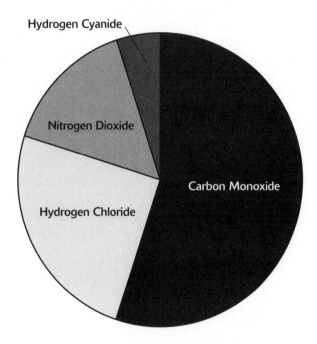

Percentages of Deaths Associated with Toxic Atmospheres in 2010

4. Using the information from the pie chart, you may determine the toxic atmosphere considered to be MOST deadly is

   A. hydrogen chloride.
   B. nitrogen dioxide.
   C. carbon monoxide.
   D. hydrogen cyanide.

Directions (5–8): Answer the following questions solely on the basis of this passage.

Your fire department is dispatched to the scene of a multiple-vehicle crash involving four vehicles. A 2009 red Toyota Prius driven by Paula Wolfe stopped suddenly to avoid hitting a deer that ran across the street in front of her. This caused Nicollet Boone, who was driving a 2011 black Lincoln MKZ behind Wolfe, to <u>veer</u> out of her lane and into oncoming traffic to avoid hitting Wolfe's vehicle. Boone then hit a 2007 white Toyota Rav driven by Marlene Shusta that caused Shusta to hit a 2010 blue Ford Taurus driven by Harold Maxim.

Ms. Wolfe was wearing her seatbelt at the time of the accident and complained of left elbow pain. She did not appear to have any injuries. She had one passenger, her teenage daughter, who was sitting in the front passenger seat and wearing her seatbelt. She complained of moderate neck and back pain.

Ms. Boone was not wearing her seatbelt at the time of the accident and was unconscious when paramedics arrived. She had multiple lacerations on her face, arms, and legs and was bleeding profusely from her head and face. Firefighters noticed she was slumped over in the front seat of her vehicle with her neck bent at an unnatural angle.

Ms. Shusta was wearing her seatbelt at the time of the accident and didn't appear to have any injuries. She had one passenger, her six-year-old grandson who was restrained in a child safety seat, in the backseat of the car. He did not appear to be injured.

Mr. Maxim, who had no passengers, was wearing a seatbelt at the time of the accident. He suffered from several minor scratches on his face and arms. He also complained of sharp pain in his abdomen.

5. Based on the passage, who would appear to be the MOST seriously injured individual?

   A. Paula Wolfe
   B. Nicollet Boone
   C. Marlene Shusta
   D. Harold Maxim

6. What injury did the driver of the Ford Taurus sustain?

   A. Minor scratches on his face and arms
   B. Lacerations on his abdomen
   C. No injuries
   D. Broken neck

7. The word *veer* MOST nearly means

   A. remain.
   B. cease.
   C. swerve.
   D. hurdle.

8. According to the passage, what color was the vehicle Harold Maxim was driving?

   A. Orange
   B. Blue
   C. Black
   D. White

Directions (9–10): Answer the following questions solely on the basis of the following table.

The New York City Fire Department (FDNY) uses a color-coded shield system on helmets to differentiate between types of firefighters.

FDNY Color-Coded System	
Color of Shield	**Type of Firefighter**
Black	Engine company
Blue	Rescue company
Green	Hazardous materials; marine unit
Orange	Probationary firefighter
Red	Ladder company
White	Commanding officer
Yellow	Squad company

9. According to the preceding table, which of the following statements is true?

    A. A FDNY firefighter wearing a helmet with a red shield is part of the ladder company.
    B. A FDNY firefighter wearing a helmet with a green shield is part of the engine company.
    C. A FDNY firefighter wearing a helmet with a black shield is part of the rescue company.
    D. A FDNY firefighter wearing a helmet with a green shield is part of the squad company.

10. A FDNY firefighter involved in a situation at a chemical plant would MOST LIKELY be wearing a helmet with a

    A. black shield.
    B. red shield.
    C. yellow shield.
    D. green shield.

Answers

1. **B** According to the passage, three units were destroyed in the multifamily dwelling fire.

2. **D** The cause of the fire has been determined for the restaurant, office building, and multifamily dwelling. The cause of the school fire has not yet been determined.

3. **B** According to the passage, the restaurant fire occurred on June 7.

4. **C** Because Carbon Monoxide takes up the most space on the pie chart, you can assume that it is the most deadly toxic atmosphere.

5. **B** Based on the information in the passage, Nicollet Boone appears to be the most seriously injured individual.

6. **A** The driver of the Ford Taurus sustained minor scratches on his face and arms.

7. **C** The word *veer* is a verb that most nearly means to swerve.

8. **B** According to the passage, Harold Maxim was driving a 2010 blue Ford Taurus.

9. **A** According to the table, the statement *a FDNY firefighter wearing a helmet with a red shield is part of the ladder company* is true.

10. **D** An FDNY firefighter involved in a situation at a chemical plant would most likely be working with hazardous materials, so he would be wearing a helmet with a green shield.

B. Verbal Expression

As we previously discussed, *verbal expression* refers to how you communicate information to others. Although the word *verbal* is typically associated with the idea of speech, this section of the firefighter exam is more concerned with the way you're able to convey ideas through writing. Firefighters communicate through writing every day, whether they're filling out arson reports or simply documenting what they discovered during the days' standard inspections.

Don't worry—you don't physically have to hand-write any responses on this test. Instead, you'll be asked to read other people's writing and pick out their flaws. Do their subjects and pronouns agree with one another? Are they using the correct verb tense? Did the author just misspell the word *hydrant?* It's up to you to pick out these errors or choose the correct way to present written ideas on this section of the exam.

Topics discussed in this section include the following:

- Spelling
- Adjectives
- Pronouns
- Verbs (tense and agreement)
- Prepositions

1. Spelling

Any reports you complete as a firefighter should be both grammatically correct and free of spelling errors, especially because your documents are most likely representative of the entire department. Today, many people blame their automatic spellcheckers when they submit reports with misspellings in them. While this may sometimes be the case, your supervisor will still place the blame of the misspelling on you. After all, it's your responsibility to re-read your document after you run the spellchecker and before you send it to your supervisor. If you catch something that your spellchecker doesn't and you're still not sure, you can always pick up a dictionary.

The following list will help you brush up on spelling rules before taking the firefighter written exam:

- After a short vowel, the *ch* sound is usually spelled *tch.*
- The letter *c* is usually doubled when it follows a short vowel.
- Words are usually spelled with *-dge* if the *j* sound follows a short vowel.
- Instead of *cc,* the letters *ck* are used if the letter following the *c* sound is *e, i,* or *y.*

- Drop the *e* if it's silent before adding a suffix that begins with a vowel, such as *-ing.*
- Use the letter *i* for the *ee* sound when the sound comes before a suffix that begins with a vowel.
- The endings *-tion* and *-sion* refer to ideas or things, while the ending *-cian* always refers to a person.
- Most of the time, *i* comes before *e,* unless the *i* and the *e* appear after the *c* or if they make the *ay* sound.
- You should find two consonants between the vowel and an *-le* ending in words with a short vowel sound.
- Use the ending *-est* to create superlative adjectives, such as *quickest,* and the ending *-ist* for words referring to people, such as *orthodontist.*

Check out the commonly misspelled words in the following table. Note that they don't abide by any known or decided rules. The only way to always know them is to memorize them.

Commonly Misspelled Words		
acceptable	grateful	misspell
accommodate	guarantee	noticeable
amateur	harass	occasionally
apparent	height	occurrence
argument	ignorance	pastime
calendar	independent	personnel
category	indispensable	playwright
cemetery	inoculate	questionnaire
changeable	intelligence	recommend
collectible	jewelry	referred
committed	judgment	relevant
conscience	kernel	rhythm
discipline	leisure	separate
embarrass	license	sergeant
equipment	lightning	supersede
exceed	maintenance	vacuum
existence	millennium	
gauge	miniature	

Although commonly misspelled words can be a bit confusing at times, we have a whole other list for you of words that writers commonly confuse with one another. These words are called *homophones.* They're words that sound the same, but have entirely different meanings. Mistakes with homophones are easy to make and even easier for your spellchecker to miss.

Can you spot the error in the following sentence?

> Due to construction on the off-ramp of the highway, police officers are stationed at various points on the ramp today to ensure that drivers precede with caution.

The word *precede* is a verb that means "to come before." In this case, the writer most likely wanted to use the word *proceed,* which means "to go forward." Did you spot the error? *Proceed* and *precede* sound alike and are easy to confuse, especially when you're rushing through a report or working under a seemingly impossible deadline. Even under these circumstances, however, it's important to use the correct word. Otherwise, your readers will become confused and may obscure the meaning of your writing.

Below is a table of commonly confused words. Reviewing this table before you answer the following examples will help you choose the correct answers.

Homophones		
accept—to receive e.g. She accepted the birthday gift.	**except**—to take or leave out e.g. He folded all the laundry except the socks.	
affect—to influence e.g. Their argument affected the entire office.	**effect**—n., result; v., to accomplish e.g. Her presence had a positive effect on my performance. The manager effected change by creating a new policy.	
ascent—the act of rising or moving upward e.g. The ascent up the stairs was difficult while carrying those boxes.	**assent**—to agree to something e.g. The teens assented to the curfew their parents proposed.	
buy—to purchase e.g. She will buy her lunch in the company cafeteria every day.	**by**—in proximity to; near e.g. My house is by the river.	**bye**—the position of a participant in a tournament. e.g. The team earned a bye in the first round of playoffs.
capital—a city serving as the seat of government e.g. Boise is the capital of Idaho.	**capitol**—a building in which a legislative body meets e.g. The business and law class took a field trip to the capitol building.	
cent—monetary unit equal to $\frac{1}{100}$ of a basic unit of value e.g. Everything in this store costs less than 97 cents.	**scent**—an odor e.g. The scent of my favorite candle reminds me of gatherings around the campfire at the beach.	**sent**—past tense of send e.g. She said that she sent me an e-mail, but I never received it.
cite—to quote by way of example e.g. Our professor requires us to cite all of our sources on the last page of our papers.	**sight**—something that is seen e.g. The sight of the fog rolling into the cemetery after dark sends shivers down my spine.	**site**—the location of a structure e.g. When we were in Pennsylvania, we visited the site of the Battle of Gettysburg.
complement—n., something that completes; v., to complete e.g. The scarf is a great complement to her outfit. The seasoning Chef added at the last minute complements the dish beautifully.	**compliment**—n., praise; v., to praise e.g. The best man received many compliments after he gave his speech at the wedding reception. The husband complimented his wife on her new dress.	

(continued)

its—of or belonging to it e.g. On the way to work this morning, my shirt lost one of <u>its</u> buttons.	**it's**—contraction of it is e.g. At 5:00, <u>it's</u> finally time to go home!	
lead—a type of metal e.g. When a number of people got sick in my town, scientists tested the water for <u>lead</u> poisoning.	**led**—past tense of lead e.g. He <u>led</u> his son to the edge of the water, and the toddler began to whimper as the waves reached his feet.	
lose—to fail e.g. If we don't submit this project on time, we may <u>lose</u> the account.	**loose**—not fastened securely e.g. The player's baseball cap slid in front of his eyes because it was too <u>loose</u>.	
passed—past tense of pass e.g. When I lived in Charlotte, I always thought of my grandmother when I <u>passed</u> by her old house.	**past**—having existed or taken place in a period before the present e.g. The time capsule contains postcards and small toys from the <u>past</u>.	
precede—to come before e.g. The singing of the National Anthem <u>preceded</u> the baseball game.	**proceed**—to go forward e.g. I <u>proceeded</u> down the rocky hill carefully.	
principal—adj., most important; n., a person in authority e.g. The proposed salary was the <u>principal</u> reason I took this job. My elementary school <u>principal</u> had an amusing laugh.	**principle**—a general or fundamental law e.g. In the 101 courses, culinary students learn the <u>principles</u> of cooking and baking.	
right—adj., being in accordance with what is just or proper; n., something to which one has a just claim e.g. Reading the questions before you read the passages will help you determine the <u>right</u> answers. He has the <u>right</u> to sit anywhere he'd like in the classroom.	**rite**—a ceremonial act or action e.g. Staying home alone for the first time is a <u>rite</u> of passage for most middle school students.	**write**—to express in literary form e.g. Every night, she sits down to <u>write</u> at least 10 pages of her upcoming novel.
their—of or relating to them or themselves e.g. <u>Their</u> lives always seemed more interesting than mine.	**there**—in or at that place e.g. When I set my glass <u>there</u>, I didn't see the cat lurking nearby.	**they're**—contraction of they are e.g. <u>They're</u> not certain that they like living in Memphis yet.
threw—past tense of throw e.g. He <u>threw</u> the ball to the catcher, who missed it and allowed the runner to score.	**through**—indicates movement into one side or point and out another e.g. I put a hole in my stocking when I accidently shoved my finger <u>through</u> the material.	
to—indicates movement or action toward a place e.g. This weekend, we're going <u>to</u> the drive-in.	**too**—to an excessive degree e.g. When she has <u>too</u> much coffee, she gets headaches.	**two**—being one more than the number one e.g. I've had so much free time in the last week, I was able to finish reading <u>two</u> whole books.

In the following example questions, select the misspelled word in each sentence.

EXAMPLES:

1. When responding to a fire, firefighters frequently remove power tools from the fire aperattus and carry them to the site of the fire.

   A. responding
   B. frequently
   C. aperattus
   D. site

The correct answer is **C.** The correct spelling of *aperattus* is *apparatus.*

2. Today's fire alarm systems inable alarms to be transmitted and received by the fire department swiftly and accurately.

   A. inable
   B. transmitted
   C. received
   D. accurately

The correct answer is **A.** The correct spelling of *inable* is *enable.*

3. When Firefighter Roberts arrives on the seen, he sees three vehicles that have collided and are in danger of a gasoline fire.

   A. arrives
   B. seen
   C. vehicles
   D. gasoline

The correct answer is **B.** The correct spelling of *seen* in this sentence is *scene.*

2. Adjectives

Some questions on the written portion of the firefighter exam may ask you to identify the correct use of adjectives in a sentence. *Adjectives* are words used to describe nouns; words that describe colors, shapes, and even a person's characteristics are all considered adjectives. There are three main types of adjectives:

- **Positive adjectives:** A positive adjective stands alone, which means it's the only adjective used to describe a noun. Positive adjectives don't offer a comparison between two or more objects and don't always have to be positive in meaning. For example:

  The <u>greasy</u> pan sat in the sink all night, which made it difficult to clean the next morning.

- **Comparative adjectives:** A comparative adjective compares only two people, places, things, or ideas. If the adjective has one or two syllables, add an *-er* ending. If it has three or more syllables, place the word *more* or *less* before the adjective. For example:

  Firefighter Langdon is <u>quicker</u> than Firefighter Andrews.

  I like to think I'm <u>more athletic</u> than my brother, but he often proves me wrong.

■ **Superlative adjectives:** A superlative adjective compares three or more people, places, ideas, or items. If the adjective has one or two syllables, add *-est* ending. If it contains three or more syllables, use the word *most* or *least* before the adjective. For example:

Captain Brady is probably the smartest man I know.

Of the gifts I received for my last birthday, Margie's was the most interesting.

We think you should be familiar with one other type of adjective. This adjective is known as the *possessive adjective.* We'll discuss this more in the "Pronouns" section later in this chapter.

In the following example questions, choose the word or phrase that best completes the sentence.

EXAMPLES:

---

1. When they march in our local parade, each firefighter wears a _____ polo and black pants.

   A. blue
   B. more blue
   C. bluer
   D. least blue

The correct answer is **A.** Because you only have to describe one noun, *polo,* you can use a positive adjective.

---

2. The _____ way to reach a victim trapped on the top floor of a burning building is to take the stairs.

   A. safe
   B. safer
   C. safest
   D. most safe

The correct answer is **C.** In this sentence, you're comparing taking the stairs to all other forms of rescue during a fire, so you need to use the superlative adjective *safest.* If you were only comparing the stairs to one other form of rescue, you would use the comparative form, *safer.*

---

3. Saving a fire victim's life is _____ than preventing property damage.

   A. important
   B. importanter
   C. more important
   D. most important

The correct answer is **C.** Because you're only comparing two ideas (saving a life and preventing property damage), you can use the comparative adjectival phrase *more important.*

3. Pronouns

You'll most likely encounter questions that ask you to choose the correct pronoun to use in a sentence when you're taking the verbal section of the written firefighter exam. While a *noun* is the word used to represent a person, place, item, or idea, a *pronoun* is a word used in place of a noun. The noun that the pronoun replaces and refers to is called the *antecedent.* Writers like to use pronouns so their sentences don't contain the same noun again and again, making their writing difficult (and frustrating) to read.

Although you don't necessarily *have* to memorize the following list of pronouns, you can only benefit by doing so. It's important that you're able to know when you should use each type of pronoun so you can answer grammar questions correctly when you see them on the exam. There are six different categories of pronouns:

- **Subject pronouns:** These words are substituted for the subject of a sentence. The subject usually appears in a sentence before the verb or after *than* and *as.* Subject pronouns can also be used when a compound subject contains a noun and a pronoun. Subject pronouns include *I, you, he, she, it, we, you, they,* and *who.*

- **Object pronouns:** These words can be substituted for the object of a sentence. The object is usually found after the verb in a sentence. Use an object pronoun when a compound object contains a noun and a pronoun. Object pronouns can also appear as the object of a prepositional phrase. Object pronouns include *me, you, him, her, it, us, them,* and *whom.*

- **Possessive pronouns:** These words show ownership, or possession. Possessive pronouns include *its, yours, his, hers, ours, theirs,* and *mine.* Although possessive adjectives may look similar to possessive pronouns (and also show ownership), they're actually used to modify nouns. Possessive adjectives include *its, your, his, her, our, their,* and *my* and should be used before nouns ending in *-ing.*

Tip: Neither possessive pronouns nor possessive adjectives need apostrophes to show possession, so don't add them!

- **Demonstrative pronouns:** These words refer to the nouns or pronouns that stand in for objects that may be near or far away from the narrator. Demonstrative pronouns include *that, this, those,* and *these.*

- **Indefinite pronouns:** These words don't refer to a specific person or thing and may be singular or plural. If another pronoun appears in the sentence with a singular indefinite pronoun, it should also be singular. Singular indefinite pronouns include *another, anybody, anyone, anything, each, either, everybody, everything, everyone, nobody, no one, nothing, somebody, someone,* and *something.* Plural indefinite pronouns include *few, many, others,* and *several.*

- **Reflexive pronouns:** These words are used to reference a previous word in the sentence. Reflexive pronouns include *myself, yourself, yourselves, ourselves, herself,* and *himself.*

In the following example questions, choose the word or words that best complete the sentence.

EXAMPLES:

1. Someone forgot _____ notebook in the bunk area this morning.
   - **A.** his
   - **B.** their
   - **C.** its
   - **D.** his or her

The correct answer is **D.** Because the indefinite pronoun *Someone* is singular, it needs a singular possessive adjective. Because you don't know the sex of the person who forgot the notebook, you need to use the phrase *his or her*.

---

2. My department chief is a better cook than _____.

    A.   I
    B.   me
    C.   us
    D.   they

The correct answer is **A.** In this sentence, use the subject pronoun, *I,* after *than* or *as.* Sometimes it helps to complete the sentence in your head: My department chief is a better cook than *I am.*

---

3. _____ coming to work late doesn't surprise me; you do it all the time.

    A.   You
    B.   Your
    C.   Yours
    D.   Yourself

The correct answer is **B.** Because the adjective comes before a noun ending in *-ing* (*coming*), you need to use the possessive adjective *your* instead of *you.*

4. Verbs

Verbs are words that tell the reader what's going on (action) or the state of being (emotion or condition).

Look at the following sentence:

> I ride my bike to work each day.

The word *ride* is the verb because it shows the action in the sentence.

All verbs have a *tense* that tells the reader *when* the action or state of being is happening, such as in the past, present, or future. The form of the verb changes when the tense of a sentence changes. All sentences must have a subject and verb and these two parts must agree in number. If you have a singular verb, you need a singular subject and if you have a plural subject, you should have a plural verb.

a. Tense

The previous example is set in the present tense. If you changed the sentence to the past tense, then the form of the verb would have to change to the past tense. The same is true if you change the sentence to the future tense.

Look at the following sentence that shows an action that happened in the past:

> I rode my bike to work each day last week.

Notice how the verb tense changes to *rode* to describe an action that took place in the past.

Look at the following sentence that describes an action that will take place in the future:

> I <u>will ride</u> my bike to work each day next week.

Notice how the verb tense changes to *will ride* to describe an action that will take place in the future.

On the firefighter exam, you'll encounter several types of questions that ask you to identify or use the correct verb tense. Review the following verb-tense examples:

- **Present Tense:** A verb in the present tense expresses an action that is happening right now. It also describes an action that happens continually or regularly. For example:

  > I <u>drink</u> coffee every morning while I <u>wait</u> for the bus.

  > The sight of the mother bird feeding its babies <u>is</u> adorable.

- **Past Tense:** A verb in this tense describes an action that was completed at a particular point in the past. For example:

  > I <u>walked</u> two miles with my dogs last evening.

  > He <u>cooked</u> pot roast and potatoes for dinner last Sunday.

- **Future Tense:** A sentence written in the future tense describes an action that will take place at a certain point in the future. For example:

  > I <u>will take</u> a class in economics next semester.

  > They <u>will plant</u> the garden next weekend.

- **Present-Perfect Tense:** A verb in the present-perfect tense describes an action that began in the past and either continues in the present or is completed in the present. For example:

  > My mother <u>has lived</u> in the same house for more than 50 years.

  > I <u>have dreaded</u> this moment for weeks.

- **Past-Perfect Tense:** This tense describes an action that began in the past and was completed in the past. For example:

  > She <u>had saved</u> enough money to purchase a car by the time she graduated.

  > She <u>had finished</u> the project by 5:00 p.m.

- **Future-Perfect Tense:** This tense describes an action that will begin in the future and will be completed at a specific time in the future. For example:

  > By this time next year, I <u>will have moved</u> to California.

  > In a few months, she <u>will have saved</u> enough money to go on vacation.

You must also determine if a verb is regular or irregular. It's important to learn the difference between regular and irregular verbs so you know how to conjugate them, or change them from one verb form to another. **Regular verbs** can be transformed into the past tense by adding *–d* or *–ed*. For example, the present-tense verb *train* is changed to the past tense by adding *–ed* to make the past-tense verb *trained*. In this case, the past participle of the word *train* is also *trained*. The **past participle** often uses an auxiliary verb to describe an action that took place in the past. For example:

> I <u>have trained</u> for the marathon for six months.

Unlike regular verbs, **irregular verbs** don't always use –d or –ed to form the past tense or the past participle. Think about the word *write*. It would be incorrect to say *The author writed 20 novels in the past five years.* In this case, the past tense of *write* is *wrote* and the past participle is *written.* For example:

    Past Tense: The author <u>wrote</u> 20 novels in the past five years.

    Past Participle: The author <u>has written</u> 20 novels in the past five years.

About 200 irregular verbs exist in the English language, but unfortunately, there is no rhyme or reason as to how irregular verbs are conjugated. The only way to learn the different forms is through memorization. The following table shows common irregular verbs:

Common Irregular Verbs					
Present Tense	**Past Tense**	**Past Participle**	**Present Tense**	**Past Tense**	**Past Participle**
am, be	was, were	been	ring	rang	rung
begin	began	begun	rise	rose	risen
break	broke	broken	run	ran	run
bring	brought	brought	see	saw	seen
catch	caught	caught	set	set	set
choose	chose	chosen	shake	shook	shaken
come	came	come	show	showed	shown
do	did	done	sing	sang, sung	sung
drive	drove	driven	sink	sank, sunk	sunk
eat	ate	eaten	speak	spoke	spoken
fall	fell	fallen	spring	sprang, sprung	sprung
fight	fought	fought	steal	stole	stolen
fly	flew	flown	swear	swore	sworn
freeze	froze	frozen	swim	swam	swum
give	gave	given	swing	swung	swung
go	went	gone	take	took	taken
grow	grew	grown	tear	tore	torn
hide	hid	hidden	throw	threw	thrown
know	knew	known	wake	woke, waked	waked
lead	led	led	wear	wore	worn
ride	rode	ridden	write	wrote	written

In the following example questions, choose the word or words that best complete the sentence.

EXAMPLES:

> 1. By the end of the month, members of the Lanceyville Fire Department _____ 12 training classes.
>
>   A. complete
>   B. completes
>   C. has completed
>   D. will have completed

The correct answer is **D.** Because the sentence describes an action that will both begin and end in the future, it needs a verb set in the future-perfect tense (*will have completed*).

---

2. Yesterday, the firefighters _____ to an accident scene involving four vehicles.

    A. respond
    B. responded
    C. will have responded
    D. has responded

The correct answer is **B.** Because the sentence begins with the word *yesterday,* it alerts you that the action in the sentence happened in the past, so it needs a verb set in the past tense (*responded*).

---

3. Firefighter Mullens _____ every fire alarm each week at the senior citizen center.

    A. inspect
    B. inspects
    C. will inspected
    D. have inspected

The correct answer is **B.** Because the sentence is set in the present tense, it needs a verb set in the present tense (*inspects*).

b. Agreement

In addition to answering questions about correct verb tense on the firefighter exam, you will also be tested on subject-verb agreement. While agreement can be tricky at times, just remember that subjects and verbs must be in agreement based on the number of people or things that are performing the action. For example:

Singular subject and singular verb: <u>Nancy</u> <u>wears</u> boots when it snows.

The singular subject (*Nancy*) should be followed by the singular form of the verb (*wears*).

Plural subject and plural verb: The <u>teachers</u> <u>sign</u> the contract.

The plural subject (*teachers*) should be followed by a plural form of the verb (*sign*).

Review the following agreement rules:

- Use a plural verb with a plural subject.
- Use a singular verb with a singular subject.
- Use a singular verb with *neither/nor* or *either/or.*
- Use a singular verb when dealing with time or money.
- Use a singular verb with collective nouns such as *team* and *group.*
- Use a plural verb when at least two subjects are connected by *and.*
- Use a singular verb when two singular subjects are connected by *or* or *nor.*
- Use a singular verb in sentences with *each, everyone, every one, someone, somebody, anyone,* and *anybody.*

- If a phrase appears between the subject and the verb, make sure the verb agrees with the subject, not the phrase.
- If *there* or *here* begins a sentence, the subject of the sentence should follow the verb. The verb should agree with the subject.
- If a compound subject has both a singular and a plural subject joined by *or* or *nor,* the verb should agree with the part of the subject that appears closest to the verb.

In the following example questions, choose the word or words that best complete the sentence.

EXAMPLES:

---

1. Shelley and I _____ kickboxing class every Tuesday after our shifts end.

   A. will attends
   B. attending
   C. attend
   D. attends

The correct answer is **C.** When two singular subjects are connected by the conjunction *and,* use the plural form of the verb (*attend*).

---

2. A group of firefighters _____ the stairs, looking for trapped victims.

   A. climb
   B. climbs
   C. climbing
   D. have climbed

The correct answer is **B.** A singular verb (*climbs*) should be used with the collective pronoun *group.*

---

3. Seven dollars _____ the price of the barbecue chicken dinner.

   A. be
   B. is
   C. are
   D. were

The correct answer is **B.** A singular form of the verb should be used when dealing with time or money, so the verb *is* is correct.

5. Prepositions

A preposition is the part of the sentence that establishes a relationship between a noun (or pronoun) and links it to another word in the sentence. It usually expresses a position in space or time. The following table contains the most common prepositions:

Common Prepositions			
about	between	like	till
above	beyond	near	to
across	but	of	toward
after	by	off	under
against	despite	on	underneath
along	down	onto	until
among	during	out	up
around	except	outside	upon
at	for	over	with
before	from	past	within
behind	in	since	without
below	inside	through	
beneath	into	throughout	

The word or phrase that the preposition introduces is called the object of the preposition. A prepositional phrase begins with a preposition and contains the object of the preposition, and adjectives or adverbs. For example:

Maryann searched feverishly <u>for her house keys.</u>

The prepositional phrase *for her house keys* contains a prepositional object (*keys*) and adjectives (*her* and *house*).

A prepositional phrase can sometimes function as a noun, an adjective, or an adverb. (See the previous section, "Adjectives," for more information on adjectives.) For example:

Maryann dropped her keys <u>on the floor.</u>

The prepositional phrase *on the floor* acts as an adverb in this sentence, modifying the verb *dropped. On the floor* specifies where the dropping occurred.

> **Tip:** When answering questions about prepositions on the firefighter exam, read the sentence carefully and substitute each answer choice to choose the word that makes the most sense.

In the following example questions, choose the word that best completes the sentence.

EXAMPLES:

1. The firefighter searched _____ the rubble for victims.
   - **A.** after
   - **B.** until
   - **C.** beneath
   - **D.** from

The correct answer is **C**. The sentence makes the most sense if you insert the preposition *beneath,* which establishes the relationship between the verb *searched* and the object of the preposition *rubble.*

---

2. Firefighter Manuel propped the pike pole _____ the wall so he could wipe the sweat from his brow.

   A. between
   B. against
   C. inside
   D. about

The correct answer is **B**. The sentence makes the most sense if you insert the preposition *against,* which establishes the relationship between the verb *propped* and the object of the preposition *wall.*

---

3. The firefighter maneuvered the firetruck _____ the cloud of smoke.

   A. below
   B. despite
   C. since
   D. toward

The correct answer is **D**. The sentence makes the most sense if you insert the preposition *toward,* which establishes the relationship between the verb *maneuvered* and the object of the preposition *cloud.*

Practice

Directions (1–4): Choose the word that best completes the sentence.

---

1. The firefighter placed the mask on his face _____ he entered the burning building.

   A. about
   B. despite
   C. before
   D. since

2. Everyone made it safely out of the burning house _____ a pet turtle.

   A. except
   B. for
   C. inside
   D. against

3. There _____ many reasons the house may have caught fire.

    A.   be

    B.   is

    C.   are

    D.   was

4. The student, as well as his classmates, _____ to pass the firefighter exam.

    A.   hope

    B.   hopes

    C.   hoping

    D.   will hope

Directions (5–6): Select the misspelled word in each sentence.

5. To turn off a supply of gas, firefighters need to apply an automatic shut-off devise.

    A.   supply

    B.   apply

    C.   automatic

    D.   devise

6. After arriving on the scene, firefighters may feel distracted or overwelmed by growing crowds of spectators.

    A.   distracted

    B.   overwelmed

    C.   crowds

    D.   spectators

Directions (7–10): Choose the word that best completes the sentence.

7. In some situations, foam is _____ when putting out fires than high-pressure water.

    A.   better

    B.   effective

    C.   best

    D.   more effective

8. Although we all know better, we still let Firefighter Mifflin think he's the _____ man in the firehouse.

    A.   stronger

    B.   strongest

    C.   more strong

    D.   most strong

9. Each of the women in our department agreed to play in the charity softball tournament and to pay for _____ own T-shirt.

   A. their
   B. them
   C. its
   D. her

10. It didn't take Firefighter Nelson long to determine that _____ are the tools he needs to complete his task.

    A. that
    B. these
    C. this
    D. them

Answers

1. **C** The sentence makes the most sense if you insert the preposition *before,* which establishes the relationship between the verb *placed* and the object of the preposition *building.*

2. **A** The sentence makes the most sense if you insert the preposition *except,* which establishes the relationship between the verb *made* and the object of the preposition *turtle.*

3. **C** Because the subject of the sentence (*reasons*) is plural, the plural verb *are* is correct.

4. **B** If a phrase appears between the subject and the verb, the verb agrees with the subject, not the phrase, so because *student* is singular, it would take the singular form of the verb (*hopes*).

5. **D** The correct spelling of *devise* in this sentence is *device.*

6. **B** The correct spelling of *overwelmed* is *overwhelmed.*

7. **D** Because this sentence compares two things (*foam* and *water*), you can use a comparative adjectival phrase such as *more effective* to describe the difference between the two items.

8. **B** Because this sentence is comparing Firefighter Mifflin to all of the men in the firehouse, you need to use a superlative adjective. Because *strong* only has one syllable, you can add -*est* to the end of the word to form *strongest.*

9. **D** Because *Each* is singular, a singular adjective is needed to complete the sentence. Because the team is assumedly all female, *her* is the correct possessive adjective to use to modify the noun *T-shirt.*

10. **B** The demonstrative pronoun *these* represents objects (*the tools*) that are near or far away. Because Firefighter Nelson needs multiple tools, the demonstrative pronoun has to be plural.

VII. Deductive, Inductive, and Logical Reasoning; Information Ordering; and Problem Sensitivity

Many questions on the written firefighter exam test your ability to make good decisions. Firefighters must make decisions under pressure every day, whether they're in the station house with their superiors or in a structure engulfed by flames. As a firefighter, your ability to quickly examine the situation, weigh the pros and cons, and then act will undoubtedly save lives.

In this chapter, we discuss the types of questions that ultimately test your reasoning skills. Your future employers will want to know if you can identify problems on your own, avoid dangerous situations, and think on your feet. Firefighters need to keep their heads on straight at all times—their priority must always be to save lives. Firefighters should also never let their own emotions and opinions get in the way of their duties. Keep this in mind as you continue to prepare for the firefighter exam.

In addition to having stellar reasoning skills, firefighters also need to be able to quickly organize information they receive and detect problems that may arise on the scene. The written firefighter exam tests these abilities using information ordering questions and problem sensitivity questions.

A. Topics Covered on the Exam

Reasoning questions cover topics such as firefighting operations and procedures, in addition to public and international relations. These topics appear in lists and reading passages, which are a few related paragraphs, and require you to read between the lines. The following list explains each of these topics:

1. Firefighting Operations

These questions are designed to show your future employers that you can follow directions and act appropriately in emergency situations. You may be presented with a passage that places you at the scene of an emergency such as a traffic accident, hazardous spill, or structural fire. You need to read the passage, imagine yourself in the situation, and then read the question. Most of the time, you're asked to examine the answer choices and choose the action you should perform first. No matter what the situation is, a firefighter's priorities should always remain the same:

1. Save lives.
2. Reduce property damage.
3. Stop or prevent fire.

Like all other questions on the written firefighter exam, you don't necessarily need to know anything about firefighting to answer reasoning and judgment questions. All the information you need to answer these questions is on the page in front of you—all you have to do is find it.

> **Remember: No matter the situation presented to you, the answer you choose should always keep everyone (victims, bystanders, fellow emergency personnel, etc.) safe. It should also present a quick solution to the problem. If property is involved, think about the choice that will save the owner the most money.**

2. Following Procedures

These questions contain a list of directions or instructions accompanying a short passage or a single line of text. They test your ability to follow directions. You have to be careful with following-procedures questions, as the lists provided aren't always in chronological order. Sometimes you may be asked to order the steps chronologically; other times, you may be asked which actions you should perform first or last. To answer these questions correctly, you need to understand what the question is asking. Look for words such as *first, next, last, before,* and *after* to help you choose the correct answer. These questions don't test your judgment skills as much as they test your ability to comprehend information and act reasonably.

> **Tip: Read every piece of information you're given when answering questions about following procedures. This includes introductory paragraphs and notes at the end of the list. All parts of these passages are fair game, which means the information in these areas may help you choose the correct answer to questions on the exam.**

3. Public Relations

These questions test your ability to interact with civilians whether you're consoling them after their home was damaged in a fire or simply stopping to say hello in the parking lot of a hardware store. You should always treat civilians with respect, and when you don't think you can answer their questions, point them in the direction of someone who can. It's important that all members of the community know that they can depend on their town's firefighters. It's especially important that children feel safe when firefighters are around, and that they know they can trust their town's fire company to help them if they are in need.

Judgment and reasoning questions about public relations on the written firefighter exam typically appear as short passages. The question asks you to choose the appropriate action based on the information in the passage. Keep in mind that the correct answer should show a firefighter treating all civilians with respect while simultaneously following department policies.

> **Remember: Read every answer choice carefully when dealing with questions about public relations. Even though multiple answer choices may seem right, only one of them will show a firefighter following the rules and being respectful to the civilian in question. Think of the effects of each answer choice. If you choose Choice C, would anyone be angry? Would the department be negatively affected in any way? After reading each choice, draw a line through the ones that hurt feelings, put the department in a negative light, or break protocol. What you have left is most likely the best answer.**

4. Interpersonal Relations

Interpersonal relations questions test your ability to interact with others, but these questions require you to read passages about firefighters working with their co-workers and supervisors instead of with members of the community. Like public relations questions, the correct answer choice always shows firefighters following protocol and respecting authority.

As a firefighter candidate, it's important that you realize how vital a good relationship with your fellow firefighters truly is—how are you supposed to feel safe and confident in a burning building while standing alongside men and women you don't trust? Your fellow firefighters will become like a second family to you. You'll learn to respect one another's opinions and become comfortable with the idea of depending on them to help you in dangerous situations. Even though you can lean on others in times of need, it's always important to take full responsibility for your actions and decisions.

Questions on the firefighter exam that test your interpersonal skills appear as short passages or paragraphs. They ask you to imagine yourself in a certain situation and then respond accordingly. Read the entire question and cross out any answer choices that don't show the firefighter being honest or respectful.

> **Tip: Although the majority of interpersonal relations questions on the written firefighter exam will ask you about teamwork, you'll encounter a few questions that require you to consider your relationship with authority figures. If the scenario takes place at an emergency scene, always choose the answer choice that has you following your superiors' instructions, even if you don't agree with them. If you want to talk to your captain about an issue you're having, ask for a private meeting and keep your side of the conversation polite and respectful. Never point fingers or throw one of your fellow firefighters or your superiors under the bus.**

B. Reasoning

Many of the questions you'll answer on the written firefighter exam are designed to test your ability to make decisions. You have to weigh the pros and cons of each situation and then choose the best answer choice. These questions test your ability to reason, or in other words, to comprehend the information given to you and form judgments based on that information. In this section, we discuss the three most common forms of reasoning questions on the exam: deductive, inductive, and logical.

1. Deductive Reasoning

Deductive reasoning questions come in two forms: short, informative paragraphs and lists of definitions. These paragraphs and lists provide you with a small amount of general information about various topics. You then have to take this new information and apply it to a specific situation to form a conclusion. The process of taking general information and applying it to a single circumstance is called *deductive reasoning*.

Consider this statement: All dogs are mammals. You have a pet Chihuahua named Chance. A Chihuahua is a type of dog. Using deductive reasoning, you could reach the conclusion that Chance is a mammal. Do you see how simple that was? You made a general statement about all dogs into a specific and accurate statement about Chance.

These types of questions are similar to many of the reading comprehension questions we discussed in Chapter VI. As we discussed earlier, everything you need to know to answer the majority of questions on the firefighter exam is on the test. Carefully read every passage, examine every list you come across, and read every single question and its answer choices multiple times. Be sure you understand what the question is asking you before choosing an answer.

The following is an example of a deductive reasoning passage and questions you may see on the written firefighter exam:

EXAMPLES:

Questions 1–3 refer to the following information.

Couplings are used to join hoses, and may be used to divide the stream or join several streams. Firefighters may use various types of couplings, including:

- **Double female:** To connect two "male" couplings together or adapt different sizes.
- **Double male:** Two male-threaded connectors, used to join two "female" couplings.
- **Siamese:** Used to merge two streams into one.
- **Storz:** A sexless coupling that secures with a quarter turn. The coupling may have a locking device. Storz couplings require adapters for use with threaded hose.
- **Wye:** Used for splitting one line into two or more outlets. Gated Wyes may have separate valves for each outlet.

---

1. At a brush fire there is only one hydrant in the neighborhood to which you have attached a primary line. The shift commander orders two teams to attack the fire from two positions. Based on the information provided, what type of coupling do you use to attach two hoses to the main line?

   A. Wye
   B. Storz
   C. Siamese
   D. Double male

The correct answer is **A.** Information in this deductive reasoning passage tells you that the Wye coupling allows you to split the stream and attach two hoses. Choice C is incorrect because the Siamese coupling is used to bring two streams together, not split them apart. Choices B and D are also incorrect; the passage does not state that the double male coupling or the Storz coupling can be used to attach two hoses to the main line.

---

2. You're responding to a two-alarm structure fire, joining a neighboring municipality's fire department in a mutual-response effort to control a fire in an office building. Your superior officer tells you the hoses on your truck are not the same diameter as those of the local department, but must be joined to reach the upper floors of the building. Based on the information provided, what type of coupling do you need to join the hoses?

   A. Wye
   B. Storz
   C. Siamese
   D. Double female

The correct answer is **D.** The deductive reasoning passage states that the double female coupling may be used to adapt different sizes. This means that you'll be able to use your department's hoses along with the neighboring municipality's hoses. Choices A, B, and C are incorrect because the passage does not state that Wye, Storz, or Siamese couplings can be used to adapt different sizes of hoses.

3. A number of new office buildings have been built in your city, and additional hoses have been purchased for the fire engine. These additional lengths will allow your department to reach the upper floors should there be a fire. Unfortunately, due to a clerical error, the threads on the new hose don't match those your department already has. Using the information in the passage, what type of coupling will allow you to connect both the old and new hoses?

A. Wye
B. Storz
C. Siamese
D. Double male

The correct answer is **B.** The Storz is a sexless coupling that does not require threads, but can be joined to a threaded hose using an adapter. You know this because this information appears directly in the deductive reasoning passage. Because the Storz coupling is sexless, male and female couplings can be connected, thus increasing the number of hoses that can be used during a fire. Choices A, C, and D are incorrect because the passage does not include evidence that Wye, Siamese, or Double male couplings can connect to both old and new hoses.

2. Inductive Reasoning

Inductive reasoning questions can easily be mistaken for deductive reasoning questions; however, there's one big difference—inductive reasoning questions ask you to rely on general information you already know. Instead of applying general information to specific circumstances, inductive reasoning questions force you to take bits and pieces of specific information, combine them with general information you already know, and then come to a conclusion. This conclusion may help you develop a rule or even figure out how seemingly unrelated events are actually connected to each other. This entire thought process allows you to use your inductive reasoning skills.

Consider this situation: On the way to work, Doug briefly lost control of his car. At the time, he said he had just finished adjusting the heat in his car so the windows would defrost. When he got to work, he shook snow out of his hair and hung up his coat to dry. Using inductive reasoning, why did Doug most likely lose control of his car?

Think of what you know about Doug's predicament: He lost control of his car, he needed heat in his car so the windows would defrost, he had snow in his hair, and his coat was damp. From these clues, you know that this happened to Doug during the winter season, which probably means that Doug lost control of his car because there was ice on the road. The situation doesn't explicitly say that Doug hit a patch of ice and briefly lost control of his car, but by studying the clues you were given and linking these clues to what you already know, you have a good chance of figuring out why Doug had difficulty driving to work.

The following are examples of inductive reasoning passages and questions you may see on the written firefighter exam:

EXAMPLES:

Question 1 refers to the following passage.

> You receive a call to tend to a child found unconscious in a neighborhood park. When you arrive, you find the boy under a tree, still unconscious, surrounded by neighbors. A woman tells you she found the boy there, but apparently no one saw what happened. The neighbor has sent her husband to the boy's house on the next block to find his parents. The boy has a few fresh scratches but no serious injuries are apparent. The neighbors say he has no known medical conditions. As you check for injuries, you hear a dog barking in a nearby yard and, from above, you hear a plaintive meow.

1. Based on the information in the passage, what is the *most likely* reason the boy came to be unconscious under the tree?

    A. He was attacked by a dog and fell trying to escape.
    B. He tripped over the tree roots and hit his head.
    C. He fell out of the tree trying to rescue a cat.
    D. He was hit by a car and landed under the tree.

The correct answer is **C**. The boy is on the ground, under the tree. Though no witnesses saw him climb the tree, you hear a meow up in the branches. You know that cats meow and occasionally get stuck in trees. The most likely answer is that he fell out of the tree trying to rescue a cat. There is no evidence to suggest that he was attacked by a dog and fell trying to escape; therefore, Choice A is incorrect. The passage does not mention the tree's roots or any cars; therefore, you can eliminate Choices B and D as viable answer choices.

Question 2 refers to the following passage.

> You arrive at a 2 p.m. fire call at a multifamily dwelling and observe a woman in the street. She is screaming in a language you do not understand and pointing to the upper floors of the structure. Heavy smoke is pouring out of the door and you can see the roof is in flames. The woman is prevented from entering the building by the landlord, who tells you all the tenants have day jobs and the building is empty. Near the woman's feet is a plastic shopping bag, out of which has fallen a package of extra-small diapers and several new baby bottles.

2. Based on the information in this passage, what is the woman trying to communicate?

    A. She wants you to start fighting the fire.
    B. Her property is being destroyed.
    C. The fire is on the top floor.
    D. An infant is still inside the building.

The correct answer is **D**. You know from the items the woman has purchased that someone has recently had a baby; the landlord may not know this, or the woman may be caring for the child of a tenant or family member. Although she may be worried that her property is being destroyed and that the fire is on the top floor, you can safely assume that she is more concerned about the child trapped inside. This information will help you eliminate Choice B.

Tip: Inductive reasoning questions may also appear as tables or charts. Sometimes, you may be asked to read through a paragraph or two, study a graph or table, and then answer questions based on that information in combination with your own prior knowledge. Like deductive reasoning questions, inductive reasoning questions are easier to answer when you read every piece of information presented to you and then read the question and the answer choices. Be sure you understand what you're being asked to do. Watch for keywords like **most likely** and **least likely**.

Question 3 refers to the following figure.

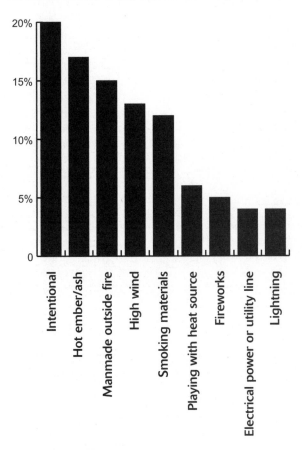

Causes of Brush, Grass, and Forest Fires, 2004–2008

Data from the National Fire Protection Association

3. According to information presented in the bar graph above, you may conclude that

    A. natural forces cause the most brush, grass, and forest fires.

    B. lightning causes more fires than fireworks and high winds combined.

    C. people are responsible for the majority of brush, grass, and forest fires.

    D. children who play with fire cause a high percentage of brush, grass, and forest fires.

The correct answer is **C.** Your prior knowledge of what is natural and what is manmade should tell you that the only natural forces that appear on this table are hot ember/ash, high winds, and lightning. This fact helps you eliminate Choices A and B. Although children may play with fire if not supervised, the graph does not specify the age of the people who play with heat sources and set brush, grass, and forest fires; therefore, you can eliminate Choice D. The rest of the fires are caused by people. Fires set intentionally are the result of man. People also control manmade outside fires, smoking materials, fireworks, and electrical/utility lines.

> **Tip: Always pay attention to how each question is worded. Watch for capitalized, italicized, underlined, and even bold words. When you see words such as *all, always, every, except, never,* and *not,* reread the sentence so you know what the question is asking. These words will help you eliminate the wrong answers and choose the correct one.**

3. Logical Reasoning

Logical reasoning questions that appear on the written firefighter exam may be a bit more challenging than deductive and inductive reasoning questions, but don't let these questions intimidate you. Finding the correct answer to these questions is as easy as using your ability to think critically. Firefighters need to think critically—and quickly—every day. They have to organize the information they do know and interpret brand new information they receive. They need to make split-second decisions and they need to do so responsibly. You may see two different types of logical reasoning questions on the exam: series and sequences and logical ordering.

a. Series and Sequences

One type of logical reasoning question tests your ability to complete patterns or find missing pieces of information, thus proving that you can use sound reasoning without relying on words. Instead, you'll be asked to study series of numbers, letters, and even images. These are called series and sequences questions.

Following are two different types of series and sequences questions that you may see on the written firefighter exam.

EXAMPLES:

---

1. Look at the sequence of letters below. Choose the letter that correctly completes this sequence.

   A Z B Y C X D ____

   A.   R
   B.   W
   C.   V
   D.   E

The correct answer is **B.** The sequence follows this pattern: first letter of the alphabet, last letter of the alphabet, second letter of the alphabet, second to last letter of the alphabet, etc. *D* is the fourth letter in the alphabet, and *W* is the fourth from last letter.

Tip: When you come across a pattern or series that has numbers in it, see if you can detect the connection between the numbers. How do they change from one part to the next? Do they increase? Decrease? By 2? Or maybe 4? Do any of the numbers repeat? This will help you determine the pattern and complete the series.

2.

A.

B.

C.

D.

The correct answer is **B.** The pattern in this problem is simple: The second shape is a black reflection of the first white shape. Because the pattern leaves off with half of a white hexagon, you know that it must end with the second half of the hexagon in black. Choice A is incorrect because the shape is white. Choice C is incorrect because the shape is white and a half of a seven-sided polygon. Choice D is incorrect because even though it's black, it's half an octagon.

Remember: If you're given scrap paper during the written firefighter exam, use it! When facing logical reasoning questions that involve images, try sketching the pattern that you believe belongs in the missing space. Then, compare your drawing to your answer choices and choose the one that matches best.

b. Logical Ordering

The second type of logical reasoning question you'll encounter on the exam consists of short lists sometimes accompanied by introductory information. These lists may include steps to completing a task that you must rearrange in a logical order or they may be rules that you must prioritize (most important to least and vice versa). To answer these questions correctly, look for a theme that is present in every part of the list.

The following is an example of a logical-ordering question you may see on the written firefighter exam:

EXAMPLE:

The question refers to the following information.

Firefighters have to don their gear before they leave the station when they're called to emergency scenes. The following are instructions for donning protective gear in no particular order:

1. Step into your boots. Pull the suspenders attached to your bunker pants up over your shoulders and fasten the front of the pants.

2. Put your helmet over your head and secure it.

3. Pick up your SCBA and slide your arms into the straps one at a time.

4. Lay out your gear on the floor in front of you, making sure your pants are folded down so the tops of the boots stick through the pants.

5. Pull your flame-resistant hood over your head with the opening in front, and then pull your SCBA mask over your head and secure it over your face.

6. Put your gloves on after all your other gear is secure.

7. Slide first one arm, then the other, into the jacket sleeves and close the front of the jacket.

Using the information above, choose the most logical sequence for putting on bunker gear.

A. 7, 1, 4, 3, 2, 6, 5

B. 3, 4, 7, 1, 5, 2, 6

C. 4, 1, 7, 3, 5, 2, 6

D. 4, 1, 3, 7, 6, 5, 2

The correct answer is **C.** You can use logic and word clues to determine the correct order, even if you've never donned bunker gear. Laying out the gear is a logical beginning, so 4 should be your first step. You see in Step 1 that you must pull suspenders over your shoulders, so stepping into your boots and putting on the pants must come before putting on the jacket, Step 7. The SCBA (3) obviously goes on outside the jacket, and the hood and SCBA mask (5) must go on before the helmet (2). All that remains is to put on the gloves, and Step 6 clearly states this is to be done after all other gear is secure, so logically that is the final step.

Practice

Directions (1–10): Select the best answer for each question.

Questions 1–2 refer to the following information.

You recently transferred to a different fire station. You look over the monthly chore schedule and see that you are to make dinner three times this month. These are the recipes you are considering and the ingredients you will need:

- **Mom's three-alarm vegetarian chili:** Vegetarian burger crumbles; cans of green chile peppers, tomatoes, kidney beans, garbanzo beans, black beans, and corn

- **Meat lover's lasagna:** Ground beef, pork sausage, canned tomatoes, ricotta cheese, mozzarella cheese, eggs, and lasagna noodles

- **Aunt Julie's baked fried chicken:** Chicken, eggs, and cornflakes

- **Dad's crock pot seafood gumbo:** Canned tomatoes, shrimp, crab meat, and rice

- **Lazy pigs-in-a-blanket casserole:** Cabbage, ground beef, tomato soup, and rice

1. Firefighter Fortuna stops you at work. She tells you she is lactose intolerant and asks you to prepare dairy-free meals when it's your turn to make dinner. Which dish should you avoid making to comply with her request?

   A. Dad's crock pot seafood gumbo
   B. Aunt Julie's baked fried chicken
   C. Meat lover's lasagna
   D. Lazy pigs-in-a-blanket casserole

2. Firefighter Adams lets you know he's allergic to shellfish, and asks you to be careful not to include any in your cooking. Which dish should you avoid making to ensure his safety?

   A. Lazy pigs-in-a-blanket casserole
   B. Meat lover's lasagna
   C. Mom's three-alarm vegetarian chili
   D. Dad's crock pot seafood gumbo

Questions 3–5 refer to the following passage.

The driver of a minivan is distracted by a ringing cell phone and runs a red light at Kennedy Boulevard and Eisenhower Avenue. She hits an SUV broadside, and the impact pushes the second vehicle into a utility pole. The driver of the SUV calls 911 and escapes with her husband's help through the rear door. Both were wearing seatbelts at the time of the accident. The dispatch center alerts police, the fire rescue units, and emergency medical services.

Firefighters arrive on the scene and assess the situation. The utility pole appears to be stable and no electrical lines are down. Fluids leaking from the minivan appear to be nonflammable, though firefighters continue to monitor the damaged vehicle for any dangers that might develop and stretch a hose line.

The SUV is empty. The driver is complaining of moderate back pain, and her passenger complains of severe neck and shoulder pain. They move to the curb and decline your help, saying they will wait for the paramedics while you check the other victims. The driver tells you there is an unconscious child in the minivan, but she could not open the doors to get to him.

The driver of the minivan, who was wearing her seatbelt at the time of the accident, is trapped. She has numerous scratches on her neck, arms, and face; is in pain; and is bleeding from her left shoulder. She cannot move the fingers on her left hand and is screaming for you to check her children in the back seat, because she cannot reach them. The passengers are a male, approximately seven years old, and a female, approximately two years old. The female child is crying. She is strapped into a child safety seat and appears to be uninjured. The male is wearing his seatbelt. The restraints are loose. He has cuts on his arms and face and is bleeding from the head. Firefighters note the boy is conscious but does not respond to their questions. While they work with the hydraulic spreader to open the doors, the boy vomits.

The individuals from the SUV are evaluated by paramedics and decide to see their family doctor for follow-up care. The individuals from the minivan are transported to the trauma center.

3. The male child is displaying symptoms of what serious condition?

   A. flu
   B. concussion
   C. broken arm
   D. whiplash

4. According to the passage, which of the following statements is true?

   A. Everyone on the scene is in danger of being electrocuted.
   B. A seven-year-old male and a two-year-old female are stuck in the SUV.
   C. Firefighters connected a hose line just in case the leaking fluids catch fire.
   D. The driver of the minivan hit the SUV because she was changing the radio station.

5. What symptoms of the minivan driver MOST LIKELY indicate a broken arm?

   A. She is in pain.
   B. She cannot move her fingers.
   C. Her left shoulder is bleeding.
   D. Her arms have multiple scratches.

6. 0, 1, 1, 2, 3, 5, 8, 13, 21, _____

   A. 34
   B. 33
   C. 28
   D. 29

7. 2, 6, 18, _____, 172, 516

   A. 42
   B. 64
   C. 54
   D. 88

8. S M T _____ T F S

   A. S
   B. M
   C. U
   D. W

Question 9 refers to the following information.

Instructions for using a standard fire extinguisher are listed below:

1. Squeeze the handle. Move in toward the fire when you can see the extinguisher is having an effect, keeping the extinguisher focused on the base of the fire.
2. Sweep the fire extinguisher from side to side and keep doing so until the fire is out.
3. Aim the nozzle low, keeping the extinguisher upright.
4. Hold the extinguisher upright. Remove the plastic tie from the handle, and pull the pin from the handle.

9. Using the information above, choose the most logical sequence for using a fire extinguisher.

   A. 3, 4, 2, 1
   B. 4, 3, 1, 2
   C. 1, 4, 3, 2
   D. 4, 3, 2, 1

10. A pair of firefighters has been sent to the roof of a structure with orders to open the stairwell door and ventilate the building. They climb the ladder and have just arrived on the roof when they hear cries. A man two floors below is waving from a window and calling for help. What is the first thing the pair of firefighters on the roof should do?

   A. Initiate a rescue attempt.
   B. Open the stairwell door.
   C. Give the man instructions to escape.
   D. Radio their superior officer, giving the man's location.

Answers

1. **C** Firefighter Fortuna is lactose intolerant. You know that lactose intolerant means she cannot consume dairy products. According to the passage, the meat lover's lasagna includes both ricotta and mozzarella cheeses, which you know are dairy foods. The crock pot seafood gumbo, baked fried chicken, and lazy pigs-in-a-blanket casserole do not appear to contain any dairy-based ingredients; therefore, Firefighter Fortuna should be able to eat any of those meals. This means Choices A, B, and D are incorrect.

2. **D** According to the passage, the gumbo contains shrimp and crab. Because shrimp and crab are both shellfish, Firefighter Adams cannot eat them. This means that you should avoid making Dad's crock pot seafood gumbo. The lazy pigs-in-a-blanket casserole, meat lover's lasagna, and three-alarm vegetarian chili don't appear to contain shellfish; therefore, Firefighter Adams should be able to eat these dishes. This means Choices A, B, and C are incorrect.

3. **B** Based on the information in the passage, the child is exhibiting symptoms of a concussion. The driver of the SUV noted the child was unconscious immediately following the accident, and the boy's disorientation and vomiting, as well as the head wound, would likely indicate a concussion. Although the passage doesn't definitively state that the child has a concussion, you know that the child is not suffering from the flu, a broken arm, or whiplash; therefore, the only answer choice left is B.

4. **C** Based on the information in the passage, firefighters connected a hose line just in case the leaking fluids catch fire. Although firefighters at the scene determined that the leaking fluids were most likely not flammable, they still stretched a hose line. This information, combined with what you already know about motor vehicle accidents, fires, and flammable liquids, should help you determine that the firefighters connected the hose line as an additional safety precaution.

5. **B** According to the passage, the driver of the minivan is unable to move her fingers; this fact most likely indicates a broken arm. Although she is in pain, her shoulder is bleeding, and she has multiple scratches on her arms, these factors may not indicate that her arm is broken. This means that Choices A, C, and D are incorrect.

6. **A** This number sequence is found by adding the two previous numbers together: $0 + 1 = 1$. $1 + 1 = 2$. $2 + 3 = 5$. $5 + 8 = 13$. $13 + 21 = 34$. Therefore, Choice A is correct.

7. **C** The number sequence is found by multiplying by three each time: $2 \times 3 = 6$; $6 \times 3 = 18$; $18 \times 3 = $ ____; ____ $\times 3 = 162$; and $172 \times 3 = 516$. To determine the numbers in the first blank, you would multiply 18 by 3 to get 54. Then to confirm that 54 is the correct answer, you can multiply 54 by 3 to get 162. To brush up on your math skills, check out Chapter VIII.

8. **D** The letters represent the days of the week; *W* for Wednesday is missing in the sequence.

9. **B** The most logical sequence is to remove the pin (4) and aim the nozzle (3) before you squeeze the handle (1). You should then continue until the fire is out (2), using a sweeping motion.

10. **D** The most logical first choice is to alert your superior officer; therefore, Choice D is correct. Although you were sent onto the roof to open the stairwell door, the victim's safety should be your first priority. Because you're already on the roof, you should alert your superior officer of the situation and then wait for instructions. He or she may tell you to initiate a rescue attempt, but you should not decide to do so on your own. You also shouldn't instruct the man to leave the building. A crew on the ground tasked specifically with search and rescues will most likely come to the man's aid. Choices A, B, and D are incorrect.

C. Information Ordering

Information-ordering questions further test your ability to make sound judgments, organize information, and follow directions. As we discussed in the earlier sections of this chapter, these skills are essential for a firefighter. You need to show your superiors that you're going to follow their orders in every situation. You also need to prove that in the presence of new information, you'll be able to comprehend what you've learned and make appropriate decisions based on that knowledge.

This type of question typically comes in the form of a paragraph accompanied by a short list. The paragraph provides you with a scenario. For example, you may find that you must imagine yourself at the scene of a motor vehicle accident, a house fire, or even in the garage of your fire hall. You'll learn of a problem you must solve or task you must perform and then you'll read the list of instructions that accompany the paragraph to find out what you would need to do in that particular situation. Once you've studied the list, you'll read another brief scenario. This time, however, the scenario will describe you or another firefighter completing the task. You'll then be asked to identify which step was completed out of order, which step must be completed next, or which step was missed.

> **Tip:** Sometimes you won't see a numbered list accompanying information ordering questions. Instead, instructions or directions may be in the form of paragraphs or passages. You'll have to read this information and pay close attention to key words such as *first, next, after, then,* and *last*.

The following is an example of an information ordering passage and questions you may see on the written firefighter exam.

EXAMPLES:

Questions 1–2 refer to the following information.

When too much smoke, fire, or embers are trapped inside of a building, firefighters are often instructed to ventilate the building. If they cannot do so by opening doors or windows, they may have to climb onto the roof to cut a hole that will act as a ventilator. Below are instructions to ventilating a roof:

1. Place a ladder or other means of reaching the roof as well as a secondary means of escape.
2. Climb to the roof, taking an axe, a saw with a multipurpose blade, and a roof ladder if necessary.
3. Place the roof ladder hooks over the peak of a pitched roof and continue climbing.
4. Locate the roof supports by hitting the roof with an axe. If the impact sounds dull and solid, it is likely to be a support beam. If the axe bounces, you have found a hollow spot that can be cut.
5. Use the axe to scratch a line on the roof marking the area where you want to cut.
6. Use the saw to cut a large opening and remove layers of roofing material. Continue cutting through roofing material as needed until you make an opening.

Note: If the roof has existing openings, such as skylights, vent the roof through them.

Your engine responds to a structure fire in a subdivision at 4 a.m. The interior of the structure is dark and filled with smoke, and you can see flames at a side window. You and Firefighter Pashinski are ordered to ventilate the roof. You remove two ladders from the truck and place them at the front and rear of the house, away from the visible flames. You and Pashinski collect axes, a saw, and a roof ladder, and together get yourselves and your equipment to the roof. Pashinski moves up the roof ladder, hitting the roof with his axe, until he finds a hollow spot between the support beams. You hand him the saw and he cuts the ventilation opening. You help by pulling layers of shingles and tarpaper out of the hole with your axe. He cuts through more materials and you both cautiously pull the last of the roofing materials away with your axes. Smoke billows through the ventilation hole and you return to the extension ladder, bracing the roof ladder against the skylight before climbing over the edge and back to the ground.

---

1. What step did Firefighter Pashinski skip in cutting the roof vent?

    A.   He did not cut through the beams.
    B.   He did not allow his partner to help find a hollow spot.
    C.   He did not mark out the area where he was going to cut.
    D.   He did not use his axe to pull roofing material out of the hole.

The answer is **C.** Firefighter Pashinski began using the saw without mapping out the area to be cut by scratching a line on the roof with his axe. Step 4 of the instructions state that you must find a hollow spot to cut before making any marks in the roof. Firefighter Pashinski then takes the saw from you instead of scratching a line in the roof marking the area where he wants to cut, as Step 5 states.

> **2.** What procedural rule did you both overlook?
>
> **A.** Use a roof ladder for safety on a pitched roof.
> **B.** Ventilate the roof through an existing opening.
> **C.** Use an axe to pull layers of roofing material out of the hole.
> **D.** Locate a hollow section of roof by hitting spots with your axe until the axe bounces.

The answer is **B.** As noted at the end of the instructions to ventilate a roof, you should ventilate the roof through available skylights and other existing openings before choosing to cut a hole in the roof. This decreases the amount of property damage. You know that this particular roof has a skylight because you braced the roof ladder against the skylight before climbing over the edge and back onto the ground.

> Tip: If you have a hard time organizing your thoughts, try marking up your test booklet (if allowed!) so that you can see what the passage is telling you. In the example above, you could have crossed out the steps in the list as you and Firefighter Pashinski completed them. After reading the questions and studying the list, you would have been left with two possible options, which would make choosing the correct answer for each even easier. For more tips on understanding what you read on the written firefighter exam, turn to Chapter VI.

Practice

Directions (1–10): Select the best answer for each question.

Questions 1–3 refer to the following information.

At serious accident scenes, firefighters and paramedics must first perform triage when they arrive. This means they quickly assess the problems on the scene. They determine the resources, skills, and information immediately available to them to address each problem. Three components of the severe accident scene must be considered:

1. **Stabilization of the scene.** The responders must identify actions that are necessary to prevent the problem from escalating.
2. **Injury evaluation.** The responders must determine how serious the injuries of each individual are.
3. **Resource evaluation.** The responders must identify the capabilities of the resources available at the scene and call for the correct additional help when necessary.

Engine 20 and the Rescue Response Team arrive on the scene of a serious accident on the Highland Expressway. They find a compact car on its side with two occupants, an adult female and a child, still inside. The driver, an adult male, is on the shoulder of the road, about 10 yards from the vehicle. Captain Gregory orders a hose line on standby in case fuel leaking from the vehicle ignites and sends a team to stabilize the vehicle. He then orders the firefighters to evaluate the passengers and provide aid. Firefighters remove some of the windows of the vehicle and quickly remove the child. He is in good condition with minor cuts and bruises. The female passenger, the child's mother, has major physical trauma. She is bleeding profusely from the nose and from a deep cut in her leg. The driver is on his back with his leg bent at an unnatural angle. He has major physical trauma, is unconscious and is not breathing.

1. Firefighters and paramedics arriving at a severe accident scene must *first*

   A. put on protective gear.
   B. perform triage.
   C. stabilize the vehicle.
   D. remove the victims from the vehicle.

2. What is the first command Captain Gregory gives when he arrives on the scene?

   A. Call for backup.
   B. Prepare a hose line.
   C. Evaluate the passengers.
   D. Remove the windows of the vehicle.

3. In responding to the accident described in the passage, which of the following injuries might you treat immediately?

   A. bleeding profusely
   B. minor cuts and bruises
   C. unconscious and not breathing
   D. leg bent at an unnatural angle

Questions 4–5 refer to the following information.

Hoses are packed into apparatus hose beds based on the unit's needs. The fire unit's needs are determined by the area's water supply system and the majority of the types of structures. A hose bed that runs from side to side across the apparatus, usually behind the crew cabin, is called a transverse bed.

Hoses are loaded in three basic ways:

- **The accordion load:** The hose is folded front to rear. The flat side of the hose faces the side wall and the hose is worked across the hose bed, back and forth, until it is filled. Additional layers can be added. This load can be used for lines that require hand stretching. The many folds can cause wear on the hose, but it is easy for firefighters to unload.

- **The flat load:** This is a front to rear, back-and-forth load as well. The flat side of the hose is placed on the base of the hose bed. Additional sections are stacked beside the first until all of the hose is loaded. This load can be used for lines that require hand stretching as well. The numerous folds can cause wear on the hoses, but the flat load is easy to unload.

- **The horseshoe load:** The hose is wrapped around the outer edge of the hose bed. It is then wrapped in nesting U shapes back around the bed. This load type is useful for laying out lines with the apparatus. It causes less wear and tear on the hose than the accordion load, but can be more difficult to unload.

Note: It is necessary to consider the conditions of deployment before loading hose. Do you need to use a forward lay? If so, the apparatus will stop at the water supply first and you will need to load the male hose butt first. If you need to use a reverse lay, the apparatus will stop at the fire first, the female hose butt is loaded first.

4. You begin your shift and an officer instructs you to work with several other firefighters to load the hose bed using the accordion load for forward lay. You lay out the hose and load the female hose butt first and then load the hose with the flat side facing the side wall. You work across the hose bed, filling it. You load second and third layers into the hose bed in the same way. The officer who assigned you the task walks by and tells you to unload it and load it again—this time correctly. What part of the procedure has not been done in line with the officer's orders?

    A. The female hose butt was loaded first.
    B. The flat side faced the side wall of the bed.
    C. The hose bed held multiple layers.
    D. The hose was loaded back and forth.

5. You're about to load a hose into the bed of the truck using the flat loading method. What do you need to do *first*?

    A. Identify the male and female hose butts.
    B. Wrap the hose around the outer edge of the hose bed.
    C. Place the flat side of the hose on the base of the hose bed.
    D. Determine if you need to use a forward or reverse lay.

Questions 6–7 refer to the following passage.

Each firefighter on an emergency scene has specific duties to perform. The first engine company on scene at a single-family structure positions the apparatus at the front of the structure. The driver then breaks the supply line and connects to the pump panel. He or she then facilitates communications with the crew and monitors the water supply. The officer establishes an incident command until he or she is relieved by a higher ranking officer. The officer then provides an initial incident report, which includes confirming the location of the fire, determining the conditions, relaying the unit's location, and any other information pertinent to the call. Firefighter 1 begins fire confinement and extinguishment procedures or initiates search and rescue if no other unit is on scene.

When the first truck company arrives, the driver also positions the apparatus in front of the structure. He or she deploys ground ladders if necessary and lights the exterior of the structure. Firefighter 1 initiates search-and-rescue operations, forcibly entering the structure if necessary, with Firefighter 2. The team initiates ventilation of the structure, advises the engine company of conditions, and provides interior lighting as needed. The truck company also controls utilities.

The primary responsibility of the second arriving engine company is ensuring adequate water supply for the first engine company. The personnel advances a second attack line; if a third engine company arrives, it takes the rear structure position.

6. A structure fire is reported on Meadow Drive in the Riverwynde development. Smoke is evident along the roofline of the single-family structure as your engine arrives on the scene first. The driver positions the apparatus at the front and proceeds to connect the pump panel to the supply line. You, Firefighter 1, unload hose and work to contain the fire. The first truck company arrives and the driver positions the apparatus. Firefighter 1 initiates search and rescue as the driver positions ground ladders and lights. Where should the driver of the first arriving truck have positioned the apparatus?

   A. behind the structure
   B. at the nearest hydrant
   C. between the engine and the structure
   D. in front of the structure

7. What should have been your first duty when you arrived on the scene?

   A. Set up ground ladders.
   B. Ventilate the structure.
   C. Initiate search and rescue.
   D. Establish a water supply.

Questions 8–10 refer to the following passage.

Firefighters may follow some general guidelines when individuals are trapped in an inoperative elevator. Personnel with portable radios should be dispatched to the elevator equipment room and the floor where the elevator is accessible. Personnel on the landing floor will coordinate rescue procedures. Rescuers should establish voice contact with the elevator passengers and determine if conditions are stable and if any are in need of medical assistance. Passengers should only be rescued using forcible entry if they are in need of immediate medical care. If conditions are stable, passengers should be assured they are safe and will be removed as soon as possible. Trapped passengers should be kept informed of actions being taken. Passengers should locate and activate the Emergency Stop Button. They will be instructed to find and push the Door Open Button, if the elevator is equipped with one.

Personnel sent to the equipment room should check the electrical circuits. If the elevator has power, turning it off for at least 30 seconds and on again may reset the relays. Passengers are then instructed to try the Door Open Button again. If the power is off in the equipment room and the elevator car is within inches of the landing floor, passengers should manually try to open the car door. If the elevator has a recall system, use the key to recall the elevator to the ground floor. If the doors do not open, passengers should push the Door Open Button.

8. Firefighters respond to a college dormitory where six students are trapped in an elevator nearly on the fourth floor. A team is dispatched to the elevator equipment room and determines the power is on. What is the next step they should take?

   A. Turn off the power for 30 seconds and turn it back on.
   B. Tell passengers to push the Emergency Stop Button.
   C. Send a firefighter into the car to evaluate passengers.
   D. Instruct the passengers to push the Door Open Button.

9. During an elevator rescue, what is the first thing rescue personnel stationed on the landing floor should do?

   A. Establish voice contact with passengers who are trapped.
   B. Find the equipment room and determine if the power is on.
   C. Use forcible entry to reach passengers needing medical assistance.
   D. Push and hold the Door Open Button and the Emergency Stop Button.

10. What has to happen before passengers try to manually open the elevator car door?

   A. The power has to be on.
   B. The car must be near the landing floor.
   C. Rescuers need to enter the elevator car.
   D. Passengers need to receive a radio from rescuers.

Answers

1. **B** According to the information provided, responders must first evaluate the situation before they take action. This means that they must perform triage. Triage is a system of assessing, clarifying, and making decisions about the situation at hand. It helps you determine the location of victims, bystanders, and other emergency personnel as well as the severity of damage and injury.

2. **B** Captain Gregory first tells his fellow firefighters to prepare a hose line in case fuel leaking from the vehicle ignites. He then sends them to evaluate the passengers. To extricate the passengers, they must remove the windows of the vehicle. The passage doesn't mention if Captain Gregory calls for backup.

3. **C** Although the injuries in the answer choices all appear to be serious, a passenger who is not breathing is in immediate need of attention. You would then attempt to stop the bleeding and stabilize the broken leg.

4. **A** According to the information provided, the male hose butt should be loaded first for a forward lay, not the female hose butt. If the supervisor had requested a reverse lay, then he would have been satisfied with the placement of the male hose butt.

5. **D** Before you load a hose into the bed of a truck using the flat hose method, you must determine if you need to use a forward or reverse lay. This information will help you decide whether to place the male hose butt or female hose butt in the bed first. Whether you need to use a forward lay or a reverse lay depends on how you will use the hose.

6. **D** According to the information provided, standard operating procedure is to position the truck in front of the structure. Once the driver breaks the supply line and connects the pump panel, he can then begin communicating with the crew while he monitors the water supply.

7. **C** As you already know, saving lives is always a priority at the scene of a house fire. According to the information provided, unless a truck company or another engine crew has begun searching, Firefighter 1's primary duty is to initiate search and rescue.

8. **A** Once the team in the elevator equipment room determines the power is on, they should turn off the power for 30 seconds and then turn it back on. This will reset the system and possibly return the elevator to the fourth floor. Because the team in the equipment room is not situated near the elevator

itself, team members won't be instructing elevator passengers to perform any actions. They also won't be able to enter the elevator car to perform any medical evaluations.

9. **A** The first thing rescue personnel stationed on the landing floor should do is establish voice contact with passengers who are trapped. Once they establish this connection, they can then either use forcible entry to reach trapped passengers or tell passengers to hold the Door Open Button or the Emergency Stop Button. A separate team of firefighters will find the equipment room and determine if the power is on.

10. **B** Before passengers try to manually open the elevator car door, they need to be sure that the elevator car is near the landing floor. If it's nowhere near the landing floor, they should not try to open the doors to escape the car without rescue personnel's help.

D. Problem Sensitivity

The final kind of judgment and reasoning question you'll encounter on the written firefighter exam is referred to as problem sensitivity. These questions ask you to notice when a problem is present and then identify the cause. You don't, however, have to recommend a solution or try to solve the problem. Answering these questions correctly proves that you're aware of when a situation is unsafe or when a fellow firefighter may be going through a rough patch. It shows that you'll be able to draw your own conclusions by evaluating what's in front of you, even if you're under a fair amount of stress.

Problem sensitivity questions on the firefighter exam typically involve other fellow firefighters. You'll be given a scenario about the firefighter's behavior on the job and then have to determine if a problem is present and why the problem may be occurring.

The following is an example of a problem sensitivity question in which another firefighter is involved. You'll see plenty of these on the written firefighter exam.

EXAMPLE:

The question refers to the following passage.

Firefighter Patil has frequently been arriving late for his shift. He has been distracted when performing routine duties and has had to be reminded to clean and check his gear after a call. He has stopped contributing to the fund for the team's regular Friday night pizza order. One night you find him in the kitchen long after everyone else has gone to sleep and ask him if he's okay. He nods, but doesn't answer you. Instead, he shuffles through a stack of papers that look like bills. You remember that several weeks ago he mentioned his mother, who lives alone nearby, had been diagnosed with cancer. As you leave, you hear him muttering about insurance companies.

Based on the information in the passage, what is *most likely* bothering Patil?

A. He no longer wants to be a firefighter.
B. He thinks his mother is very demanding.
C. He is afraid he will lose his job because he is late.
D. He is worried about paying his mother's medical expenses.

The answer is **D.** Patil is most likely worried about paying for his mother's medical care expenses, and this worry is probably affecting his work performance. You can make this assumption because you already know his mother was diagnosed with cancer, he muttered about insurance companies, and he's clearly stressed. Evidence is not present in this paragraph that suggests he no longer wants to be a firefighter, so Choice A is incorrect. There is also no evidence in this paragraph that supports the claim that his mother is demanding or that he fears he'll lose his job; therefore, Choices B and C are also incorrect options.

Not all problem sensitivity questions will ask you to identify the needs of a fellow firefighter. Sometimes, you may be asked to read a scenario and determine if a problem is present at the scene of a motor vehicle accident, a gas spill, a building fire, or even a routine fire drill. You'll have to read all the information presented to you and then identify the issue, the cause of the problem, or the fact that a problem is not present. Like all questions on the firefighter exam, you don't need to know anything about firefighting (beyond the obvious) to answer these questions. All the information you need is in the passage, questions, and answer choices presented to you.

Practice

Directions (1–10): Select the best answer for each question.

Questions 1–3 refer to the following passage.

> Personnel from your fire department were dispatched to the scene of a multiple-vehicle accident in front of Elmhurst Elementary School at 7:57 a.m. According to eyewitness accounts, a 1999 GMC Sierra pickup driven by William Tucker passed a school bus discharging students and struck a 2002 Ford Explorer driven by Casey Carter. Mr. Carter was stopped in the oncoming lane, as required by law, while the bus lights were flashing red. The force of the impact pushed the Explorer into another vehicle, a 1994 Honda Accord driven by Ellen Bogdanovicz. The bus was not involved in any collisions, and no students being transported by bus were injured.
>
> Mr. Tucker, who was not wearing his seatbelt at the time of the accident, sustained severe lacerations of the face and torso and was bleeding profusely from the mouth. He complained of head and neck pain.
>
> Mr. Carter, who was wearing his seatbelt at the time of the accident, was dropping off his son, Lyle Carter, at school. The boy, age 12, was wearing his seatbelt at the time of the accident and was in the front seat. Mr. Carter's young daughters, Maria and Miranda Carter, were in the rear seat and were strapped into child safety seats. Maria Carter appeared to be uninjured. Miranda Carter was bleeding from her lip. Mr. Carter reported the force of the airbag deployment had bruised him, and he and his son complained of slight neck pain. Lyle Carter exhibited signs of anxiety. While firefighters spoke to Mr. Carter, the boy began sweating profusely and struggled to breathe. Mr. Carter indicated that his son had left his inhaler in his school locker. Firefighters observed that Lyle Carter's lips were beginning to turn blue.
>
> Ms. Bogdanovicz, who was wearing a seatbelt at the time of the accident, was traveling with her mother, Kathy Wilson, and uncles, Robert Anderson and Lloyd Anderson, all of whom were wearing seatbelts at the time of the accident. Both women complained of neck pain. Though both women were protected from front impact by airbags, Ms. Wilson said her head had hit the side window, and she had a laceration on the right side of her head. Robert Anderson and Lloyd Anderson both said they were uninjured.

1. Based on the information in the passage, which of the following individuals would appear to be *most* in need of medical assistance?

   A. Kathy Wilson
   B. William Tucker
   C. Lyle Carter
   D. Casey Carter

2. Based on the information in the passage, which of the occupants of the 2002 Ford Explorer would appear to be the LEAST seriously injured?

   A. Casey Carter
   B. Maria Carter
   C. Miranda Carter
   D. Lyle Carter

3. Based on the information in the passage, which of the following individuals would appear to be the MOST seriously injured?

   A. Casey Carter
   B. Miranda Carter
   C. Ellen Bogdanovicz
   D. Kathy Wilson

Question 4 refers to the following passage.

Firefighter Edwards has been observing the behavior of Firefighter Hernandez, who has been with the fire department for three years. Hernandez became engaged to Eddie Richards on her birthday, four months after they met and began dating. She has been excitedly planning her wedding for several weeks. Last week, however, she had little to say when a fellow firefighter asked her how the wedding plans were going. Edwards heard Hernandez having an argument with her fiancé in front of the fire station recently, and several times last week thought he saw Richards parked across the street from the fire station while Hernandez was on duty. Today Edwards noticed a large bruise on Hernandez's upper arm. When he asked her about it, she said she had tripped.

4. Based on the information in the passage, if Hernandez were having a problem, it would *most likely* be

   A. domestic violence.
   B. drug abuse.
   C. financial troubles.
   D. job stress.

Question 5 refers to the following passage.

5. Your fire department receives all of the following notifications in one day. Of these notifications, which should be considered the MOST urgent?

   A. a request to install smoke detectors in a duplex
   B. a report of smoke at a chemical plant
   C. a report of a cyclist who may have a broken arm
   D. a report of a shed burning in a rural field

Question 6 refers to the following passage.

6. Engine 3 responds to a report of an explosion. You arrive at the scene to find a duplex with significant roof damage and numerous broken windows. An elderly couple is outside, the man supporting his wife as she grips her walker. They tell you they live in one half of the residence. A young family lives in the other side, where the explosion took place; the parents are at work, and the two children are in school. The man, who says he smelled gas inside after the explosion, tells you his son lives with them but is at work. The woman interrupts him, insisting you turn off the water because the pipes have burst, and the water is ruining the carpets and floors. The MOST urgent problem facing you now is

   A. accounting for the couple's son.
   B. shutting off the water.
   C. shutting off the gas.
   D. stabilizing the roof.

7. Firefighter Watson misses an important meeting. Later at lunch you mention some procedural changes discussed, but Watson doesn't remember being informed to attend the meeting. Another veteran firefighter teases him about ruining his 30-year perfect record. Watson has been losing his keys and misplacing items for several months, and recently had trouble remembering the captain's first name. If Watson were having a problem, it would *most likely* be related to

   A. alcohol.
   B. drugs.
   C. marital issues.
   D. medical issues.

8. Firefighter Wagner is mopping the locker room when Firefighter Roberts enters. Roberts seems surprised to see someone there, and goes directly to her locker. After Roberts leaves, Wagner can smell alcohol near the lockers. Roberts arrived late for work that morning after an argument with her husband and has appeared disheveled and unfocused lately. What type of problem is Roberts MOST likely having?

   A. marital
   B. mental health
   C. drug-related
   D. alcohol-related

Questions 9–10 refer to the following passage.

Personnel from your fire department were dispatched to the scene of a motor vehicle accident. Eyewitnesses said a 1999 Chevrolet Silverado driven by Rachel Parry swerved to avoid a child on a bicycle and struck a 1991 Toyota Camry operated by Hugo Wilson. A 2010 Vespa GTS 300 Super operated by Bethany Mann was following close behind the Silverado and also swerved. Mann lost control of the Vespa and the scooter slid under the wheels of an oncoming 2000 Dodge Caravan driven by Maryanne May.

Ms. Parry, who was wearing her seatbelt at the time of the accident, complained of moderate neck and back pain. She had numerous minor lacerations and scrapes on her face and arms. When firefighters pried open her door, she insisted on getting out and checking on the crate in the bed of the pickup. Firefighters helped her remove a dog from the crate and she agreed to wait for paramedics to examine her.

Mr. Wilson, who was wearing his seatbelt at the time of the accident, was traveling with his wife, Marilyn Wilson. Mr. Wilson complained of severe neck, back, and leg pain. He had multiple lacerations on his face and head. Ms. Wilson complained of severe neck and shoulder pain. She also had multiple lacerations on her face. Mr. Wilson's immediate concern was that his wife, who had been diagnosed with hypertension, remained calm.

Ms. Mann, who was wearing a helmet at the time of the accident, was ejected from her scooter in the slide and collided with both the scooter and the Caravan. When firefighters arrived, she was unconscious and her legs appeared to be broken. Ms. Mann had numerous large abrasions on her arms, back, and legs. Her helmet was intact. One boot had been ripped away and her foot was bleeding profusely. Her breathing was shallow and firefighters found her blood pressure low.

Ms. May, who was wearing her seatbelt at the time of the accident, had no visible injuries. She complained of slight shoulder pain, but declined treatment in favor of seeing her family physician.

9. Based on the information in the passage, which of the following individuals would appear to be MOST seriously injured?

    A. Bethany Mann
    B. Maryanne May
    C. Marilyn Wilson
    D. Rachel Parry

10. Based on the information in the passage, which of the following individuals would appear to be LEAST seriously injured?

    A. Bethany Mann
    B. Rachel Parry
    C. Marilyn Wilson
    D. Hugo Wilson

Answers

1. **C** Lyle Carter is exhibiting signs of an asthma attack. It is obvious from the color of his lips that he is having difficulty breathing. While William Tucker's lacerations are serious, Lyle Carter's condition is life threatening.

2. **B** Maria Carter appeared to be uninjured, according to the information provided. Casey Carter, Lyle Carter, and Miranda Carter all sustained minor injuries in the wreck.

3. **D** Kathy Wilson's head wound appears to be the most serious injury. Casey Carter suffered only bruises from the airbag. Miranda Carter sustained a cut on her lip from the collision. Ms. Bogdanovicz complained of neck pain.

4. **A** The sudden engagement and stalking behavior indicate Hernandez is being controlled. The unexplained bruise is a sign that her fiancé may be physically violent; therefore, domestic violence may be an issue in this relationship.

5. **B** A chemical fire could endanger lives in a large radius. An isolated, burning shed is unlikely to spread quickly or threaten lives or property. Installing smoke detectors is important, but not urgent. Also, the fire department may not be called if a cyclist broke his arm. Instead, paramedics and police may respond.

6. **C** Leaking gas creates a dangerous condition. The gas could ignite and cause an explosion and fire. Choice A is incorrect because the son is accounted for; Choices B and D are concerns that should be addressed after the gas leak has been corrected.

7. **D** Watson may be experiencing dementia, which is a medical condition. There are no indications of alcohol or drug use or marital problems in the passage, so Choices A, B, and C are incorrect.

8. **D** There are no indications of mental health issues or drug use in the passage, so choices B and C can be eliminated. Her problems have been developing over time, so although Roberts argued with her husband that morning, the dispute was likely a result of ongoing alcohol use.

9. **A** Though Marilyn Wilson has a preexisting medical condition, she does not appear to be in immediate danger. Maryanne May has minor pain, and Rachel Parry has some severe pain and lacerations. Bethany Mann, however, is unconscious and bleeding profusely. She appears to have broken bones and her vital signs indicate she may be going into shock.

10. **B** Rachel Parry has slight cuts and moderate pain. She is ambulatory, whereas the Wilsons are in severe pain. Bethany Mann's injuries are very serious.

VIII. Mathematics

Firefighters are routinely involved in situations that require them to perform calculations. They might have to determine how many feet of fire hose are needed, how tall a ladder needs to be to reach a building, what percentage of a building is on fire, or how many gallons of water per minute is needed to extinguish a fire.

It's vital that they're able to solve these calculations—and solve them quickly—as lives may be at stake. They typically only have a mere second to determine the ratio of firefighters to victims at an accident scene or how long it will take them to reach a fire scene. Familiarizing yourself with formulas, equations, and rules will prepare you for the mathematics section of the firefighter exam and prepare you to work in the field as a firefighter.

The firefighter exam contains a mathematics section with problems on basic operations, algebra, geometry, and more. If you thought you'd never need math again and have since forgotten how to solve most math problems, don't fret because we explain how to solve the different types of math problems you may see on the firefighter exam and provide you with rules, tips, formulas, and equations.

A. Basic Math Review

If you break down even the most complex mathematics problem, you'll find that you need to use basic operations such addition, subtraction, multiplication, and division to solve it. While you probably won't see a simple addition or multiplication problem on the firefighter exam, you'll need these skills to solve other types of problems. Use this section to brush up on the basics, so you can use these skills to solve more complex problems. Memorize the rules in this section along with any formulas or conversions provided since you may not be allowed to use a calculator during the exam. You'll be allowed to use scrap paper, however, to work out problems so you don't have to do it all in your head. Take advantage of the scrap paper and use it to write out the steps of each problem, so you're more likely to get the correct answer.

1. Addition and Subtraction

While you won't be asked to solve simple addition and subtraction questions on the mathematics section of the firefighter exam, you'll use these basic skills to solve problems that are more complicated. That's why you'll need to review simple addition and subtraction problems.

> **Tip: Remember, some problems you may encounter on the firefighter exam many contain key words that indicate you'll need to use addition (*all together, greater, more, sum,* and *total*) or subtraction (*difference, fewer, left over, less,* and remain).**

In addition problems, the *sum,* or total, should always be greater than the *addends* (numbers added together) in the equation. This means you can automatically eliminate any answer choices that are less than or equal to the addends.

For example, you have three ladders on your truck: one is 8 feet long, one is 15 feet long, and one is 25 feet long. What is the total length of the three ladders? First, you should scan the answer choices and eliminate any numbers less than 25 feet because the sum must be greater than the addends, and 25 is the greatest addend.

To solve this problem, add the length of the three ladders: 8 + 15 + 25 = 48.

In subtraction problems, the *difference,* or the remainder (the answer), should never be greater than the *minuend,* or largest number. This means you can automatically eliminate any answer choices that are greater than the minuend.

For example, you have two ladders on your truck: one is 19 feet long and the other is 12 feet long. How many feet longer is the first ladder? Before you begin to solve this problem, you should scan the answer choices and eliminate any numbers that are larger than 19 feet because the difference should never be greater than the minuend.

To solve this problem, subtract the length of the second ladder from the first ladder: 19 – 12 = 7.

As we mentioned previously, you won't be asked to solve simple addition and subtraction questions on the mathematics section of the firefighter exam, but you should be familiar with these types of problems because they're the building blocks of the types of questions you may see on the exam.

EXAMPLES:

---

1. The Barrington Fire Department has three fire engines in service. Engine 12 carries 19 different pieces of apparatus, Engine 14 carries 22 pieces of apparatus, and Engine 17 carries 14 pieces of apparatus. How many total pieces of apparatus do fire engines 12 and 14 carry?

   A. 33
   B. 41
   C. 49
   D. 55

The correct answer is **B.** Together fire engines 12 and 14 carry 41 pieces of apparatus. To solve this problem, add the number of pieces of apparatus that Engine 12 carries to the number of pieces of apparatus that Engine 14 carries: 19 + 22 = 41.

Questions 2–3 refer to the following passage.

To accommodate their growing number of volunteers, the Looming Fire Station recently built a new facility. The old facility had six rooms plus eight individual sleeping quarters. The new facility has 10 rooms plus 16 individual sleeping quarters.

---

2. How many rooms total does the new facility have?

   A. 10
   B. 16
   C. 26
   D. 30

The correct answer is **C**. The new facility has a total of 26 rooms. To solve this problem, add together the number of rooms and individual sleeping quarters the new facility has: $10 + 16 = 26$.

---

3. How many more rooms does the new facility have than the old facility?

    A. 4
    B. 6
    C. 8
    D. 12

The correct answer is **D**. The new facility has 12 more rooms than the old facility. To solve this problem, first add together the number of rooms and individual sleeping quarters the old facility had and then add together the number of rooms and individual sleeping quarters the new facility has. Next, subtract the total number of rooms the old facility had from the total number of rooms the new facility has: $6 + 8 = 14$; $10 + 16 = 26$; $26 - 14 = 12$.

2. Multiplication and Division

You'll be asked to use multiplication and division to solve problems on the firefighter exam, but these types of questions—like addition and subtraction—will usually be part of more complicated problems. Multiplication can be looked at as just another way to add. You may remember memorizing timetables in grade school or various mnemonic devices to help with multiplication. The numbers you multiply together are called *factors* and the answer is called the *product*. Remember the following tips when solving multiplication problems:

- Any number multiplied by 0 will always equal 0.
- Any number multiplied by 1 will equal itself.
- When multiplying by 2, double the number.
- When multiplying by 4, double the number twice.
- To multiply by 5, count by 5s.
- To multiply by 10, attach a 0.

Division problems break down large numbers into smaller parts. The number being divided (usually the larger number) is called the *dividend*, while the number it's being divided by is called the *divisor*. The answer to a division problem is usually called the *quotient*, which is also the number of times the divisor will go into the dividend. Some numbers don't divide equally into other numbers, so the leftover is called the *remainder*, or the number that is less than the divisor and is too small to be divided by the divisor to form a whole number. Remember the following tips when solving division problems:

- Zero divided by any other number is always 0.
- You cannot divide by 0.
- Any number ending in 0 is divisible by 10.
- Any number divided by 1 always equals itself.
- All even numbers are divisible by 2.
- If a number is divisible by 2 and 3, it's also divisible by 6.
- All numbers ending in a 5 or a 0 are always divisible by 5.

Tip: Remember, some problems you may encounter on the firefighter exam many contain key words that indicate you'll need to use multiplication (*of, product,* and *times*) or division (*each* and *per* such as in *per hour, per day,* or *per mile*).

One type of division question you may see on the firefighter exam involves finding an average. An *average,* also called a *mean,* is the number in a set of numbers that is somewhere in the middle. To find an average of a set of numbers, add the set of numbers and divide by the number of numbers within the set. For example, to find the average of 3, 5, 7, and 9, add the numbers together and divide by how many numbers you're adding together: $3 + 5 + 7 + 9 = 24$; $24 \div 4 = 6$. The average of 3, 5, 7, and 9 is 6.

Tip: Sometimes averages may have a remainder. To avoid decimals or fractions in answers, some average questions on the firefighter exam may ask you to round to the nearest value.

EXAMPLES:

1. The Mahoning Fire Department paid a total of $1,750 for 8 new hoses for the fire department. How much did each individual hose cost if each hose cost the same amount of money?

   A. $150.25
   B. $218.75
   C. $322.50
   D. $420.00

The correct answer is **B.** Each individual hose cost $218.75. To solve this problem, divide the total paid for the new hoses by the number of hoses: $1,750 \div 8 = 218.75.

2. If Sergeant Fernando bought lunch for each of the 12 firefighters in the fire department and paid $6 for each lunch, what is the total he paid for lunch for the firefighters?

   A. $48
   B. $56
   C. $60
   D. $72

The correct answer is **D.** The total cost of lunch for the 12 firefighters was $72. To solve this problem, multiply the number of firefighters by the cost of lunch for each one: $12 \times $6 = 72.

3. The Aloysius Fire Department responded to 14 fires over the course of 3 days. How many fires did the fire department respond to on average each day? Round to the nearest whole number.

   A. 3
   B. 4
   C. 5
   D. 6

The correct answer is **C.** The Aloysius Fire Department responded to an average of 5 fires each day. To find the average, divide the number of fires by the number of days $14 \div 3 = 4.66$, which rounds to 5.

3. Exponents

Exponents stand for repeated multiplication of the same number (or variable) by itself. For example, 4^3 means $4 \times 4 \times 4$. The number being multiplied is the base, and the exponent is the number of times the base is being multiplied by itself. In this case, 4 is the base and 3 is the exponent. Solving or simplifying exponents is also called "raising to the power," so in the above example, 4 is raised to the third power, which is also called cubed. Any number raised to the second power is typically called squared.

You should use the following rules when solving exponents:

- Any number raised to the 0 power is equal to 1: $4^0 = 1$
- Any number raised to the 1 power equals itself: $4^1 = 4$
- To multiply powers with the same base, add the exponents: $(4^2)(4^3) = 4^{2+3} = 4^5$
- To divide powers with the same base, subtract the exponents: $4^5 \div 4^3 = 4^{5-3} = 4^2$
- If the powers have different bases, you can't simplify them any further: $x^4 y^4$
- When a product has an exponent, each factor is raised to that power: $(xy)^4 = x^4 y^4$
- When a power is raised to a power, multiply the exponents: $(x^4)^3 = x^{4 \times 3} = x^{12}$
- A power with a negative exponent equals the base's reciprocal with a positive exponent: $4^{-2} = \frac{1}{4^2} = \frac{1}{4 \times 4} = \frac{1}{16}$

EXAMPLES:

---

1. $(x^9)(x^6) =$

   A. x^2
   B. x^3
   C. x^{15}
   D. x^{54}

The correct answer is **C**. To multiply powers with the same base, add the exponents: $(x^9)(x^6) = x^{9+6=15}$, so x^{15} is correct.

---

2. $3x^{15} \div 3x^{14}$

   A. $3x$
   B. $3x^2$
   C. $9x^{29}$
   D. $3x^{210}$

The correct answer is **A**. To divide powers with the same base, subtract the exponents: $3x^{15-14=1}$, so $3x$ is correct.

3. $(5^4)(x^4) =$

   A. 1

   B. $5x$

   C. $(5x)^4$

   D. $(5x)^8$

The correct answer is **C.** Because you can't simplify powers with different bases, the answer is $(5x)^4$.

4. Order of Operations

While many math problems can be solved in a multitude of ways, there is only one correct answer. To get this correct answer—no matter how difficult or simple the problem—you must remember to follow the order of operations, which is a mathematical rule that clarifies which procedures to do first in a mathematical expression.

For example, look at this problem: $4 + 5 \times 2$. How would you solve this problem? Should you add first and then multiply to get 18? Or should you multiply first and then add to get 14? Which way is correct?

Using order of operations helps you determine the correct way to solve this problem:

1. Parenthesis
2. Exponents
3. Multiplication and division
4. Addition and subtraction

You might recall the acronym PEMDAS or maybe the clever mnemonic device: <u>P</u>lease <u>E</u>xcuse <u>M</u>y <u>D</u>ear <u>A</u>unt <u>S</u>ally as a way to remember the correct order of operations.

This means you should solve what is inside the parenthesis first. Then, solve the exponents. After this, you must multiply and divide (you can do either first) and last, add and subtract. (The same goes for these, you can do either first.) For the above problem, $4 + 5 \times 2$, you would multiply first and then add to get the correct answer of 14.

Let's try an example:

$$6 + 3(5 - 2)^2$$

First, find the value inside the parenthesis: $5 - 2 = 3$.

$$6 + 3(3)^2$$

Next, solve the exponents: $3^2 = 3 \times 3 = 9$

$$6 + 3(9)$$

Next, multiply: $3(9) = 27$

$$6 + 27$$

Last, add: 6 + 27 = 33

As long as you follow the order of operations, solving these types of problems shouldn't be that difficult. Now try some on your own.

EXAMPLES:

---

1. Simplify the expression: $4 + 5(6 + 2)^3$

   A.   36
   B.   368
   C.   2,564
   D.   4,608

The correct answer is **C.** If you correctly followed the order of operations, you would get 2,564. First, solve what's inside the parenthesis: (6 + 2) = 8; next, solve the exponent: 8^3 = 512; then, multiply: 5(512) = 2,560; last, add: 2,560 + 4 = 2,564.

---

2. Simplify the expression: $(9 \times 3)(4 + 5)^2$

   A.   133
   B.   452
   C.   1,989
   D.   2,187

The correct answer is **D.** If you correctly followed the order of operations, you would get 2,187. First, solve what's inside the parenthesis: (9 × 3) = 27 and (4 + 5) = 9; next, solve the exponent: 9^2 = 81; then multiply: 27 × 81 = 2,187.

---

3. Simplify the expression: $7 + 3(7 + 4)^4$

   A.   43,930
   B.   44,667
   C.   45,001
   D.   46,742

The correct answer is **A.** If you correctly followed the order of operations, you would get 43,930. First, solve what's inside the parenthesis: (7 + 4) = 11; next, solve the exponent: 11^4 = 14,641; then, multiply: 3 (14,641) = 43,923; last, add: 7 + 43,923 = 43,930.

5. Units of Measurement

Some math questions on the firefighter exam may involve units of measurement, such as distance, time, length, weight, or temperature. For these types of questions, you should be familiar with the traditional measurement system used in the United States and the metric system, because you'll most likely have to convert some measurements to solve the problems. These conversions will not be provided to you on the exam, so you should memorize the following tables before taking the exam.

Converting Traditional Measurements to the Metric System

Traditional	Metric
1 inch	2.54 centimeters
1 mile	1.6 kilometers
1 pound	454 grams
1 quart	946 milliliters or 0.946 liters
1 yard	0.9144 meters

Converting Metric Measurements to the Traditional System

Metric	Traditional
1 centimeter	0.394 inches
1 gram	0.035 ounces
1 kilogram	2.2 pounds
1 kilometer	0.62 miles
1 liter	1.06 quarts

Common Measurement Conversions

Length	Time	Volume	Weight
1 foot = 12 inches	1 minute = 60 seconds	1 pint = 2 cups	1 pound = 16 ounces
1 yard = 3 feet	1 hour = 60 minutes	1 quart = 4 cups	1 ton = 2,000 pounds
1 mile = 5,280 feet	1 day = 24 hours	1 gallon = 4 quarts	

Tip: To convert the measurements in the tables, just multiply. For example, if you need to convert miles to kilometers, multiply the number of miles by 1.6 to determine the distance in kilometers.

Another type of measurement question you may find on the firefighter exam involves temperature. These types of questions ask you to convert temperatures measured in degrees Celsius (°C) to degrees Fahrenheit (°F) and vice versa. To solve these types of problems, plug the values you know into the following formulas:

To convert Celsius to Fahrenheit, use the formula: $F = \frac{9}{5}C + 32$

To convert Fahrenheit to Celsius, use the formula $C = (F - 32)\frac{5}{9}$

Here's an example of a math problem involving temperature:

> You're traveling overseas with a few of your fellow firefighters and their families for vacation. You've been told the average temperature at your destination is 54.5°C. What is the temperature in degrees Fahrenheit (°F)?

To solve this problem, use the Celsius to Fahrenheit temperature formula: $F = \frac{9}{5}C + 32$

Plug the numbers you know from the problem into the formula and solve:

$$F = \frac{9}{5}C + 32$$
$$= \frac{9}{5}(54.5) + 32$$
$$= \frac{9 \times 54.5}{5 \times 1} + 32$$
$$= \frac{490.5}{5} + 32$$
$$= 98.1 + 32$$
$$= 130.1$$

The answer in degrees Fahrenheit is 130.1°F.

EXAMPLES:

---

1. How many grams are in 47.5 pounds?

   A. 4,236 g
   B. 9,995 g
   C. 16,448 g
   D. 21,565 g

The correct answer is **D**. To determine how many grams are in 47.5 pounds, multiply the number of grams in 1 pound by the number of pounds: 454 grams = 1 pound; 454 × 47.5 = 21,565. There are 21,565 grams in 47.5 pounds.

---

2. How many minutes are in 4 days?

   A. 1,440 min.
   B. 3,550 min.
   C. 5,760 min.
   D. 6,100 min.

The correct answer is **C**. To determine how many minutes are in 4 days, first determine how many minutes are in 1 day by multiplying the number of minutes in 1 day by the number of hours in 1 day: 60 × 24 = 1,440. Next, multiply the number of minutes in 1 day by 4 days: 1,440 × 4 = 5,760. There are 5,760 minutes in 4 days.

---

3. Covert 79.8°F to °C. Round to the nearest tenth.

   A. 26.6°C
   B. 32.8°C
   C. 45.5°C
   D. 63.2°C

The correct answer is **A**. To solve this problem, plug the numbers you know into the Fahrenheit to Celsius formula and solve:

$$C = (F - 32)\frac{5}{9}$$

$$= (79.8 - 32)\frac{5}{9}$$

$$= (47.8)\frac{5}{9}$$

$$= 26.55$$

$$= 26.6$$

B. Fractions, Decimals, and Percentages

In this section, we focus on questions that ask you to determine a piece of a whole. Thinking of fractions, decimals, and percentages in this way may help you solve these types of questions.

1. Fractions

Don't be alarmed if you don't remember how to solve problems involving fractions. The easiest way to think of a fraction is $\frac{\text{part}}{\text{whole}}$ or "a part over a whole." You can turn any number into a fraction by putting it over 1. This means you can turn the number 4 into a fraction by putting it over 1: $\frac{4}{1}$. The top part of a fraction is called the *numerator* while the bottom is called the *denominator*. These are also called *terms*. You'll see three different types of fractions on the firefighter exam:

- **Proper fraction:** A proper fraction has a smaller number in the *numerator* and a larger number in the *denominator*. EXAMPLES: $\frac{1}{2}$, $\frac{2}{3}$, or $\frac{5}{6}$.
- **Improper fraction:** An improper fraction has a larger number in the numerator and a smaller number in the denominator. All numbers, except 1or 0, become improper fractions when placed over 1. EXAMPLES: $\frac{4}{1}$, $\frac{12}{3}$, or $\frac{20}{5}$.
- **Mixed number:** A mixed number includes a whole number and a proper fraction. EXAMPLES: $1\frac{2}{3}$, $4\frac{3}{4}$, or $6\frac{1}{2}$.

Fractions are rational numbers that can be added, subtracted, multiplied, divided, and cross-multiplied. The bad news is that each of these operations has separate rules. The good news is that we'll explain how to solve each operation every step of the way.

a. Converting Fractions

You may be asked to convert mixed numbers to improper fractions and improper fractions to mixed numbers.

> Tip: Proper fractions cannot be converted, so you don't have to worry about converting them.

To convert a mixed number to an improper fraction, use multiplication and addition. First, multiply the whole number by the fraction's denominator to get the *product*. Next, add the product to the numerator. Last, place this new number over the original denominator.

Here's an example:

Convert $6\frac{3}{4}$ to an improper fraction.

First, multiply the whole number by the fraction's denominator: $6 \times 4 = 24$.

Next, add this number to the numerator: $24 + 3 = 27$.

Last, place this number over the original denominator: $\frac{27}{4}$.

To convert an improper fraction to a mixed number, use division. First, divide the numerator by the denominator. The number of times the denominator *evenly* divides into the numerator becomes the whole number part of the mixed number. The remainder (if there is one) is placed over the original denominator and becomes the fraction part of the mixed number.

Here's an example:

Covert $\frac{25}{7}$ to a mixed number.

First, divide the numerator by the denominator: $25 \div 7$. Because 7 does not evenly divide into 25, you'll get 3 as the whole number with a remainder of 4.

Last, place the remainder over the original denominator: $3\frac{4}{7}$.

b. Reducing Fractions and Increasing Terms

Two fractions having a different denominator and numerator can be equal to each other. For example, $\frac{1}{2} = \frac{4}{8}$ and $\frac{2}{3} = \frac{6}{9}$. Some math problems require you to reduce a fraction to its lowest terms (simplify). A fraction is reduced to its lowest terms when the numerator and denominator have no common factors. Follow these steps when reducing a fraction:

- List the prime factors of the numerator and denominator.
- Divide the numerator and denominator by all common factors. (This is called canceling the common factors.)

Here's an example:

Reduce $\frac{9}{12}$ to its lowest terms.

First, list the prime factors:

$$\frac{9}{12} = \frac{3 \times 3}{3 \times 4}$$

Next, cancel the common factors:

$$\frac{\cancel{3} \times 3}{\cancel{3} \times 4}$$

So, $\frac{9}{12} = \frac{3}{4}$.

Some math problems require you to increase a fraction's terms. To increase a fraction's terms without changing the value of the fraction, multiply the fraction by a fraction that is equal to 1. All fractions that have the same numerator and denominator are always equal to 1: $\frac{1}{1}, \frac{2}{2}, \frac{3}{3}, \frac{4}{4}$, etc. For example: $\frac{1}{4} = \frac{1 \times 4}{4 \times 4} = \frac{4}{16}$.

c. Adding and Subtracting Fractions

When adding and subtracting denominators, make sure the denominators match, or have a common denominator. If the denominators match, just add or subtract the numerators. For example, $\frac{1}{4} + \frac{2}{4} = \frac{3}{4}$ or $\frac{3}{6} - \frac{2}{6} = \frac{1}{6}$.

If the denominators are different, you must find a common denominator before you can add the numerators. For example, if you want to add $\frac{1}{12}$ and $\frac{2}{3}$, first find a common multiple. Some multiples of 12 are 12, 24, 36, etc. Some multiples of 3 are 6, 9, 12, 15, etc. Note that the common multiple for 12 and 3 is 12, so you can use 12 as the common denominator. Next, you have to multiply the numerator and denominator of each fraction by the number that gets you equal to that denominator. As you learned in the previous section, to increase a fraction's terms without changing the value of the fraction, multiply the fraction by a fraction that is equal to 1. For example, $\frac{1}{12} \times \frac{1}{1} = \frac{1}{12}$ and $\frac{2}{3} \times \frac{4}{4} = \frac{8}{12}$.

So, $\frac{1}{12} + \frac{8}{12} = \frac{9}{12}$ and this reduces to $\frac{3}{4}$.

> **Tip: Remember, you must find a common denominator before you can add or subtract fractions.**

You subtract fractions the same way. Find a common denominator, multiply, and then subtract.

Here's an example:

$$\frac{4}{6} - \frac{1}{3}$$

$$\frac{4}{6} \times \frac{1}{1} = \frac{4}{6}$$

$$\frac{1}{3} \times \frac{2}{2} = \frac{2}{6}$$

$$\frac{4}{6} - \frac{2}{6} = \frac{2}{6} = \frac{1}{3}$$

d. Multiplying and Dividing Fractions

Multiplying and dividing fractions is much easier than adding and subtracting fractions because you don't need to find a common denominator. To multiply fractions, multiply the numerators and then multiply the denominators. Then reduce to lowest terms. For example, $\frac{1}{2} \times \frac{2}{3} = \frac{2}{6} = \frac{1}{3}$.

Dividing fractions is just as easy. To divide fractions, take the *reciprocal* of the second fraction, which means you invert, or flip it over, and then multiply the numerators and then multiply the denominators, just like when you multiply fractions.

> **Tip: You don't need to find a common denominator when multiplying or dividing fractions.**

Here's an example:

$$\frac{1}{2} \div \frac{2}{3} = \frac{1}{2} \times \frac{3}{2} = \frac{3}{4}$$

e. Cross-Multiplication

Like multiplying and dividing fractions, you don't need to find a common denominator to cross-multiply fractions. Cross-multiplication is typically used to solve proportions. (We'll talk more about proportions in the later section "Ratios and Proportions.") A proportion is a problem that has two fractions that are equal to each other, with one containing a variable that is usually represented by a letter such as x or y that stands for a value.

To cross-multiply fractions, multiply the denominator of one fraction by the numerator of the other. Next, solve the variable in the equation. To solve equations, you have to use inverse operations. If one side of the equation uses multiplication, use division to cancel out that information on the other side and solve for the variable. Remember, when you solve an equation, you must get both sides to be equal.

Tip: Any operation you perform to one side of an equation, you must perform to the other side of an equation.

Look at this example:

$$\frac{3}{5} = \frac{x}{15}$$

First, multiply the denominator of one fraction by the numerator of the other:

$$\frac{3}{5} = \frac{x}{15}$$
$$5x = 45$$

Next, divide each side by 5:

$$\frac{\cancel{5}x}{\cancel{5}} = \frac{45}{5}$$
$$x = \frac{45}{5}$$
$$x = 9$$

EXAMPLES:

1. Convert $4\frac{5}{10}$ to an improper fraction. Reduce your answer to lowest terms.

   A. $\frac{2}{9}$

   B. $\frac{3}{4}$

   C. $\frac{9}{2}$

   D. $\frac{11}{2}$

The correct answer is **C**. To solve this problem, first, multiply the whole number by the fraction's denominator: $4 \times 10 = 40$; next, add this number to the numerator: $40 + 5 = 45$; last, place this number over the original denominator and reduce to lowest terms: $\frac{45}{10} = \frac{9}{2}$.

---

2. What is the total of the following fractions: $\frac{1}{4} + \frac{2}{5} + \frac{3}{20}$? Reduce your answer to lowest terms.

   A. $\frac{2}{10}$

   B. $\frac{4}{5}$

   C. $\frac{7}{5}$

   D. $\frac{3}{2}$

The correct answer is **B**. Because the denominators are different, you must find a common denominator before you can add the numerators. A common multiple of 4, 5, and 20 is 20. Next, multiply the numerator and denominator of each fraction by the number that gets you equal to that denominator: $\frac{1}{4} \times \frac{5}{5} = \frac{5}{20}$ and $\frac{2}{5} \times \frac{4}{4} = \frac{8}{20}$ and $\frac{3}{20}$.

Next, add the numerators $\frac{5}{20} + \frac{8}{20} + \frac{3}{20} = \frac{16}{20}$ and this reduces to $\frac{4}{5}$.

---

3. Solve this equation: $\frac{4}{12} = \frac{x}{24}$

   A. 2
   B. 4
   C. 6
   D. 8

The correct answer is **D**. First, multiply the denominator of one fraction by the numerator of the other:

$$\frac{4}{12} = \frac{x}{24}$$
$$12x = 96$$

Next, divide each side by 12:

$$\frac{12x}{12} = \frac{96}{12}$$
$$x = \frac{96}{12}$$
$$x = 8$$

2. Decimals

A decimal, like a fraction, is a part of a whole. A decimal is a whole number with a decimal point. Its position represents its value and its name (such as one tenth, one hundredth, etc.). If the decimal point is moved one place to the left, the value of the number decreases.

For example,

$0.1 = \text{one tenth} = \frac{1}{10}$

$0.01 = \text{one hundredth} = \frac{1}{100}$

$0.001 = \text{one thousandth} = \frac{1}{1,000}$

If the decimal point is moved one place to the right, the value of the number increases.

$0.01 = \text{one hundredth} = \frac{1}{100}$

$0.1 = \text{one tenth} = \frac{1}{10}$

$1.0 = \text{one} = 1$

a. Converting Decimals to Fractions and Vice Versa

Some questions on the firefighter exam may ask you to convert decimals to fractions and fractions to decimals. Some questions may be easier to solve by converting them. To convert a decimal to a fraction, the numerals to the right of the decimal point become the numerator. The denominator is the name of the decimal (one tenth, one hundredth, etc.) and can be found by counting the number of numerals (or places) after the decimal point.

EXAMPLE:

Convert 0.25 to a decimal point.

First, place the numerals to the right of the decimal point (25) as the numerator. Next, count the number of places after the decimal point (2, which is hundredths) and use this number as the denominator: $\frac{25}{100}$. This reduces to $\frac{1}{4}$.

To convert a fraction to a decimal, divide the numerator by the denominator. It helps to use long division and to add a decimal point and a zero for every decimal place needed to the end of the numerator to solve these types of problems:

$$\frac{3}{4} = 4\overline{)3.00}^{.75}$$
$$\underline{-28}$$
$$20$$
$$\underline{-20}$$
$$0$$

b. Adding and Subtracting Decimals

Adding and subtracting decimals is just like adding and subtracting whole numbers. Just be sure to align the decimal points when you set up your problem.

Tip: Add a zero to the end of any number to make the decimal points line up.

EXAMPLE:

0.75
3.25
+2.30
6.30 or 6.3

c. Multiplying and Dividing Decimals

Multiplying and dividing decimals isn't as easy as adding and subtracting them. The easiest way to solve multiplication problems involving decimals is to remove the decimal points from the problem, solve it, and then put the decimal back in the correct place. After you multiply without the decimals, add the number of decimal places in each number and move the decimal this many places.

Let's look at an example:

4.6×0.36

First you would change 4.6×0.36 to 46×36.

Next, multiply to get $46 \times 36 = 1,656$.

Last, add together the number of decimal places (2 + 1 = 3) and place the decimal three places to the right of the number:1.656.

To solve division problems involving decimals, first move the decimal point in the *divisor* (the number by which you're dividing) to the right until it becomes a whole number. Then, move the decimal point in the *dividend* (the number you're dividing) the same number of places to the right. Now, put a decimal point in the *quotient* (the answer) directly above the decimal point in the dividend. Now leave the decimal point alone and divide.

For example, to divide 63.44 by 1.22, you would first move the decimal point in the divisor two places to the right to get a whole number. Therefore, 1.22 becomes 122. Now that you've moved the decimal point two places to the right in the divisor, you have to move it two places to the right in the dividend. Therefore, 63.44 becomes 6344:

$$1.22\overline{)63.44}^{\;x} \rightarrow 122\overline{)6344}^{\;x} \rightarrow 122\overline{)6344}^{\;52}$$

EXAMPLES:

1. The Minersville Fire Department typically responds to two types of calls: emergency and nonemergency. If $\frac{2}{3}$ of the calls that the Minersville Fire Department responds to each week are for emergencies, such as fires and accidents, and they typically respond to 96 calls per week, how many of those calls are for nonemergency calls?

   A. 9
   B. 16
   C. 32
   D. 64

The correct answer is **C.** The Minersville Fire Department responds to *32* nonemergency calls each week. To find the number of emergency calls, use cross-multiplication:

$$\frac{2}{3} = \frac{x}{96}$$
$$3x = 192$$
$$\frac{\cancel{3}x}{\cancel{3}} = \frac{192}{3}$$
$$x = 64$$

Next, subtract this number from the number of total calls each week: $96 - 64 = 32$.

---

2. $\frac{3}{4} \times 0.56 + \frac{7}{6} - \frac{6}{24} = ?$ Round to the nearest hundredth.

    A.   1.11
    B.   1.34
    C.   1.56
    D.   1.78

The correct answer is **B.** To solve this problem, first convert the fractions to decimals by dividing the numerators by the denominators: $\frac{3}{4} = 0.75$; $\frac{7}{6} = 1.17$; and $\frac{6}{24} = 0.25$. Next, substitute the decimals into the problem: $= 0.75 \times 0.56 + 1.17 - 0.25$ and solve using the order of operations. $0.75 \times 0.56 = 0.42 + 1.17 = 1.59 - 0.25 = 1.34$.

---

3. $\frac{9}{3} + \frac{12}{18} - \frac{3}{6} + \frac{4}{9} - \frac{2}{3} = ?$ Round to the nearest hundredth.

    A.   0.96
    B.   1.98
    C.   2.44
    D.   3.17

The correct answer is **D.** To solve this problem, first find a common denominator: 18. Next, multiply each fraction to achieve the common denominator: $\frac{9}{3} \times \frac{6}{6} = \frac{54}{18}$, $\frac{12}{18} \times \frac{1}{1} = \frac{12}{18}$, $\frac{3}{6} \times \frac{3}{3} = \frac{9}{18}$, $\frac{4}{9} \times \frac{2}{2} = \frac{8}{18}$, and $\frac{2}{3} \times \frac{6}{6} = \frac{12}{18}$. Next, substitute the new fractions into the problem, and then add and subtract: $\frac{58}{18} + \frac{12}{18} - \frac{9}{18} + \frac{8}{18} - \frac{12}{18} = \frac{57}{18} = 3.17$.

3. Percentages

A percentage of something is a part of a whole, just like a fraction and decimal. *Percent* means "per 100 parts" and is part of a fraction that always has a denominator of 100. Percentages can be represented as percents, fractions, or decimals:

$$50 \text{ percent or } \frac{50}{100} \text{ or } 0.50$$

As long as you know how to work with fractions and decimals, you shouldn't have trouble answering percentage problems on the firefighter exam. You can solve percentage problems in two ways: by converting them to fractions and using cross-multiplication or by converting them to decimals.

Tip: A percentage represented as a fraction is always set over 100.

a. Converting Percentages to Fractions and Using Cross-Multiplication

You can use cross-multiplication (see the heading "Cross-Multiplication" earlier in this chapter for more information) to solve percentage problems on the firefighter exam. To do this, convert the percentage into a fraction, set up a proportion, and then cross-multiply.

EXAMPLE:

What is 45 percent of 70?

First, place the percent over 100:

$$\frac{45}{100}$$

Next, set up a proportion x:

$$\frac{45}{100} = \frac{x}{70}$$

Last, solve for x:

$$\frac{45}{100} = \frac{x}{70}$$
$$100x = 45 \times 70$$
$$100x = 3150$$
$$\frac{100x}{100} = \frac{3150}{100}$$
$$x = 31.5$$

45% of $70 = 31\frac{1}{2}$ or 31.5

b. Converting Percentages to Decimals

You can also convert a percentage to a decimal to solve percentage problems on the firefighter exam. To change a percentage to a decimal, remove the percentage sign and move the decimal point two places to the left. Remember, in these types of problems, you can substitute a multiplication sign for the word "of" in percentage problems.

EXAMPLE:

What is 45 percent of 70?

First, convert the percentage to a decimal:

$$45\% = 0.45$$

Next, multiply:

$$0.45 \times 70 = 31.5$$

So, 45% of $70 = 31\frac{1}{2}$ or 31.5.

Notice that we ended up with the same answer even though we solved the problem two different ways. One way is not more right than the other, so use the way you are most comfortable with.

EXAMPLES:

Directions (1–3): Select the best answer for each question.

---

1. What is 55 percent of 35?

   A. 19.25
   B. 27
   C. 43.75
   D. 65

The correct answer is **A.** You can solve this problem in two ways to determine that 55 percent of 35 = 19.25. To solve this problem using cross-multiplication:

$$\frac{55}{100} = \frac{x}{35}$$
$$100x = 1{,}925$$
$$\frac{100x}{100} = \frac{1{,}925}{100}$$
$$x = 19.25$$

To solve this problem by converting the percentage to a decimal: $0.55 \times 35 = 19.25$

---

2. What percent of 325 is 46? Round to the nearest tenth.

   A. 9.4 percent
   B. 11.1 percent
   C. 14.2 percent
   D. 17.3 percent

The correct answer is **C**. To verify that 46 is 14.2 percent of 325, you can use one of two methods. To solve this problem using cross-multiplication:

$$\frac{46}{325} = \frac{x}{100}$$
$$325x = 4,600$$
$$\frac{325x}{325} = \frac{4,600}{325}$$
$$x = 14.2$$

To solve this problem by converting the percentage to a decimal, divide: $46 \div 325 = 0.142$ or 14.2 percent.

---

3. On your last 24-hour shift, you spent 9 hours fighting fires, 4 hours at the scene of a car accident, and your remaining hours at the station. What percent of your shift was spent at the station? Round to the nearest whole number.

   A. 11 percent
   B. 20 percent
   C. 34 percent
   D. 46 percent

The correct answer is **D**. You spent 46 percent of your shift at the station. Because you spent 9 hours fighting fires and 4 hours at the scene of a car accident, you were not at the station during 13 hours. Subtract this number from the total number of hours of your shift to get the number of hours you spent at the station: $24 - 13 = 11$. You spent 11 hours out of 24 at the station or $\frac{11}{24}$. Next, convert this fraction to a percentage by dividing: $11 \div 24 = 0.458$, which rounds to 0.46 or 46 percent.

C. Ratios and Proportions

A *ratio* is a comparison of two numbers, and as we mentioned previously, a *proportion* is a problem that has two fractions that are equal to each other, with one containing a variable that is usually represented by a letter such as x or y that stands for a value. Ratios and proportions are used to compare things. Firefighters use ratios and proportions to compare the number of victims to the number of firefighters at the scene of a fire; the number of feet a fire hydrant is located away from the scene of a fire to the length of a fire hose; and so on. A ratio can be written either as a fraction $\left(\frac{2}{3}\right)$ or a notation (2:3). They're part of proportion problems, which are solved by using cross-multiplication.

Here's an example of a ratio: The Plains Fire Department has 7 volunteer firefighters and the Brownville Fire Department has 4 volunteer firefighters. The ratio of Plains volunteer firefighters to Brownville volunteer firefighters is 7:4 and can also be expressed as $\frac{7}{4}$.

Here's an example of a proportion: 7:4::9:12 or $\frac{7}{4} = \frac{9}{12}$.

On the firefighter exam, you're not given all the values in a proportion problem and must solve for the unknown variable.

EXAMPLE:

Your fire department is hosting a bake sale, and you're in charge of baking cookies to sell. If it takes 2 cups of flour per 36 cookies, how many cookies can you bake with 7 cups of flour?

To solve this problem, set up a proportion to represent the number of cookies to the number of cups of flour and use cross-multiplication:

$$\frac{36}{2} = \frac{x}{7}$$
$$2x = 36 \times 7$$
$$2x = 252$$
$$\frac{2x}{2} = \frac{252}{2}$$
$$x = 126$$

You can bake 126 cookies with 7 cups of flour.

EXAMPLES:

1. Your fire department is hosting a spaghetti dinner, and you're in charge of making the meatballs. If it takes 4 cups of breadcrumbs per 60 meatballs, how many meatballs can you make with 18 cups of breadcrumbs?

   A. 65
   B. 120
   C. 270
   D. 465

The correct answer is **C.** You can make 270 meatballs with 18 cups of breadcrumbs. To solve this problem, set up a proportion to represent the number of meatballs to the number of cups of breadcrumbs and use cross-multiplication:

$$\frac{60}{4} = \frac{x}{18}$$
$$4x = 1,080$$
$$\frac{4x}{4} = \frac{1,080}{4}$$
$$x = 270$$

2. If Firefighter Stephenson can run up 14 flights of stairs in 4 minutes, how many flights of stairs can he run up in 9 minutes?

   A. 19
   B. 27.5
   C. 30
   D. 31.5

The correct answer is **D.** Firefighter Stephenson can run up 31.5 flights of stairs in 9 minutes. To solve this problem, set up a proportion to represent the number of minutes to the number of flights of stairs and use cross-multiplication:

$$\frac{14}{4} = \frac{x}{9}$$
$$4x = 126$$
$$\frac{\cancel{4}x}{\cancel{4}} = \frac{126}{4}$$
$$x = 31.5$$

---

3. If Firefighter Lamir can complete 75 push-ups in 3 minutes, how many push-ups can she complete in 15 minutes?

   A. 375
   B. 395
   C. 425
   D. 465

The correct answer is **A.** Firefighter Lamir can complete 375 push-ups in 15 minutes. To solve this problem, set up a proportion to represent the number of minutes to the number of push-ups and use cross-multiplication:

$$\frac{75}{3} = \frac{x}{15}$$
$$3x = 1,125$$
$$\frac{\cancel{3}x}{\cancel{3}} = \frac{1,125}{3}$$
$$x = 375$$

D. Algebra

If the thought of algebra conjures up bad memories of junior-high math class, don't worry, we'll tell you what you need to know to solve algebra problems on the firefighter exam. An algebraic equation, or expression, contains information that you must use to solve for an unknown variable, usually represented by the letter x or y. To do this, you must perform inverse operations to get the variable by itself on one side of the equation. This means that if one side of the equation uses subtraction, you have to use addition to cancel out that information and solve for the variable.

1. Algebraic Equations/Expressions

When you solve an algebraic equation, or expression, you must get both sides to be equal. Any operation you perform to one side of the equation, you must perform to the other side of the equation. Many types of algebraic equations exist, but they're all solved using the basic operations of addition, subtraction, multiplication, or division or a combination of a few or all of these operations.

Here's an example of a simple algebraic equation:

$$x - 5 = 10$$
$$x - 5 + 5 = 10 + 5$$
$$x = 15$$

Because the equation uses subtraction, you need to add 5 to the left of the equal sign to cancel out 5, and then add 5 to the opposite side.

Tip: What you do to one side of the equation, you must do to the other. For example, if you multiply one side by 2, you must multiply the other side by 2 to ensure both sides are balanced.

EXAMPLES:

1. $9x + 9 = 7(3 + 6)$

   A.   3
   B.   6
   C.   12
   D.   14

The correct answer is **B.** To solve this problem, first use the order of operations to solve the right side (parenthesis first, then addition): $7(3 + 6) = 7(9) = 63$. Because the equation uses addition, subtract 9 from each side: $9x + 9 - 9 = 63 - 9 = 9x = 54$. Last, divide each side by 9 to get 6:

$$9x + 9 = 7(3+6)$$
$$9x + 9 = 7(9)$$
$$9x + 9 = 63$$
$$9x + 9 - 9 = 63 - 9$$
$$9x = 54$$
$$\frac{9x}{9} = \frac{54}{9}$$
$$x = 6$$

2. $\frac{3x - 3}{6} = 48$

   A.   15
   B.   32
   C.   63
   D.   97

The correct answer is **D.** To solve this problem, first multiply each side by 6. Then, add 3 to each side. Last, divide each side by 3 to get 97:

$$\frac{3x-3}{6} = 48$$

$$(6)\frac{3x-3}{6} = 48(6)$$

$$3x - 3 = 288$$

$$3x - 3 + 3 = 288 + 3$$

$$3x = 291$$

$$\frac{3x}{3} = \frac{291}{3}$$

$$x = 97$$

---

3. $5x - 12 = 4(11 - 4)$

   A. 8
   B. 12
   C. 16
   D. 24

The correct answer is **A.** To solve this problem, first use the order of operations to solve the right side: $4(11 - 4) = 4(7) = 28$. Next, add 12 to each side: $5x - 12 + 12 = 28 + 12 = 5x = 40$. Last, divide each side by 5 to get 8:

$$5x - 12 = 4(11 - 4)$$

$$5x - 12 = 4(7)$$

$$5x - 12 = 28$$

$$5x - 12 + 12 = 28 + 12$$

$$5x = 40$$

$$\frac{5x}{5} = \frac{40}{5}$$

$$x = 8$$

2. Binomials (FOIL)

A *binomial* is an algebraic equation that has two terms, which are either numbers, variables, or a combination of both, that are separated from the rest of the problem by a plus or minus sign. In the binomial $4x - 6$, the two terms are $4x$ and -6. On the firefighter exam, you may see problems that include two binomials wrapped in parenthesis, such as $(x + 4)(2x - 5)$. The answer to these problems is usually a *trinomial,* which is an algebraic equation containing three terms, such as $2x^2 + 3x - 20$.

To solve binomial problems, use the FOIL method. *FOIL* is a mnemonic, or memory, device that helps you remember the steps in solving binomials. FOIL works like this:

- **First:** Multiply the first terms in each set of parentheses.
- **Outer:** Multiply the outer terms in each set of parentheses.
- **Inner:** Multiply the inner terms in each set of parentheses.
- **Last:** Multiply the last terms in each set of parentheses.

The last step is to simplify by either adding or subtracting the like terms.

Let's look at an example:

$(3x + 7)(3x + 9)$

Perform the FOIL method:

First: $3x \times 3x = 9x^2$
Outer: $3x \times 9 = 27x$
Inner: $7 \times 3x = 21x$
Last: $7 \times 9 = 63$

Now, add the like terms and simplify:

$9x^2 + 27x + 21x + 63$
$9x^2 + 48x + 63$

Tip: Remember to look at your signs when multiplying. A negative number multiplied by another negative number results in a positive number. A positive number multiplied by a negative number results in a negative number. A positive number multiplied by a positive number results in a positive number.

EXAMPLES:

1. $(-6x - 3)(4x - 8)$

   A. $-24x^2 - 60x - 24$
   B. $-24x^2 + 36x + 24$
   C. $24x^2 - 36x - 12$
   D. $24x^2 + 60x + 12$

The correct answer is **B.** To solve this problem, use the FOIL method:

First $= -6x \times 4x = -24x^2$
Outer: $-6x \times -8 = 48x$
Inner: $-3 \times 4x = -12x$
Last: $-3 \times -8 = 24$

Now, combine like terms: $48x + -12x = 36x$; the correct answer is $-24x^2 + 36x + 24$.

2. $(3x + 4)(-5x - 7)$

    A. $-15x^2 - 41x - 28$
    B. $-15x^2 - x + 11$
    C. $15x^2 + x + 11$
    D. $15x^2 + 41x + 28$

The correct answer is **A.** To solve this problem, use the FOIL method:

First $= 3x \times -5x = -15x^2$

Outer: $3x \times -7 = -21x$

Inner: $4 \times -5x = -20x$

Last: $4 \times -7 = -28$

Now, combine like terms: $-21x + -20x = -41x$; the correct answer is $-15x^2 - 41x - 28$.

3. $(-8x - 5)(-3x + 9)$

    A. $-24x^2 - 87x + 25$
    B. $-24x^2 + 57x + 45$
    C. $24x^2 - 87x - 25$
    D. $24x^2 - 57x - 45$

The correct answer is **D.** To solve this problem, use the FOIL method:

First $= -8x \times -3x = 24x^2$

Outer: $-8x \times 9 = -72x$

Inner: $-5 \times -3x = 15x$

Last: $-5 \times 9 = -45$

Now, combine like terms: $-72x + 15x = -57x$; the correct answer is $24x^2 - 57x - 45$.

E. Geometry

Geometry isn't just about triangles and formulas. Firefighters use geometry to determine basic calculations such as the volume of a tank, the perimeter of a location, etc. Solving geometry problems isn't much different from solving algebraic equations. You're given information that you typically plug into a formula and then solve for the unknown variable.

The geometry problems on the mathematics section of the firefighter exam may be about perimeter, circumference, area, and volume. Others may involve shapes such as triangles, rectangles, squares, and circles. You should memorize the formulas provided in the following tables before you take the firefighter exam.

1. Perimeter and Circumference

Perimeter refers to the distance around shapes, such as rectangles, squares, and triangles, and is equal to the total length of all of a shape's sides. *Circumference* is the distance around a circle. Different formulas are used for each shape. The following table shows a few of the different perimeter and circumference formulas:

Perimeter and Circumference Formulas	
Shape	**Formula**
Square	Perimeter = length + length + length + length ($P = l + l + l + l$)
Rectangle	Perimeter = length + length + width + width ($P = l + l + w + w$)
Triangle	Perimeter = the lengths of the three sides ($P = a + b + c$)
Circle	Circumference = two times the length of the radius multiplied by pi ($\pi = 3.14$) ($C = 2 \times \pi \times r$)

Tip: The radius of a circle is the distance from the center of the circle to a point on the circle, and the diameter is the distance across a circle. The diameter of a circle is equal to twice the radius ($D = 2r$).

Let's try an example:

Find the perimeter of a rectangle with a length of 4 feet and a width of 8 feet.

Plug the values into the perimeter formula for a rectangle ($P = l + l + w + w$): $P = 4 + 4 + 8 + 8 = 24$. The perimeter of the rectangle is 24 feet.

Sometimes, you may see questions on the firefighter exam that give you the perimeter (or circumference) of an object and ask you to find its length or width (or radius).

Here's an example:

A rectangle's perimeter is 24 feet and its length is 4 feet. What is the width?

Plug the values into the perimeter formula for a rectangle ($P = l + l + w + w$): $24 = 4 + 4 + w + w = 24 = 8 + w + w$.

Next, subtract 8 from both sides: $24 - 8 = 8 - 8 + w + w = 16 = (2)w$ (or $w + w$). Last, divide each side by 2:

$$\frac{16}{2} = \frac{(2)w}{2}$$
$$8 = w$$

The width of the rectangle is 8 feet.

Tip: Pi (π) is a Greek letter used in the circumference formula. It's equal to 3.14159265, but is rounded to 3.14.

EXAMPLES:

1. Find the perimeter of the triangle shown below.

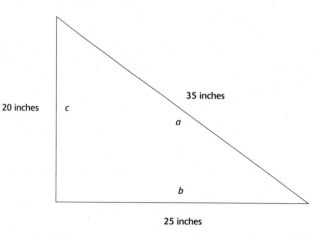

35 inches

20 inches   *c*

a

b

25 inches

   A. 40 in.
   B. 60 in.
   C. 80 in.
   D. 100 in.

The correct answer is **C.** The perimeter of the triangle is 80 inches. To solve this problem, use the perimeter formula for a triangle ($P = a + b + c$) and plug in the values: $P = 35 + 25 + 20 = 80$.

2. Find the circumference of the circle shown below. Round your answer to the nearest whole number.

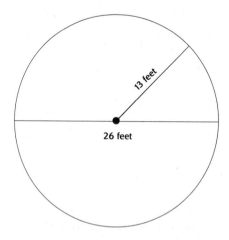

13 feet

26 feet

   A. 64 ft.
   B. 82 ft.
   C. 125 ft.
   D. 163 ft.

The correct answer is **B.** The circumference of the circle is 82 feet. To solve this problem, use the circumference formula ($C = 2 \times \pi \times r$) and plug in the values: $C = 2 \times 3.14 \times 13 = 81.64$. Now, round 81.64 to the nearest whole number to get 82.

---

3. A circle's diameter is 84 inches. What is the radius?

    A.   42 in.
    B.   101 in.
    C.   168 in.
    D.   263 in.

The correct answer is **A.** If a circle's diameter is 84 inches, its radius is 42 inches. Because a circle's radius is half its diameter, divide 84 by 2 to get 42.

2. Area

The area of a shape is the number of squares it takes to cover the shape completely. Area is measured in square units and all measurements must be in the same units. For example, you can't multiply inches by feet. The following table gives you a few of the different area formulas:

Area Formulas	
Shape	**Formula**
Square	Area = length × width ($A = lw$)
Rectangle	Area = length × width ($A = lw$)
Triangle	Area = $\frac{1}{2}$ × base × height $\left(A = \frac{1}{2}bh \right)$
Circle	Area = π × radius × radius ($A = \pi r^2$)

Here's an example:

    Find the area of a triangle with a base of 16 feet and a height of 9 feet.

Use the area formula for a triangle $\left(A = \frac{1}{2}bh \right)$ and plug in the values: $A = \frac{1}{2} \times 16 \times 9 = \frac{1}{2} \times 144 = 72$ feet^2. A triangle with a base of 16 feet and a height of 9 feet has an area of 72 feet^2.

Just as with the perimeter problems, you may see questions on the firefighter exam that give you the area of an object and ask you to find its length, width, base, height, or radius.

Take a look at this example:

    A rectangle's area is 108 inches, and its width is 12 inches. What is its length?

Use the area formula for a rectangle: $A = l \times w$ and plug in the values: $108 = l \times 12$.

To solve for l, divide both sides of the equation by 12:

$$108 = l \times 12$$
$$\frac{108}{12} = l \times \frac{12}{12}$$
$$9 = l$$

The length of the rectangle is 9 inches^2.

Tip: Make sure your answers for area problems contain square units.

EXAMPLES:

---

1. Find the area of the circle shown below. Round your answer to the nearest whole number.

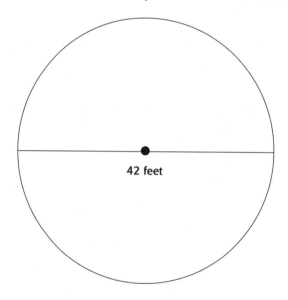

42 feet

   A.   436 ft.^{2}
   B.   769 ft.^{2}
   C.   1,385 ft.^{2}
   D.   1,596 ft.^{2}

The correct answer is **C.** The area of the circle is 1,385 feet^2. To solve this problem, first find the radius. Because the diameter is twice the radius, divide the diameter by 2 to find the radius: $42 \div 2 = 21$. Next, use the area formula for a circle ($A = \pi \times r \times r$) and plug in the values: $A = 3.14 \times 21 \times 21 = 1,384.74$, which rounds to 1,385 feet^2.

2. Find the area of the rectangle shown below.

11 inches

19 inches

A.   30 in.²
B.   60 in.²
C.   209 in.²
D.   239 in.²

The correct answer is **C.** The area of the rectangle is 209 inches². To solve this problem, use the area formula for a rectangle ($A = l \times w$) and plug in the values: $A = 11 \times 19 = 209$ inches².

3. A triangle's area is 140 inches, and its base is 14 inches. What is its height?

A.   10 in.
B.   20 in.
C.   30 in.
D.   40 in.

The correct answer is **B.** The height of the triangle is 20 inches. To solve this problem, use the area formula for a triangle $\left(A = \frac{1}{2}bh \right)$ and plug in the values: $140 = \frac{1}{2}(14)h$. Next, multiply each side by 2, and then divide each side by 14:

$$140 = \frac{1}{2}(14)h$$
$$(2)140 = (2)\frac{1}{2}14h$$
$$280 = 14 \times h$$
$$\frac{280}{14} = \frac{14}{14} \times h$$
$$20 = h$$

3. Volume

While perimeter, circumference, and area problems typically refer to flat shapes, volume problems refer to three-dimensional objects, such as cubes, cylinders, and prisms. If you take a flat shape, such as a rectangle or triangle, and give it height, you get a *prism.* Volume measures the amount of fluid (such as gas or liquid) that a three-dimensional object can hold. Volume is measured in cubic units and all measurements must be in the same units. The following table gives you a few of the different volume formulas:

Volume Formulas	
Three-Dimensional Object	**Formula**
Cube	$V = a^3$ (a = 1 side)
Cylinder	$V = \pi r^2 h$
Triangular prism	Volume = $\frac{1}{2}$ × base × height × length $\left(V = \frac{1}{2}bhl\right)$
Rectangular prism	Volume = length × width × height ($V = lwh$)

Let's try a volume problem:

What is the volume of the rectangular prism shown below?

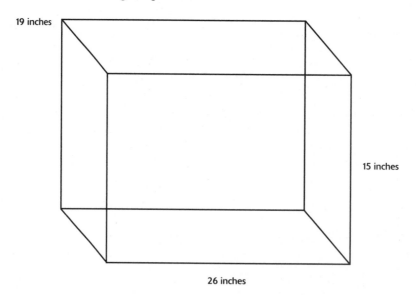

To solve this problem, use the volume formula for a rectangular prism ($V = l \times w \times h$), and plug in the values: $V = 26 \times 15 \times 19 = 7,410$ inches³.

Tip: Make sure your answers for volume problems contain cubic units.

Sometimes questions on the firefighter exam give you the volume of an object and ask you to find its length, width, base, height, or radius. For example:

A cylinder's volume is 50 inches^3 and its radius is 25 inches. What is its height?

Use the volume formula for a cylinder ($V = \pi r^2 h$) and plug in the values:

$$50 = 3.14(25)^2 h$$
$$= 3.14 \times 625 \times h$$
$$= 1,962.5 \times h$$

Last, divide each side by 50:

$$\frac{50}{50} = \frac{1,962.5}{50} \times h$$
$$39.25 = h$$

The cylinder's height is 39.25 inches.

EXAMPLES:

1. What is the volume of the triangular prism shown below?

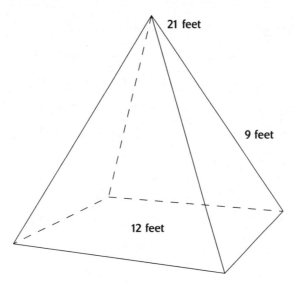

21 feet

9 feet

12 feet

A. 986 ft.^{3}
B. 1,134 ft.^{3}
C. 1,997 ft.^{3}
D. 2,268 ft.^{3}

The correct answer is **B.** The volume of the triangular prism is 1,134 feet^3. To solve this problem, use the volume formula for a triangular prism $\left(V = \frac{1}{2}bhl\right)$ and plug in the numbers:

$$V = \frac{1}{2}(12)(21)(9)$$

Next, multiply each side by 2, and then divide each side by 2:

$$V = \frac{1}{2} \times 12 \times 21 \times 9$$

$$(2)V = (2)\frac{1}{2} \times 12 \times 21 \times 9$$

$$2V = 12 \times 21 \times 9$$

$$2V = 2,268$$

$$\frac{2V}{2} = \frac{2,268}{2}$$

$$V = 1,134$$

---

2. A cylinder's volume is 35 inches^3, and its radius is 18 inches. What is its height? Round your answer to the nearest hundredth.

   A. 29.07 in.
   B. 33.56 in.
   C. 45.95 in.
   D. 59.10 in.

The correct answer is **A.** The height of the cylinder is 29.07 inches. To solve this problem, use the volume formula for a cylinder ($V = \pi r^2 h$) and plug in the numbers: 35 = 3.14 × (18)^2 × h = 35 = 3.14 × 324 × h = 35 = 1017.36 × h. Next, divide each side by 35 and round your answer:

$$\frac{35}{35} = \frac{1,017.36}{35} \times h$$

$$29.0674 = h$$

$$29.07 = h$$

3. What is the volume of the cube shown below?

21 feet

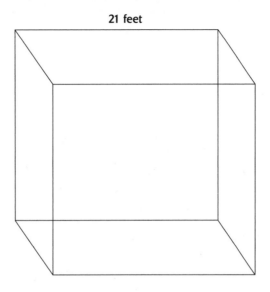

A. 441 ft.³
B. 5,465 ft.³
C. 8,493 ft.³
D. 9,261 ft.³

The correct answer is **D.** The volume of the cube is 9,261 feet³. To solve this problem, use the volume formula for a cube ($V = a^3$) and plug in the numbers: $V = 21^3 = 21 \times 21 \times 21 = 9,261$.

F. Word Problems

Many of the questions you'll see on the mathematics portion of the firefighter exam are word problems. These types of questions typically contain a short passage that ranges in size from a sentence or two to a few paragraphs. Word problems give you information that you must plug into an equation to solve.

> **Tip:** Sometimes word problems contain irrelevant information that's just there to confuse you. Be sure to read the entire word problem carefully to determine which information you need to solve the problem. Ignore the irrelevant information. Sometimes it's helpful to list the important information from word problems to help you solve them.

1. Basic Word Problems

After you've read through a word problem and figured out which information you need, you have to determine what operation (or operations) you should use to solve the problem. Word problems usually contain key words that alert you of the correct operation to use. Look out for the following key words:

- **Addition:** altogether, greater, more, sum, total
- **Subtraction:** difference, fewer, left over, less, remain
- **Multiplication:** of, product, times
- **Division:** each, per

> **Tip: Many word problems on the firefighter exam involve distance (number of miles traveled), rate (speed of travel), and time (how long it takes to travel a distance). Use the formula: distance = rate of speed × time $(d = r \times t)$ to solve these problems.**

Here's an example of a word problem:

In the past 5 days, the Lehman Township Fire Department responded to 6 house fires, 8 car accidents, and 11 emergency situations. How many total incidents did the fire department respond to in the past 5 days?

After reading the word problem, you can determine that the number of days (5) is irrelevant information and ignore it. You can also determine that you need to use addition to solve this problem because of the key word *total*. To solve this problem, add together the number of house fires (6), the number of car accidents (8), and the number of emergency situations (11):

$$6 + 8 + 11 = 25$$

The Lehman Township Fire Department responded to 25 total incidents in the past 5 days.

EXAMPLES:

---

1. You're responding to the scene of an accident involving 2 vehicles and 6 victims, located 7 miles from the station. If you travel at an average speed of 35 miles per hour, how many minutes will it take for you to arrive at the scene?

   A. 3 min.
   B. 6 min.
   C. 12 min.
   D. 15 min.

The correct answer is **C**. It will take you 12 minutes to arrive at the scene. To solve this problem, use the distance formula $(d = r \times t)$ and plug in the numbers. Next, divide each side by 35 miles per hour and solve to get $\frac{1}{5}$ hours $= t$:

$$d = rt$$

$$7 \text{ miles} = 35 \text{ miles per hour} \times t$$

$$\frac{7 \text{ miles}}{35 \text{ miles per hour}} = \frac{35 \text{ miles per hour}}{35 \text{ miles per hour}} \times t$$

$$\frac{1}{5} \text{ hours} = t$$

Because your answer is in hours and the question asks for the answer in minutes, you have to multiply $\frac{1}{5}$ by the number of minutes in 1 hour (60):

$$\frac{1}{5 \text{ hours}} \times \frac{60 \text{ minutes}}{1} = \frac{60 \text{ minutes}}{5 \text{ hours}} = 12 \text{ minutes}$$

---

2. In the past 30 days, the Monroe Fire Department responded to 16 accidents, 27 emergency situations, and 40 fires. How many more fires than accidents did the fire department respond to in the past 30 days?

   A. 13
   B. 24
   C. 56
   D. 83

The correct answer is **B**. The Monroe Fire Department responded to 24 more fires than accidents in the past 30 days. The number of emergency situations responded to is irrelevant information that is not needed to solve this problem, so you should ignore the number of emergency situations (27). To solve this problem, subtract the number of accidents (16) from the number of fires (40): $40 - 16 = 24$.

---

3. A fire engine responds to an activated fire alarm at a building that is 12 miles from the fire station. If the fire engine arrives at the building in 9 minutes, what was the average speed the fire engine traveled on the way to the building?

   A. 40 m.p.h.
   B. 55 m.p.h
   C. 65 m.p.h.
   D. 80 m.p.h.

The correct answer is **D**. The fire engine traveled at an average speed of 80 miles per hour on the way to the building. To solve this problem, use the distance formula ($d = r \times t$) and plug in the numbers. Next, divide each side by 9 minutes to get $\frac{4 \text{ miles}}{3 \text{ minutes}}$:

$$d = rt$$

$$12 \text{ miles} = r \times 9 \text{ minutes}$$

$$\frac{12 \text{ miles}}{9 \text{ minutes}} = r \times \frac{9 \text{ minutes}}{9 \text{ minutes}}$$

$$\frac{12}{9} = r$$

$$\frac{4 \text{ miles}}{3 \text{ minutes}} = r$$

Because your answer is in miles per minute and the question asks for the answer in miles per hour, multiply $\frac{4}{3}$ by the number of minutes in 1 hour (60):

$$\frac{4 \text{ miles}}{3 \text{ minutes}} \times \frac{60 \text{ minutes}}{1 \text{ hour}} = \frac{240}{3} = 80 \text{ miles per hour}$$

2. Mathematical Reasoning

Mathematical reasoning questions on the firefighter exam are word problems requiring you to use both math and reasoning skills. To solve these problems, you have to choose the correct operation(s) to use. Sometimes you will have to draw a conclusion about what you are given based on the information presented in the problem. As with other word problems, some of the information you are given may not be needed to solve the problem.

Tip: Sometimes, you have to consider information presented in a table or chart to solve mathematical reasoning questions.

Here's an example:

> While training to be firefighters, recruits are given a physical fitness test that tests their ability to do physical activities, such as running and doing push-ups. Use the following table to determine which statement MOST ACCURATELY describes the relationship between the number of push-ups done by one firefighter and the time it takes to complete them.

Total Time	Number of Push-Ups
1 minute, 15 seconds	25
3 minutes,15 seconds	50
5 minutes,15 seconds	65
7 minutes,15 seconds	75

    A.   As the time increases, the number of push-ups completed is doubled.
    B.   As the time increases, the number of push-ups completed is tripled.
    C.   As the time increases, the number of push-ups completed is decreased by 45 percent.
    D.   As the time increases, the push-ups are completed at a slower rate.

The correct answer is **D.** If you examine the information in the table, you can identify a specific pattern. The table shows that as the time is increased, the number of push-ups completed are done at a slower rate because you can assume that as time goes on, it gets harder to complete the push-ups. The table does not show that the number is doubled, tripled, or decreased by 45 percent.

EXAMPLES:

Questions 1–2 refer to the following passage.

> Firefighters working at the Grenada Fire Company receive a yearly raise based on the number of years of service with the company. Firefighters who have been with the company less than five years

typically receive a raise that is 2 percent of their yearly salary. Firefighters who have been with the company for 5 to 10 years receive a raise that is 3.5 percent of their salary. Firefighters who have dedicated 10 to 15 years with the same company receive a raise that is 5 percent of their yearly salary.

1. Based on the information in the passage, if the trend continues, what percentage of their yearly salary would firefighters with 20 to 25 years of service with the same company receive as their raise?

   A. 6.5 percent
   B. 8 percent
   C. 9.5 percent
   D. 11 percent

The correct answer is **B.** If the trend continues, firefighters with 20 to 25 years of service with the same company will receive an 8 percent raise. If you examine the information in the passage, you can determine that for every five years of service, firefighters get a 1.5 percent raise.

2. If the rate of the current raise is increased by 3 percent, what percentage of their yearly salary would firefighters with 25 to 30 years of service with the same company receive as their raise?

   A. 5 percent
   B. 9.5 percent
   C. 12.5 percent
   D. 15 percent

The correct answer is **C.** If the rate of the current raise is increased by 3 percent, firefighters with 25 to 30 years of service with the same company will receive a 12.5 percent raise. To solve this problem, add 3 percent to each rate. Firefighters who have been with the company less than five years typically receive a raise that is 5 percent of their yearly salary. Firefighters who have been with the company for 5 to 10 years receive a raise that is 6.5 percent of their salary. Firefighters who have dedicated 10 to 15 years with the same company receive a raise that is 8 percent of their yearly salary. Firefighters who have dedicated 15 to 20 years with the same company receive a raise that is 9.5 percent of their yearly salary. Firefighters who have dedicated 20 to 25 years with the same company receive a raise that is 11 percent of their yearly salary.

3. Use the following table to determine which statement MOST ACCURATELY describes the relationship between the ladder length and the number of firefighters needed to carry a ladder.

Number of Firefighters Needed to Carry a Ladder	Ladder Length
1	12 ft.
2	16 ft.
3	20 ft.
4	24 ft.

   A. As the ladder length is increased by 4 feet, the number of firefighters needed to carry it is doubled.
   B. As ladder length increases, the number of firefighters needed to carry it decreases.
   C. As ladder length decreases, the number of firefighters needed to carry it increases.
   D. As the ladder length is increased, one additional person is needed for each 4-foot increase.

The correct answer is **D.** If you examine the information in the table, you can identify a specific pattern. The table shows that as the ladder length is increased, one additional person is needed for each 4-foot increase. The table does not show that the number is doubled (Choice A). It also does not show that, as the ladder length increases, the number of firefighters needed to carry it decreases, and vice versa (Choices B and C).

3. Number Facility

Number-facility questions are another type of word problem on the firefighter exam that tests your mathematical ability. For these types of questions, you need to use the information provided to determine which basic operation (or operations) you should use to solve the problem. These types of questions are straightforward and solved using the information provided and typically don't contain any irrelevant information.

For example:

> A firefighter enters a smoke-filled room on the top floor of a building and needs to ventilate it. He uses a pike pole to make a 3-foot by 6-foot opening in the roof. How large is the opening?

To solve this problem, multiply 3 by 6: $3 \times 6 = 18$ feet^2. The hole is 18 feet^2.

> **Tip: Make sure you pay close attention to units when solving word problems and include squared and cubed units in your answers.**

EXAMPLES:

---

1. If the average height of a story in an apartment building is 15 feet, what size ladder is needed to reach the top floor of a building with 19 stories?

    A. 34 ft.
    B. 120 ft.
    C. 285 ft.
    D. 319 ft.

The correct answer is **C.** A ladder measuring 285 feet is needed to reach the top floor of a building with 19 stories. To solve this problem, multiply the height of each story by the number of stories: $15 \times 19 = 285$.

---

2. The Newell Fire Department has 3 fire engines and 24 firefighters. If an equal number of firefighters rode in each engine, how many firefighters would fit on each fire engine?

    A. 6
    B. 8
    C. 9
    D. 11

The correct answer is **B.** Exactly 8 firefighters would fit on each fire engine. To solve this problem, divide the number of firefighters by the number of fire engines: $24 \div 3 = 8$.

3. If Fire Engine No. 9 can hold 7 pike poles and Fire Engine No. 56 can hold 14 pike poles, how many pike poles can the two fire engines hold total?

   A. 7
   B. 16
   C. 21
   D. 47

The correct answer is **C.** The two fire engines can hold 21 pike poles total. To solve this problem, add the number of pike poles Fire Engine No. 9 can hold to the number of pike poles Fire Engine No. 56 can hold: $7 + 14 = 21$.

Practice

Directions (1–20): Select the best answer for each question.

Question 1 refers to the following figure.

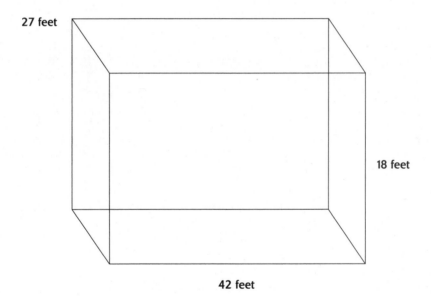

27 feet

18 feet

42 feet

1. What is the volume of the rectangular prism?

   A. 2,986 ft.^{3}
   B. 8,698 ft.^{3}
   C. 12,454 ft.^{3}
   D. 20,412 ft.^{3}

2. $(9x^{15})(x^7) =$

    A. $9x^7$

    B. $9x^8$

    C. $9x^{22}$

    D. $9x^{105}$

3. If Firefighter Wallace can complete 18 training exercises in 24 minutes, how many training exercises can she complete in 32 minutes?

    A.   18

    B.   24

    C.   36

    D.   44

4. $(-8x + 2)(9x - 5)$

    A. $-72x^2 - 22x + 10$

    B. $-72x^2 + 58x - 10$

    C. $72x^2 - 58x + 10$

    D. $72x^2 + 22x - 10$

5. If Sergeant Manning bought 6 new fire hoses for the fire department and paid $750 for each hose, what is the total he paid for all 6 fire hoses?

    A. $2,000

    B. $4,500

    C. $5,000

    D. $7,500

6. You're responding to the scene of a multi-vehicle accident located 15 miles from the station. If you travel at an average speed of 45 miles per hour, how many minutes will it take for you to arrive at the scene?

    A.   7 minutes

    B.   13 minutes

    C.   18 minutes

    D.   20 minutes

7. What is the total of the following fractions: $\frac{4}{3} + \frac{8}{9} + \frac{15}{27}$? Reduce your answer to lowest terms.

    A. $\frac{3}{4}$

    B. $\frac{12}{14}$

    C. $\frac{25}{27}$

    D. $\frac{25}{9}$

8. Simplify the expression: $5 + 8(3 + 2)^3$

   A. 954
   B. 1,005
   C. 1,625
   D. 2,465

9. A triangle's area is 180 inches^2 and its base is 40 inches. What is its height?

   A. 9 in.
   B. 18 in.
   C. 24 in.
   D. 36 in.

10. $(-9x - 3)(-12x - 4)$

    A. $-108x^2 - 72x - 12$
    B. $-72x^2 + 36x - 12$
    C. $72x^2 - 36x + 12$
    D. $108x^2 + 72x + 12$

11. $\frac{2}{3} \times 0.99 - \frac{4}{7} + \frac{9}{21} = ?$ Round to the nearest hundredth.

    A. -0.34
    B. -0.10
    C. 0.52
    D. 1.12

12. The Hilldale Volunteer Fire Department responded to 86 fires over the course of 30 days. How many fires did the fire department respond to on average each day? Round to the nearest whole number.

    A. 3
    B. 5
    C. 9
    D. 11

13. Solve this equation: $\frac{8}{12} = \frac{x}{36}$

    A. 9
    B. 14
    C. 21
    D. 24

Question 14 refers to the following information.

The inspector at the fire department is in charge of writing reports that detail the causes of all fires. He can fill out some reports in less time than other reports. The table below shows the average time it takes the inspector to fill out reports.

Total Time	Number of Reports
4 hours, 30 minutes	10
6 hours, 45 minutes	15
9 hours	20
11 hours, 15 minutes	25

14. How many reports can the inspector complete in 18 hours?

   A.   30
   B.   35
   C.   40
   D.   45

15. What is 43 percent of 95?

   A.   24.50
   B.   29.65
   C.   36.40
   D.   40.85

16. Covert 38.2°C to °F. Round to the nearest tenth.

   A.   65.5
   B.   75.3
   C.   98.6
   D.   100.8

17. If fire engine L can carry up to 16 people, and fire engine G can carry up to 10 people, how many people can the two fire engines carry?

   A.   10
   B.   16
   C.   18
   D.   26

Question 18 refers to the following figure.

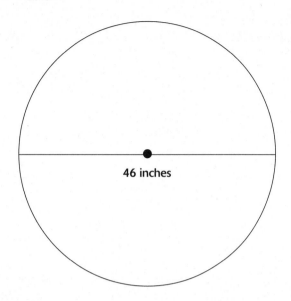

46 inches

18. Find the circumference of the circle. Round your answer to the nearest whole number.

   A.   72 in.
   B.   98 in.
   C.   144 in.
   D.   289 in.

19. On your last 24-hour shift, you spent 11 hours fighting fires, 8 hours at the scene of a car accident, and your remaining hours at the station. What percentage of your shift was spent at the station? Round to the nearest whole number.

   A.   19 percent
   B.   21 percent
   C.   55 percent
   D.   79 percent

20. $2x + 15 = 3(7 + 9)$

   A.   9
   B.   14
   C.   16.5
   D.   31.5

Answers

1. **D** The volume of the rectangular prism is 20,412 feet³. To solve this problem, use the volume formula for a rectangular prism ($V = l \times w \times h$) and plug in the values: $V = 42 \times 18 \times 27 = 20{,}412$ feet³.

2. **C** The correct answer is $9x^{22}$. To multiply powers with the same base, add the exponents: $(9x^{15})(x^{7}) = 9x^{15+7=22}$.

3. **B** Firefighter Wallace can complete 24 training exercises in 32 minutes. To solve this problem, set up a proportion to represent the number of minutes to the number of training exercises and use cross-multiplication:

$$\frac{18}{24} = \frac{x}{32}$$
$$24x = 576$$
$$\frac{24x}{24} = \frac{576}{24}$$
$$x = 24$$

4. **B** The correct answer is $-72x^2 + 58x - 10$. To solve this problem, use the FOIL method. First: $-8x \times 9x = -72x^2$; Outer: $-8x \times -5 = 40x$; Inner: $2 \times 9x = 18x$; and Last: $2 \times -5 = -10$. Now, combine like terms: $40x + 18x = 58x$ to get $-72x^2 + 58x - 10$.

5. **B** The total cost for all 6 fire hoses was $4,500. To solve this problem, multiply the number of fire hoses by the cost of each hose: $6 \times \$750 = \$4{,}500$.

6. **D** It will take you 20 minutes to arrive at the scene. To solve this problem, use the distance formula ($d = r \times t$) and plug in the numbers. Next, divide each side by 45 miles per hour and solve to get $\frac{1}{3}$ hours $= t$:

$$d = rt$$
$$15 \text{ miles} = 45 \text{ miles per hour} \times t$$
$$\frac{15 \text{ miles}}{45 \text{ miles per hour}} = \frac{45 \text{ miles per hour}}{45 \text{ miles per hour}} \times t$$
$$\frac{15}{45} \text{ hours} = t$$
$$\frac{1}{3} \text{ hours} = t$$

Because your answer is in hours and the question asks for the answer in minutes, you msut multiply $\frac{1}{3}$ by the number of minutes in 1 hour (60):

$$\frac{1}{3 \text{ hours}} \times \frac{60 \text{ minutes}}{1} = \frac{60 \text{ minutes}}{3 \text{ hours}} = 20 \text{ minutes}$$

7. **D** The correct answer is $\frac{25}{9}$. Because the denominators are different, you must find a common denominator before you can add the numerators. A common multiple of 3, 9, and 27 is 27. Next, multiply the numerator and denominator of each fraction by the number that gets you equal to that denominator: $\frac{4}{3} \times \frac{9}{9} = \frac{36}{27}$ and $\frac{8}{9} \times \frac{3}{3} = \frac{24}{27}$ and $\frac{15}{27}$. Next, add the numerators $\frac{36}{27} + \frac{24}{27} = \frac{15}{27} = \frac{75}{27}$ and this reduces to $\frac{25}{9}$.

8. **B** If you correctly followed the order of operations, you would get 1,005. First, solve what's inside the parenthesis: $(3 + 2) = 5$. Next, solve the exponent: $5^3 = 125$. Then, multiply: $8(125) = 1,000$; last, add: $5 + 1,000 = 1,005$.

9. **A** The height of the triangle is 9 inches. To solve this problem, use the area formula for a triangle $\left(A = \frac{1}{2}bh\right)$ and plug in the values: $180 = \frac{1}{2}(40)h$. Next, multiply each side by 2, and then divide each side by 40:

$$180 = \frac{1}{2}40h$$
$$(2)180 = (2)\frac{1}{2}40h$$
$$360 = 40h$$
$$\frac{360}{40} = \frac{40h}{40}$$
$$9 = h$$

10. **D** The correct answer is $108x^2 + 72x + 12$. To solve this problem, use the FOIL method. First: $-9x \times -12x = 108x^2$; Outer: $-9x \times -4 = 36x$; Inner: $-3 \times -12x = 36x$; and Last: $-3 \times -4 = 12$. Now, combine like terms: $36x + 36x = 72x$ to get $108x^2 + 72x + 12$.

11. **C** To solve this problem, first convert the fractions to decimals by dividing the numerators by the denominators: $\frac{2}{3} = 0.67$; $\frac{4}{7} = 0.57$; and $\frac{9}{21} = 0.43$. Next, substitute the decimals into the problem: $0.67 \times 0.99 - 0.57 + 0.43$. Solve using the order of operations. $0.67 \times 0.99 = 0.66 - 0.57 = 0.09 + 0.43 = 0.52$.

12. **A** The Hilldale Volunteer Fire Department responded to an average of 3 fires each day. To find the average, divide the number of fires by the number of days $86 \div 30 = 2.86$, which rounds to 3.

13. **D** The correct answer is 24. This problem can be solved using the cross-multiplication method. First, multiply the denominator of one fraction by the numerator of the other:

$$\frac{8}{12} = \frac{x}{36}$$
$$12x = 288$$

Next, divide each side by 12:

$$\frac{12x}{12} = \frac{288}{12}$$
$$x = 24$$

14. **C** The inspector can complete 40 reports in 18 hours. If you examine the information in the passage and table, you can determine that the inspector can complete 5 reports in 2 hours and 15 minutes. Based on this number, you can determine he can complete 30 reports in 13 hours, 30 minutes; 35 reports in 15 hours, 45 minutes; 40 reports in 18 hours; and 45 reports in 20 hours, 15 minutes.

15. **D** You can determine that 43 percent of 95 equals 40.85 using two methods. To solve this problem using cross-multiplication:

$$\frac{43}{100} = \frac{x}{95}$$
$$100x = 4{,}085$$
$$\frac{100x}{100} = \frac{4{,}085}{100}$$
$$x = 40.85$$

To solve this problem by converting the percentage to a decimal: $0.43 \times 95 = 40.85$.

16. **D** The correct answer is 100.8°F. To solve this problem, plug the numbers you know into the Celsius to Fahrenheit formula and solve:

$$F = \frac{9}{5}C + 32$$
$$= \frac{9}{5}(38.2) + 32$$
$$= \frac{9 \times 38.2}{5 \times 1} + 32$$
$$= \frac{343.8}{5} + 32$$
$$= 68.76 + 32$$
$$= 100.76$$
$$\approx 100.8$$

17. **D** Together fire engines L and N can carry up to 26 people. To solve this problem, add the number of people that fire engine L can carry to the number of people that fire engine G can carry: $16 + 10 = 26$.

18. **C** The circumference of the circle is 144 inches. To solve this problem, first find the radius using the formula $D = 2r$:

$$D = 2r$$
$$46 = 2r$$
$$\frac{46}{2} = \frac{2r}{2}$$
$$23 = r$$

Next, use the circumference formula ($C = 2 \times \pi \times r$) and plug in the values: $C = 2 \times 3.14 \times 23 = 144.44$. Now, round 144.44 to the nearest whole number to get 144.

19. **B** You spent 21 percent of your shift at the station. Because you spent 11 hours fighting fires and 8 hours at the scene of a car accident, you were not at the station during 19 hours. Subtract this number from the total number of hours of your shift to get the number of hours you spent at the station: $24 - 19 = 5$. You spent 5 hours out of 24 at the station or $\frac{5}{24}$. Next, convert this fraction to a percentage by dividing: $5 \div 24 = 0.208$, which rounds to 0.21 or 21 percent.

20. **C** The correct answer is 16.5. To solve this problem, first use the order of operations to solve the right side: $3(7 + 9) = 3(16) = 48$. Next, subtract 15 from each side: $2x + 15 - 15 = 48 - 15 = 2x = 33$. Last, divide each side by 2 to get 16.5:

$$2x + 15 = 3(7 + 9)$$
$$2x + 15 = 3(16)$$
$$2x + 15 = 48$$
$$2x + 15 - 15 = 48 - 15$$
$$2x = 33$$
$$\frac{2x}{2} = \frac{33}{2}$$
$$x = 16.5$$

IX. Mechanical Aptitude

Mechanical aptitude is the ability to work with tools and machines and understand how they work. On the mechanical aptitude portion of the firefighter exam, you'll be asked how to use simple tools and machines. Firefighters are required to work with tools and machines when they are called to fight a fire or to the scene of an accident. If you arrive at the scene of an accident and a person is trapped inside a vehicle, you need to know which tools to use to extract the victim. Firefighters must know how to use various tools to be able to do their job.

You probably have some mechanical-aptitude experience and don't even know it. Have you ever changed a flat tire? You need mechanical knowledge to complete this task. And don't worry if you've never changed a flat tire. In this chapter, you'll learn what you need to know to answer mechanical-aptitude questions on the firefighter exam. We'll also describe the various firefighting tools and tell you how to apply mechanical aptitude to everyday situations.

A. Tools

Firefighters use an array of different tools from everyday hand-held tools such as shovels and hammers to forcible-entry tools such as pike poles and crowbars. While you don't need to be a tool expert to pass the firefighter exam, you need to be able to recognize the most common firefighting tools and know how to use them. Questions related to tools on the test may ask you to identify a pictured tool or give a tool's function. They may also present a scenario or an illustration and ask you to identify the best tool to use based on this information.

In this chapter, we break down the various firefighter tools into the following five categories:

- Cutting tools
- Hand-held tools
- Pushing/Pulling tools
- Prying tools
- Striking tools

Cutting tools, pushing/pulling tools, prying tools, and striking tools are considered *forcible-entry tools,* which are used to breach inaccessible areas. Firefighters may need to ventilate structures or pry open locked doors while extinguishing fires and need the right tools to be able to do so. For example, they may need to use a sledgehammer to create an opening in a wall so they can get to a trapped victim in a house fire.

Note: It would be impossible to name and describe every tool a firefighter may come into contact with on the job, so we describe the most common tools in this chapter—those that are most likely to appear on the test. This list is not comprehensive and many more tools exist.

In addition to knowing how to use a tool correctly, firefighters must follow safety precautions when using tools. They must wear protective clothing, including gloves and goggles, look behind them before they swing a tool such as a sledgehammer so that they don't hit anyone who might be close in range, and know where the on/off switch on a tool is located.

1. Cutting Tools

Cutting tools are used just as their name suggests: to cut. A variety of cutting tools exist, such as axes and saws, and each is used for a specific job. Imagine cutting a piece of paper with a handsaw. It wouldn't work well, would it? A pair of scissors, which are used primarily to cut through paper or fabric, is a better tool for the job. Handsaws are mainly used to cut through wood or metal and not light materials such as paper.

Situations that require the use of cutting tools vary greatly. For example, suppose a utility pole is hit by lightning and falls to the ground. The utility company is on the scene and cuts the electricity from the pole but the workers need help moving it. The firefighters on the scene use a chainsaw to cut through the utility pole, which is made of wood, and easily move the smaller pieces from the ground.

The following table lists some commonly used cutting tools.

Cutting Tools			
Tool	**Use**	**Description**	**Figure**
Bolt Cutter	to cut through metal objects such as chains, iron bars, or metal fences	a hand-held tool with long handles and short blades	
Chainsaw	to cut through trees, lumber, or concrete	a power-operated saw with a chain featuring teeth	

Tool	Use	Description	Figure
Cutting Torch	to slice through thick metals	a device that uses a gas-powered flame (similar to a welding torch)	
Flat-Head Axe	to cut through floors, roofs, or ceilings	a long-handled tool with a 6- or 8-lb steel head (can also be used as a striking tool)	
Handsaw	to cut through wood or metal	a hand-held tool with a variety of handles and blades (examples include carpenter's handsaw, coping saw, keyhole saw, or hacksaw)	
Pick-Head Axe	to cut through floors or roofs (axe side); to pry up floorboards (pick end)	a long-handled tool with a 6- or 8-lb steel head and a pick on one end (can also be used as a prying tool)	

(continued)

Tool	Use	Description	Figure
Reciprocating Saw	uses a push-and-pull motion to cut through a variety of materials	a power-operated saw with a short straight blade	
Rotary (Circular) Saw	to cut through wood, plastic, metal, or concrete	a power-operated saw with circular removable blades	
Ventilation Saw	to make quick cuts in roofs, walls, or ceilings; should never be used to cut metal	a power-operated saw with a chain featuring teeth; similar to a chainsaw	

2. Hand-Held Tools

You're probably familiar with the various types of hand-held tools and may have even used a few of them before to fix things around your home. For example, if you've ever fixed a loose screw, you probably used a screwdriver. These types of tools are found in the toolboxes in most people's garages and include screwdrivers, hammers, pliers, rope, and wrenches.

Firefighters use ordinary hand-held tools every day because these tools come in handy for many firefighting-related tasks. They may use a length of rope to rescue a child stuck in a well or a shovel to move debris at the scene of a house fire.

The following table lists some commonly used hand-held tools.

Hand-Held Tools

Tool	Use	Description	Figure
Clamp	to tightly hold two or more objects together	a fastening device that comes in a variety of shapes and sizes; usually has two adjustable arms that lock together	
Cutters	to cut through materials such as wire, tree limbs, or metal	a hand-held tool with two handles and a set of pincers used to crimp or cut through materials such as wire, tree limbs, or metal	
Hammer	to drive and remove nails; break up materials	a hand-held tool with a short handle and a metal head	
Pliers	to grip objects; bend and cut wire	a hand-held tool with two handles and a set of pincers	
Rake	to break up or smooth out soil or gather materials such as leaves or debris into a pile	a long-handled tool with several prongs	

(continued)

Tool	Use	Description	Figure
Rope	to hoist, secure, or lower objects or persons	a long cord of twisted or braided fibers	
Screwdriver	to tighten and loosen screws	a hand-held tool with a cylindrical handle and thin metal blade (examples include Phillips and flat-head screwdrivers)	
Shovel	to dig holes or carry and move materials such as soil, gravel, or small debris	a long-handled tool with a scoop on one end	
Utility Knife	to cut through light materials such as paper, fabric, or cardboard	a lightweight cutting tool with a retractable blade	
Wrench	to tighten or loosen bolts, nuts, or pipes	a double-ended hand-held tool usually made solely of metal (examples include nonadjustable, adjustable, open-end, and box-end wrenches)	

3. Pushing/Pulling Tools

Firefighters use pushing/pulling tools to check for fire in walls or ceilings or to ventilate structures. One of the most common pushing/pulling tools is the pike pole, which has a long handle either made of wood, fiberglass, or metal, and a metal head with a point and a hook that can be used to push through and pull down a ceiling to check for fire. Pushing/pulling tools all have long handles, but the different heads on them have specific uses.

The following table lists common pushing/pulling tools.

Pushing/Pulling Tools			
Tool	**Use**	**Description**	**Figure**
Clemens Hook	to remove plaster or siding; ventilate ceilings	a long-handled tool that has a curved groove at the end rather than a hook	
Drywall Hook	to remove drywall, wood, plaster, or sheet metal on walls or ceilings	a pole with a long handle and a wide hook featuring teeth; looks like a small rake	
Multipurpose Hook	to remove walls, ceilings, or roofs	a long pole with a multipurpose hook	
New York Hook	heavy-duty prying and pulling; also used for leverage	a long pole with a metal handle and hook	
Pike Pole	to create a hole in a ceiling by pushing (point end); to pull down a ceiling to check for flames (hook end)	a pole with a long, slender body and a metal head that includes a point and hook	
San Francisco Hook	to ventilate and turn off a gas line	a long pole with a built-in gas shut-off and directional slot	

4. Prying Tools

Prying tools are used to force open doors, locks, or windows, which can hamper a firefighter's ability to get inside a burning building. Some prying tools may also be used as a lever to help move heavy objects. A firefighter may use a Hux bar to turn on a fire hydrant at the scene of a fire or a pry bar to help open a door.

The following table lists some commonly used prying tools.

Prying Tools			
Tool	**Use**	**Description**	**Figure**
Claw Tool	to pull up floorboards, baseboards, window casements, or door frames	a heavy-duty prying tool with a hook on one end and a fork on the other end	
Crowbar	to force apart objects; to remove objects such as nails or staples; also used as a lever to move heavy objects	one end is inclined for prying and the other end is curved	
Flat Bar	to pry up objects	a flat metal bar with a curved fork on one end and a flat, slightly inclined fork on the other end	
Halligan Bar	to pry open locked doors	a short bar with a claw at one end and a combination pick/blade at the other end	

Tool	Use	Description	Figure
Hux Bar	to turn hydrants on or off	a wrench with a spur on one end and two receptacles on the other end	
Hydraulic Door Opener	to open doors	a tool operated by a hand pump that uses hydraulic pressure; also called a rabbit tool	
Hydraulic Spreader	to help remove trapped car accident victims	a power-operated tool that uses hydraulic pressure to push apart metal using two arms	
Kelly Tool	to pry and strike	a straight steel bar with a chisel at one end and an adze (a tool with a thin, arched blade) at the other end (can also be used as a striking tool)	
Pry Axe	to pry	a long-handled tool that has a wooden shaft with an axe on one end and a pick on the other end	

(continued)

Tool	Use	Description	Figure
Pry Bar	to gain leverage to open doors or remove boards or concrete blocks	a straight bar; similar to the crowbar, but is not curved; also called a pinch bar	

5. Striking Tools

Striking tools are an important part of forcible-entry operations. They usually have a weighted head and a long handle and are used to break, crush, or hit materials. Firefighters use striking tools in a multitude of situations, such as using a punch to safely shatter a window without harming themselves or those inside or a battering ram to break down a locked door.

The following table lists some commonly used striking tools.

Striking Tools			
Tool	**Use**	**Description**	**Figure**
Battering Ram	to break down objects such as locked doors	a heavy metal bar with handles	
Chisel	used in combination with a striking tool such as a hammer to cut through wood, metal, or stone	a metal tool with a sharp edge	
Mallet	to deliver a soft blow to an object	a hand-held tool with a barrel-shaped head	
Maul	to split wood along the grain; one side can be used as a sledgehammer	a long, hammer-like tool with a dual-sided head; one side resembles an axe	

Tool	Use	Description	Figure
Pick	to break up earth or stone	a heavy-duty tool with a long handle and a metal head with one or two points	
Punch	to shatter windows safely during emergency rescues	a spring-loaded tool; also called a window punch	
Sledgehammer	to initiate heavy-duty pounding or breaking	a long-handled tool with a large metal head	

Practice

Directions (1–15): Answer the following questions based on the information provided.

Question 1 refers to the following figure.

1. This tool would MOST LIKELY be used to

   A. cut through a padlock.
   B. ventilate ceilings.
   C. move heavy objects.
   D. deliver a soft blow to an object.

2. Which of these tools would MOST LIKELY be used to shut off a gas line?

   A. Hux bar
   B. crowbar
   C. San Francisco hook
   D. pliers

3. What do a utility knife, a circular saw, and a flat-head axe have in common?

   A. They are used to tighten or loosen bolts.
   B. They are used to cut through materials.
   C. They are used to pry open locked entryways.
   D. They are used to cut through metals.

4. Which of these tools could be used as both a striking tool and a cutting tool?

   A. pick-head axe
   B. mallet
   C. punch
   D. flat-head axe

Question 5 refers to the following figure.

5. This tool should NOT be used to cut

   A. wood.
   B. metal.
   C. concrete.
   D. plastic.

6. Which of these tools is also called a rabbit tool?

A.

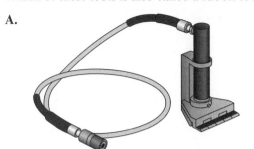

B.

C.

D.

7. Which of these could be used as both a prying tool and a striking tool?

    A.   chisel

    B.   Kelly tool

    C.   Clemens hook

    D.   hammer

Question 8 refers to the following figure.

8. During forcible-entry operations, this tool would MOST LIKELY be used for

    A. cutting.
    B. pulling.
    C. prying.
    D. pushing.

Question 9 refers to the following figure.

9. During forcible-entry operations, this tool would MOST LIKELY be used for

    A. prying.
    B. pushing.
    C. cutting.
    D. pulling.

Question 10 refers to the following figure.

10. What is the name of this tool?

    A. wrench
    B. maul
    C. bolt cutter
    D. clamp

11. What do a sledgehammer, a pick-head axe, and a maul have in common?

    A. They all have dual-sided heads.
    B. They are all prying tools.
    C. They all have a pick on one end.
    D. They are all cutting tools.

12. Which of these tools would MOST LIKELY be used to clean up a fire scene?

    A. New York hook
    B. shovel
    C. punch
    D. pry bar

Questions 13–14 refer to the following figure.

13. What is the name of this tool?

    A. mallet
    B. Pike pole
    C. chisel
    D. sledgehammer

14. What would the tool MOST LIKELY be used for?

    A. to lift heavy objects
    B. to hoist and lower objects
    C. to break a hole in a wall
    D. to cut through materials

15. Which of these tools would MOST LIKELY be used to break down a door?

    A.

    B.

    C.

    D.

Answers

1. **C** The tool pictured is a crowbar, which would most likely be used as a lever to move heavy objects. Bolt cutters would most likely be used to cut through a padlock; a Clemens hook would most likely be used to ventilate ceilings; and a mallet would most likely be used to deliver a soft blow to an object.

2. **C** The San Francisco hook would most likely be used to shut off a gas line. A Hux bar would most likely be used to turn fire hydrants on or off; a crowbar would most likely be used as a lever to move heavy objects or force apart objects; and pliers would most likely be used to grip objects and bend and cut wire.

3. **B** A utility knife, a circular saw, and a flat-head axe are all used to cut through materials.

4. **D** The flat-head axe, which has a 6- or 8-pound steel head with an axe on one side, could be used as both a striking and cutting tool.

5. **B** The tool pictured is a ventilation saw, which is used to make quick cuts in roofs, walls, or ceilings. It should never be used to cut metal.

6. **A** The hydraulic door opener, which is a tool operated by a hand pump that uses hydraulic pressure, is also called a rabbit tool. The other tools are a sledgehammer, a hydraulic spreader, and a chainsaw.

7. **B** The Kelly tool, which has a chisel on one end and an adze on the other end, could be used as both a prying tool and a striking tool.

8. **A** The tool pictured is a cutting torch, which is used to cut through thick metals. It would most likely be used for cutting in forcible-entry operations.

9. **A** The tool pictured is a pry bar, which is used to gain leverage to open doors. It would most likely be used for prying in forcible-entry operations.

10. **D** The tool pictured is a clamp, which is a device used to hold two or more objects tightly together.

11. **A** A sledgehammer, a pick-head axe, and a maul all have dual-sided heads.

12. **B** A shovel would most likely be used to clean up a fire scene. A New York hook is used for heavy-duty prying and pulling as well as leverage; a punch is used to shatter glass typically during emergency rescues; and a pry bar is used for leverage to open doors or remove boards or concrete blocks.

13. **C** The tool pictured is a chisel.

14. **D** The chisel is typically used in combination with a tool, such as a hammer, to cut through materials such as wood, metal, or stone.

15. **C** A battering ram would most likely be used to break down a door. A pike pole would most likely be used to pull down a ceiling to check for flames; a pry axe would most likely be used to pry up materials or pry open objects; and a rake would most likely be used to break up, smooth out, or gather materials.

B. Mechanical Devices

Mechanical devices are tools or machines that help make everyday tasks easier. For example, you can lift a heavy item such as a box with your arms, but you're restricted by the amount of weight you can lift. To make this task easier, you can use a lever or a pulley to lift the box. Mechanical devices aren't technically necessary to complete a job, but they make certain jobs less difficult.

Because firefighters are required to work with machinery, tools, and safety equipment, they should understand how to predict the outcome of specific mechanical activities using the following devices:

- Gears
- Inclined planes
- Levers
- Pulleys
- Screws
- Springs
- Wheels and axles

These machines give firefighters a mechanical advantage, which is the number of times a machine multiplies an applied force. These types of questions on the firefighter exam ask you to predict the outcome of various mechanical activities and may ask you the purpose of specific mechanical devices.

Questions on the firefighter exam about mechanical devices require mathematical skills such as multiplication and division. For more information about solving math problems on the firefighter exam, see Chapter VIII.

1. Gears

A *gear* is a rotating wheel that has teeth or cogs that fit together with another gear to transmit torque, or a force that produces rotation. A gear is a form of a wheel and axle, which consists of a large wheel that rotates around a smaller wheel. (You will learn more about wheels and axles later in this section.)

Everyday items such as bicycles, clocks, and can openers have gears. When two gears' teeth interlock, the gears rotate in opposite directions. When two gears are joined by another object, such as a chain, they spin in the same direction. Keep in mind that smaller gears rotate faster and at more revolutions than a larger gear. Gears of the same size and that have the same number of teeth rotate the same number of revolutions per minute, or at the same speed.

To answer questions about gears on the firefighter exam, keep in mind the following tips:

- Identify the *driver gear,* which is the gear for which the direction of rotation is provided. This gear's movement determines the movement of the other gears it makes contact with. For example, if the driver gear is spinning counterclockwise, the gear it is in contact with is spinning clockwise.
- For questions that ask you to figure out the direction a gear is rotating, but the gear is not in contact with the driver gear, you should first determine the direction of the gears that are in contact with the driver gear.

Tip: The easiest way to answer questions about gears on the firefighter exam is by drawing a diagram of exactly what the question is describing, if one is not already provided. Use arrows to indicate which direction each gear is rotating, so you don't get confused.

EXAMPLE:

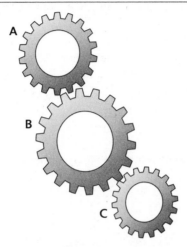

Based on the figure above, if Gear B rotates in a clockwise direction, Gear A rotates

A. clockwise.
B. in the same direction of Gear B.
C. in the opposite direction of Gear C.
D. counterclockwise.

The correct answer is **D**. According to the illustration, the teeth of Gear B and Gear A are interlocked, so the gears must spin in opposite directions. Gear B is the driver gear because you're given the direction of its rotation. This means if Gear B rotates in a clockwise direction, then Gear A and Gear C would have to rotate in a counterclockwise direction.

2. Inclined Planes

An *inclined plane* is a flat surface that makes an angle with the plane of the horizon. This means it is slanted and is higher on one end. A few examples of an inclined plane are ramps, sliding boards, and hills. Objects move from the top of an inclined plane to the bottom and vice versa. Think about how fast a child slides down a slide. Now think about how slow a child moves back up the slide. This means objects travel down inclined planes much faster than they travel up them. When you're answering questions about inclined planes, you should consider the size and weight of the object moving up or down the inclined plane as well as the way forces such as gravity or friction affect an object's movement.

Tip: The steeper the inclined plane, or the larger the angle of an inclined plane, the faster an object will move down it. Therefore, the smaller the angle of an inclined plane, the slower an object will move down it.

Keep these tips in mind when answering questions about inclined planes on the firefighter exam:

- Objects traveling straight down move faster than objects traveling down an inclined plane.
- Objects traveling straight up move slower than objects traveling up an inclined plane.
- It takes more force to move an object up an inclined plane because gravity pulls down on the object and slows it down.
- It takes less force to move an object down an inclined plane because gravity pulls down on the object and speeds it up.
- Objects with a larger surface-to-surface contact area move up and down the inclined plane slower than objects with a smaller surface-to-surface contact area because more friction occurs where the surface of the object meets the surface of the inclined plane.
- Objects with a smaller surface-to-surface contact area move up and down the inclined plane faster than objects with a larger surface-to-surface contact area because less friction occurs where the surface of the object meets the surface of the inclined plane.

Tip: Keep factors such as gravity and friction in mind when answering questions about inclined planes on the firefighter exam.

EXAMPLE:

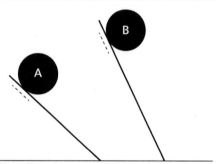

*Dotted line represents friction

Ball A and B are the same size and weight. Based on the figure above, what will MOST LIKELY happen?

- **A.** Ball A will reach the bottom before Ball B.
- **B.** Ball A and B will reach the bottom at the same time.
- **C.** Ball B will reach the bottom before Ball A.
- **D.** Ball B will roll, but Ball A will not move.

The correct answer is **C**. Remember, the steeper an inclined plane, the faster an object will travel down it. Because Ball B is on a steeper inclined plane than Ball A, it will roll faster and more quickly than Ball A. This means Ball B will reach the bottom before Ball A.

3. Levers

A *lever* is a device used to lift heavy objects. A lever is made by placing a metal bar (such as the crowbar that you learned about earlier in this chapter) or a wooden bar on a fixed point called a fulcrum. Think about how a seesaw at the playground works. A child sits on one end of the seesaw that is sitting on a fixed point (the fulcrum is in the middle) and another child sits on the other end of the seesaw. The weight of one child causes the child on the other side to be lifted into the air. Levers work in the same way as seesaws do.

A heavy object is placed on the end of a lever and the lever is positioned over a fulcrum. A person applies force to the other side of the lever to lift the object. The force required to lift the object is less than what the person would need to lift the object with his or her arms and is usually much less than the weight of the object.

> **Tip: The closer the object is to the fulcrum, the less force you have to apply to lift the object. The farther away the object is from the fulcrum, the more force you have to apply to lift the object. If the fulcrum is located in the center of the lever, such as a seesaw, then the lever provides no mechanical advantage as it only works to lift the same amount of weight on both sides.**

Questions on the firefighter exam about levers ask you to determine the force necessary to lift an object using the following formula:

$$w \times d_1 = f \times d_2$$

In other words, the weight of the object multiplied by the distance from the object to the fulcrum is equal to the force necessary to lift the object multiplied by the distance from the fulcrum to you.

EXAMPLE:

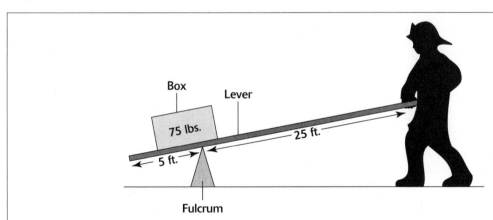

Based on the figure above, how many pounds of force must the firefighter apply to the lever to lift the box?

A. 5
B. 15
C. 75
D. 125

The correct answer is **B.** To answer this question, use the formula $w \times d_1 = f \times d_2$ and plug the information you know into the formula. The weight of the object is 75 pounds, so $w = 75$. The distance from the box to the fulcrum is 5 feet, so $d_1 = 5$. The distance from the firefighter to the fulcrum is 25 feet, so $d_2 = 25$. Solve for force (f):

$$w \times d_1 = f \times d_2$$
$$75 \times 5 = f \times 25$$
$$\frac{375}{25} = \frac{25f}{25}$$
$$15 = f$$

The firefighter would need to exert 15 pounds of force to lift the 75-pound box.

4. Pulleys

A *pulley,* like a gear, is another variation of the wheel and axel. It includes a wheel with a grooved rim and a rope or belt that runs along the groove. It's used to change the direction of an applied force to lift heavy objects. In simpler terms, you pull down to lift something up. Pulleys operate many everyday items such as mini blinds and flags. You tug at the rope to raise the blind or flag and the rope gets longer as the blind or flag goes up.

Pulleys can either have one wheel and a rope or two wheels connected by a belt or chain—which is similar to the gears on a bicycle that are connected by a chain. In a two or more pulley setup, also called a *belt-drive pulley,* one wheel's rotation causes the belt to turn, which causes the other wheel to rotate. A few examples of belt-drive pulleys include a fan belt in a car's engine or the conveyor belt at the grocery store. All wheels in a belt-drive pulley setup rotate in the same direction regardless of size unless the belt is crossed. If the belt is crossed in a belt-drive pulley setup, the wheels rotate in the opposite direction.

Tip: Just like gears, small pulleys rotate at a faster speed and make more revolutions per minute than larger pulleys.

EXAMPLE:

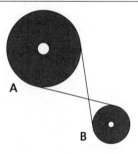

Based on the figure above, Pulley A spins

A. slower than Pulley B.
B. clockwise.
C. faster than Pulley B.
D. counterclockwise.

The correct answer is **A.** From the figure, you can't determine which direction either pulley is turning, so choices B and D are incorrect. You can determine, however, that Pulley A is larger than Pulley B, which means that Pulley A spins slower than Pulley B and therefore, makes fewer revolutions per minute.

5. Screws

A *screw* is a cylinder with an inclined plane wrapped around it. A perfect example of what a screw looks like is a spiral slide at a playground. Screws are inserted into another object by rotating them clockwise into the object. They are removed from an object by rotating them counterclockwise.

Screws have ridges around them called *threads.* These threads either fit into an object's grooves to hold it in place or cut into an object to lock it in place. A nut is an example of an object with grooves that fit a screw. Reverse-thread screws are rotated counterclockwise into an object and rotated clockwise when removed from an object. The space between the threads is called the *pitch* of the screw. The slope of the inclined plane determines the pitch. If the slope is steep, the screw will have wide threads—which are more difficult to rotate into an object than a screw with narrow threads.

Tip: By rotating a screw clockwise into an object, it creates a tight bond. By rotating a screw counterclockwise out of an object, it creates a loose bond. To help you remember the correct way to turn a screw to either tighten or loosen it, repeat the phrase "righty-tighty, lefty-loosey."

EXAMPLE:

A B

Based on the figure above, which of the following statements is true?

A. Screw A is more difficult to insert into an object than Screw B.

B. Screw A is a reverse-thread screw, and Screw B is a standard-thread screw.

C. Screw B is more difficult to insert into an object than Screw A.

D. Screw B is a reverse-thread screw, and Screw A is a standard-thread screw.

The correct answer is **C.** Based on the figure, you cannot determine if Screw A or Screw B are standard-thread or reverse-thread screws. You can determine, however, that Screw B has wider threads than Screw A. Wider threads make a screw more difficult to rotate into an object.

6. Springs

A *spring* is an elastic coil typically made out of metal that is able to retain its shape after being stretched or compressed. Springs can be found in everyday objects such as clocks, ink pens, and cars. As a child, you may have played with a toy called a Slinky, which is a perfect example of a spring that bounces and stretches.

For the questions about springs on the firefighter exam, you can assume that all springs return to their original shape—even when they have been stretched too far, exceeding their elastic limit—and behave linearly. This means that a spring that stretches 2 inches under a pull of 25 pounds will stretch 4 inches under a pull of 50 pounds.

These questions will deal with springs that are either arranged parallel (side-by-side) or in a series (end-to-end). When springs are arranged parallel, the pulling force is divided equally between each spring. Let's say you have 3 springs of the same size and each one stretches 3 inches under a pull of 9 pounds on each. If you set them up parallel under a pull of 9 pounds, each spring only bears one-third of the weight, or 3 pounds, and will stretch one-third as much, or 1 inch. When springs are arranged in a series, the pulling force passes through each spring. Let's use the same example above: You have three springs of the same size and each spring stretches 3 inches under a pull of 9 pounds on each. If you arrange them in a series, each spring will stretch 3 inches under a pull of 9 pounds.

EXAMPLE:

> A spring bearing a 5-pound weight stretches 1 inch. If you were to increase the weight to 20 pounds, how many inches would the spring stretch?
>
> **A.** 2 in
> **B.** 3 in
> **C.** 4 in
> **D.** 5 in

The correct answer is **C.** To solve this problem, first determine how many times heavier the new weight is than the old weight. To do this, divide the new weight by the old weight: $20 \div 5 = 4$. Next, multiply this number by the number of inches the spring stretches under the old weight: $4 \times 1 = 4$. If you increase the weight by four times, the spring would stretch 4 inches.

7. Wheels and Axles

The wheel and axle is a simple machine that consists of a large wheel connected to a smaller one, which is called an axle. The wheel rotates around the axle and both rotate at the same time. The wheel moves a larger distance than the axle does in one full rotation. Think about how a Ferris wheel works. A large wheel is connected to a smaller wheel. Both wheels turn, but the larger wheel moves a larger distance than the smaller one. The same is true for a doorknob or a faucet. A wheel and axle work in the same way as a lever and fulcrum do—the wheel rotates around the axle.

Tip: Turning the axle takes great force, but the wheel gives you a mechanical advantage and allows you to turn the axle with much less force.

Questions on the firefighter exam about wheels and axles require you to determine the mechanical advantage by dividing the radius of the wheel by the radius of the axle, using the following formula:

$$\text{Mechanical Advantage (MA)} = \frac{\text{radius of wheel}}{\text{radius of axle}}$$

EXAMPLE:

If the radius of a wheel is 48 inches and the wheel's axle is 8 inches, what is the mechanical advantage?

A.   4
B.   6
C.   8
D.   12

The correct answer is **B**. To answer this question, plug the information given into the equation:

$$\text{Mechanical Advantage (MA)} = \frac{\text{radius of wheel}}{\text{radius of axle}}$$

$$\text{MA} = \frac{48}{8}$$

$$\text{MA} = 6$$

The mechanical advantage is 6.

Practice

Directions (1–15): Answer the following questions based on the information provided.

Question 1 refers to the following figure.

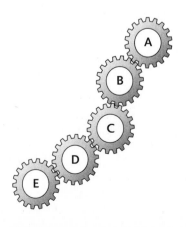

1. The figure shows five gears of the same size. If Gear D rotates in a counterclockwise direction, which other gear(s) will rotate in the same direction?

   A. Gears A, C, and E
   B. Gear B only
   C. Gears C and D
   D. Gear A only

Questions 2–3 refer to the following figure.

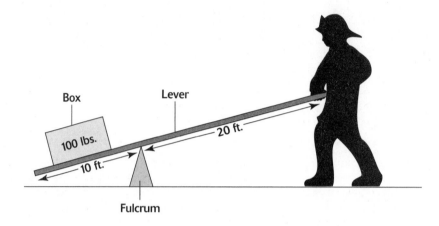

2. How many pounds of force must the firefighter apply to the lever to lift the box?

   A. 25
   B. 50
   C. 75
   D. 100

3. If the firefighter moved the fulcrum 10 feet farther from the box, how many pounds of force would he have to apply to the lift the box?

   A. 12.5
   B. 50
   C. 100
   D. 125.5

Question 4 refers to the following figure.

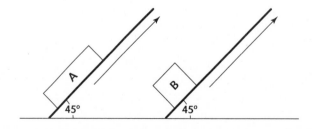

4. Boxes A and B are made of the same material and are the same weight. Which box will require more effort to push it up the inclined plane?

    A. Box A will require more effort to push it up the inclined plane.
    B. Box B will require more effort to push it up the inclined plane.
    C. The boxes will require the same amount of effort to be pushed up the inclined plane.
    D. The boxes will require no effort to be pushed up the inclined plane.

Questions 5–6 refer to the following figure.

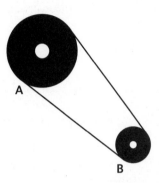

5. Wheel A is twice the size of Wheel B. If Wheel B makes 60 revolutions per minute, how many revolutions per minute does Wheel A make?

    A. 15
    B. 30
    C. 45
    D. 60

6. Which of the following statements about the pulley setup is true?

    A. If Wheel A spins clockwise, Wheel B spins counterclockwise.
    B. If Wheel A spins counterclockwise, Wheel B spins clockwise.
    C. Neither wheel can spin in the pulley setup.
    D. If Wheel A spins clockwise, Wheel B spins clockwise.

Question 7 refers to the following figure.

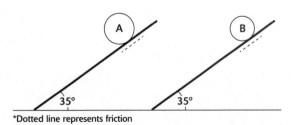

*Dotted line represents friction

7. Ball A and Ball B are different sizes, but they're made of the same material and are the same weight. They're also positioned on equal inclined planes. What will MOST LIKELY happen if both balls begin to roll at the same time?

    A.   Ball A will roll faster than Ball B.
    B.   Ball B will roll faster than Ball A.
    C.   Balls A and B will roll at the same speed.
    D.   Ball A will roll, but Ball B will not move.

8. If the radius of a wheel is 432 inches and the wheel's axle is 12 inches, what is the mechanical advantage?

    A.   6
    B.   18
    C.   24
    D.   36

9. What will happen if you turn a nut on a standard-thread screw clockwise?

    A.   It will be difficult to turn.
    B.   It will move down the screw.
    C.   It will not turn on a standard-thread screw.
    D.   It will move up the screw.

10. If a spring stretches 6 inches under a pull of 12 pounds, how many inches will the spring stretch under a pull of 60 pounds?

    A.   12 in
    B.   18 in
    C.   24 in
    D.   30 in

11. If the radius of a wheel is 112 inches and the wheel's axle is 14 inches, what is the mechanical advantage?

    A.   4
    B.   8
    C.   14
    D.   28

Question 12 refers to the following figure.

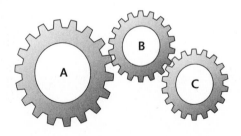

12. Which of the following statements about the gears is true?

    A. Gear A makes fewer revolutions per minute than Gears B and C.
    B. Gears B and C make the same number of revolutions as Gear A.
    C. Gear C makes fewer revolutions per minute than Gear A.
    D. Gears A and C make more revolutions per minute than Gear B.

Questions 13–14 refer to the following figure. The four springs in the figure are the same size.

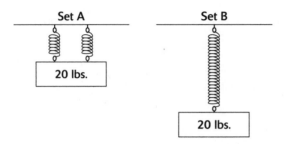

13. In Set A, the stretch of each spring caused by the 20-pound weight is

    A. one-half as much as each spring in Set B.
    B. the same as each spring in Set B.
    C. two times as much as each spring in Set B.
    D. four times as much as each spring in Set B.

14. If the springs in Set B stretched 5 inches under a pull of 20 pounds, how many inches will the springs stretch under a pull of 80 pounds?

    A. 7.5 in
    B. 10 in
    C. 12.5 in
    D. 20 in

Question 15 refers to the following figure.

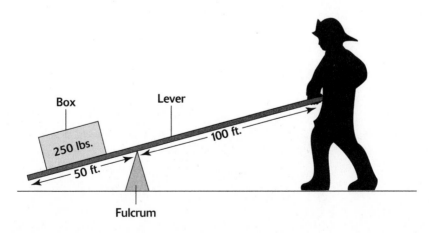

15. How many pounds of force must the firefighter apply to the lever to lift the box?

    A.   25

    B.   75

    C.   125

    D.   200

Answers

1. B If Gear D rotates in a counterclockwise direction, then the two gears its teeth are interlocked with (Gears C and E) must rotate in the opposite direction, so Gears C and E must rotate clockwise. Because Gear C is rotating clockwise and interlocked with Gear B, then Gear B must rotate counterclockwise. Because Gear B is rotating counterclockwise and interlocked with Gear A, then Gear A must rotate clockwise. Therefore, Gear B is the only gear that is rotating in the same direction as Gear D.

2. B To answer this question, use the formula $w \times d_1 = f \times d_2$ and plug the information you know into the formula. The weight of the object is 100 pounds, so $w = 100$. The distance from the box to the fulcrum is 10 feet, so $d_1 = 10$. The distance from the firefighter to the fulcrum is 20 feet, so $d_2 = 20$. Solve for force (f):

$$w \times d_1 = f \times d_2$$
$$100 \times 10 = f \times 20$$
$$\frac{1000}{20} = \frac{20f}{20}$$
$$50 = f$$

3. C To answer this question, use the formula $w \times d_1 = f \times d_2$ and plug the information you know into the formula. The weight of the object is 100 pounds, so $w = 100$. The distance from the box to the fulcrum is 20 feet, so $d_1 = 20$. The distance from the firefighter to the fulcrum is 10 feet, so $d_2 = 10$. Solve for force (f):

$$w \times d_1 = f \times d_2$$
$$100 \times 20 = f \times 10$$
$$\frac{2000}{10} = \frac{10f}{10}$$
$$100 = f$$

4. A The only difference between the two boxes is the size. They weigh the same, are made of the same material, and are positioned at the same angle on the inclined planes. Box A is larger than Box B and therefore, has a larger surface-to-surface contact area with the inclined plane. This means more friction exists between the surface of Box A. Therefore, Box A will require more effort to push it up the inclined plane.

5. B Because Wheel A is twice the size of Wheel B, it rotates half as fast as Wheel B. If Wheel B rotates 60 revolutions per minute, then Wheel A makes half as many revolutions, so 60 divided in half is 30. Wheel A rotates 30 revolutions per minute.

6. **D** All wheels in a belt-drive pulley setup rotate in the same direction regardless of size unless the belt is crossed. Because the belt is not crossed, Wheel A and Wheel B would spin in the same direction, so if Wheel A spins clockwise, Wheel B spins clockwise.

7. **B** The only difference between the two balls is the size. They weigh the same, are made of the same material, and are positioned at the same angle on the inclined planes. Because Ball B is smaller than Ball A, Ball B has a smaller surface-to-surface contact area with the inclined plane and will roll down the inclined plane faster than Ball A.

8. **D** To answer this question, plug the information given into the equation:

$$\text{Mechanical Advantage (MA)} = \frac{\text{radius of wheel}}{\text{radius of axle}}$$
$$\text{MA} = \frac{432}{12}$$
$$\text{MA} = 36$$

The mechanical advantage is 36.

9. **D** When a standard-thread screw is turned clockwise, it will tighten, so this means the nut will move up the screw.

10. **D** To solve this problem, first determine how many times heavier the new weight is than the old weight. To do this, divide the new weight by the old weight: $60 \div 12 = 5$. Next, multiply this number by the number of inches the spring stretches under the old weight: $5 \times 6 = 30$. If you increase the weight by five times, the spring would stretch 30 inches.

11. **B** To answer this question, plug the information given into the equation:

$$\text{Mechanical Advantage (MA)} = \frac{\text{radius of wheel}}{\text{radius of axle}}$$
$$\text{MA} = \frac{112}{14}$$
$$\text{MA} = 8$$

The mechanical advantage is 8.

12. **A** Because Gear A is larger than Gears B and C, Gear A makes fewer revolutions per minute than Gears B and C. Because Gears B and C are the same size, they make the same number of revolutions per minute.

13. **A** The springs in Set A distribute the 20 pounds of weight evenly therefore, each spring bears 10 pounds. The springs in Set B bear the full 20 pounds of weight. Since 10 is half of 20, each spring in Set A bears one-half as much as each spring in Set B.

14. **D** To solve this problem, first determine how many times heavier the new weight is than the old weight. To do this, divide the new weight by the old weight: $80 \div 20 = 4$. Next, multiply this number by the number of inches the springs stretch under the old weight: $4 \times 5 = 20$. If you increase the weight by four times, the springs would stretch 20 inches.

15. C To answer this question, use the formula $w \times d_1 = f \times d_2$ and plug the information you know into the formula. The weight of the object is 250 pounds, so $w = 250$. The distance from the box to the fulcrum is 50 feet, so $d_1 = 50$. The distance from the firefighter to the fulcrum is 100 feet, so $d_2 = 100$. Solve for force (f):

$$w \times d_1 = f \times d_2$$
$$250 \times 50 = f \times 100$$
$$\frac{12500}{100} = \frac{100f}{100}$$
$$125 = f$$

X. Full-Length Practice Test with Answer Explanations

Answer Sheet

Section 1

1 Ⓐ Ⓑ Ⓒ Ⓓ	6 Ⓐ Ⓑ Ⓒ Ⓓ	11 Ⓐ Ⓑ Ⓒ Ⓓ	16 Ⓐ Ⓑ Ⓒ Ⓓ
2 Ⓐ Ⓑ Ⓒ Ⓓ	7 Ⓐ Ⓑ Ⓒ Ⓓ	12 Ⓐ Ⓑ Ⓒ Ⓓ	17 Ⓐ Ⓑ Ⓒ Ⓓ
3 Ⓐ Ⓑ Ⓒ Ⓓ	8 Ⓐ Ⓑ Ⓒ Ⓓ	13 Ⓐ Ⓑ Ⓒ Ⓓ	18 Ⓐ Ⓑ Ⓒ Ⓓ
4 Ⓐ Ⓑ Ⓒ Ⓓ	9 Ⓐ Ⓑ Ⓒ Ⓓ	14 Ⓐ Ⓑ Ⓒ Ⓓ	19 Ⓐ Ⓑ Ⓒ Ⓓ
5 Ⓐ Ⓑ Ⓒ Ⓓ	10 Ⓐ Ⓑ Ⓒ Ⓓ	15 Ⓐ Ⓑ Ⓒ Ⓓ	20 Ⓐ Ⓑ Ⓒ Ⓓ

Section 2

1 Ⓐ Ⓑ Ⓒ Ⓓ	6 Ⓐ Ⓑ Ⓒ Ⓓ	11 Ⓐ Ⓑ Ⓒ Ⓓ	16 Ⓐ Ⓑ Ⓒ Ⓓ
2 Ⓐ Ⓑ Ⓒ Ⓓ	7 Ⓐ Ⓑ Ⓒ Ⓓ	12 Ⓐ Ⓑ Ⓒ Ⓓ	17 Ⓐ Ⓑ Ⓒ Ⓓ
3 Ⓐ Ⓑ Ⓒ Ⓓ	8 Ⓐ Ⓑ Ⓒ Ⓓ	13 Ⓐ Ⓑ Ⓒ Ⓓ	18 Ⓐ Ⓑ Ⓒ Ⓓ
4 Ⓐ Ⓑ Ⓒ Ⓓ	9 Ⓐ Ⓑ Ⓒ Ⓓ	14 Ⓐ Ⓑ Ⓒ Ⓓ	19 Ⓐ Ⓑ Ⓒ Ⓓ
5 Ⓐ Ⓑ Ⓒ Ⓓ	10 Ⓐ Ⓑ Ⓒ Ⓓ	15 Ⓐ Ⓑ Ⓒ Ⓓ	20 Ⓐ Ⓑ Ⓒ Ⓓ

Section 3

1 Ⓐ Ⓑ Ⓒ Ⓓ	6 Ⓐ Ⓑ Ⓒ Ⓓ	11 Ⓐ Ⓑ Ⓒ Ⓓ	16 Ⓐ Ⓑ Ⓒ Ⓓ
2 Ⓐ Ⓑ Ⓒ Ⓓ	7 Ⓐ Ⓑ Ⓒ Ⓓ	12 Ⓐ Ⓑ Ⓒ Ⓓ	17 Ⓐ Ⓑ Ⓒ Ⓓ
3 Ⓐ Ⓑ Ⓒ Ⓓ	8 Ⓐ Ⓑ Ⓒ Ⓓ	13 Ⓐ Ⓑ Ⓒ Ⓓ	18 Ⓐ Ⓑ Ⓒ Ⓓ
4 Ⓐ Ⓑ Ⓒ Ⓓ	9 Ⓐ Ⓑ Ⓒ Ⓓ	14 Ⓐ Ⓑ Ⓒ Ⓓ	19 Ⓐ Ⓑ Ⓒ Ⓓ
5 Ⓐ Ⓑ Ⓒ Ⓓ	10 Ⓐ Ⓑ Ⓒ Ⓓ	15 Ⓐ Ⓑ Ⓒ Ⓓ	20 Ⓐ Ⓑ Ⓒ Ⓓ

Section 4

1 Ⓐ Ⓑ Ⓒ Ⓓ	6 Ⓐ Ⓑ Ⓒ Ⓓ	11 Ⓐ Ⓑ Ⓒ Ⓓ	16 Ⓐ Ⓑ Ⓒ Ⓓ
2 Ⓐ Ⓑ Ⓒ Ⓓ	7 Ⓐ Ⓑ Ⓒ Ⓓ	12 Ⓐ Ⓑ Ⓒ Ⓓ	17 Ⓐ Ⓑ Ⓒ Ⓓ
3 Ⓐ Ⓑ Ⓒ Ⓓ	8 Ⓐ Ⓑ Ⓒ Ⓓ	13 Ⓐ Ⓑ Ⓒ Ⓓ	18 Ⓐ Ⓑ Ⓒ Ⓓ
4 Ⓐ Ⓑ Ⓒ Ⓓ	9 Ⓐ Ⓑ Ⓒ Ⓓ	14 Ⓐ Ⓑ Ⓒ Ⓓ	19 Ⓐ Ⓑ Ⓒ Ⓓ
5 Ⓐ Ⓑ Ⓒ Ⓓ	10 Ⓐ Ⓑ Ⓒ Ⓓ	15 Ⓐ Ⓑ Ⓒ Ⓓ	20 Ⓐ Ⓑ Ⓒ Ⓓ

Section 5

1 Ⓐ Ⓑ Ⓒ Ⓓ	6 Ⓐ Ⓑ Ⓒ Ⓓ	11 Ⓐ Ⓑ Ⓒ Ⓓ	16 Ⓐ Ⓑ Ⓒ Ⓓ
2 Ⓐ Ⓑ Ⓒ Ⓓ	7 Ⓐ Ⓑ Ⓒ Ⓓ	12 Ⓐ Ⓑ Ⓒ Ⓓ	17 Ⓐ Ⓑ Ⓒ Ⓓ
3 Ⓐ Ⓑ Ⓒ Ⓓ	8 Ⓐ Ⓑ Ⓒ Ⓓ	13 Ⓐ Ⓑ Ⓒ Ⓓ	18 Ⓐ Ⓑ Ⓒ Ⓓ
4 Ⓐ Ⓑ Ⓒ Ⓓ	9 Ⓐ Ⓑ Ⓒ Ⓓ	14 Ⓐ Ⓑ Ⓒ Ⓓ	19 Ⓐ Ⓑ Ⓒ Ⓓ
5 Ⓐ Ⓑ Ⓒ Ⓓ	10 Ⓐ Ⓑ Ⓒ Ⓓ	15 Ⓐ Ⓑ Ⓒ Ⓓ	20 Ⓐ Ⓑ Ⓒ Ⓓ

CUT HERE

Section 6

1 Ⓐ Ⓑ Ⓒ Ⓓ	6 Ⓐ Ⓑ Ⓒ Ⓓ	11 Ⓐ Ⓑ Ⓒ Ⓓ	16 Ⓐ Ⓑ Ⓒ Ⓓ
2 Ⓐ Ⓑ Ⓒ Ⓓ	7 Ⓐ Ⓑ Ⓒ Ⓓ	12 Ⓐ Ⓑ Ⓒ Ⓓ	17 Ⓐ Ⓑ Ⓒ Ⓓ
3 Ⓐ Ⓑ Ⓒ Ⓓ	8 Ⓐ Ⓑ Ⓒ Ⓓ	13 Ⓐ Ⓑ Ⓒ Ⓓ	18 Ⓐ Ⓑ Ⓒ Ⓓ
4 Ⓐ Ⓑ Ⓒ Ⓓ	9 Ⓐ Ⓑ Ⓒ Ⓓ	14 Ⓐ Ⓑ Ⓒ Ⓓ	19 Ⓐ Ⓑ Ⓒ Ⓓ
5 Ⓐ Ⓑ Ⓒ Ⓓ	10 Ⓐ Ⓑ Ⓒ Ⓓ	15 Ⓐ Ⓑ Ⓒ Ⓓ	20 Ⓐ Ⓑ Ⓒ Ⓓ

Section 7

1 Ⓐ Ⓑ Ⓒ Ⓓ	6 Ⓐ Ⓑ Ⓒ Ⓓ	11 Ⓐ Ⓑ Ⓒ Ⓓ	16 Ⓐ Ⓑ Ⓒ Ⓓ
2 Ⓐ Ⓑ Ⓒ Ⓓ	7 Ⓐ Ⓑ Ⓒ Ⓓ	12 Ⓐ Ⓑ Ⓒ Ⓓ	17 Ⓐ Ⓑ Ⓒ Ⓓ
3 Ⓐ Ⓑ Ⓒ Ⓓ	8 Ⓐ Ⓑ Ⓒ Ⓓ	13 Ⓐ Ⓑ Ⓒ Ⓓ	18 Ⓐ Ⓑ Ⓒ Ⓓ
4 Ⓐ Ⓑ Ⓒ Ⓓ	9 Ⓐ Ⓑ Ⓒ Ⓓ	14 Ⓐ Ⓑ Ⓒ Ⓓ	19 Ⓐ Ⓑ Ⓒ Ⓓ
5 Ⓐ Ⓑ Ⓒ Ⓓ	10 Ⓐ Ⓑ Ⓒ Ⓓ	15 Ⓐ Ⓑ Ⓒ Ⓓ	20 Ⓐ Ⓑ Ⓒ Ⓓ

Section 8

1 Ⓐ Ⓑ Ⓒ Ⓓ	6 Ⓐ Ⓑ Ⓒ Ⓓ	11 Ⓐ Ⓑ Ⓒ Ⓓ	16 Ⓐ Ⓑ Ⓒ Ⓓ
2 Ⓐ Ⓑ Ⓒ Ⓓ	7 Ⓐ Ⓑ Ⓒ Ⓓ	12 Ⓐ Ⓑ Ⓒ Ⓓ	17 Ⓐ Ⓑ Ⓒ Ⓓ
3 Ⓐ Ⓑ Ⓒ Ⓓ	8 Ⓐ Ⓑ Ⓒ Ⓓ	13 Ⓐ Ⓑ Ⓒ Ⓓ	18 Ⓐ Ⓑ Ⓒ Ⓓ
4 Ⓐ Ⓑ Ⓒ Ⓓ	9 Ⓐ Ⓑ Ⓒ Ⓓ	14 Ⓐ Ⓑ Ⓒ Ⓓ	19 Ⓐ Ⓑ Ⓒ Ⓓ
5 Ⓐ Ⓑ Ⓒ Ⓓ	10 Ⓐ Ⓑ Ⓒ Ⓓ	15 Ⓐ Ⓑ Ⓒ Ⓓ	20 Ⓐ Ⓑ Ⓒ Ⓓ

Section 9

1 Ⓐ Ⓑ Ⓒ Ⓓ	6 Ⓐ Ⓑ Ⓒ Ⓓ	11 Ⓐ Ⓑ Ⓒ Ⓓ	16 Ⓐ Ⓑ Ⓒ Ⓓ
2 Ⓐ Ⓑ Ⓒ Ⓓ	7 Ⓐ Ⓑ Ⓒ Ⓓ	12 Ⓐ Ⓑ Ⓒ Ⓓ	17 Ⓐ Ⓑ Ⓒ Ⓓ
3 Ⓐ Ⓑ Ⓒ Ⓓ	8 Ⓐ Ⓑ Ⓒ Ⓓ	13 Ⓐ Ⓑ Ⓒ Ⓓ	18 Ⓐ Ⓑ Ⓒ Ⓓ
4 Ⓐ Ⓑ Ⓒ Ⓓ	9 Ⓐ Ⓑ Ⓒ Ⓓ	14 Ⓐ Ⓑ Ⓒ Ⓓ	19 Ⓐ Ⓑ Ⓒ Ⓓ
5 Ⓐ Ⓑ Ⓒ Ⓓ	10 Ⓐ Ⓑ Ⓒ Ⓓ	15 Ⓐ Ⓑ Ⓒ Ⓓ	20 Ⓐ Ⓑ Ⓒ Ⓓ

Section 10

1 Ⓐ Ⓑ Ⓒ Ⓓ	6 Ⓐ Ⓑ Ⓒ Ⓓ	11 Ⓐ Ⓑ Ⓒ Ⓓ	16 Ⓐ Ⓑ Ⓒ Ⓓ
2 Ⓐ Ⓑ Ⓒ Ⓓ	7 Ⓐ Ⓑ Ⓒ Ⓓ	12 Ⓐ Ⓑ Ⓒ Ⓓ	17 Ⓐ Ⓑ Ⓒ Ⓓ
3 Ⓐ Ⓑ Ⓒ Ⓓ	8 Ⓐ Ⓑ Ⓒ Ⓓ	13 Ⓐ Ⓑ Ⓒ Ⓓ	18 Ⓐ Ⓑ Ⓒ Ⓓ
4 Ⓐ Ⓑ Ⓒ Ⓓ	9 Ⓐ Ⓑ Ⓒ Ⓓ	14 Ⓐ Ⓑ Ⓒ Ⓓ	19 Ⓐ Ⓑ Ⓒ Ⓓ
5 Ⓐ Ⓑ Ⓒ Ⓓ	10 Ⓐ Ⓑ Ⓒ Ⓓ	15 Ⓐ Ⓑ Ⓒ Ⓓ	20 Ⓐ Ⓑ Ⓒ Ⓓ

CUT HERE

Section 1: Observation

Time: 25 minutes

20 questions

Directions (1–20): Answer the following questions solely on the basis of the information provided.

Questions 1–4 refer to the following figure and passage.

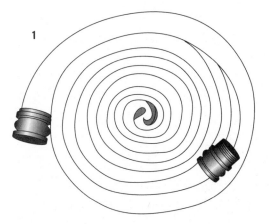

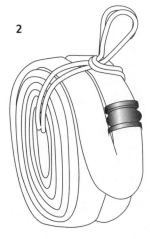

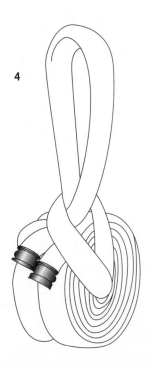

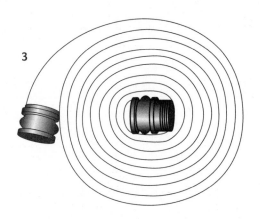

When hoses are not in use, firefighters must roll them and then store them properly. The way firefighters roll a hose depends on what the hose will be used for in the future. Four of the most common types of rolls are the straight roll, the donut roll, the twin donut roll, and the self-locking twin donut roll. No matter which roll firefighters use, they must also make sure the couplings are protected.

A *straight roll* is used for easy loading and rack storage. Sometimes, firefighters even use a straight roll when they know the hoses will be washed at the firehouse later on. To form a straight roll, firefighters start with the male coupling and roll the hose toward the other end. When the entire length of the hose has been rolled, the female coupling should hang loose.

Firefighters use a *donut roll* when they plan on using the hose, deploying it straight from the roll. Donut rolls are advantageous because they allow for both couplings to be exposed, thus they can be quickly accessed in the event of a fire. Many firefighters favor donut rolls because they know that when the hose is unraveled, it is less likely to tangle or kink than a straight roll.

When employing a *twin-donut roll,* firefighters also need a strap that will help hold the hose together and make carrying it to the scene easier. Many firefighters choose to offset both ends of the hose by about 1 foot when they're wrapping the hose. This allows for the male and female couplings to join together on the outside of the hose, which makes both couplings available at all times. Oftentimes, two firefighters are needed to complete this type of roll. Once a firefighter finishes coupling the hose, he or she then ties a strap through the middle of it and slings it comfortably onto his or her shoulder.

Finally, some firefighters like to use a *self-locking twin-donut roll* when rolling hoses. This type of roll is constructed and looks similar to a twin-donut roll, except part of the hose itself acts as a carrying strap. Instead of coupling the ends of the hoses, both are left exposed and unattached. Firefighters who use this rolling method typically adjust the length of the strap so they can easily carry the hose over one shoulder.

1. Using information from the passage above, you can conclude that Hose 2 was rolled using which method?

   A. donut roll
   B. straight roll
   C. twin-donut roll
   D. self-locking twin-donut roll

2. Which two rolls can easily be carried over a firefighter's shoulder?

   A. Hose 1 and Hose 2
   B. Hose 2 and Hose 3
   C. Hose 3 and Hose 4
   D. Hose 2 and Hose 4

3. As your engine company approaches the scene of a house fire, you spot a rolled hose near the door. Both male and female couplings are exposed, but uncoupled. When you arrive at the scene, you grab the hose and immediately get to work connecting it to the nearest water source. Which of the following rolling methods was *most likely* used on the hose you're using?

   A. donut roll
   B. straight roll
   C. twin-donut roll
   D. self-locking twin-donut roll

4. At the station, Firefighter Brady unloads the engine and places the clean hoses on a rack, where they'll sit until they're needed. Because Firefighter Brady didn't need to re-roll any of the hoses, they were *most likely* rolled to look like

   A. Hose 1.
   B. Hose 2.
   C. Hose 3.
   D. Hose 4.

Questions 5–9 refer to the following figure.

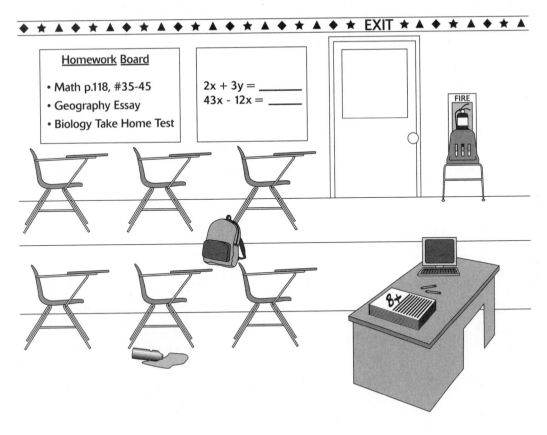

5. How many homework assignments do the students in the classroom have?

   A. one
   B. two
   C. three
   D. four

6. Which tripping hazard is in the middle of the aisle of desks?

   A. papers
   B. pencils
   C. backpack
   D. water bottle

7. The fire extinguisher is located directly to the

   A. left of the teacher's desk.
   B. right of the classroom door.
   C. right of the homework board.
   D. left of the last row of students' desks.

8. If you stood at the front of the classroom and walked down the aisle, in which order would you pass these items?

   A. fire extinguisher, backpack, math board, extra chair
   B. pencils, math board, spilled water, homework board
   C. computer, spilled water, math board, fire extinguisher
   D. exit, homework board, math board, backpack

9. Which of the following is true regarding this illustration?

   A. The students have science homework.
   B. An extra chair is blocking the classroom's exit.
   C. There are no tripping hazards in this classroom.
   D. A pile of graded assignments sits on the teacher's desk.

Questions 10–14 refer to the following figure and passage.

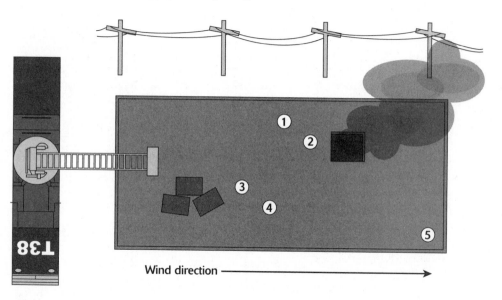

Wind direction ──────────→

When firefighters must work on the roof of a building, they must take many safety precautions to ensure that they don't fall through any ventilation openings, unnecessarily damage any property, or get trapped on the roof. Most departments recommend that when firefighters are working on the roof of a building, they work in pairs and stick together at all times. They must be aware of unsafe roof conditions such as melting asphalt or spongy (unstable) roofs. Firefighters should always work with the wind at their backs, especially when creating an opening in the roof. They also need to be aware of any obstructions on the roof, such as heavy materials. Firefighters must keep in mind that as buildings burn, the ceiling and its structural supports may weaken.

Before climbing onto a roof, firefighters should be sure they're wearing the proper Self Contained Breathing Apparatus (SCBA) gear. When they reach the roof, they should ensure that they have at least two ways to exit the roof. They may leave the roof via roof ladders, emergency staircases, or elevated platforms. If power lines are nearby, they must pay close attention to the location of the lines. If the lines break during the event, they risk electrocution.

10. Which of the following poses the MOST danger to the firefighters on the roof in this diagram?

A. wind direction

B. one means of escape

C. broken electrical lines

D. heavy materials on the roof

11. When there's an opening on the roof, one firefighter is typically assigned the task of guarding the opening to be sure his fellow firefighters don't fall through. In the diagram above, which firefighter is *most likely* performing this task?

A. Firefighter 1

B. Firefighter 2

C. Firefighter 4

D. Firefighter 5

12. Based on information provided, firefighters should always be aware of obstructions on the roof because an obstruction may

A. be too heavy for firefighters to lift.

B. electrocute all firefighters on the roof.

C. place extra strain on the roof and cause it to collapse.

D. prevent firefighters from rescuing people in the building.

13. According to the passage, which of the following is NOT true?

A. Melting asphalt may create dangerous conditions for firefighters working on a roof.

B. All firefighters are responsible for only themselves when on the roof of a burning building.

C. When ventilating a roof, firefighters should create the opening with the wind at their backs.

D. Firefighters that climb onto the roof of a building must be wearing their department-issued helmets.

14. Which of the following firefighters in the diagram is putting himself at the MOST risk?

A. Firefighter 1

B. Firefighter 3

C. Firefighter 4

D. Firefighter 5

Questions 15–17 refer to the following figure and passage.

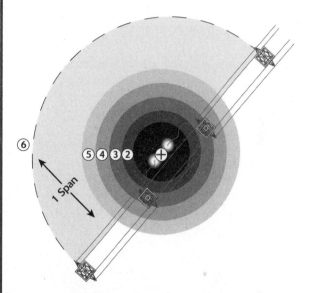

Firefighters regularly respond to emergencies that involve active electrical lines. Despite the frequency of these calls, this type of emergency remains one of the most dangerous firefighters face every day. If firefighters do not act appropriately, they may be injured or even killed. When firefighters arrive on the scene of an electrical emergency, they should assume that all lines are energized and request help from the utility company. While the utility company works, firefighters may control the scene.

While controlling the scene, firefighters are required to keep all untrained personnel, victims, and bystanders away from any dangerous areas. These include all areas that have wire fences or other metal objects. This also includes the area where the downed electrical line has fallen (called the point of contact) and areas close by. Firefighters should work at a distance of at least one span between utility poles until the power has been shut off.

15. Firefighters on the scene of an electrical emergency would be *least likely* to

    A.   control the scene.

    B.   rescue trapped victims.

    C.   turn off the power supply.

    D.   avoid the point of contact.

16. Assuming the electrical lines are energized, which firefighter in the diagram above is the safest on the scene?

    A.   Firefighter 3

    B.   Firefighter 4

    C.   Firefighter 5

    D.   Firefighter 6

17. What is the MAIN reason bystanders and firefighters should avoid areas with wire fences at the scene of an electrical emergency?

    A.   Fences may catch fire and burn them.

    B.   Fences may collapse, trapping them beneath.

    C.   Their clothing may get caught on any broken pieces of fences.

    D.   They may be electrocuted if they touch fences that have been energized.

Questions 18–20 refer to the following figure.

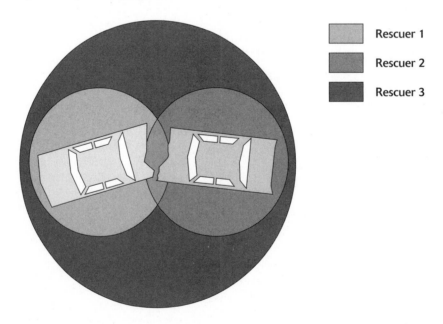

Rescuer 1

Rescuer 2

Rescuer 3

At the scene of a motor vehicle accident, firefighters must assess the need for extrication activities before taking any direct action. To thoroughly assess the accident, the number of firefighters needed is equal to the number of cars involved in the wreck. If extra personnel are available, they can check the area around the cars to ensure there are no additional issues. These issues may include victims who have been thrown from their vehicles, damage to structures or utility poles that may cause further damage to the vehicles involved, and spills involving flammable liquids. If the firefighters inspecting the vehicles find victims who are both trapped and not trapped, they should help the victims who are not trapped from the car before attempting to rescue victims who are stuck.

18. Why do firefighters MOST LIKELY remove victims who are not trapped in damaged cars before victims who are?

   A. to make room for personnel to extricate the trapped victims
   B. to assess and treat victims who may have life-threatening injuries
   C. to give firefighters trained in first-aid more responsibilities
   D. to get all victims out of looming danger, such as power lines

19. The fewest number of firefighters needed to thoroughly assess the accident depicted above is

   A. one.
   B. two.
   C. three.
   D. four.

20. According to the passage, if Rescuer 3 were available to work the scene of the accident in the above diagram, he or she would look for all of the following EXCEPT

   A. utility poles with energized lines.
   B. victims who are stuck in their cars.
   C. spills of flammable liquid, such as gas or oil.
   D. trees that may be cracked or in danger of collapsing.

IF YOU FINISH BEFORE TIME IS CALLED, CHECK YOUR WORK ON THIS SECTION ONLY. DO NOT WORK ON ANY OTHER SECTION IN THE TEST.

Section 2: Memory

Time: 45 minutes

20 questions

Directions (1–20): Study the information provided for 10 minutes. Then turn the page and answer the questions. Don't look back.

Questions 1–5 refer to the following passage.

In late December, firefighters from Department 623 receive a report of a residential fire at 8:10 p.m. The fire is located at a single-family dwelling at 512 Blueberry Lane. The firefighters put on their gear and load their equipment in Engine 5 and Engine 8. On the way to the fire, Engine 5 has engine trouble and the driver pulls over to see what's wrong.

Engine 8 reaches the scene of the fire at 8:25 p.m., and firefighters see flames shooting from the front of the structure. Two firefighters lay a supply line from a hydrant located two blocks north of the fire, while the remaining six firefighters initiate incident command. It's unclear if any victims are trapped inside. A neighbor tells the firefighters that a husband and wife live in the home with two young children, but he is unsure if they are home. Three firefighters proceed into the burning two-story home and keep in contact with the other firefighters outside the home via radio.

In the meantime, a firefighter from Engine 5 contacts the unit from Engine 8 to tell them they are on their way and are four minutes from the scene. The three firefighters emerge from inside the house and report there are no victims inside. Some firefighters rush back inside to fight the blaze, which is contained to the walls of a large living room located at the front of the house.

Engine 5 arrives on the scene at 8:40 p.m. and the firefighters onboard give some of the firefighters from Engine 8 a rest. Two firefighters lay an additional line and begin to attack the fire as a third goes inside the structure to help other firefighters already inside.

By 9:05 p.m., the fire has been extinguished, and Engine 8 begins to pack up both engines' equipment, while firefighters from Engine 5 perform salvage duties. Investigators on the scene determine the cause of the fire to be a short in a string of lights on a withering Christmas tree. Both engines arrive back at the firehouse at 10:10 p.m.

1. What time did Engine 5 arrive at the scene of the fire?

   A. 8:25 p.m.
   B. 8:40 p.m.
   C. 9:05 p.m.
   D. 10:10 p.m.

2. How many firefighters from Engine 8 went inside the structure?

   A. three
   B. four
   C. five
   D. six

3. How many people live in the home?

   A. two
   B. three
   C. four
   D. five

4. What was the cause of the fire?

   A. lights on a Christmas tree
   B. a candle left unattended
   C. the pilot light on a gas stove
   D. unknown

5. What was the location of the fire?

   A. 119 Huckleberry Lane
   B. 128 Raspberry Lane
   C. 215 Blackberry Lane
   D. 512 Blueberry Lane

Questions 6–15 refer to the following figure.

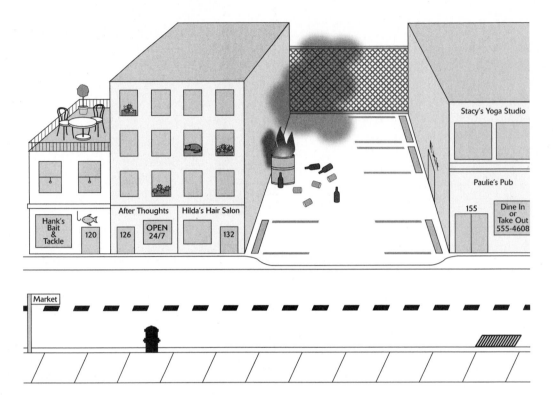

6. The fire in this illustration is located in the

   A. street.
   B. restaurant.
   C. parking lot.
   D. apartment building.

7. How many trees are in this image?

   A. one
   B. two
   C. three
   D. four

8. All of the following are house numbers that appear in this illustration EXCEPT

   A. 120.
   B. 132.
   C. 145.
   D. 155.

9. Which of the following is true about this fire scene?

   A. Hilda's Hair Salon exits into the alley.
   B. Apartments are located above Paulie's Pub.
   C. A fire hydrant is located directly across the street from After Thoughts.
   D. There are five parking spaces in the lot between Hilda's Hair Salon and Paulie's Pub.

10. Which crime has clearly been committed in this illustration?

   A. arson
   B. littering
   C. breaking and entering
   D. destruction of private property

11. Which phone number would you dial to place a take-out order from Paulie's Pub?

   A. 555-0914
   B. 555-4608
   C. 555-8872
   D. 555-0249

12. Which of the following businesses is always open?

   A. Hank's Bait and Tackle
   B. Hilda's Hair Salon
   C. After Thoughts
   D. Stacy's Yoga Studio

13. Which business is located on the second floor of one of the buildings in this illustration?

   A. restaurant
   B. hair salon
   C. yoga studio
   D. bait and tackle shop

14. A storm drain is located across the street from

   A. Paulie's Pub.
   B. After Thoughts.
   C. Hilda's Hair Salon.
   D. Hank's Bait and Tackle.

15. Where is the cat in this image?

   A. on the roof of the bait and tackle shop
   B. in the window above the hair salon
   C. on the fence behind the parking lot
   D. in the lot between the hair salon and the pub

Questions 16–20 refer to the following passage.

In July, firefighters from Department 638 receive a report of a fire at a commercial property at 10:30 p.m. They dress quickly and load their gear into Engine 9 and Engine 11. On the way to the location, Engine 11 is forced to find another route when a vehicle traveling in front of it on Barnhart Avenue has engine trouble and stalls in the lane. Engine 9 arrives at the scene of the fire at 15 Commerce Avenue at 10:45 p.m.

Half of the firefighters lay a supply line from a hydrant located on Drinker Avenue, which runs parallel to the scene, while the others initiate incident command. Three firefighters proceed into the burning structure, which houses a pizza shop, and find that the 42-year-old owner is inside. The firefighters outside the structure contact dispatch via radio to let them know the exact location of the fire, the conditions of the fire, and that they need a paramedic to check the person they found inside the structure.

Engine 11 arrives on the scene at 10:55 p.m. Firefighters with Engine 9 emerge from the structure with the rescued victim at 11:05 p.m. Firefighters with Engine 11 lay an additional line and assist in attacking the fire. The firefighters find that the fire started in the kitchen of the pizza shop, and smoke and flames quickly traveled throughout the one-level structure.

By 11:35 p.m., police and paramedics have arrived and the blaze is under control. Firefighters from both engines perform salvage duties, and department investigators determine the fire was started when a cardboard pizza box fell on a lit stovetop burner. At 12:30 a.m., Engine 9 and Engine 11 pull into Department 638's garage. Firefighters hang and store their equipment, and the department chief begins his paperwork.

16. What was the first thing the firefighters did upon arriving at the scene?

   A. Contact dispatch.

   B. Proceed inside the structure.

   C. Rescue the 42-year-old inside.

   D. Lay a supply line from a hydrant.

17. Why was Engine 11 detained in getting to the scene?

   A. a flat tire

   B. engine trouble

   C. a vehicle stalled in the road

   D. a detour due to construction

18. What time did Engine 9 arrive on the scene?

   A. 10:15 p.m.

   B. 10:45 p.m.

   C. 10:55 p.m.

   D. 11:05 p.m.

19. What was the location of the fire?

   A. 11 Commerce Avenue

   B. 15 Drinker Avenue

   C. 10 Barnhart Avenue

   D. 15 Commerce Avenue

20. Approximately how much time passed between the initial report of fire and when the engines pulled into the station's garage?

   A. 1 hour

   B. 1.5 hours

   C. 2 hours

   D. 4.5 hours

IF YOU FINISH BEFORE TIME IS CALLED, CHECK YOUR WORK ON THIS
SECTION ONLY. DO NOT WORK ON ANY OTHER SECTION IN THE TEST.

Section 3: Spatial Orientation

Time: 25 minutes

20 questions

Directions (1–20): Answer the following questions solely on the basis of the figure provided. For maps of streets, remember to follow the legal direction of the flow of traffic.

Questions 1–5 refer to the following map.

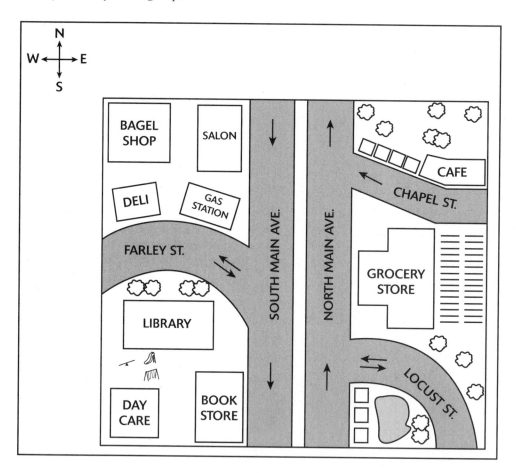

1. If you are at the bookstore, what direction would you walk to get to the café?

   A. northeast

   B. southwest

   C. northwest

   D. southeast

2. You exit the grocery store and proceed to walk west until you reach Farley Street, at which point you turn north and follow South Main Avenue. Following this route, which location will be the last on your left?

   A. bookstore
   B. gas station
   C. salon
   D. library

3. You are standing at the intersection of Locust Street and North Main Avenue. If you walk to the bookstore, proceed north to the intersection of Farley Street and South Main Avenue, and then turn and walk to the east, which location will you eventually arrive at?

   A. deli
   B. grocery store
   C. café
   D. gas station

4. You have just exited the grocery store. You walk to the nearby pond and then start heading west. You see two buildings ahead of you. You pass the first one and enter the second. Where are you?

   A. book store
   B. deli
   C. bagel shop
   D. day care

5. If you are at the salon, what direction would you walk to get to the day care?

   A. northeast
   B. southwest
   C. northwest
   D. southeast

Questions 6–10 refer to the following floor plan.

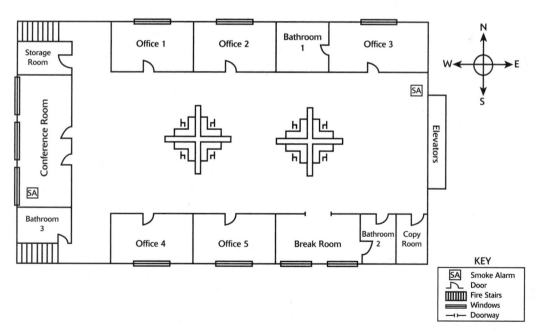

6. You respond to an activated fire alarm at an office building. Upon your arrival on the scene, you ascend the fire stairs on the south side of the building, proceed around the corner, and enter the first room you find on your right. Where are you?

   A. Office 1
   B. Office 2
   C. Office 4
   D. Office 5

7. Upon arriving at the scene of a fire, you learn that a fast-moving fire in the southwest corner of the building has prevented a number of workers in the break room from reaching the emergency stairs they are assigned to use. Which of the following would be the safest way to rescue these victims?

   A. Instruct the victims to proceed north across the main floor until they reach Office 2 and then proceed to the fire stairs at the northwest corner of the building.
   B. Instruct the victims to leave the break room and proceed to the elevators that they will use to escape.
   C. Instruct the victims to crawl on their hands and knees to their assigned emergency exit.
   D. Instruct the victims to prepare to be rescued through the break room's windows.

8. During a fire at the office building, you find yourself facing a bank of elevators. You turn left and then turn left again and proceed forward until you arrive at the second door on your right. At this point, you are standing in front of

   A. Office 2.
   B. the break room.
   C. a bathroom.
   D. Office 3.

9. As you embark on a search-and-rescue mission, you enter the office from the fire stairs on the north side of the building. Once inside, you place your right hand on the wall on your right side. You carefully follow the wall south until you arrive at a door. Finding this door locked, you proceed forward until you reach a second door. Because this door is unlocked, you enter the room and find yourself in

   A. Office 2.
   B. a storage closet.
   C. Office 1.
   D. the conference room.

10. If a fire on a lower floor of the office building prevents the use of both sets of fire stairs, which of the following rooms would BEST be used as an extraction point on victims trapped on this floor?

   A. bathroom
   B. break room
   C. copy room
   D. conference room

Questions 11–15 refer to the following map.

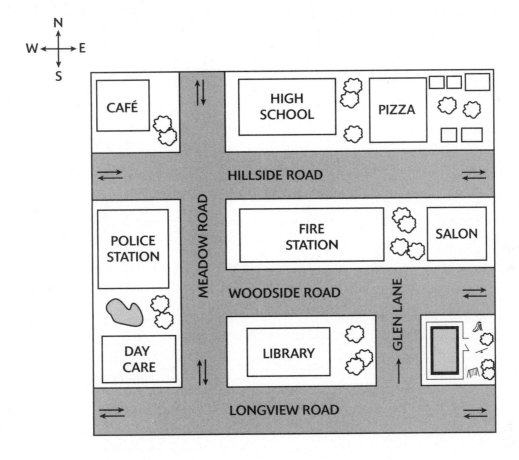

11. Starting at the intersection of Hillside and Meadow Roads, if you walked south, turned left, turned right and then turned right again, you would be closest to the

    A. salon.
    B. fire station.
    C. day care.
    D. library.

12. What is the quickest route to drive from the pizza shop to the day care?

    A. west on Hillside Road, south on Meadow Road, west on Longview Road
    B. west on Woodside Road, south on Meadow Road, west on Longview Road
    C. west on Hillside Road, north on Meadow Road, west on Longview Road
    D. west on Hillside Road, south on Meadow Road, east on Woodside Road

13. You exit the library onto Longview Road. You walk west to the end of the block and turn north. You then walk two blocks north and turn east. Which building are you now standing in front of?

    A. day care
    B. café
    C. fire station
    D. police station

14. If you are at the café, what direction would you walk to get to the library?

    A. northeast
    B. southwest
    C. northwest
    D. southeast

15. If you start from the intersection of Glen Lane and Woodside Road, turn left, turn left again, and then turn right, you will be closest to the

    A. high school.
    B. police station.
    C. day care.
    D. library.

Questions 16–20 refer to the following floor plan.

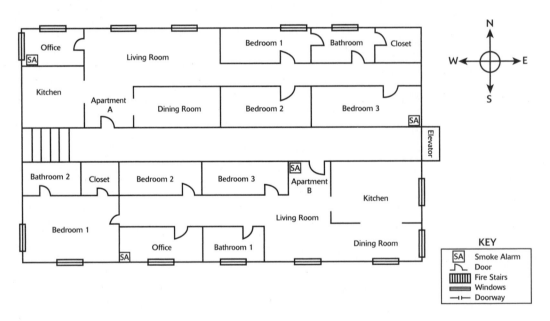

16. You are on the scene of a fire. You have just secured Apartment A and you are asked to check Apartment B for trapped victims. You exit Bedroom 3 and stand in the hallway in Apartment A, facing the living room. If you proceed forward with your left hand on the wall to your left, how many room entrances will you pass by before reaching the exit to the corridor between apartments?

   A. one
   B. two
   C. three
   D. four

17. You arrive at the scene of a fire and proceed up the main stairs. When you reach the floor where the fire is located, you proceed down the main hallway to the first door on your right. You enter this apartment and proceed forward before turning right. You reach the first door on the wall. Where are you?

   A. Bedroom 3 in Apartment B
   B. Bedroom 3 in Apartment A
   C. office in Apartment B
   D. office in Apartment A

18. How many smoke alarms are installed in each apartment?

   A. one
   B. two
   C. three
   D. four

19. You are sent to search for victims in Apartment B. After entering the apartment, you walk straight forward until you find a window directly in front of you. Facing the window, you turn to your left and proceed along the wall until you reach and pass through the entrance to another room. What room are you now in?

   A. bathroom
   B. dining room
   C. kitchen
   D. Bedroom 3

20. You are searching for victims in Apartment A. You exit the office and follow the wall to your left. After passing two windows and turning a corner, you eventually arrive at the entrance to another room. You enter the room and follow the wall to your right and find another doorway, which you quickly enter. In what room are you now standing?

   A. Bedroom 1
   B. Bedroom 2
   C. bathroom
   D. closet

IF YOU FINISH BEFORE TIME IS CALLED, CHECK YOUR WORK ON THIS SECTION ONLY. DO NOT WORK ON ANY OTHER SECTION IN THE TEST.

Section 4: Reading Comprehension

Time: 25 minutes

20 questions

Directions (1–20): Answer the following questions solely on the basis of the information provided.

Questions 1–4 refer to the following information.

The following fires were reported in the town of Kingston. The following descriptions of each fire are based on its determined cause.

- **Restaurant (May 3):** A cook overloaded the deep fryer, which overflowed, causing the oil to catch fire. The kitchen sustained minor damage because the owner used a fire extinguisher to put out the fire before firefighters arrived on the scene. Smoke damage was limited to the kitchen area. The cause of the fire was determined to be accidental.

- **Single-family dwelling (May 14):** A candle was left unattended and ignited some papers. The fire spread to the furniture and draperies. The living room and attic sustained major fire damage. The cause of the fire was determined to be negligence.

- **Trash fire (May 18):** The fire began inside the largest trash receptacle and spread to debris piled beside it. Damage was limited to the waste receptacles, which were not located close to any structures. The cause of the fire was determined to be arson and is under investigation.

- **Multi-family dwelling (May 21):** The third floor sustained major fire damage and the roof was destroyed while the lower floors suffered major water damage. The cause of the fire has not yet been determined.

1. On which day did the trash fire occur?

   A. May 18
   B. May 3
   C. May 21
   D. May 14

2. The cause of the fire has been determined for all of the fires, EXCEPT the

   A. trash fire.
   B. multi-family dwelling.
   C. restaurant.
   D. single-family dwelling.

3. How many structures were damaged by fire on May 18?

   A. one
   B. two
   C. three
   D. none

4. The cause of the single-family dwelling fire is

   A. accidental.
   B. undetermined.
   C. negligence.
   D. arson.

Questions 5–9 refer to the following passage.

Your fire department is dispatched to the scene of a multiple-vehicle crash involving four vehicles on the Davenport Beltway North. A 2010 blue Ford Fiesta driven by Danni Davis was entering the highway from an entrance ramp. Ms. Davis collided with a 1988 black Honda Civic driven by Tyler Miller that entered the right lane from the left between two other vehicles, a 2011 white Toyota Venza driven by Emilio Cruz in front and a 2009 red Chevrolet Malibu driven by Charlotte Santi in the rear. The Civic then struck the Venza, which veered off the road and into a ditch. Ms. Santi was unable to stop and hit the Fiesta.

Mr. Cruz was wearing his seat belt at the time of the accident and complained of moderate neck pain. He had a passenger, a minor child restrained in a child-safety seat, in the back seat. She did not appear to be injured. Both individuals were seated on the berm when rescue personnel arrived.

Ms. Davis was wearing her seat belt at the time of the accident. She had minor scratches to her face and arms and complained of severe pain in her left shoulder. Ms. Davis had exited her vehicle and called 911 immediately following the crash.

Mr. Miller was not wearing his seat belt at the time of the accident and was unconscious when paramedics arrived. He had multiple lacerations on his head, face, and arms. Firefighters noticed he had an open fracture of the left humerus. Mr. Miller had two passengers, a middle-aged male and a teenage female. The male passenger, who was sitting in the rear left seat and was wearing his seat belt, had minor scratches on his face and arms and complained of moderate shoulder and neck pain. The female passenger, who was in the front seat and was wearing her seat belt, had multiple lacerations on her head, face, and arms, and complained of severe neck pain.

All three individuals in the Civic were trapped and had to be removed using hydraulic spreaders. The female passenger stated that Mr. Miller had changed lanes in anticipation of taking an upcoming exit.

Ms. Santi was wearing her seat belt at the time of the accident. She did not appear to be injured, was ambulatory when paramedics arrived, and was checking on other victims when firefighters arrived.

5. The word *ambulatory* (in the last paragraph) MOST nearly means

   A. paralyzed by fear.
   B. hysterical.
   C. able to move about.
   D. confused.

6. Based on the information in the passage, who appears to be the MOST seriously injured individual?

   A. Emilio Cruz
   B. Charlotte Santi
   C. Danni Davis
   D. Tyler Miller

7. How many accident victims were NOT wearing seat belts?

   A. one
   B. two
   C. three
   D. four

8. How many passengers were trapped in vehicles and had to be removed by rescue personnel?

   A. two
   B. three
   C. one
   D. none

9. According to the information in the passage, what color was the vehicle driven by Charlotte Santi?

   A. blue
   B. white
   C. red
   D. black

Questions 10–13 refer to the following table.

Types of Nozzles Firefighters Use	
Type	**Description and Use**
Bresnan Cellar	Has a rotating nozzle tip with two or more outlets that form water jets; the water jets propel the tip, spraying water in a circular pattern; useful for dousing flames in a basement through a hole cut in the floor above.
Penetrator	Long and narrow, this hardened steel tip is designed to be forced through an obstruction such as a wall and deliver water to the other side.
Smooth Bore	Provides the greatest reach and the largest drops of water.
Water Curtain	Involves combustible metals like sodium, uranium, and magnesium; shoots water into the air and, as it falls, covers the area on fire in addition to surrounding areas.

10. Which nozzle would be used to prevent a fire from igniting a nearby dwelling?

    A. smooth bore
    B. penetrator
    C. Bresnan cellar
    D. water curtain

11. Which type of nozzle sprays water jets that cause it to rotate?

    A. water curtain
    B. penetrator
    C. Bresnan cellar
    D. smooth bore

12. Which nozzle allows firefighters to create a hole in an obstruction?

    A. Bresnan cellar
    B. penetrator
    C. smooth bore
    D. water curtain

13. According to the information in the table, which of the following statements is true?

    A. The water curtain nozzle has a rotating tip.
    B. The smooth bore nozzle may only be used when firefighters can get close to the fire.
    C. The penetrator nozzle provides the greatest reach.
    D. The Bresnan cellar nozzle can be inserted through a hole in the floor to attack a basement fire.

Questions 14–17 refer to the following information.

Firefighter Falcone inspected a local commercial/residential property on March 1. She compiled a list of safety violations for the property owner, who was preparing the upper floors of the three-story building for residential occupancy:

- Fire extinguisher on the second floor expired
- Emergency exit signs on the third floor not illuminated due to burned-out bulbs
- Window exits to the fire escape on the second and third floors sealed by paint
- Faulty smoke detector in the second-floor hallway
- Boxes of office supplies partially blocking the stairway exit located beside the ground-floor real-estate office

14. How many violations did Firefighter Falcone find on the second floor?

   A. one

   B. two

   C. three

   D. none

15. How many floors of the building were used for residential purposes?

   A. two

   B. three

   C. four

   D. none

16. What violations did Firefighter Falcone find on the third floor?

   A. The window exit was painted shut and a smoke detector was faulty.

   B. Boxes blocked the stairway exit and the window exit was painted shut.

   C. A fire extinguisher was expired and a smoke detector was faulty.

   D. The window exit was painted shut and emergency exit signs were not illuminated.

17. What was located on the ground floor of the building?

   A. a real-estate office

   B. apartment units

   C. a law office

   D. the property owner's residence

Questions 18–19 refer to the following graph.

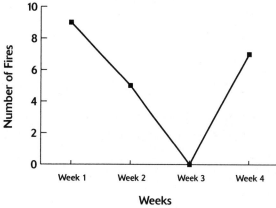

Number of Accidental Fires Each Week in July

18. According to the information in the graph, which of the following statements is true?

   A. The same number of fires occurred in week 1 as in weeks 2 and 3 combined.

   B. Fewer fires occurred in week 4 than in weeks 2 and 3 combined.

   C. Most of the fires in July occurred in week 1.

   D. The least number of fires in July occurred in week 4.

19. According to the information in the graph, how many fires occurred in weeks 3 and 4 combined?

   A. 7

   B. 12

   C. 14

   D. 16

20. According to the information in the graph, which week had the FEWEST number of fires?

   A.   week 1
   B.   week 2
   C.   week 3
   D.   week 4

IF YOU FINISH BEFORE TIME IS CALLED, CHECK YOUR WORK ON THIS SECTION ONLY. DO NOT WORK ON ANY OTHER SECTION IN THE TEST.

Section 5: Verbal Expression

Time: 25 minutes

20 questions

Directions (1–8): Select the misspelled word in each sentence.

1. Water should not be used to douse a fire involving flammible liquids because it can cause the liquids to splatter and spread the fire.

   A. douse
   B. involving
   C. flammible
   D. spread

2. The firefighters responded to a grass fire in a field adjacent to the cemetary at the end of town.

   A. responded
   B. field
   C. adjacent
   D. cemetary

3. On approaching the apartment building, Firefighter Nelson had to altar his plan to use the front entrance when he found it blocked by debris.

   A. approaching
   B. altar
   C. entrance
   D. debris

4. There was a noticable smell of gas at the school; the firefighters who responded contacted the gas company immediately.

   A. noticable
   B. responded
   C. contacted
   D. immediately

5. Firefighter Rodriguez entered the offices on the fourth floor and serched for victims who may have been trapped by the heavy smoke and flames.

   A. entered
   B. fourth
   C. serched
   D. trapped

6. The crew arrived at the apartment building and used the elavator to reach the overheating unit on the roof.

   A. arrived
   B. elavator
   C. overheating
   D. roof

7. The exaust hood was obscured by flames as the grease fire filled the restaurant kitchen with smoke.

   A. exaust
   B. obscured
   C. grease
   D. restaurant

8. Central Fire Station equipment has standardized threads on all its hose cuplings.

   A. equipment
   B. standardized
   C. threads
   D. cuplings

Directions (9–15): Choose the word that best completes the sentence.

9. The firefighter climbed _____ the window to rescue the child inside the building.

   A. around
   B. over
   C. through
   D. along

10. The children listened attentively to the firefighters _____ the 30-minute fire safety demonstration.

    A. after
    B. before
    C. since
    D. during

11. _____ asking for a raise was unexpected because last week they were reprimanded for poor performance.

    A. Their
    B. Theirs
    C. Them
    D. Theirselves

12. The firefighter _____ four certification courses in the last two years without giving up.

    A. will attempt
    B. has attempted
    C. have attempted
    D. will have attempted

13. The chief _____ the media to a demonstration of the new engine before he learned highway construction had delayed delivery.

    A. inviting
    B. invites
    C. will invite
    D. had invited

14. Firefighter Campbell had to carefully maneuver the rescue engine down the dark and _____ street.

    A. narrowest
    B. most narrow
    C. narrow
    D. narrower

15. In areas where residue would be a problem, such as computer rooms, halotron is a _____ extinguishing agent than foam.

    A. good
    B. better
    C. best
    D. more better

Directions (16–17): Select the misspelled word in each sentence.

16. Firefighters may have to climb to the roof of a structure and cut a hole to provide adequate ventilacion before they can begin extinguishing the flames.

    A. structure
    B. adequate
    C. ventilacion
    D. extinguishing

17. Every comercial kitchen should be equipped with a fire extinguisher and all employees should be instructed on its use.

    A. comercial
    B. equipped
    C. extinguisher
    D. instructed

Directions (18–20): Choose the word that best completes the sentence.

18. Carbon monoxide, hydrogen chloride, hydrogen cyanide, and nitrogen dioxide _____ toxic atmospheres associated with fire.

    A. is
    B. are
    C. has
    D. was

19. The fire suppression system _____ activated by heat-sensitive valves and extinguished the flames before they spread beyond the storage closet.

    A. was
    B. has
    C. are
    D. were

20. The second fire engine _____ more hose next year when the planned industrial complex is built.

    A. will have carried
    B. had carried
    C. has carried
    D. will carry

IF YOU FINISH BEFORE TIME IS CALLED, CHECK YOUR WORK ON THIS SECTION ONLY. DO NOT WORK ON ANY OTHER SECTION IN THE TEST.

Section 6: Deductive/Inductive/Logical Reasoning

Time: 25 minutes

20 questions

Directions (1–20): Answer the following questions solely on the basis of the information provided.

Questions 1–4 refer to the following information.

In addition to normal firefighters, a fire department also relies on special personnel to carry out specific duties for the department. Some of these positions include:

- **Fire prevention officer:** Enforces and ensures compliance with fire prevention and fire control laws, ordinances, and regulations
- **Fire/arson investigator:** Investigates fire scenes and makes analytical judgments to determine the origin and cause of a fire
- **Public fire safety instructor:** Responsible for educating the public about fire hazards, fire causes, fire safety, fire prevention, and other fire-related topics
- **Fire protection engineer:** Works with department administrations and assists in the design and implementation of fire protection and prevention systems

1. Your fire department responds to a late-night fire at a downtown business. After a relatively short effort, the flames are extinguished. Although the scene has been secured, the origin of the fire is not immediately apparent and a cause needs to be established. This situation requires the expertise of which fire professional?

   A. fire prevention officer
   B. fire/arson investigator
   C. public fire safety instructor
   D. fire protection engineer

2. Reports indicate that a local nightclub is regularly exceeding its established occupancy limit and may be in violation of other fire-code regulations. Your department needs to address this issue. This situation requires the expertise of which fire professional?

   A. fire prevention officer
   B. fire/arson investigator
   C. public fire safety instructor
   D. fire protection engineer

3. A new office building is being built in a nearby commercial business park. The builders request your department's assistance in designing and installing an appropriate fire prevention system for the building. This situation requires the expertise of which fire professional?

   A. fire prevention officer
   B. fire/arson investigator
   C. public fire safety instructor
   D. fire protection engineer

4. A local elementary school is hosting a fire prevention week seminar for its students. Your department is asked to make a presentation for several classes. This situation requires the expertise of which fire professional?

   A. fire prevention officer
   B. fire/arson investigator
   C. public fire safety instructor
   D. fire protection engineer

Questions 5–8 refer to the following passage.

Two vehicles are traveling at a moderately high rate of speed in opposite directions on a rural road late at night. One of the drivers is feeling drowsy and momentarily closes his eyes. This causes the driver to drift into the other lane and strike the oncoming vehicle head-on. The force of the impact leaves both vehicles heavily damaged and disabled in the middle of the roadway.

Firefighters arrive on the scene and proceed to assess the situation. The driver of the first car is a 35-year-old male who appears dazed and disoriented. He has numerous cuts and scratches from flying shards of glass. He appears to be holding his right arm at an unnatural angle. He also presents with a severe bruise on the right side of his chest and irregular breathing sounds.

The driver of the second vehicle was found sitting on the ground outside his car. He is visibly upset and shaken. He presents with a severe laceration near the top of his forehead that is bleeding heavily and reports a painful headache. He is holding his left ankle at an unnatural angle, but says that it is not painful. He complains of severe abdominal pain and visual examination reveals notable distention and discoloration. Firefighters begin transport procedures to move the patients to a local medical center for further evaluation and treatment.

5. What symptom of the driver of the first vehicle MOST LIKELY indicates a concussion?

   A. He presents with numerous lacerations.
   B. He appears dazed and disoriented.
   C. His right arm is held at an unnatural angle.
   D. He presents with chest bruising and irregular breathing sounds.

6. Why would firefighters MOST LIKELY suspect that the driver of the second car has an internal injury?

   A. He is visibly upset and shaken.
   B. He presents with abdominal distention and discoloration.
   C. He has a severe cranial wound and a painful headache.
   D. He holds his left ankle at an unnatural angle.

7. The driver of the first car seems to have impacted the dashboard with his

   A. head.
   B. right side.
   C. left side.
   D. abdomen.

8. An appropriate title for this passage is

   A. "Nighttime Driving Protocols."
   B. "First Aid in the Field."
   C. "On-Scene Victim Assessment."
   D. "The Dangers of Driving While Tired."

9. Consider the following sequence of numbers:

   2, 7, 12, 17, _____, 27

   Which number correctly completes the sequence?

   A. 18
   B. 19
   C. 21
   D. 22

Question 10 refers to the following series of images.

10. Which image correctly completes the series?

A.

B.

C.

D.

11. Consider the following sequence of numbers:

1, 5, 17, _____, 161, 485

Which number correctly completes the sequence?

A. 53
B. 78
C. 121
D. 145

Question 12 refers to the following series of images.

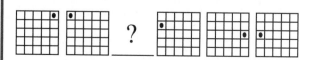

12. Which image correctly completes the series?

A.

B.

C.

D.

Questions 13–15 refer to the following passage.

On occasion, often in instances of explosions or natural disasters, firefighters may be dispatched to the scene of a structural collapse. In the event that a search-and-rescue operation is required to extricate victims trapped within a fallen structure, it is vitally important for firefighters to understand the structural nature of the collapse they are dealing with. Firefighters should be familiar with the four important types of structural collapses:

- **Pancake collapse:** A pancake collapse occurs when two opposing exterior walls of a structure fail. When this happens, the roof and upper floors collapse in on each other and take the form of a stack of pancakes. This type of collapse pattern is unlikely to produce voids wherein survivors may be found.

- **V-shaped collapse:** A V-shaped collapse occurs when the floor and/or roof fail, but the outer walls remain intact. This type of collapse often results in the formation of habitable voids on either side of the collapse where survivors would likely be found.

- **Lean-to collapse:** A lean-to collapse occurs when one outer wall fails, but the opposing wall remains intact. This type of collapse often results in the formation of a single, large void created when the side of the roof that was supported by the failed wall drops to the ground while the other side remains elevated. Survivors are likely to be found in this void.

- **Cantilever collapse:** A cantilever collapse occurs when one of a building's side walls collapses, but the rest of the structure remains intact. This type of collapse is likely to produce numerous habitable voids under the supported ends of the floor.

13. Your department is dispatched to a structural collapse in which one wall of a two-story residential home has failed. As you arrive on the scene, you note that while one-half of the roof has fallen to the ground along with the wall, the other half remains in its original position. This scenario would BEST be described as a

    A. pancake collapse.
    B. V-shaped collapse.
    C. lean-to collapse.
    D. cantilever collapse.

14. Your department is dispatched to a structural collapse in which one wall of a four-story apartment building has collapsed. As you arrive on the scene, you note that the support wall has failed, but the rest of the structure remains intact, although it's exposed. This scenario would BEST be described as a

    A. pancake collapse.
    B. V-shaped collapse.
    C. lean-to collapse.
    D. cantilever collapse.

15. Your department is dispatched to a structural collapse that has occurred because of excessive snow cover on the roof of a local fast-food restaurant. As you arrive on the scene, you note that all four supporting walls are still intact, but the roof has collapsed in on the building. This scenario would BEST be described as a

    A. pancake collapse.
    B. V-shaped collapse.
    C. lean-to collapse.
    D. cantilever collapse.

Question 16 refers to the following information.

The following table shows the number of smoke detectors and the amount of property damages reported in May 2011.

Number of Smoke Detectors in Home	Total Property Damage
1	$16,000
2	$13,000
3	$10,000
4	$7,000
5	$4,000
6	Less than $1,000

16. According to information presented in the table, you may conclude that

    A. homes with more smoke detectors suffer less property damage than homes with fewer smoke detectors.
    B. the number of smoke detectors in a home does not affect the amount of property damage.
    C. homes with more smoke detectors suffer from more fires than homes with fewer smoke detectors.
    D. homes with fewer smoke detectors suffer less property damage than homes with more smoke detectors.

Questions 17–18 refer to the following passage.

Brush fires are wind driven, and each edge of these types of fires is classified and given a name. A moving brush fire's leading edge is called the *head* of the fire. The opposite side is called the *rear*. When viewing the fire from the rear, the left side is the *left flank* and the right side of the blackened area is the *right flank*. Any unburned sections of shrubs or trees within the blackened area of the brush fire are called *pockets*. Firefighters should try to control the head of a brush fire, but should never attempt a frontal assault.

17. Which of the following is the MOST appropriate title for this passage?

    A. "Dangers of Fighting Brush Fires"
    B. "How a Brush Fire Spreads"
    C. "How to Fight a Brush Fire"
    D. "The Parts of a Brush Fire"

18. What is the MOST dangerous area around a brush fire?

    A. rear
    B. head
    C. left flank
    D. pockets

Questions 19–20 refer to the following information.

Large fires may be classified into the following categories:

- **Conflagrations** are major fires with flames that spread over a large area, which often threaten structures as well as woodlands. A wildfire is an example of a conflagration.

- **Group fires** are events of major building-to-building fires spread within adjacent buildings in a city block or within an industrial complex.

- **Large-loss fires** are fires that cause $5 million or more of direct property loss. These fires generally occur in office, manufacturing, and storage structures.

19. Firefighters respond to a fire in a warehouse in an industrial complex. The isolated structure is engulfed and unoccupied. Firefighters determine the warehouse, which is used to store electronic equipment and textbooks for five area schools, is unsafe and unsalvageable. They work to contain and extinguish the fire from outside. The security guard tells the firefighters that the warehouse contains electronic equipment and textbooks valued at more than $1.5 million for each school. How should this fire be categorized?

    A. group fire
    B. conflagration
    C. group conflagration
    D. large-loss fire

20. Engine 4 responds to a structure fire at 345 Maple Avenue. The fire is in an apartment on the top floor of an older three-story building. The block comprises four apartment buildings that are similar in size and located close together. If the fire spreads, it would be categorized as a

    A. conflagration.
    B. group fire.
    C. large-loss fire.
    D. large-loss conflagration.

IF YOU FINISH BEFORE TIME IS CALLED, CHECK YOUR WORK ON THIS SECTION ONLY. DO NOT WORK ON ANY OTHER SECTION IN THE TEST.

Section 7: Information Ordering

Time: 25 minutes

20 questions

Directions (1–20): Answer the following questions solely on the basis of the information provided.

Questions 1–4 refer to the following passage.

    Firefighters from the Dewdrop Fire Department are trained in triage, meaning they assess victims involved in motor-vehicle accidents and treat them according to the degree of their injuries. For example, upon arriving at the scene of an accident, firefighters first treat victims in need of cardiopulmonary resuscitation (CPR)—that is, those who are not breathing or for whom no pulse is detected. Next, firefighters treat bleeding wounds, such as deep lacerations. Then they treat victims suffering from shock, followed by victims with broken bones. Minor scrapes and bruises are treated last.

    One November day, Dewdrop firefighters respond to a three-car motor-vehicle accident involving five victims. Kyle John, who was driving one of the vehicles, is a 35-year-old male with a deep laceration on his cheek that is bleeding. Sarah Gerard, a 72-year-old female who suffered a heart attack at which point she lost control of her vehicle and caused the accident, is not breathing. James Monroe is a 47-year-old man whose left ankle is bent in an unnatural position. His son, Pat Monroe, is a 15-year-old with a large contusion on his left arm. James's wife, Cheryl Monroe, is a 45-year-old woman who is in shock.

1. Based on the information, which of the following victims should be treated *first*?

    A.   Kyle John
    B.   Cheryl Monroe
    C.   Sarah Gerard
    D.   James Monroe

2. Based on the information, which of the following people should be treated *last*?

    A.   Kyle John
    B.   Pat Monroe
    C.   Cheryl Monroe
    D.   Sarah Gerard

3. Based on the information, Cheryl Monroe should be treated *directly after*

    A.   Kyle John.
    B.   Sarah Gerard.
    C.   Pat Monroe.
    D.   James Monroe.

4. The injuries sustained by the five victims of this vehicular accident are listed below, in no particular order. Based on Dewdrop Fire Department's triage procedure, determine the order in which the injuries/conditions should be treated.

    1.   shock
    2.   broken ankle
    3.   heart attack
    4.   large contusion
    5.   deep-bleeding laceration

    A.   4, 2, 3, 5, 1
    B.   3, 5, 1, 2, 4
    C.   3, 1, 2, 4, 5
    D.   1, 3, 4, 5, 2

Questions 5–7 refer to the following passage.

The axe is an important tool used by firefighters. Rarely are firefighters seen entering a burning building without at least one axe, most commonly a flat-head axe. A flat-head axe has a blade on one end and a flat head on the other. The blade side of the axe can be used to cut through doors while the flat head can be used to force open doors, break locks, and provide leverage. Before using an axe, firefighters will first clear the area around the spot to be cut and will make sure that it is safe to swing the axe. Then they will chop in a circular motion, making many small cuts rather than attempting to cut through on each swing. The firefighters' cuts enter the surface at a 60-degree angle. When cutting roofs for ventilation purposes, firefighters will cut the sheathing first and will then cut the roof boards, making sure not to cut on top of roof joists or in the center of the bay. Cuts should be made 2 inches from the joist.

5. What is the *first* thing a firefighter should do before swinging an axe?

   A. Make sure the axe is sharpened.
   B. Inspect the axe for any defects.
   C. Clear the area where the cut is to be made.
   D. Be sure the cutting edge is facing forward.

6. According to the passage, after cutting a roof's sheathing, firefighters will then cut

   A. on top of the roof joists.
   B. through all the boards at once.
   C. the boards at a 75° angle.
   D. the roof boards using a circular motion.

7. You and two of your fellow firefighters enter a building ablaze. You hear children calling for help behind a closed door. You try to open the door but it is locked and the children are unable to unlock it. One of the other firefighters hands you an axe; you make sure the area is clear, and then you swing the axe and hit the door at a 90-degree angle with all your might. You do the same thing two more times. What should you have done *after* making sure the area was clear instead of swinging the axe and hitting the door at a 90° angle?

   A. Chop in full thrusts, at a 45° angle.
   B. Chop in a straight line, at a 60° angle.
   C. Chop in a crooked pattern, at a 90° angle.
   D. Chop in a circular motion, at a 60° angle.

Questions 8–12 refer to the following information.

The use of elevators during fires requires advanced training and knowledge to safely operate the transporters. To improve safety, many elevators have been equipped with a special firefighter service. Firefighter service can be activated in two ways—by a designated key switch in the lobby or in the elevator car itself. The three-position key switch in the lobby recalls the elevator to the lobby. Once the elevators have been recalled to the lobby, firefighters can take the following steps (not shown in any particular order) to use the elevators to get people inside the building to safety.

1. Push the button for the desired floor.
2. When the desired floor is reached, push and hold the door-open button until the door stops.
3. When the elevator begins moving, test the call-cancel button.
4. Choose firefighter service.
5. If the elevator stops at the next floor, push the button for the desired floor.
6. Push the button to close the door.

8. What is the logical order of the steps given in the passage?

   A. 4, 6, 1, 3, 5, 2
   B. 1, 4, 6, 5, 3, 2
   C. 6, 1, 4, 3, 5, 2
   D. 4, 1, 6, 5, 2, 3

9. According to the information above, what step should you perform *directly after* you choose firefighter service?

   A. Push the button for the desired floor.
   B. Push the button to close the door.
   C. When the elevator begins moving, test the call-cancel button.
   D. When the desired floor is reached, push and hold the door-open button until the door stops.

10. You and two members of your firefighting team need to get to a fire on the fifteenth floor. The elevators are still working properly and residents are using them to vacate the building. What is the *first* thing you should do in order to use the elevators?

    A. Tell residents the elevators are out of service.
    B. Have the facilities manager redirect residents to the stairs.
    C. Use the three-position key to recall the elevators to the lobby.
    D. Initiate firefighter service by pressing the button inside the elevator car.

11. You are traveling in an elevator and see water dripping from the ceiling of the car. After pushing the call-cancel button, you should

    A. continue traveling to the desired floor.
    B. use the three-position key to return to the lobby.
    C. tell the facilities manager the elevator is not working properly.
    D. exit the car by pushing and holding the door-open button at the next floor.

12. If you are in the lobby and want to use the elevators to rescue people, what should you do *first*?

    A. Wait patiently for the elevator to return to the lobby.
    B. Use the three-position key to recall the elevator to the lobby.
    C. Initiate firefighter service when the elevator returns to the lobby.
    D. Make an announcement in the building to return the elevator to the lobby.

Questions 13–16 refer to the following passage.

Fire Chief Barrett ordered several department veterans to drill new firefighters on the specific actions required when completing a search-and-rescue mission in burning structures.

During a search-and-rescue mission, the firefighters should first ensure they wear full protective gear and use a functioning breathing apparatus, which should be double-checked before any rescue attempt.

Firefighters should always enter a burning building in groups of at least two and search on their hands and knees to increase their visibility. They should begin their search along an outside wall, so they can locate exterior windows, which may be opened for ventilation.

Once a room has been thoroughly searched, the firefighters should leave hang tags on the door handles to indicate that the room has been searched.

Any victims removed from a building should not be left unattended. They should either be placed in the care of emergency personnel, if needed, or in the custody of someone who will prevent them from reentering the building.

13. At the scene of a two-story structure fire, Firefighter Hoffman takes the lead on a search, with Firefighter Davis on his team. They both check their gear and enter the front door, immediately dropping to their hands and knees in the smoke-filled building. Hoffman heads right along the outside wall, searching a living room, which is empty, and then proceeds to the next room with an outside wall. He continues to search until the first floor is clear. The team then searches the second floor in the same manner and finds a woman on the floor in a bedroom. She is conscious, but coughing and weak. Hoffman relays their position via radio and notifies paramedics. He and Davis remove the woman from the building and take her to the paramedics. Meanwhile, a second search-and-rescue team enters the structure through the rear door and begins searching the ground floor. What is *most likely* the reason the second team begins searching the ground floor?

A. They are searching rooms with outside walls.

B. The first team did not leave hang tags on doors of searched rooms.

C. They were looking for windows for ventilation.

D. They were following orders to recheck the floor.

14. A firefighter conducts a search and rescue in a burning trailer. She checks her gear and crawls through the trailer, leaving hang tags as she completes her search of each room. The firefighter finds a young adult male in the bedroom and drags him outside. He does not seem to require immediate medical attention, so she leaves him with a neighbor until the ambulance arrives. What procedure has the firefighter neglected?

A. Firefighters should not leave victims unattended.

B. Firefighters should leave hang tags on the door handles of searched rooms.

C. Firefighters should search on their hands and knees.

D. Firefighters should always enter a burning building in groups of at least two.

15. Soon after entering a burning structure, the team leader, Firefighter Harris, pulls Firefighter Evans out of the building. She helps him to the paramedics, who put an oxygen mask over his face. What procedure has Evans *most likely* omitted from the search-and-rescue attempt?

A. He did not check his breathing apparatus.

B. He did not crawl on his hands and knees.

C. He did not leave hang tags on doors of searched rooms.

D. He did not enter the building in teams of two.

16. A team of three firefighters has been ordered to search a burning structure. They check their gear—including their breathing apparatus—enter on their hands and knees, and search rooms with outside walls first. Firefighter Barber leaves a hang tag on each room's door after it has been searched. He completes the search of the last room, radios the commander, and leads the team outside. What step has the team missed in this search-and-rescue mission?

   A. The team left unharmed fire victims unattended.
   B. They did not check their breathing apparatus before entering the building.
   C. They forgot to place hang tags on the rooms they searched.
   D. They did not miss any steps in the search-and-rescue mission.

Questions 17–20 refer to the following information.

The mission of a firefighter includes fighting fires and rescuing victims during these fires. After a victim is found, precautions must be taken to ensure the victim is not further injured during the rescue. Firefighters should follow these steps when performing a two- or three-person lift onto a gurney:

1. Firefighters acting as rescuers should determine a lead rescuer and follow his command.
2. Rescuers should ensure the gurney is placed in a safe area away from fire.
3. Rescuers should leave the gurney in a position that will allow them to place the victim on it, without moving the victim too much, such as in a fully raised position.
4. All rescuers should position themselves as close as they can to the victim, crouching or kneeling, and keeping their backs straight.

5. The lead rescuer should support the victim's head with one hand and use his other hand and arm to support the victim's upper back.
6. The other rescuers should place their arms under the victim's body.
7. Together, the rescuers should carefully roll the victim toward their chests and stand up, lifting the victim.
8. The rescuers should carry the victim to the location of the gurney.
9. Once at the gurney, the rescuers should reverse the above steps to lower the victim to the gurney.

17. Based on the information, which of these steps should be performed *before* the lead rescuer supports the victim's head?

   A. The rescuers should carry the victim to the location of the gurney.
   B. The rescuers should kneel as close as they can to the victim.
   C. The rescuers should lower the victim onto the gurney.
   D. The other rescuers should place their arms under the victim's body.

18. What is the *first* step that must be done when lowering the victim to the gurney?

   A. The rescuers should lower the gurney.
   B. The rescuers should ensure the gurney is placed in a safe area.
   C. The rescuers should carefully roll the victim away from their chests.
   D. The rescuers should stand at least one foot away from the gurney.

19. Based on the information, which of these steps should be performed *first*?

    A. Rescuers should ensure the gurney is placed in a safe area away from fire.
    B. Rescuers should roll the victim toward their chests and stand up.
    C. Rescuers should place their arms under the victim's body.
    D. Rescuers should kneel beside the victim.

20. Firefighters find one victim during a search-and-rescue mission. The woman is unconscious, but firefighters are unsure whether the woman is injured, so they perform a three-person lift to get her from the floor to a nearby gurney. After a firefighter is designated the lead rescuer, they all kneel next to her. They then slide their arms under the victim's body and roll the victim toward them as they lift her. They then carry her to the gurney. Which of these steps was omitted during the lift?

    A. Rescuers did not appoint a lead rescuer.
    B. Rescuers did not lower the gurney to the floor.
    C. The lead rescuer did not call paramedics.
    D. The lead rescuer did not support the victim's head with one hand.

IF YOU FINISH BEFORE TIME IS CALLED, CHECK YOUR WORK ON THIS SECTION ONLY. DO NOT WORK ON ANY OTHER SECTION IN THE TEST.

Section 8: Problem Sensitivity

Time: 25 minutes
20 questions

Directions (1-20): Answer the following questions solely on the basis of the information provided.

Questions 1–3 refer to the following passage.

Personnel from your fire department were dispatched to the scene of a two-car motor vehicle accident. Several individuals involved in the accident were injured. According to the testimony of those involved and eyewitness reports, a gray 2005 Ford Escape, driven by Carmen Alvarez, swerved to avoid a pedestrian and accidentally crossed into the opposite lane where it struck a black 2003 Hyundai Sonata, driven by Timothy Hansen, head-on.

Mr. Alvarez, who had been wearing a seat belt at the time of the accident, suffered numerous severe cuts and bruises because of broken glass. He also complained of pain in his right wrist, which he held at a slightly unnatural angle.

Maria Alvarez, Mr. Alvarez's wife, was seated in the front passenger's seat and was wearing her seat belt. She suffered numerous cuts and bruises and complained of neck pain.

Mr. Hansen, who had not been wearing his seat belt, also suffered severe cuts and bruises. He appeared to be bleeding heavily from the mouth and appeared to be missing several teeth. In addition, he complained of severe pain on the right side of his chest and difficulty breathing. Firefighters noticed that his airbag failed to deploy.

Mr. Hansen was driving with three passengers: his brother Steven, who was seated in the front passenger's seat, and his sons, Michael and Jonathan, who were both seated in the rear of the vehicle. Steven, who was wearing his seat belt, sustained severe cuts and bruises and reported severe pain in his right hand. Two of his fingers were positioned at an unnatural angle. Michael, who was wearing his seat belt, suffered only a few minor cuts and had no complaints. Jonathan, who was not wearing his seat belt, was reported thrown into the back of the front passenger's seat and complained of severe pain in his neck and right shoulder. He had difficulty moving his right arm.

1. Based on the information in the passage, which of the following individuals would appear to be the LEAST seriously injured?

   A. Maria Alvarez
   B. Steven Hansen
   C. Michael Hansen
   D. Carmen Alvarez

2. Based on the information in the passage, which of the following individuals would appear to be the MOST seriously injured?

   A. Carmen Alvarez
   B. Timothy Hansen
   C. Maria Alvarez
   D. Steven Hansen

3. Based on the information in the passage, which occupant in the 2003 Hyundai Sonata was the MOST seriously injured?

   A. Timothy Hansen
   B. Steven Hansen
   C. Michael Hansen
   D. Jonathan Hansen

Question 4 refers to the following passage.

Firefighter Mitchell has been observing the behavior of Firefighter Parker, an experienced member of the department who is known for his keen abilities and bravery. Several months ago, Parker was fighting a house fire when a nearby gas stove suddenly exploded. Though he managed to escape serious injury, Parker has not been himself since. From the time Parker returned to the department, he has seemed edgy and often had a short fuse with his co-workers. On scene, he frequently seems hesitant and reluctant to get involved. Parker has denied that anything is wrong, but his behavior clearly seems to indicate otherwise.

4. Based on the information in the passage, if Parker were having a problem, it would MOST LIKELY be

   A. health-related.
   B. drug-related.
   C. financial.
   D. marital.

Question 5 refers to the following passage.

Firefighter Johnson has been observing the behavior of Firefighter Cohen, who has been one of the fire department's most reliable members for the last 10 years. Over the last few months, however, Johnson has noted a distinct change in Cohen's behavior. He has been signing up for more shifts than usual, often spending full-shift rotations on duty. He rarely ever orders food with his co-workers any more, preferring instead to eat whatever scraps of food he brings with him from home. He has also been arriving at work on a bicycle instead of in his car, even though he lives quite a distance from the station. When he's not on duty, a number of other firefighters have reported seeing him at the local casino.

5. Based on the information in the passage, if Cohen were having a problem, it would most likely be

   A. marital.
   B. financial.
   C. drug-related.
   D. health-related.

6. Your fire department receives the following notifications in one day. Of these notifications, which should be considered the MOST urgent?

   A. a report of a single-car accident with no injuries
   B. a request to conduct a fire-prevention seminar
   C. a report of a wildfire in a remote forested area
   D. a call about a kitchen fire in an apartment building

Question 7 refers to the following passage.

Firefighter Peters has been observing the behavior of Firefighter Grant, who has been a member of the department for 15 years. Over the last two months, Grant, who is normally one of the department's most positive and upbeat members, has become increasingly depressed and withdrawn. He seems to be quite distressed about something, but refuses to discuss the matter with any of his co-workers. On several occasions, he has been overheard having emotionally charged phone conversations with his wife. A number of times, he has decided not to go home and to sleep overnight at the fire station even though he was not on duty.

7. Based on the information in the passage, if Grant were having a problem, it would MOST LIKELY be

   A. drug-related.
   B. financial.
   C. marital.
   D. health-related.

Questions 8–10 refer to the following passage.

Personnel from your fire department were dispatched to a traffic accident involving three cars on a local interstate highway. The driver of a 1992 Cadillac DeVille, Meredith Simmons, attempted to merge into the left lane to exit the interstate. As she attempted to merge, she failed to notice a 2001 Acura Integra, driven by Eric Leonard, attempting to pass her. As a result, Simmons's vehicle collided with the front side of the Integra. The impact of the collision caused Simmons to lose control, spin into the shoulder, and strike the retaining wall. The Integra also spun out of control and was struck head-on by a 2005 Dodge Ram truck driven by Gene Howard. The impact of this collision forced the Integra into the rear of the DeVille. All three vehicles came to a stop on the shoulder.

Mrs. Simmons, who was wearing her seat belt at the time of the accident, was traveling with three passengers. Simmons suffered a number of serious cuts and bruises and appeared to be a bit disoriented. Marilyn Thomas, who was sitting in the front passenger's seat, was not wearing a seat belt. She had severe cuts and noticeable swelling on the right side of her head. Through she was also disoriented, she complained of a severe headache and terrible pain in her right forearm, which she held at an unnatural angle. Isabelle Kaczynski, who was sitting in the rear driver's side and was wearing her seat belt, suffered minor cuts and scratches and complained of neck pain. Martha Hughes, who was sitting in the rear passenger's side and was wearing her seat belt, suffered only minor cuts, but complained of severe pain in her right shoulder and an inability to move her right arm.

Mr. Leonard, who was traveling alone, was wearing his seat belt at the time of the accident. The force of both the first and second impacts resulted in extensive damage to his vehicle. Leonard was pinned in and had to be extricated with the Jaws of Life. When paramedics first arrived on the scene, Leonard was bleeding severely and complaining of intense back pain and an inability to feel his lower extremities. He also complained of chest pain and difficulty breathing. He appeared to be coughing up some blood.

Mr. Howard, who was also traveling alone, was wearing his seat belt. He complained of neck pain that he thought was probably related to whiplash. He did not suffer any cuts or bruises.

8. Based on the information in the passage, which of the following individuals would appear to be the MOST seriously injured?

   A. Martha Hughes
   B. Gene Howard
   C. Eric Leonard
   D. Marilyn Thomas

9. Based on the information in the passage, which of the following individuals would appear to be the LEAST seriously injured?

   A. Isabelle Kaczynski
   B. Eric Leonard
   C. Meredith Simmons
   D. Gene Howard

10. Based on the information in the passage, which occupant in Simmons's vehicle was the MOST seriously injured?

   A. Meredith Simmons
   B. Isabelle Kaczynski
   C. Marilyn Thomas
   D. Martha Hughes

Question 11 refers to the following passage.

Firefighter Rizzo has been observing the behavior of Firefighter Harris, a veteran firefighter who has been working with the department for the last 25 years. Several months ago, Harris's brother died unexpectedly. Since then, Harris has been depressed and sullen. Over time, his behavior has worsened. He often appears disheveled and unkempt. When he works the morning shift, he frequently arrives looking exhausted and appears to be at least a little disoriented. On more than one occasion, other firefighters have seen his car parked outside the bar near the fire department.

11. Based on the information in the passage, if Harris were having a problem, it would MOST LIKELY be related to

    A.   alcohol.
    B.   finances.
    C.   job stress.
    D.   marital problems.

Question 12 refers to the following passage.

Firefighter Fitzgerald has been observing the behavior of Firefighter McGowan, who, with more than 30 years of experience, is one of the department's most veteran members. Over the years, McGowan has always kept himself in top physical condition and was known for his ability to outwork even the youngest firefighters in the department. During the past few months, McGowan, usually an even-tempered and friendly fellow, has become increasingly agitated and temperamental. Some of his fellow firefighters have noticed that he has been less active than normal on calls lately and seems to stick mostly with the less physically taxing jobs. Some of his co-workers have tried to ask him if anything is wrong, but he simply brushes them off and insists everything is fine.

12. Based on the information in the passage, if McGowan were having a problem, it would MOST LIKELY be related to

    A.   finances.
    B.   health.
    C.   drugs.
    D.   family.

13. Your fire department receives all of the following notifications in one day. Of these notifications, which should be considered the MOST urgent?

    A.   a report of a contained shed fire
    B.   a request to repair a faulty fire hydrant
    C.   a call about an accident involving hazardous materials
    D.   a call involving an elderly fall victim

Question 14 refers to the following passage.

Firefighter Walters has been observing the behavior of Firefighter Thompson, a young firefighter who recently transferred from another department. During his first few weeks with the department, Thompson has often seemed stressed and edgy. Though polite, he is curt with many of his co-workers and seems reluctant to interact with them. He has demonstrated his skill as a firefighter consistently, but he continues to appear uncomfortable and distant around his co-workers. The firefighters at his former station have said he never acted like this when he was working there.

14. Based on the information in the passage, if Thompson were having a problem, it would MOST LIKELY be

    A.   drug-related.
    B.   job stress.
    C.   financial.
    D.   domestic violence.

Questions 15–17 refer to the following passage.

Personnel from your fire department responded to a three-vehicle traffic accident involving a car fire. The primary accident occurred when a 1999 Chevrolet Blazer, driven by Charles White, ran a red light and was struck by a 2010 Dodge Charger, driven by Marcus Jordan, which was proceeding through the intersection at a high rate of speed. This collision, which occurred when the left front of the Charger struck the right rear of the Blazer, caused White to lose control and crash into a nearby tree. The vehicle burst into flames upon impact. Mr. White and his passenger were able to free themselves and escape the flames after a short time. Simultaneously, a 2006 Toyota Camry, driven by Jessica Reynolds and traveling behind Jordan, was unable to stop in time and rear-ended the Charger.

Mr. White, who was wearing his seat belt and traveling with his girlfriend, Michelle Davis, suffered numerous cuts and bruises. He sustained second- and third-degree burns on his legs and arms. His right knee appeared to be severely swollen and slightly displaced. He had a large wound on the top of his head that was bleeding profusely. At the time of paramedics' arrival on the scene, he was nearly unconscious and completely incoherent. Davis, his passenger, suffered first- and second-degree burns to her legs and arms and complained of moderate neck pain. She had numerous cuts and bruises.

Mr. Jordan, who was wearing his seat belt, sustained only minor cuts and bruises. He reported that his airbag did not deploy and, as a result, he struck the steering wheel with great force. He complained of intense, searing pain in the center of his chest and near his collar on the right side. His passenger, Sam Maxwell, suffered only a single significant cut on the right side of his forehead. He complained of severe pain in his right hand and arm. He was wearing his seat belt.

Ms. Reynolds, who was wearing her seat-belt, complained of neck and shoulder pain. She had no obvious injuries. Two of her children were traveling with her. Her son, Ronald, was not wearing a seat belt and was thrown into the dashboard. He complained of extreme abdominal pain and difficulty breathing. Visual examination revealed distension and discoloration of the abdomen. The region was very sensitive to palpitation. The other passenger, Reynolds's daughter Ashley, was sitting in the rear of the vehicle and was wearing her seat belt. She did not show any signs of injury or make any complaints.

15. Based on the information in the passage, which individual would appear to be MOST in need of immediate medical attention?

   A. Ronald Reynolds
   B. Michelle Davis
   C. Marcus Jordan
   D. Charles White

16. Based on the information in the passage, which individual would appear to be the LEAST in need of immediate medical attention?

   A. Sam Maxwell
   B. Jessica Reynolds
   C. Charles White
   D. Ashley Reynolds

17. Based on the information in the passage, which of the following passengers is MOST in need of medical attention?

   A. Michelle Davis
   B. Sam Maxwell
   C. Ronald Reynolds
   D. Ashley Reynolds

18. Your fire department receives all of the following notifications in one day. Of these notifications, which should be considered the MOST urgent?

    A. a request to conduct a vehicular extraction demonstration
    B. a call regarding a multicar highway accident
    C. a dispatch to investigate a residential gas leak
    D. an EMS call regarding a commercial airplane accident

Question 19 refers to the following passage.

Firefighter Perez has been observing the behavior of Firefighter Clarke, who recently returned to the fire department after spending a few years working at a busy inner-city fire department. Since his return, many of the other firefighters have commented that Clarke does not seem to be the same person he once was. He regularly arrives late for his shift looking bleary-eyed and scruffy. His behavior has become erratic; he is often very short-tempered with his co-workers, but also experiences bouts of severe depression and anxiety.

19. Based on the information in the passage, if Clarke were having a problem, it would MOST LIKELY be related to

    A. health issues.
    B. drugs.
    C. marital.
    D. finances.

Question 20 refers to the following passage.

Firefighter Quinn has been observing the behavior of Firefighter Williams, who has been working with the fire department for seven years. Normally, Firefighter Williams is a bright, outgoing, and unflappably positive young woman. Over the last few months, however, she has grown increasingly reserved and depressed. Numerous times, she has been overheard sobbing in the bathroom. For weeks, her co-workers have noticed that she regularly has numerous bumps and bruises. She claims they are work-related. Last week, she arrived at work with a large welt above her right eye that she claimed was from accidentally walking into a door.

20. Based on the information in the passage, if Williams were having a problem, it would MOST LIKEY be related to

    A. finances.
    B. health issues.
    C. domestic violence.
    D. drug problems.

IF YOU FINISH BEFORE TIME IS CALLED, CHECK YOUR WORK ON THIS SECTION ONLY. DO NOT WORK ON ANY OTHER SECTION IN THE TEST.

Section 9: Mathematics

Time: 25 minutes

20 questions

Directions (1–20): Select the best answer for each question.

1. $(4x - 6)(-3x + 8) =$

   A. $-12x^2 - 50x + 48$
   B. $-12x^2 + 50x - 48$
   C. $12x^2 - 14x - 48$
   D. $12x^2 + 14x + 48$

2. You are traveling out of the country for a firefighter conference. You've been told the average temperature at your destination is 44.6°F. What is the temperature in degrees Celsius (°C)?

   A. 7
   B. 9.3
   C. 12
   D. 14.9

3. What is the total of the following fractions: $\frac{3}{4} + \frac{7}{8} + \frac{5}{12}$? Reduce your answer to lowest terms.

   A. $\frac{7}{9}$

   B. $\frac{9}{12}$

   C. $\frac{2}{3}$

   D. $\frac{49}{24}$

4. Simplify the expression: $(4 \times 3)(7 + 2)^2$

   A. 489
   B. 638
   C. 972
   D. 1,554

Question 5 refers to the following information.

Fire Chief Norris is responsible for filling out employee evaluations at the end of each fiscal year. He needs to complete evaluations for all 12 firefighters at the First Valley Hose Company. The table below shows the average time it takes Fire Chief Norris to complete evaluations.

Total Time	Number of Evaluations
1 hour, 45 minutes	2
3 hours, 30 minutes	4
5 hours, 15 minutes	6

5. How long will it take Fire Chief Norris to complete 12 evaluations?

   A. 7 hours
   B. 8 hours, 15 minutes
   C. 8 hours 45 minutes
   D. 9 hours

6. A cylinder's volume is 80 inches³ and its radius is 12 inches. What is its height? Round your answer to the nearest tenth.

   A. 4.3 in
   B. 5.7 in
   C. 6.3 in
   D. 7.1 in

7. You're responding to the scene of a fire located 27 miles from the station. If you travel at an average speed of 55 miles per hour, how many minutes will it take for you to arrive at the scene? Round your answer to the nearest whole number.

   A. 29 minutes
   B. 31 minutes
   C. 45 minutes
   D. 62 minutes

8. If Firefighter Jameson can run 4 miles in 28 minutes, how many miles can he run in 84 minutes?

   A. 7
   B. 9
   C. 12
   D. 15

9. $(y^{11})(y^{19}) =$

   A. y^{-8}
   B. y^{8}
   C. y^{30}
   D. y^{209}

10. $\frac{9}{5} + \frac{12}{10} + \frac{3}{25} - \frac{4}{50} - \frac{2}{100} = ?$ Round to the nearest hundredth.

    A. 0.30
    B. 3.02
    C. 30.20
    D. 32.002

11. Simplify the expression: $7^2(9 - 4)^3$

    A. 925
    B. 2,000
    C. 4,950
    D. 6,125

12. $\frac{4}{9} \times 0.78 + \frac{16}{3} - \frac{6}{27} = ?$ Round to the nearest hundredth.

    A. 5.45
    B. 9.25
    C. 25.90
    D. 60.42

Question 13 refers to the following figure.

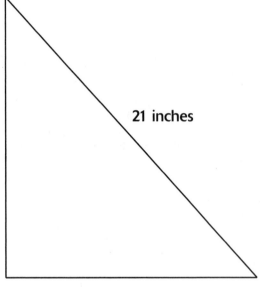

13. Find the area of the triangle.

    A. 72 in^2
    B. 147 in^2
    C. 294 in^2
    D. 588 in^2

14. What is 12 percent of 598?

    A. 52.35
    B. 68.96
    C. 71.76
    D. 82.45

15. If Firefighter Latona can complete 45 sit-ups in 90 seconds, how many sit-ups can he complete in 156 seconds?

    A. 60
    B. 78
    C. 99
    D. 110

16. A firefighter enters a smoke-filled room and needs to ventilate it. He uses a sledgehammer to make a 6-foot by 9-foot opening in the wall. How large is the opening?

    A. 15 ft.^{2}
    B. 54 ft.^{2}
    C. 90 ft.^{2}
    D. 120 ft.^{2}

17. Solve this equation: $\frac{250}{15} = \frac{x}{6}$

    A. 50
    B. 75
    C. 100
    D. 125

18. A fire engine responds to an activated fire alarm at a bakery that is located 13 miles from the fire station. If the fire engine arrives at the business in 11 minutes, what was the average speed the fire engine traveled on the way to the building? Round your answer to the nearest whole number.

    A. 24 m.p.h.
    B. 40 m.p.h.
    C. 65 m.p.h.
    D. 71 m.p.h.

19. $(x^{-6})(x^{-8})$

    A. $\frac{1}{x^{48}}$
    B. $\frac{1}{x^{4}}$
    C. $x{-}48$
    D. x^{-14}

20. On your last 24-hour shift, you spent 6 hours fighting fires, 2 hours at the scene of a car accident, and your remaining hours at the station. What percent of your shift was spent at the station? Round your answer to the nearest whole number.

    A. 8 percent
    B. 16 percent
    C. 52 percent
    D. 67 percent

IF YOU FINISH BEFORE TIME IS CALLED, CHECK YOUR WORK ON THIS SECTION ONLY. DO NOT WORK ON ANY OTHER SECTION IN THE TEST.

Section 10: Mechanical Aptitude

Time: 25 minutes

20 questions

Directions (1–20): Answer the following questions solely on the basis of the information provided.

Question 1 refers to the following figure.

1. Look at the tool shown above. During forcible entry operations, this tool would MOST LIKELY be used for

   A. prying.
   B. pulling.
   C. pushing.
   D. cutting.

Questions 2–3 refer to the following figure.

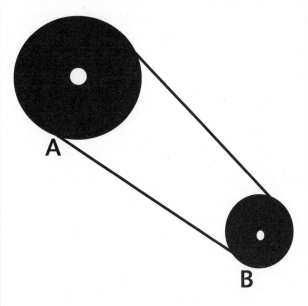

2. Wheel A is twice the size of Wheel B. If Wheel B makes 90 revolutions per minute, how many revolutions per minute does Wheel A make?

   A. 30
   B. 45
   C. 90
   D. 180

3. Which of the following statements about the pulley setup is true?

A. Wheel B spins slower than Wheel A.
B. If Wheel A spins clockwise, Wheel B spins counterclockwise.
C. Neither wheel can spin in the pulley setup.
D. If Wheel A spins clockwise, Wheel B spins clockwise.

4. If the radius of a wheel is 549 inches and the wheel's axle is 18 inches, what is the mechanical advantage?

A. 30.5
B. 49
C. 63.7
D. 80

5. Which of the following statements is true?

A. Reverse-thread screws are more difficult to rotate into an object than standard-thread screws.
B. Standard-thread screws are more difficult to rotate into an object than reverse-thread screws.
C. Standard-thread screws are rotated clockwise when removed from an object.
D. Reverse-thread screws are rotated clockwise when removed from an object.

6. If a spring stretches 9 feet under a pull of 120 pounds, how many feet will the spring stretch under a pull of 480 pounds?

A. 27 ft.
B. 36 ft.
C. 45 ft.
D. 54 ft.

Question 7 refers to the following figure.

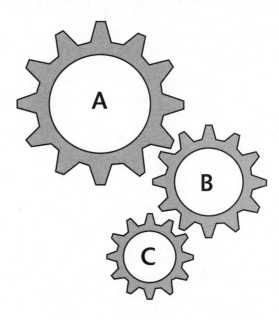

7. The image shows three gears of different sizes. If Gear C rotates in a counterclockwise direction, which other gear(s) will rotate in the same direction?

A. Gear A only
B. Gear B only
C. Gears A and B
D. none of the gears

Question 8 refers to the following figure.

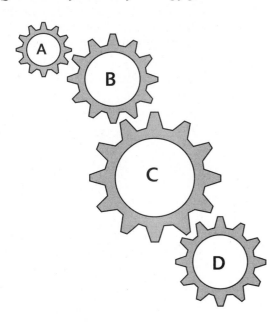

8. Based on the image, which gear will make the fewest revolutions per minute?

   A. Gear A
   B. Gear B
   C. Gear C
   D. Gear D

Question 9 refers to the following figure.

9. Look at the tool shown above. What is the name of this tool?

   A. Halligan bar
   B. wrench
   C. hammer
   D. claw tool

Question 10 refers to the following figure.

10. What is another name for this tool?

    A. circular saw
    B. ventilation saw
    C. cutting torch
    D. bolt cutter

Questions 11–12 refer to the following figure.

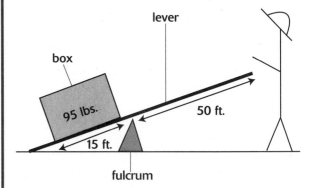

11. Based on the image, how many pounds of force must the firefighter apply to the lever to lift the box?

    A. 15 lbs.
    B. 22.5 lbs.
    C. 28.5 lbs.
    D. 40 lbs.

12. Based on the image, if the weight of the box was increased to 195 pounds and the fire-fighter moved the fulcrum 5 feet closer to the box, how much force would he have to apply to lift the box?

   A. 12.5 lbs.
   B. 19 lbs.
   C. 21.5 lbs.
   D. 39 lbs.

13. What do a clamp, pliers, and a rope have in common?

   A. They are used to cut through wire.
   B. They are used to hold an object in place.
   C. They are used to break up materials.
   D. They are used to turn off a gas line.

14. A San Francisco hook would MOST LIKELY be used to

   A. remove plaster or siding.
   B. shut off a gas line.
   C. help remove trapped accident victims.
   D. deliver a soft blow to an object.

15. All of these tools can be used to cut through various materials, including metal, EXCEPT:

   A. a ventilation saw.
   B. a reciprocating saw.
   C. a bolt cutter.
   D. a handsaw.

Question 16 refers to the following figure.

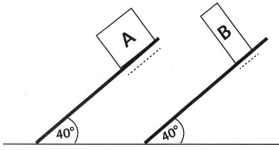

*Dotted line represents friction

16. Box A and Box B are different sizes, but they're made of the same material and are the same weight. They're also positioned on equal inclined planes. Based on the image, what will MOST LIKELY happen if both boxes begin to slide down the inclined plane at the same time?

   A. Box A will slide faster than Box B.
   B. Box A will slide, but Box B will fall over.
   C. Boxes A and B will slide at the same speed.
   D. Box B will slide faster than Box A.

17. Which of these tools would MOST LIKELY be used to cut through light materials?

   A.

   B.

   C.

   D.

18. Which of these tools is also called a pinch bar?

A.

B.

C.

D.

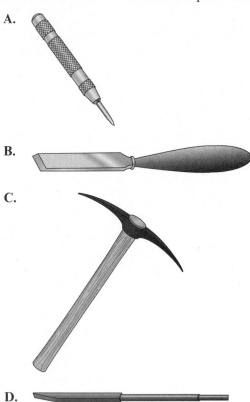

19. Which of these tools would MOST LIKELY be used to move heavy objects?

A.

B.

C.

D.

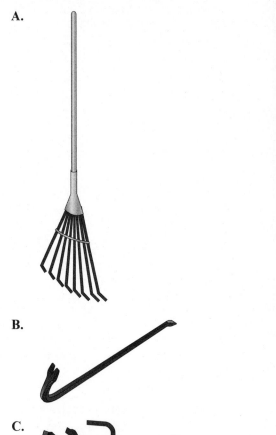

Question 20 refers to the following figure.

20. What is the name of this tool?

    A.   claw tool
    B.   battering ram
    C.   chainsaw
    D.   pike pole

IF YOU FINISH BEFORE TIME IS CALLED, CHECK YOUR WORK ON THIS
SECTION ONLY. DO NOT WORK ON ANY OTHER SECTION IN THE TEST.

Answer Key

Section 1: Observation

1. C	6. C	11. B	16. D
2. D	7. B	12. C	17. D
3. A	8. B	13. B	18. A
4. C	9. D	14. D	19. B
5. C	10. B	15. C	20. B

Section 2: Memory

1. B	6. C	11. B	16. D
2. A	7. A	12. C	17. C
3. C	8. C	13. C	18. B
4. A	9. C	14. A	19. D
5. D	10. B	15. B	20. C

Section 3: Spatial Orientation

1. A	6. C	11. D	16. B
2. C	7. A	12. A	17. A
3. B	8. A	13. C	18. B
4. D	9. D	14. D	19. C
5. B	10. B	15. C	20. C

Section 4: Reading Comprehension

1. A	6. D	11. C	16. D
2. B	7. A	12. B	17. A
3. D	8. B	13. D	18. C
4. C	9. C	14. C	19. A
5. C	10. D	15. A	20. C

Section 5: Verbal Expression

1. C	6. B	11. A	16. C
2. D	7. A	12. B	17. A
3. B	8. D	13. D	18. B
4. A	9. C	14. C	19. A
5. C	10. D	15. B	20. D

Section 6: Deductive/Inductive/Logical Reasoning

1. B	6. B	11. A	16. A
2. A	7. B	12. C	17. D
3. D	8. C	13. C	18. B
4. C	9. D	14. D	19. D
5. B	10. B	15. B	20. B

Section 7: Information Ordering

1. C	6. D	11. D	16. D
2. B	7. D	12. B	17. B
3. A	8. A	13. B	18. C
4. B	9. B	14. D	19. A
5. C	10. C	15. A	20. D

Section 8: Problem Sensitivity

1. C	6. D	11. A	16. D
2. B	7. C	12. B	17. C
3. A	8. C	13. C	18. D
4. A	9. D	14. B	19. B
5. B	10. C	15. D	20. C

Section 9: Mathematics

1. B	6. B	11. D	16. B
2. A	7. A	12. A	17. C
3. D	8. C	13. B	18. D
4. C	9. C	14. C	19. D
5. C	10. B	15. B	20. D

Section 10: Mechanical Aptitude

1. D	6. B	11. C	16. D
2. B	7. A	12. D	17. C
3. D	8. C	13. B	18. D
4. A	9. B	14. B	19. B
5. D	10. A	15. A	20. A

Answer Explanations

Section 1: Observation

1. **C** Hose 2 was rolled using the twin-donut roll method. You know this because the passage tells you that when firefighters roll hoses using this method, the couplings are connected and a strap is attached so they can easily transport the hoses. The illustration of the twin-donut roll has both a strap and connected couplings. *(See Chapter V, Section A.)*

2. **D** In this diagram, Hose 2 was rolled using a twin-donut roll and Hose 4 was rolled using a self-locking twin-donut roll. Both of these hoses can easily be transported on a firefighter's shoulder using the strap. As the passage states, a strap can be fastened to a hose rolled using a twin-donut approach. Hoses rolled using a self-locking twin-donut roll have a built-in carrying strap that locks over the couplings to make for easy transport. That strap can be thrown over a firefighter's shoulder. *(See Chapter V, Section A.)*

3. **A** The hose you're working with was most likely rolled using the donut roll method. The passage states that both the male and female couplings are exposed, so you know that you're not handling a straight roll. Straight rolls (Choice B) only expose one of the couplings, normally the male. Because the couplings aren't connected to each other, you know it's not a twin-donut roll (Choice C). Also, because the rolling method lacks a strap, you know it can't be a self-locking twin-donut roll (Choice D). This leaves you with a donut roll, which exposes both the male and female couplings and is designed to deploy quickly at the scene of an emergency. *(See Chapter V, Section A.)*

4. **C** According to the passage, straight rolls are used when the hose is to be stored. Hose 3 depicts a straight roll. You know this because only one of the couplings is exposed, and the other is tucked within the rest of the hose. Choice A is incorrect because Hose 1 is a donut roll. Choices B and D are incorrect because Hose 2 is a twin-donut roll and Hose 4 is a self-locking twin-donut roll. *(See Chapter V, Section A.)*

5. **C** Students in the classroom in the illustration have three homework assignments: a math assignment, a geography assignment, and a biology assignment. You know this because these assignments are written on the Homework Board. *(See Chapter V, Section A.)*

6. **C** A backpack is in the middle of the aisle of desks. This presents a tripping hazard for any teachers or students who may need to walk down the aisle. Although a water bottle is on the floor and would definitely be considered a tripping hazard, it's not located between the aisles of desks in this illustration. *(See Chapter V, Section A.)*

7. **B** The fire extinguisher is located directly to the right of the classroom door. Choice A is incorrect because a student's desk is located to the left of the teacher's desk. Choice C is incorrect because the math board is located to the right of the homework board. Choice D is incorrect because the illustration doesn't show anything to the left of the last row of students' desks. *(See Chapter V, Section A.)*

8. **B** If you stood at the front of the classroom and walked down the aisle, you would pass pencils, the math board, spilled water, and the homework board. The pencils are on the teacher's desk, located at the front of the room. The math board is located on the wall, and the spilled water is located behind the first row of students' desks. Finally, the homework board is on the wall on the left-hand side of the illustration. *(See Chapter V, Section A.)*

9. **D** The statement *A pile of graded assignments sits on the teacher's desk* is true regarding this illustration. Choice A is incorrect because the students have geography homework, not geometry homework. Choice B is incorrect because the extra chair is blocking the classroom's fire extinguisher, not the exit. Finally, Choice C is incorrect because there are at least two tripping hazards in the classroom: the spilled water and the backpack. *(See Chapter V, Section A.)*

10. **B** The firefighters in this diagram are in danger because they only have one means of escape. The only way for them to exit the roof is by using the ladder truck. As the passage states, firefighters should always have at least two ways of getting off a roof. Nothing in this diagram indicates that the building has an emergency exit. The wind direction is not an issue, as the firefighters in the diagram don't appear to be cutting a hole in the roof. The electrical lines in this diagram are intact, so they don't present a risk of electrocution. The materials on the roof may be dangerous, but there is nothing to indicate that the fire is directly under the boxes. *(See Chapter V, Section A.)*

11. **B** In this diagram, Firefighter 2 is most likely guarding the opening on the roof to be sure that none of his or her fellow firefighters fall in. Firefighter 2 is closest to the opening; therefore, one can assume that this is the task he or she is performing. *(See Chapter V, Section A.)*

12. **C** Firefighters should always be aware of any obstructions on the roof because an obstruction may place extra strain on the roof and cause it to collapse. Although the passage doesn't directly state this, it does say that firefighters must always be aware of heavy materials. When a building is on fire, the ceiling may weaken, and its structural supports may break or burn away. Heavy materials on the roof will place extra strain on a weakened ceiling, thus causing its collapse. *(See Chapter V, Section A.)*

13. **B** According to the passage, all firefighters are directed to work in teams of two when they're on the roof of a burning building. This means that it is incorrect to assume that all firefighters are responsible for only themselves when on the roof of a burning building. A firefighter's first priority is to save lives. Although his or her own life is important, a firefighter is also responsible for the lives of the other men and women he or she works beside. Choices A and C are incorrect because melting asphalt does create dangerous conditions, and firefighters should work with the wind to their backs when creating a hole on the roof. Choice D is incorrect because firefighters working on the roof of a burning building must wear all of their SCBA gear, which includes their department-issued helmets. *(See Chapter V, Section A.)*

14. **D** Firefighter 5 is putting his life at risk because he's by himself on the roof of a burning building. As the passage states, firefighters should team up when they're on the roof. He should not be working by himself. *(See Chapter V, Section A.)*

15. **C** Firefighters on the scene of an electrical emergency would be least likely to turn off the power supply. When they get to the scene, or when they're en route, the fire company contacts the utility company. Workers for the utility company will arrive on the scene to turn off the power supply and make it a safer environment to perform rescues or put out fires. Firefighters on the scene will attempt to control the scene while waiting for utility workers to shut off the power, so Choice A is incorrect. Choice B is incorrect because a firefighter's priority on the scene of any emergency is to save lives; therefore, if victims are trapped, he or she may attempt to rescue them. Choice D is incorrect because firefighters will try to avoid the point of contact, the area where the downed electrical line rests, so they are not electrocuted. *(See Chapter V, Section A.)*

16. **D** According to information in the passage, Firefighter 6 is the safest on the scene. Firefighters are instructed to keep a distance of at least one span between utility poles until the power has been shut off. Firefighters 3, 4, and 5 may be away from the point of contact, but they're still too close to the

most dangerous area of the scene. Firefighter 6 is working in a safe space, more than one span away from the point of contact. *(See Chapter V, Section A.)*

17. **D** Bystanders and firefighters should avoid areas with wire fences at the scene of an electrical emergency because they may be electrocuted if they touch fences that have been energized. The passage states that firefighters should always assume the lines are energized until they're told that the power has been turned off. Metal objects, such as wire fences, are natural conductors of electricity and therefore may electrocute anyone who touches them. *(See Chapter V, Section A.)*

18. **A** Firefighters most likely remove victims who are not trapped in damaged cars before victims who are to make room for personnel to extricate trapped victims. As indicated in the first sentence of the paragraph, firefighters need to assess the need for extrication activities before they actually perform the extrication. This means once they find that extrication is necessary, they must do what they can to extricate the victims quickly and safely. The area needs to be cleared of all harmful debris and additional victims before the extrication can occur. Choice B is incorrect because victims who are not trapped may not have life-threatening injuries. Choice C is incorrect because firefighters with first-aid experience have many responsibilities on the scene and don't need to be tasked with more than they can handle. Choice D is incorrect because the question asks about the removal of victims who are not trapped, not the removal of all victims. *(See Chapter V, Section A.)*

19. **B** The fewest number of firefighters needed to thoroughly assess the accident in the diagram is two. As the paragraph states, the number of firefighters needed is equal to the number of cars involved in the accident. Because two cars are involved in the accident, at least two firefighters are needed to assess the scene. If more personnel are available, however, they can also assess the scene. *(See Chapter V, Section A.)*

20. **B** If Rescuer 3 was available to work the scene of the accident in the diagram, he or she would look for all of the following except victims who are stuck in their cars. This is the responsibility of the firefighter assigned to specific cars. Once Rescuer 3 inspected the area for issues such as utility poles with energized lines, spills of flammable liquids, and trees that may be cracked or are in danger of collapsing, then Rescuer 3 would be available to help Rescuer 1 or 2 inspect their assigned cars and determine whether victims need to be extricated. *(See Chapter V, Section A.)*

Section 2: Memory

1. **B** According to the passage, Engine 5 arrived at the scene of the fire at 8:40 p.m. *(See Chapter V, Section C.)*

2. **A** According to the passage, three firefighters from Engine 8 went inside the structure to search for victims. *(See Chapter V, Section C.)*

3. **C** According to the passage, a husband and wife live in the home with two young children, so four people live in the home. *(See Chapter V, Section C.)*

4. **A** According to the passage, the cause of the fire was a short in a string of Christmas lights. *(See Chapter V, Section C.)*

5. **D** According to the passage, the location of the fire was 512 Blueberry Lane. *(See Chapter V, Section C.)*

6. **C** The fire in this illustration is located in the parking lot between the apartment building and the restaurant. It started in a trash can that is positioned against the side of the apartment building. *(See Chapter V, Section B.)*

7. **A** This illustration features a single tree, which is in a pot on the roof of the building containing Hank's Bait and Tackle. The roof is surrounded by a fence. *(See Chapter V, Section B.)*

8. **C** The address of the building that hosts Hank's Bait and Tackle is 120 Market Street. The address of After Thoughts is 126 Market Street and the address of Hilda's Hair Salon is 132 Market Street. Finally, Paulie's Pub is 155 Market Street. The number 145 doesn't appear anywhere in this illustration. *(See Chapter V, Section B.)*

9. **C** The following statement is true: A fire hydrant is located directly across the street from After Thoughts. Choice A is incorrect because Paulie's Pub exits into the alley, not Hilda's Hair Salon. Choice B is incorrect because Tracy's Yoga Studio, not apartments, is located above Paulie's Pub. Finally, Choice D is incorrect because there are four parking spaces in the lot between Hilda's Hair Salon and Paulie's Pub, not five. *(See Chapter V, Section B.)*

10. **B** Bottles and crushed cans surround the trash can located in the parking lot between Hilda's Hair Salon and Paulie's Pub; therefore, you can claim that littering has occurred. Although the trash can is on fire, there is no evidence to suggest that someone intentionally lit the fire. It doesn't appear that any businesses have been broken into and graffiti or other property damage is not visible. *(See Chapter V, Section B.)*

11. **B** To place a take-out order from Paulie's Pub, you would dial 555-4608. This number is printed on the window to the right of the entrance to Paulie's Pub. It's also the only phone number that appears in the illustration. *(See Chapter V, Section B.)*

12. **C** A sign in After Thoughts' front window states that it is "Open 24/7." It is unclear, however, what type of services After Thoughts offers. Hours of operation do not appear on any other buildings in this illustration. *(See Chapter V, Section B.)*

13. **C** Stacy's Yoga Studio is located on the second floor of the same building containing a restaurant named Paulie's Pub. The hair salon and bait and tackle shop are both located on the ground floor of two separate buildings in this illustration. *(See Chapter V, Section B.)*

14. **A** A storm drain is located across the street from Paulie's Pub. A fire hydrant is across the street from the building containing After Thoughts and Hilda's Hair Salon, and a street sign is located across the street from Hank's Bait and Tackle. *(See Chapter V, Section B.)*

15. **B** In this illustration, the cat is in the window above the hair salon. The cat is most likely owned by someone who lives in the apartments above After Thoughts and Hilda's Hair Salon. It is positioned in the second row from the top, third window from the left. It is the only animal in this illustration. *(See Chapter V, Section B.)*

16. **D** According to the passage, when the firefighters first arrived at the scene, they laid a supply line from a hydrant. *(See Chapter V, Section C.)*

17. **C** According to the passage, Engine 11 arrived at the scene later because it was forced to find another route when a vehicle traveling in front of it stalled in the lane. *(See Chapter V, Section C.)*

18. **B** According to the passage, Engine 9 arrived at the scene at 10:45 p.m. *(See Chapter V, Section C.)*

19. **D** According to the passage, the location of the fire was 15 Commerce Avenue. *(See Chapter V, Section C.)*

20. **C** According to the passage, about two hours passed between the initial report of fire at 10:30 p.m. and when the engines pulled into the station's garage at 12:30 a.m. *(See Chapter V, Section C.)*

Section 3: Spatial Orientation

1. **A** The café is located on Chapel Street, and the bookstore is located on South Main Avenue, so you would have to walk northeast to reach the café from the bookstore. *(See Chapter VI, Section C.)*

2. **C** After leaving the grocery store, you will cross both North and South Main Avenues. At the intersection of South Main Avenue, you begin to head north. Following this route, the last building on your left will be the salon. *(See Chapter VI, Section C.)*

3. **B** If you head east from the intersection of Farley Street and South Main Avenue, you will cross both North and South Main Avenues and eventually arrive at the grocery store. *(See Chapter VI, Section C.)*

4. **D** The pond is located in the southeast. If you walk west from there, the two buildings you will see ahead of you are the bookstore and the day care. If you pass the first of these buildings (bookstore) and enter the second, you will find yourself in the day care. *(See Chapter VI, Section C.)*

5. **B** The day care is located in the southwest and the salon in located in the northwest, so, from the salon, you would have to walk *southwest* to reach the day care. *(See Chapter VI, Section C.)*

6. **C** If you enter the office area from the fire stairs on the south side of the building, proceed around the corner, and enter the first room you encounter on your right-hand side, you will find yourself in Office 4. *(See Chapter V, Section C.)*

7. **A** The safest way to rescue the victims would be to instruct the victims to proceed north across the main floor until they reach Office 2 and then proceed to the fire stairs at the northwest corner of the building. Because the fire is spreading at a rapid pace, it would be too dangerous for the victims to attempt to crawl on their hands and knees to their assigned emergency exit or to sit and wait to be rescued on the same side of the building the fire is burning, so Choices C and D are incorrect. In addition, elevators should never be used in the event of a fire, so Choice B is incorrect. *(See Chapter V, Section C.)*

8. **A** If you start out facing the bank of elevators and then proceed to your left, you will arrive at Office 3, which will be the first door on your right once you have turned left again. Proceeding forward again, the second door you arrive at will place you in front of Office 2. *(See Chapter V, Section C.)*

9. **D** If you enter the office from the fire stairs on the north side of the building and follow the wall on your right-hand side, you will first come to the storage closet, which is locked. If you proceed to and enter the next door along that wall, you will be standing in the conference room. *(See Chapter V, Section C.)*

10. **B** It would be best to use the break room as an extraction point for victims trapped on this floor of the office building because it has two windows through which the victims could be rescued, whereas most of the other rooms just have one. Although the conference room has more windows than the break room, the room is located above the fire and should therefore be avoided in case the floor gives way or the room grows too warm. Victims cannot be rescued from the bathroom or the copy room because these rooms don't have windows. *(See Chapter V, Section C.)*

11. **D** Heading south on Meadow Road, your first left turn would put you on Woodside Road. The next right would put you on Glen Lane, and your final right would put you on Longview Road near the *library*. This route is appropriate and abides by all laws because even though Glen Lane is a one-way street heading north, you're walking and can travel south. If you were in a car, you'd have to travel north. *(See Chapter VI, Section C.)*

12. **A** The quickest route from the pizza parlor to the day care would be west on Hillside Road, south on Meadow Road, and west on Longview Road. *(See Chapter VI, Section C.)*

13. **C** If you walk one block west from the library, you will reach the intersection of Longview and Meadow roads. Turning north, you will proceed up Meadow Road. Two blocks later, you will find yourself at the intersection of Meadow and Hillside roads. Turning east, you will find yourself in front of the fire station. *(See Chapter VI, Section C.)*

14. **D** The library is located on Longview Road, so you would have to walk southeast to get there from the café. *(See Chapter VI, Section C.)*

15. **C** The route described will take you west on Woodside Road, south on Meadow Road, and west on Longview Road, which would place you nearest to the day care. *(See Chapter VI, Section C.)*

16. **B** If you follow the instructions and route described in the question, your left hand will pass over the entrances to two rooms: Bedroom 2 and the dining room. *(See Chapter V, Section C.)*

17. **A** If you follow the instructions and route described in the question, you will find yourself standing at the entrance of Bedroom 3 in Apartment B. *(See Chapter V, Section C.)*

18. **B** Two smoke alarms are installed in each apartment. In Apartment A, one is located in the office and another is located in Bedroom 3. In Apartment B, one is located in the office and the other is located in the living room. *(See Chapter V, Section C.)*

19. **C** If you walk straight forward into the living room of Apartment B and then proceed along the wall to your left, you will eventually reach the entrance to the kitchen. *(See Chapter V, Section C.)*

20. **C** If you follow the wall to your left upon exiting the office, you will make your way along the living-room wall and into the hallway. The first entrance you encounter will take you into Bedroom 1. Once inside, if you follow the wall to the right, you will eventually find another door that leads to the bathroom. *(See Chapter V, Section C.)*

Section 4: Reading Comprehension

1. **A** According to the passage, the trash fire occurred on May 18. *(See Chapter VI, Section A.)*

2. **B** According to the passage, the cause of the multi-family dwelling has not been determined. *(See Chapter VI, Section A.)*

3. **D** According to the passage, no structures were involved in the trash fire, so none was damaged. *(See Chapter VI, Section A.)*

4. **C** The cause of the single-family dwelling fire is negligence, due to a candle being left unattended. *(See Chapter VI, Section A.)*

5. **C** *Ambulatory* is an adjective that most nearly means able to walk about, or roam. *(See Chapter VI, Section A.)*

6. **D** According to the passage, Tyler Miller appears to be the most seriously injured individual. He is unconscious and has a broken bone protruding through the skin. *(See Chapter VI, Section A.)*

7. **A** According to the passage, only one victim, Tyler Miller, was not wearing a seat belt. *(See Chapter VI, Section A.)*

8. **B** According to the passage, the three individuals in the Civic were trapped. *(See Chapter VI, Section A.)*

9. **C** According to the passage, Charlotte Santi was driving a 2009 red Chevrolet Malibu. *(See Chapter VI, Section A.)*

10. **D** According to the table, the water curtain is used to prevent items near a fire from igniting. Water curtains are similar to sprinklers; they shoot water up into the air and then the water falls, like a curtain, onto the fire and surrounding areas. *(See Chapter VI, Section A.)*

11. **C** According to the table, the Bresnan cellar nozzle rotates because outlets form water jets. *(See Chapter VI, Section A.)*

12. **B** According to the table, the penetrator nozzle has a hardened steel tip that can be forced through a wall or other obstruction. *(See Chapter VI, Section A.)*

13. **D** According to the table, the Bresnan cellar nozzle can be used to attack a basement fire when it is inserted through a hole in the floor. *(See Chapter VI, Section A.)*

14. **C** According to the passage, Firefighter Falcone found three violations on the second floor: the expired fire extinguisher, paint-sealed exit windows, and a faulty smoke detector. *(See Chapter VI, Section A.)*

15. **A** According to the passage, the building was a three-story commercial/residential property and the owner was preparing the two upper floors for residential use. *(See Chapter VI, Section A.)*

16. **D** Firefighter Falcone found a window exit that was painted shut, and bulbs in the emergency exit signs were out on the third floor. *(See Chapter VI, Section A.)*

17. **A** According to the passage, a real-estate office is located on the ground floor of the building. *(See Chapter VI, Section A.)*

18. **C** You can determine from the chart that most of the fires in July occurred in week 1. *(See Chapter VI, Section A.)*

19. **A** According to the chart, seven fires occurred in weeks 3 and 4 combined. No fires occurred in week 3, and seven fires occurred in week 4, so 0 + 7 = 7. *(See Chapter VI, Section A.)*

20. **C** According to the chart, no fires occurred in week 3, so week 3 had the fewest fires in July. *(See Chapter VI, Section A.)*

Section 5: Verbal Expression

1. **C** The correct spelling of *flammible* is *flammable*. *(See Chapter VI, Section B1.)*

2. **D** The correct spelling of *cemetary* is *cemetery*. *(See Chapter VI, Section B1.)*

3. **B** The correct spelling of *altar* in this sentence is *alter*, which means to change. *(See Chapter VI, Section B1.)*

4. **A** The correct spelling of *noticable* is *noticeable*. *(See Chapter VI, Section B1.)*

5. **C** The correct spelling of *serched* is *searched*. *(See Chapter VI, Section B1.)*

6. **B** The correct spelling of *elavator* is *elevator*. *(See Chapter VI, Section B1.)*

7. **A** The correct spelling of *exaust* is *exhaust*. *(See Chapter VI, Section B1.)*

8. **D** The correct spelling of *cuplings* is *couplings*. *(See Chapter VI, Section B1.)*

9. **C** The correct answer is the preposition *through*, which establishes the relationship between the verb *climbed* and the object of the preposition *window*. *(See Chapter VI, Section B5.)*

10. **D** The correct answer is the preposition *during*, which establishes the relationship between the verb *listened* and the object of the preposition *demonstration*. *(See Chapter VI, Section B5.)*

11. **A** Because the adjective comes before a noun ending in –ing, (*asking*), you need to use the possessive adjective *their* instead of *theirs*. *(See Chapter VI, Section B2.)*

12. **B** Because the action began in the past and continues into the present, you need to use the present-perfect tense *has attempted*. *(See Chapter VI, Section B4.)*

13. **D** Because both the actions were completed in the past, you need to use the past-perfect tense *had invited*. *(See Chapter VI, Section B4.)*

14. **C** Because you only have to describe one noun (*street*), you need to use the positive adjective *narrow*. *(See Chapter VI, Section B2.)*

15. **B** Because you are comparing two nouns, you need to use the comparative adjective *better*. *(See Chapter VI, Section B2.)*

16. **C** The correct spelling of *ventilacion* is *ventilation*. *(See Chapter VI, Section B1.)*

17. **A** The correct spelling of *comercial* is *commercial*. *(See Chapter VI, Section B1.)*

18. **B** Because at least two subjects are connected by the conjunction *and*, you need to use the plural verb *are*. *(See Chapter VI, Section B4.)*

19. **A** Because the subject (*system*) is singular, you need to use the singular verb *was*. *(See Chapter VI, Section B4.)*

20. **D** Because the action will take place in the future, you need to use the future tense *will carry*. *(See Chapter VI, Section B4.)*

Section 6: Deductive/Inductive/Logical Reasoning

1. **B** This situation would require the expertise of the fire/arson investigator, as it is this individual's responsibility to determine the source and cause of a fire. *(See Chapter VI, Section B1.)*

2. **A** This situation would require the expertise of the fire prevention officer, as it is this individual's responsibility to oversee the enforcement of all fire code regulations. *(See Chapter VII, Section B1.)*

3. **D** This situation would require the expertise of the fire protection engineer, as it is this individual's responsibility to help design and implement fire prevention and safety systems. *(See Chapter VII, Section B1.)*

4. **C** This situation would require the expertise of the public fire safety instructor, as it is this individual's responsibility to educate the public about fire safety and prevention. *(See Chapter VII, Section B1.)*

5. **B** Among the symptoms displayed by the driver of the first car, the fact that he appears dazed and disoriented most likely indicates that he has suffered a concussion. *(See Chapter VII, Section B2.)*

6. **B** Firefighters would most likely suspect that the driver of the second car has suffered an internal injury because he presents with abdominal distention and discoloration. *(See Chapter VII, Section B2.)*

7. **B** Because the driver of the first car presents with an apparent broken right arm and an injury to the right side of his chest, you can infer that he most likely impacted the dashboard with his right side. *(See Chapter VII, Section B2.)*

8. **C** The most appropriate title for this passage is "On-Scene Victim Assessment." *(See Chapter VII, Section B2.)*

9. **D** The number 22 completes this sequence. The first number in this sequence is 2. The second number is 7, which is 2 + 5. The third number is 12, which is 7 + 5. The fourth number is 17, which is 12 + 5. The fifth number is missing, but the sixth number is 27. The pattern seems to be adding 5 to each number. If you add 5 to the fourth number, you'll get 22 (17 + 5 = 22). This makes sense as 22 + 5 = 27, which fits into the sequence. *(See Chapter VII, Section B3.)*

10. **B** The pattern shows the triangle moving clockwise around the box, so the correct answer should show an image with the triangle on the right of the box. This series starts with a box with a shaded triangle on the bottom. In the second image, the triangle moves to the left of the box. In the third image, the triangle moves to the top of the box. Therefore, the fourth image should show the triangle on the right of the box because the fifth image shows the triangle on the bottom of the box again. *(See Chapter VII, Section B3.)*

11. **A** The number 53 correctly completes the pattern. The pattern in this sequence is to multiply by 3 and add 2 to each number: $1 \times 3 = 3$ and $3 + 2 = 5$; $5 \times 3 = 15$ and $15 + 2 = 17$. Therefore, to determine the next number, multiply 17 by 3 and add 2: $17 \times 3 = 51 + 2 = 53$. To check to see if 53 is the correct answer, multiply 53 by 3 and add 2: $53 \times 3 = 159 + 2 = 161$, which is the next number in the sequence. *(See Chapter VII, Section B3.)*

12. **C** This series begins with a 5×5 square with a black dot in the last column of the first row. The second image shows the same square with a black dot in the first column of the first row. The fourth image shows the same square with a black dot in the first column of the second row. The fifth image shows the same square with a black dot in the last column of the third row. The sixth image shows the same square with a black dot in the first column of the third row. Therefore, the third image should show the same square with a black dot in the last column of the second row. *(See Chapter VII, Section B3.)*

13. **C** Because only one supporting wall has failed and the opposite half of the roof remains in its original position, this scenario would best be described as a lean-to collapse. *(See Chapter VII, Section B1.)*

14. **D** Because only one supporting wall has failed and the rest of the structure remains intact, this scenario would best be described as a cantilever collapse. *(See Chapter VII, Section B1.)*

15. **B** Because all four supporting walls have remained intact and only the roof of the structure has collapsed, this scenario would best be described as a V-shaped collapse. *(See Chapter VII, Section B1.)*

16. **A** If you examine the information in the table, you can conclude that homes with more smoke detectors suffer less property damage than homes with fewer smoke detectors. While the information doesn't specifically state that, it does show a correlation between the number of smoke detectors in a home and the total property damage. The table shows that as the number of smoke detectors in a home increases by 1, the amount of property damage decreases by $3,000. *(See Chapter VII, Section B2.)*

17. **D** Though the passage begins with the information that brush fires are spread by wind, the passage is mostly about the different parts of a brush fire, so "The Parts of a Brush Fire" is an appropriate title for this passage. *(See Chapter VII, Section B2.)*

18. **B** The passage cautions against a head-on assault of the fire from the leading edge. Because the passage states that the head of the fire is the moving brush fire's leading edge, it is most likely the most dangerous position to take when fighting this type of fire. *(See Chapter VII, Section B2.)*

19. **D** This fire would be categorized as a large-loss fire. From the security guard's statement, we know that more than $5 million in property was destroyed in the fire, and according to the information in the passage, large-loss fires involve fires that have property loss of $5 million or more and typically occur in storage structures, such as warehouses. *(See Chapter VII, Section B1.)*

20. **B** The fire could be categorized as a group fire. Because the apartment buildings are close together, the fire can spread from one apartment building to another apartment building and cause a group fire. *(See Chapter VII, Section B1.)*

Section 7: Information Ordering

1. **C** In the first paragraph, it states that victims who are not breathing should be treated first. The second paragraph states that Sarah Gerard is not breathing; therefore, she should be treated first. Then, Kyle John, Cheryl Monroe, and James Monroe should be treated. *(See Chapter VII, Section C.)*

2. **B** In the first paragraph, it states that victims who have minor scrapes and bruises should be treated last. The second paragraph states that Pat Monroe has a large contusion, or bruise, on his arm; therefore, he should be treated last. Sarah Gerard, Kyle John, and Cheryl Monroe should be treated before Pat Monroe. *(See Chapter VII, Section C.)*

3. **A** In the first paragraph, it states that victims who are in shock should be treated after those with lacerations, or bleeding wounds. The second paragraph states that Kyle John has a deep laceration, so he should be treated before Cheryl Monroe, who is in shock. *(See Chapter VII, Section C.)*

4. **B** The correct order in which the injuries/conditions should be treated is heart attack, deep-bleeding laceration, shock, broken ankle, and large contusion. In the first paragraph, it states that those requiring cardiopulmonary resuscitation (CPR) should be treated first, so those suffering from a heart attack would come first. Victims with bleeding wounds, such as a deep-bleeding laceration, should be treated next. After this, victims in shock should be treated. Then, those with broken bones should be treated, and finally those with minor scrapes and bruises should be treated. *(See Chapter VII, Section C.)*

5. **C** According to the passage, the first thing a firefighter should do before swinging an axe is to make sure the area is clear so no one is injured. While making sure the axe is sharpened, inspecting the axe, and ensuring the cutting edge is facing forward are important steps, these steps were not mentioned in the passage. *(See Chapter VII, Section C.)*

6. **D** According to the passage, the best way for firefighters to cut the roof boards is in a circular motion at a 60-degree angle, so after cutting a roof's sheathing, firefighters will then cut the roof boards using a circular motion. *(See Chapter VII, Section C.)*

7. **D** According to the passage and the information provided, the firefighter should not have swung the axe and hit the door at a 90-degree angle, but should have chopped in a circular motion at a 60-degree angle. *(See Chapter VII, Section C.)*

8. **A** The first step is to choose firefighter service. The second is to push the button to close the door. The third is to push the button for the desired floor. The fourth is to test the call-cancel button. The fifth is to push the button for the desired floor if the elevator inadvertently stops at the next floor. The sixth is to push and hold the door-open button until the door stops when the desired floor is reached. *(See Chapter VII, Section C.)*

9. **B** While all the steps are performed after you choose firefighter service, the step that comes directly after choosing firefighter service is to push the button to close the elevator door. *(See Chapter VII, Section C.)*

10. **C** If you need to access the elevators quickly, you should first use the three-position key to recall the elevators to the lobby. No information is provided in the passage about directing residents, so Choices A and B are incorrect. And because you're already on the scene, firefighter service has already been initiated, so Choice D is incorrect. *(See Chapter VII, Section C.)*

11. **D** If you are in an elevator car and see water dripping inside the car, you should exit the elevator immediately. To do this, push and hold the door-open button at the next floor the elevator stops at, even if it is not your desired destination. *(See Chapter VII, Section C.)*

12. **B** If you need to access the elevators from the lobby, first you should use the three-position key to recall the elevator to the lobby. Because you need to rescue people, you should not waste time waiting for the elevator to return to the lobby, so Choice A is incorrect. Firefighter service should have already been initiated, so Choice C is incorrect. The passage does not indicate that you should make any announcements, so Choice D is not correct. *(See Chapter VII, Section C.)*

13. **B** While Choice A is part of the search-and-rescue guidelines, the first team already searched these rooms, but they failed to leave hang tags, so it's most likely that the second team doesn't know the rooms were already searched. The passage did not indicate that the second team was ordered to ventilate or recheck rooms, so Choices C and D are incorrect. *(See Chapter VII, Section C.)*

14. **D** Because the passage did not state that any other firefighters entered the burning trailer, you can assume the firefighter entered the search-and-rescue mission alone, which violates the guideline stating that firefighters should always enter a burning building in groups of at least two. The firefighter left the young man with a neighbor, so Choice A is incorrect. She left hang tags as she searched, and she crawled on her hands and knees during the search, so Choices B and C are incorrect. *(See Chapter VII, Section C.)*

15. **A** Firefighter Evans most likely forgot to check his breathing apparatus before entering the building. Because firefighters crawl on their hands and knees to increase their visibility, Choice B is incorrect. The passage does not state that Firefighter Evans checked any rooms; therefore, Choice C is incorrect. Because Firefighter Harris pulled Firefighter Evans out of the building, he was not alone, so Choice D is incorrect. *(See Chapter VII, Section C.)*

16. **D** The team correctly performed all the steps in a search-and-rescue mission. Because no fire victims were found in the burning structure, Choice A is incorrect. The passage states that the firefighters checked their breathing apparatus before entering the building and placed hang tags on searched rooms, so Choices B and C are incorrect. *(See Chapter VII, Section C.)*

17. **B** Prior to the lead rescuer supporting the victim's head, the rescuers should kneel as close as they can to the victim. After the lead rescuer supports the victim's head, the other rescuers should place their arms under the victim's body; they should carry the victim to the location of the gurney; and lower the victim onto the gurney. *(Chapter VII: Section C.)*

18. **C** The information states that rescuers should reverse the steps to lower the victim to the gurney. When lowering the victim onto the gurney, first *the rescuers should carefully roll the victim away from their chests* because they should roll the victim toward their chests to lift the victim. *(See Chapter VII, Section C.)*

19. **A** Rescuers should first ensure the gurney is placed in a safe area away from fire. Then they should kneel beside the victim, place their arms under the victim's body, and roll the victim toward their chests and stand up. *(See Chapter VII, Section C.)*

20. **D** The lead rescuer did not support the victim's head with one hand before the other rescuers slid their arms under the victim's body. The passage states that the firefighters designated a lead rescuer, so Choice A is incorrect. The information states that the gurney should be placed in a raised, not lowered, position, so Choice B is incorrect. The information does not state that the lead rescuer should call paramedics, so Choice C is incorrect. *(See Chapter VII, Section C.)*

Section 8: Problem Sensitivity

1. **C** Based on the information in the passage, it can be inferred that Michael Hansen is likely the least seriously injured individual. He appears to have suffered no serious injuries and endured only minor cuts and bruises. *(See Chapter VII, Section D.)*

2. **B** Based on information in the passage, it can be inferred that Timothy Hansen is likely the most seriously injured individual. According to the report, in addition to severe cuts and bruises, he appeared to have suffered serious oral trauma. Moreover, his complaints of chest pain and difficulty breathing would likely indicate broken ribs or some form of respiratory trauma. *(See Chapter VII, Section D.)*

3. **A** Based on the information in the passage, it can be inferred that Timothy Hansen was the most seriously injured of the occupants of the 2003 Hyundai Sonata. Steven Hansen suffered from severe cuts and bruises and reported severe pain in his right hand. Michael Hanson suffered only a few minor cuts and had no complaints. Jonathan Hanson was reported thrown into the back of the front passenger's seat and complained of severe pain in his neck and right shoulder. He also had difficulty moving his right arm. *(See Chapter VII, Section C.)*

4. **A** Parker's behavior would most likely indicate that his problem is *health-related.* His edgy, temperamental attitude with his co-workers and reluctant behavior on-scene seem to indicate that Parker's earlier accident has had a profound psychological effect and has impaired his mental well-being. *(See Chapter VII, Section D.)*

5. **B** Cohen's behavior would most likely indicate that his problem is financial. His desire to work many long hours and the fact that he no longer orders food with his co-workers or drives his car to work would likely indicate that he is having some form of financial problem. The reports of other firefighters seeing him at a casino suggest that his issue might be related to gambling. *(See Chapter VII, Section D.)*

6. **D** A call about a kitchen fire in an apartment building would most likely be the most urgent of the given notifications. Such a fire, which could easily spread through the building and endanger many lives, would present the most significant threat to public welfare and require immediate attention. While a report of a wildfire in a remote forested area is urgent, it does not present a significant threat to public welfare. A report of a single-car accident with no injuries could be handled by the police and would not be considered urgent. A request for a fire prevention seminar would not be considered an urgent request. *(See Chapter VII, Section D.)*

7. **C** Grant's behavior would most likely indicate that his problem is marital. His worsening depression, emotionally charged phone calls with his wife, and choice to sometimes sleep at the station instead of going home all suggest that Grant may be experiencing some marital issues with his spouse. *(See Chapter VII, Section D.)*

8. **C** Based on the information in the passage, it can be inferred that Eric Leonard is likely the most seriously injured individual. His inability to feel his lower extremities suggests that he may have suffered a spinal injury. In addition, his complaints of chest pain and the fact that he is coughing up blood and having difficulty breathing suggests a traumatic chest injury that may have damaged one or both of his lungs. *(See Chapter VII, Section D.)*

9. **D** Based on the information in the passage, it can be inferred that Gene Howard is likely the least seriously injured individual. He has suffered no visible injuries and only complains of minor neck pain. *(See Chapter VII, Section D.)*

10. **C** Based on the information in the passage, it can be inferred that Marilyn Thomas was the most seriously injured of the occupants of Simmons's vehicle. Her disorientation and obvious head trauma suggest that she may have suffered a severe cranial injury. It also appears that she has a broken right forearm. *(See Chapter VII, Section D.)*

11. **A** Harris's behavior would most likely indicate that his problem is related to alcohol. Based on his worsening appearance, apparent exhaustion, and the fact that firefighters have seen his car parked outside the bar near the fire department, it is likely that Harris has developed a drinking problem because of the loss of his brother. *(See Chapter VII, Section D.)*

12. **B** McGowan's behavior would most likely indicate that his problem is related to his health. Based on his switch from focusing on the more physical aspects of his job to other less-demanding aspects, you can draw the conclusion that McGowan may be experiencing difficulty performing these physical tasks possibly because of his age; the passage states that he is one of the department's most veteran members. *(See Chapter VII, Section D.)*

13. **C** A call about an accident involving hazardous materials would likely be the most urgent of the given notifications. Such an accident, which would likely require immediate containment and decontamination measures, would present the most significant threat to public welfare and require immediate attention. While a shed fire can also be urgent, a small contained shed fire is not as urgent as an accident involving hazardous materials. *(See Chapter VII, Section D.)*

14. **B** Thompson's behavior most likely indicates that his problem is related to job stress. Based on his actions and his former co-workers' statement that he never behaved this way before, you can infer that Thompson's behavior is likely tied to job stress related to his recent change in employers. *(See Chapter VII, Section D.)*

15. **D** Based on information in the passage, it can be inferred that Charles White is the individual most in need of immediate medical attention. The passage indicates that he has sustained serious burns and has likely suffered severe cranial trauma. Coupled with his obviously altered mental state, the information provided indicates that Mr. White is in more serious condition than any of the other victims. *(See Chapter VII, Section D.)*

16. **D** Based on information in the passage, it can be inferred that Ashley Reynolds is the least in need of immediate medical attention. According to the passage, she sustained no injuries and did not complain of any pain. *(See Chapter VII, Section D.)*

17. **C** Based on information in the passage, it can be inferred that Ronald Reynolds is the passenger most in need of immediate medical attention. The passage indicates that he complains of severe abdominal pain, which is accompanied by distention and discoloration. This evidence suggests that he may have sustained internal injuries. Because these injuries may pose a serious health risk, Ronald Reynolds is the passenger most in need of immediate medical care. *(See Chapter VII, Section D.)*

18. **D** An EMS call regarding a commercial airplane accident would likely be the most urgent of the given notifications. Such an accident is likely to be a mass-casualty incident that will involve a large number of victims in need of urgent medical care. Airplane accidents also pose a serious fire risk because of the large quantities of highly flammable fuels planes contain. *(See Chapter VII, Section D.)*

19. **B** Clarke's behavior would most likely indicate that his problem is related to drugs. His change in behavior and bleary-eyed and scruffy appearance indicate that Clarke most likely has a drug problem. *(See Chapter VII, Section D.)*

20. **C** Williams's behavior most likely indicates that her problem is related to domestic violence. Her change in attitude, her emotional instability, and the injuries she has been regularly displaying all hint at the possibility that she may be a victim of domestic violence. *(See Chapter VII, Section D.)*

Section 9: Mathematics

1. **B** To solve this problem, use the FOIL method. First: $4x \times -3x = -12x^2$; Outer: $4x \times 8 = 32x$; Inner: $-6 \times -3x = 18x$; Last: $-6 \times 8 = -48$. Now, combine like terms: $32x + -18x = 50x$; The correct answer is $-12x^2 + 50x - 48$. *(See Chapter VIII, Section D2.)*

2. **A** The correct answer is $7°C$. To solve this problem, plug the numbers you know into the Fahrenheit to Celsius formula and solve:

$$C = (F - 32)\frac{5}{9}$$
$$= (44.6 - 32)\frac{5}{9}$$
$$= (12.6)\frac{5}{9}$$
$$= \frac{12.6 \times 5}{1 \times 9}$$
$$= \frac{63}{9}$$
$$= 7$$

(See Chapter VIII, Section A5.)

3. **D** The correct answer is $\frac{49}{27}$. Because the denominators are different, you must find a common denominator before you can add the numerators. A common multiple of 4, 8, and 12 is 24. Next, multiply the numerator and denominator of each fraction by the number that gets you equal to that denominator: $\frac{3}{4} \times \frac{6}{6} = \frac{18}{24}; \frac{7}{8} \times \frac{3}{3} = \frac{21}{24}; \frac{5}{12} \times \frac{2}{2} = \frac{10}{24}$.

Next, add the numerators $\frac{18}{24} + \frac{21}{24} + \frac{10}{24} = \frac{49}{24}$, which cannot reduce. *(See Chapter VII, Section B1.)*

4. **C** If you correctly followed the order of operations, you would get 972. First, solve what's inside the parentheses: $(4 \times 3) = 12$ and $(7 + 2) = 9$; next, solve the exponent: $9^2 = 81$; then multiply: $12 \times 81 = 972$. *(See Chapter VIII, Section A4.)*

5. **C** It will take Fire Chief Norris 8 hours, 45 minutes to complete 12 evaluations. If you examine the information in the passage and table, you can determine that Fire Chief Norris can complete two evaluations in 1 hour and 45 minutes. Based on this number, you can determine that he can complete 8 evaluations in 7 hours and 12 evaluations in 8 hours, 45 minutes. *(See Chapter VIII, Section F2.)*

6. **B** The cylinder's height is 5.7 inches. To solve this problem, use the volume formula for a cylinder $(V = \pi r^2 h)$ and plug in the values: $80 = 3.14(12)^2 h$. $80 = 3.14 \times 144 \times h = 80 = 452.16 \times h$. Last, divide each side by 80:

$$\frac{80}{80} = \frac{452.16}{80} \times h$$
$$5.652 = h$$
$$5.7 = h$$

(See Chapter VIII, Section E3.)

7. **A** It will take you 29 minutes to arrive at the scene. To solve this problem, use the distance formula $(d = r \times t)$ and plug in the numbers. Next, divide each side by 55 miles per hour and solve to get $\frac{27}{55}$ hours $= t$:

$$d = rt$$
$$27 \text{ miles} = 55 \text{ miles per hour} \times t$$
$$\frac{27 \text{ miles}}{55 \text{ miles per hour}} = \frac{55 \text{ miles per hour}}{55 \text{ miles per hour}} \times t$$
$$\frac{27}{55} \text{ hours} = t$$

Because your answer is in hours and the question asks for the answer in minutes, you have to multiply $\frac{27}{55}$ by the number of minutes in 1 hour (60):

$$\frac{27}{55 \text{ hours}} \times \frac{60 \text{ minutes}}{1} = \frac{1,620 \text{ minutes}}{55 \text{ hours}} = 29.45 \text{ minutes} \approx 29 \text{ minutes}$$

(See Chapter VIII, Section F1.)

8. **C** Firefighter Jameson can run 12 miles in 84 minutes. To solve this problem, set up a proportion to represent the number of minutes to the number of miles and use cross-multiplication:

$$\frac{4}{28} = \frac{x}{84}$$
$$28x = 336$$
$$\frac{28x}{28} = \frac{336}{28}$$
$$x = 12$$

(See Chapter VIII, Section C.)

9. **C** The correct answer is y^{30}. To multiply powers with the same base, add the exponents: $(y^{11})(y^{19}) = y^{11+19=30}$. *(See Chapter VIII, Section A3.)*

10. **B** To solve this problem, first find a common denominator: 100. Next, multiply each fraction to achieve the common denominator: $\frac{9}{5} \times \frac{20}{20} = \frac{180}{100}$; $\frac{12}{10} \times \frac{10}{10} = \frac{120}{100}$; $\frac{3}{25} \times \frac{4}{4} = \frac{12}{100}$; $\frac{4}{50} \times \frac{2}{2} = \frac{8}{100}$; $\frac{2}{100}$. Next, substitute the new fractions into the problem, and then add and subtract: $\frac{180}{100} + \frac{120}{100} + \frac{12}{100} - \frac{8}{100} - \frac{2}{100} = \frac{302}{100}$.

Last, convert the fraction into a decimal and round to the nearest hundredth: $\frac{302}{100} = 3.02$. *(See Chapter VIII, Section B1.)*

11. **D** If you correctly followed the order of operations, you would get 6,125. First, solve what's inside the parentheses: $(9 - 4) = 5$; next, solve the exponents: $7^2 = 49$ and $5^3 = 125$; then multiply: $49 \times 125 = 6,125$. *(See Chapter VIII, Section A4.)*

12. **A** The correct answer is 2.59. To solve this problem, first convert the fractions to decimals by dividing the numerators by the denominators: $\frac{4}{9} = 0.44$; $\frac{16}{3} = 5.33$; $\frac{6}{27} = 0.22$. Next, substitute the decimals into the problem: $0.44 \times 0.78 + 5.33 - 0.22$ and solve using the order of operations: $0.44 \times 0.78 = 0.3432 + 5.33 = 5.6732 - 0.22 = 5.4532 = 5.45$. *(See Chapter VIII, Section B2.)*

13. **B** A triangle with a base of 14 feet and a height of 21 feet has an area of 147 inches^2. To solve this problem, use the area formula for a triangle $\left(A = \frac{1}{2}bh\right)$ and plug in the values:

$$A = \frac{1}{2} \times 14 \times 21$$
$$= \frac{1}{2} \times 294$$
$$= 0.5 \times 294$$
$$= 147$$

(See Chapter VIII, Section E2.)

14. **C** The correct answer is 71.76. You can solve this problem in two ways. To solve this problem using cross-multiplication:

$$\frac{12}{100} = \frac{x}{598}$$
$$100x = 7,176$$
$$\frac{100x}{100} = \frac{7,176}{100}$$
$$x = 71.76$$

To solve this problem by converting the percentage to a decimal: $0.12 \times 598 = 71.76$. *(See Chapter VIII, Section B3.)*

15. B Firefighter Latona can complete 78 sit-ups in 156 seconds. To solve this problem, set up a proportion to represent the number of seconds to the number of sit-ups and use cross-multiplication:

$$\frac{45}{90} = \frac{x}{156}$$
$$90x = 7,020$$
$$\frac{90x}{90} = \frac{7,020}{90}$$
$$x = 78$$

(Chapter VIII, Section C.)

16. B The hole is 54 feet². To solve this problem, multiply 6 by 9: $6 \times 9 = 54$ feet². *(See Chapter VIII, Section F3.)*

17. C The correct answer is 100. First, multiply the denominator of one fraction by the numerator of the other:

$$\frac{250}{15} = \frac{x}{6}$$
$$15x = 1,500$$

Next, divide each side by 15:

$$\frac{15x}{15} = \frac{1,500}{15}$$
$$x = 100$$

(See Chapter VIII, Section B1.)

18. D The fire engine traveled at an average speed of 71 miles per hour on the way to the bakery. To solve this problem, use the distance formula $(d = rt)$ and plug in the numbers. Next, divide each side by 11 minutes to get $\frac{13 \text{ miles}}{11 \text{ minutes}}$:

$$d = rt$$
$$13 \text{ miles} = r \times 11 \text{ minutes}$$
$$\frac{13 \text{ miles}}{11 \text{ minutes}} = r \times \frac{11 \text{ minutes}}{11 \text{ minutes}}$$
$$\frac{13 \text{ miles}}{11 \text{ minutes}} = r$$

Because your answer is in miles per minute and the question asks for the answer in miles per hour, you have to multiply $\frac{13}{11}$ by the number of minutes in 1 hour (60):

$$\frac{13 \text{ miles}}{11 \text{ minutes}} \times \frac{60 \text{ minutes}}{1 \text{ hour}} = \frac{780}{11} = 70.91 \approx 71 \text{ miles per hour}$$

(See Chapter VIII, Section F1.)

19. **D** The correct answer is x^{-14}. To work with negative powers, turn the exponents into fractions by taking the base's reciprocal and making the exponent positive:

$$x^{-6} = \frac{1}{x^6} \text{ and } x^{-8} \frac{1}{x^8}$$

$$\frac{1}{x^6} \times \frac{1}{x^8} = \frac{1}{x^{14}} = x^{-14}$$

(See Chapter VIII, Section A3.)

20. **D** You spent 67 percent of your shift at the station. Because you spent 6 hours fighting fires and 2 hours at the scene of a car accident, you were not at the station for 8 hours. Subtract this number from the total number of hours of your shift to get the number of hours you spent at the station: $24 - 8 = 16$. You spent 16 hours out of 24 at the station or $\frac{16}{24}$. Next, convert this fraction to a percentage by dividing: $16 \div 24 = 0.67$, which equals 67 percent. *(See Chapter VIII, Section B3.)*

Section 10: Mechanical Aptitude

1. **D** The tool pictured is a cutting torch, which uses a flame to slice through thick metals. It would most likely be used for cutting in forcible-entry operations. *(See Chapter IX, Section A.)*

2. **B** Because Wheel A is twice the size of Wheel B, it rotates half as fast as Wheel B. If Wheel B rotates 90 revolutions per minute, then Wheel A makes half as many revolutions, so 90 divided by 2 is 45. Wheel A rotates 45 revolutions per minute. *(See Chapter IX, Section B.)*

3. **D** All wheels in a belt-drive pulley setup rotate in the same direction regardless of size, unless the belt is crossed. Because the belt in the image is not crossed, Wheel A and Wheel B spin in the same direction, so if Wheel A spins clockwise, Wheel B spins clockwise. *(See Chapter IX, Section B.)*

4. **A** The mechanical advantage is 30.5. To answer this question, plug the information given into the equation:

$$\text{Mechanical Advantage (MA)} = \frac{\text{radius of wheel}}{\text{radius of axle}}$$

$$\text{MA} = \frac{549}{18}$$

$$\text{MA} = 30.5$$

(See Chapter IX, Section B.)

5. **D** Reverse-thread screws are rotated counterclockwise into an object and are rotated clockwise when removed from an object. The other statements are incorrect. *(See Chapter IX, Section B.)*

6. **B** A spring will stretch 36 feet under a pull of 480 pounds. To solve this problem, first determine how many times heavier the new weight is than the old weight. To do this, divide the new weight by the old weight: $480 \div 120 = 4$. Next, multiply this number by the number of feet the spring stretches under the old weight: $4 \times 9 = 36$ feet. *(See Chapter IX, Section B.)*

7. **A** If Gear C rotates in a counterclockwise direction, then the gear its teeth are interlocked with (Gear B) must rotate in the opposite direction, therefore Gear A must rotate counterclockwise in the same direction as Gear C. *(See Chapter IX, Section B.)*

8. **C** Based on the image, you know that Gear C is the largest gear and large gears rotate slower and at fewer revolutions than smaller gears, so Gear C will make the least revolutions per minute. *(See Chapter IX, Section B.)*

9. **B** The tool pictured is a wrench, which is a double-ended hand-held tool used to tighten or loosen bolts, nuts, or pipes. *(See Chapter IX, Section A.)*

10. **A** The tool pictured is a rotary saw, also known as a *circular saw,* which is used to cut through wood, plastic, metal, or concrete. *(See Chapter IX, Section A.)*

11. **C** The firefighter must apply 28.5 pounds of force to lift the lever. To answer this question, use the formula $w \times d_1 = f \times d_2$ and plug the information you know into the formula. The weight of the object is 95 pounds, so $w = 95$. The distance from the box to the fulcrum is 15 feet, so $d_1 = 15$. The distance from the firefighter to the fulcrum is 50 feet, so $d_2 = 40$. Solve for force (f):

$$w \times d_1 = f \times d_2$$
$$95 \times 15 = f \times 50$$
$$\frac{1,425}{50} = \frac{50f}{50}$$
$$28.5 = f$$

(See Chapter IX, Section B.)

12. **D** The firefighter must apply 39 pounds of force to lift the lever. To answer this question, use the formula $w \times d_1 = f \times d_2$ and plug the information you know into the formula. The weight of the object is 195 pounds, so $w = 195$. The distance from the box to the fulcrum is 10 feet, so $d_1 = 10$. The distance from the firefighter to the fulcrum is 50 feet, so $d_2 = 25$. Solve for force (f):

$$w \times d_1 = f \times d_2$$
$$195 \times 10 = f \times 50$$
$$\frac{1,950}{50} = \frac{50f}{50}$$
$$39 = f$$

(See Chapter IX, Section B.)

13. **B** A clamp, pliers, and a rope are all used to hold, or secure, an object in place. *(See Chapter IX, Section A.)*

14. **B** The San Francisco hook would most likely be used to shut off a gas line. A Clemens hook would most likely be used to remove plaster or siding; a hydraulic spreader would most likely be used to help remove trapped accident victims; and a mallet would most likely be used to deliver a soft blow to an object. *(See Chapter IX, Section A.)*

15. **A** A ventilation saw, reciprocating saw, bolt cutter, and handsaw can all be used to cut through various materials, but a ventilation saw should never be used to cut through metals. *(See Chapter IX, Section A.)*

16. **D** The only difference between the two boxes is the size. They weigh the same, are made of the same material, and are positioned at the same angle on the inclined planes. Because Box B is smaller than Box A, Box B has a smaller surface-to-surface contact area with the inclined plane and will slide down the inclined plane at a faster rate than Box A. *(See Chapter IX, Section B.)*

17. **C** The tool pictured is a utility knife, which is a lightweight cutting tool with a retractable blade that is used to cut through light materials such as paper, fabric, or cardboard. *(See Chapter IX, Section A.)*

18. **D** The pry bar, which is a straight bar used to gain leverage to open doors or remove boards or concrete blocks, is also called a pinch bar. The other tools are a punch, chisel, and pick. *(See Chapter IX, Section A.)*

19. **B** The crowbar, which is a bar with one end inclined for prying and the other end curved, is used as a lever to move heavy objects. A rake (Choice A) is used to break up or smooth out materials or gather materials into a pile. A hydraulic door opener (Choice C) is a tool operated by a hand pump that uses hydraulic pressure to open doors. A sledgehammer (Choice D) is a long-handled tool with a large metal head used for heavy-duty pounding or breaking. *(See Chapter IX, Section A.)*

20. **A** The tool pictured is a claw tool, which is a prying tool with a hook on one end and a fork on the other end, used to pull up floorboards, baseboards, window casements, or door frames. *(See Chapter IX, Section A.)*

Appendix A
The Candidate Physical Ability Test

You have many hurdles to cross on the way to landing a job as a firefighter—and some of them involve actual hurdles, or at least barriers.

The physical demands of the job of firefighter are so great that departments screen applicants with a strenuous physical test. Firefighters need physical strength to move quickly through burning buildings, haul equipment in heavy gear, and possibly carry victims to safety. Firefighters also need strength and endurance to set up equipment, unroll and hold hoses, and at the end of the call, clean and put away all the gear. But you weren't expecting this to be a cushy desk job, were you?

In many departments, the physical test follows the written test and is before the oral interview. This means that you have to pass the Candidate Physical Ability Test (CPAT) before you can complete the oral interview.

Of course, before you even take a physical test, you must submit a statement or form from your doctor attesting to your physical health. It's a good idea to get a physical before you even begin training for a physical test.

In this appendix, we cover the demands of physical tests and suggestions for an exercise plan to get you in top shape for the grueling activities ahead.

Remember: Physical fitness isn't just about exercise. You need to eat healthy and make sure you get enough water. Some test centers recommend eating two hours before taking the CPAT. Carbohydrates and small amounts of protein and fat are recommended, as is hydrating prior to the exam. Avoiding alcohol and caffeine the day before and day of the test is also recommended. If you're a little fuzzy on proper nutrition, consider talking to your family doctor or a registered dietitian. A wealth of resources is available in books as well as online.

What to Expect on the Candidate Physical Ability Test

Physical tests vary depending on the fire department. A fire department can give you any type of physical test it chooses. However, many fire departments test applicants by asking them to complete tasks that simulate those they might face on the job, such as the stair climb, the hose drag, and forcible entry. This type of test is called the Candidate Physical Ability Test (CPAT). Candidates must complete these tasks within a set time period. They must follow rules, such as hitting every step when climbing stairs, placing rather than dropping equipment, and lowering a ladder instead of allowing it to crash to the ground to get a better time.

Tip: Scoring often differs by gender and/or age, so find out what is expected of you by the department where you've applied. Working toward a goal will help keep you focused.

Test proctors may give candidates a prescribed number of warnings of incorrect technique on a task, but this varies depending on the department. Candidates who make excessive mistakes are disqualified.

Candidates often have to complete the CPAT in full gear (check to be sure it's provided) or while wearing heavy vests that represent the weight of firefighting gear. It's a good idea to find out what is expected, so you can work out with similarly heavy and restrictive clothing.

Scoring varies from department to department as well. Some fire departments allow candidates two shots at each task, combining the best times on each to rank candidates. If you're allowed to attempt the test twice, be cautious on the first try—be sure you can complete the test without being eliminated. Then go for a faster time on the second try.

You might be asked to walk to a finish line and ring a bell to show that you're finished. Completing this last task shows that you can think clearly when exhausted and under stress.

Some fire departments allow candidates to practice on the testing grounds. If you apply at a fire department offering this opportunity, take it.

Several elements of training may be used to evaluate fitness:

- **Aerobic or cardiorespiratory fitness:** Allows you to breathe faster and more deeply. This increases the oxygen delivered throughout your body and the efficiency of this function. Jogging, swimming, and biking are some good activities to increase your heart rate.
- **Agility or coordination training:** Allows you to change your body's position by using a combination of balance, coordination, endurance, reflexes, speed, stamina, and strength. You can increase your agility by using an agility ladder, completing exercises while wearing resistance weights, and stretching.
- **Balance training:** Minimize balance deterioration that naturally occurs with age by standing on one leg for increasing periods to improve stability or participating in activities such as tai chi.
- **Body composition:** Used to determine the amount of fat, bone, and muscle in the body. Healthy individuals should have a lower percentage of body fat compared to muscle. Some ways to increase muscle and decrease fat are by lifting weights, performing cardio activities, and eating healthy, nutritious foods.
- **Core stability:** Involves using the strength in the abdomen, lower back, and pelvis to protect the back and connect upper and lower body movements. Crunches and fitness-ball exercises increase core strength.
- **Muscular fitness:** Increases bone strength; also known as strength training. In addition to hitting the resistance machines or free weights at the gym, consider inexpensive equipment such as plastic bottles filled with water or sand, resistance bands, push-ups, abdominal crunches, and squats.
- **Stretching:** Improves range of motion in joints. It's best to stretch after exercise, when muscles are warm.

The following are examples of exercises that you may be asked to complete on a physical test, along with suggestions on how to prepare for these exercises:

- **Attic crawl:** Crawling or crab walking under barriers, the candidate must carry a simulated flashlight 20 feet and emerge without knocking over any barriers. *Training tip:* Set up a ladder on sturdy, low supports and crawl across it to simulate crawling on the rafters of a weakened ceiling. Use strings stretched 3 feet above the ladder to force yourself to stay low to the ladder.
- **Charged and dry hose deployments:** These may involve obstacles or corners around which the hoses must be placed. The candidate may have to climb, stoop, or crawl over or through obstacles with the hose. *Training tip: Locate an obstacle course in your area and practice completing it while carrying heavy objects, such as weights.*

- **Crawling search:** Following a 60-foot crawl on a fourth-floor platform, the candidate carries a hose bundle to the ground. *Training tip: In addition to core training and weight lifting, candidates can prepare for the crawling search in ways that are similar to preparing for the attic crawl. (See previous page.)*

- **Halyard raise:** The candidate raises and lowers a section of extension ladder with a rope. He or she must use only the upper body, not body weight, because the candidate must also steady and brace the ladder during the task. *Training tip:* Lift weights and do exercises that target the upper-body muscles such as push-ups, chest presses, curls, and raises.

- **Hang smoke ejector:** The candidate lifts a 40-pound fan used to eliminate smoke, carries it a prescribed distance, and hangs it atop a door jamb. A shorter candidate is at a disadvantage here and must practice lifting and controlling weight above head height. *Training tip:* Lift weights; executing lat pull-downs will develop the muscles you need.

- **Hose hoist:** The candidate carries two air bottles to the third floor of the tower. Using a rope, he or she hauls up a nozzle. The rope must not touch the railing. The candidate then pulls up the attached 100 feet of hose and returns to the ground carrying the bottles. *Training tip: Lift weights to strengthen your upper body, increasing the strength and improving the performance of your triceps.*

- **Ladder removal and carry:** It is what it says: The candidate removes a long ladder from hooks, carries it around a course, and replaces it on the hooks. Test rules may prescribe methods for carrying the ladder, such as a shoulder hold. *Training tip:* Lift weights and do exercises such as lateral raises and overhead presses to develop and strengthen shoulder muscles. Also practice carrying heavy, large objects.

- **Roof ventilation:** The candidate lifts a sledge hammer, steps onto a slanted "roof," and properly strikes the target area 30 times, lifting the hammer above helmet height each time and maintaining control of the tool. *Training tip:* Lift weights, concentrating on your biceps and triceps to develop arm strength.

- **Roof walk:** This task simulates carrying a chainsaw up a ladder to a roof and then returning to the ground. Training tip: Practice climbing stairs while holding weights.

- **Stair climb with hose:** The candidate carries a hose bundle (50 lbs.) up four flights of stairs. Women may need extra training to develop the upper-body strength needed to hoist the hose. *Training tip:* Run up stairs, such as those in a parking garage, with a bag of sand or feed on your shoulder. Wear a bulky coat and a loaded backpack during practice if the test requires turnout coat and air tanks. Practice one to three times a week, depending on your fitness level.

- **Victim removal:** The candidate drags or carries a weighted dummy around obstacles for a measured distance. Some tests include a chute or short tunnel through which the victim must be dragged. *Training tip:* Tie bags of sand in a blanket or tarp and carry or drag the bundle.

- **Wall vault:** The candidate vaults over a 4- to 6-foot barrier from a standing or running start. *Training tip:* Run uphill sprints to develop leg strength. Practice hopping fences.

Creating an Exercise Plan

Anyone embarking on a fitness plan should start out slow and, of course, get a doctor's permission. The general guidelines in this section give you an idea of where to focus your efforts as you prepare for the CPAT.

Tip: You might want to make use of the personal trainers, fitness assessments, and individualized training plans many gyms offer to get your workout off the ground.

Assessing Yourself

A fitness assessment provides a benchmark against which to measure your progress. Following are some measures you might want to record to help determine your aerobic and muscular fitness, flexibility, and body composition:

- Pulse rate before and after a 1-mile walk
- Time it takes to walk a mile
- Number of push-ups you can do at a time
- How far you can reach forward, seated on the floor with your legs in front of you
- Waist circumference above your bare abdomen, just above your hipbone
- Body mass index (you can find many online calculators)

It may take some time to build up the endurance and strength you need for the CPAT, depending on the shape you're in when you begin your exercise program. Increase the intensity, duration, and frequency of workouts as you improve. Sore or swollen joints or sharp pain indicate that you have overdone the workout.

Following a Training Schedule

Once you've assessed your current fitness, you can sketch out a fitness regimen alternating strength training and cardio workouts to prepare for the CPAT. Create a balanced routine, vary the activities to avoid boredom, and remember to alternate the muscle groups you work.

Each workout should include a warm-up and a cool-down:

- **Warming up:** Warming up helps get your cardiovascular system moving, increasing the blood flow to your muscles. Focus first on large muscle groups such as hamstrings and then add exercises more specific to your workout. Warm up for a run with a brisk 5- to 10-minute walk. Warm up for strength training by moving muscles and joints in the patterns you'll use during exercise. Warm up for swimming by swimming at a slower pace.
- **Cooling down:** Cooling down may gradually reduce the temperature of your muscles. Top athletes cool down to help regulate blood flow after intense activity. After a run, walk briskly for 5 to 10 minutes. After swimming, swim leisurely laps, varying your strokes, for 5 to 10 minutes.

> **Tip: Develop flexibility by incorporating stretching in your cool-down; stretching increases blood flow to the muscles and may decrease the risk of injury. Stretch gently. Don't bounce or stretch to the point of pain.**

You can increase the duration of your workouts as your fitness level increases. Add some moderate resistance exercise to cardio days, do some extra sit-ups, or add uphill sprints to your jog as endurance increases.

Take a look at the following general schedule for ideas:

- **Monday: Strength.** Weights 20 minutes, calisthenics 10 minutes (this combination provides a total 30 minutes of muscle training); increase calisthenics gradually.
- **Tuesday: Cardio.** Aerobic activity such as cycling or calisthenics 20 minutes.

- **Wednesday: Strength.** Weights 20 minutes, calisthenics 10 minutes (this combination provides a total 30 minutes of muscle training); increase calisthenics gradually.
- **Thursday: Cardio.** Aerobic activity such as jogging or calisthenics 20 minutes.
- **Friday: Strength.** Weights 20 minutes, calisthenics 10 minutes (this combination provides a total 30 minutes of muscle training); increase calisthenics gradually.

In addition to training, it's important to eat a healthy diet while you're preparing for the CPAT.

Tip: Remember to include rest days each week. You might still include activities such as hiking or other recreation, but keep it moderate. Your body needs time to recover and even to heal—don't push too hard, or you could end up sitting out the CPAT due to injury.

Warning: If you are in pain, short of breath, dizzy, or nauseated, take a break. If the condition continues, seek medical attention. Be flexible about your workout if you are not feeling well.

Appendix B
The Oral Interview

You've hit the books and hit the gym, now it's time to hit one out of the ballpark with your face-to-face interview.

Pressure is a big part of a firefighter's job, and the interview is an opportunity for the panel to see how you handle pressure. Remember, you want to work in a department that serves and regularly interacts with the public, so it's important to conduct yourself well and be courteous at all times.

Be sure of the date, time, and place of your interview. Allow plenty of time for travel; if you can visit the site in advance at the same time of day as your interview, you will get an idea of traffic delays you may encounter. On the day of the interview, arrive 20 minutes early, check in if necessary, and visit the restroom to freshen up.

Show respect for the panel and the position by turning your cell phone off. Not on vibrate, *off*.

When interviewing for most jobs, a candidate faces one or two interviewers, at least for the first meeting. Firefighter candidates, on the other hand, face many more interviewers. They may feel as though they're facing a tribunal, or even a firing squad. Several people will ask you questions, some from the ranks of the department, others from the municipal level, and possibly community leaders. Questions may be standardized (the same for all candidates) or based on your answers in the application process. Most of the usual job interview rules apply, however, so put on your game face and smile, it's time to prep for the questions and learn to ace the oral interview.

What to Expect

The firefighter oral interview is intimidating to most candidates. After all, you're facing a panel of professionals who have probably been told to appear neutral as you answer their questions. We're creatures of social interaction, used to feedback in the form of nods, smiles, and the occasional chuckle as we slip in a joke to break the ice. Don't take it personally, and remain friendly and respectful if you're met with poker faces. It's not that they dislike you; it's that they're evaluating you for a very important job and trying to determine your potential as a firefighter.

Tip: Remember to say "yes, sir" and "no, ma'am." Fire departments are structured by rank and the panel expects to see discipline and respect in candidates. Treat the receptionist, fellow candidates, and every person you encounter with respect, eye contact, and a smile. You can make an all-around good impression (you never know who might notice and mention it after you've gone) and get your head in the game before your interview.

You should expect open-ended questions and dilemmas that may not have a correct answer. These questions are meant to glean your ability to evaluate situations quickly and calmly. Here are some typical interview questions. Answer honestly, and try to include examples that indicate personal growth. If you think you are rambling, take a breath to collect your thoughts and get back on track.

- **Tell us about yourself.** This isn't an invitation to describe your latest fishing trip or your passion for extreme sports. Contrary to the way it sounds, this is not a personal question, it's a business question. Prepare a personal statement of what you offer and specifics about your value. Keep it to a sentence or two. You don't want to give them everything immediately. Plenty of questions are coming your way.

- **Why do you want to be a firefighter?** It's not enough to want to help people; you need to explain your strengths in serving the community in *this* profession. Your answer should address your skills and abilities. These may include physical and learning nimbleness, calm demeanor in crisis, good relationships with co-workers and the public, and tenacity.

- **What are your strengths?** They're looking for qualities here, such as honesty and dependability. Illustrate with a brief example of how that quality benefits others or served you well in a previous job.

- **What are your weaknesses? How have you worked to overcome them?** Turn a negative into a positive. Choose some trait or behavior that you have conquered, such as a fear of public speaking, and explain how you addressed it.

- **What do you know about the community?** Here's where your homework comes into play. Think about working and living there. You should know about the challenges of firefighting in the community as well as the opportunities, such as active civic groups serving the area and desirable neighborhoods in which to raise a family.

- **What are your goals with the fire service?** Give some thought to where you want to be in the future, and consider the qualities and skills you bring to the profession. Whether you want to move up in the ranks or place more importance on community outreach, your answers and reasons will give the panel information about your character and motivation.

- **How do you expect to spend free time on your shift once all equipment is serviced?** Think about how studying for advancement, getting in some exercise, or joining a pickup basketball game with your comrades highlight your skills and ambitions. Consider both personal growth and department benefits in your answer. The truth is, however, as a probationary firefighter, you may not have free time: You will be expected to learn about all the equipment and where it is stored, spend time cleaning and cooking, and go out on calls. But if you spent a lot of time with a grandparent as a child, for example, and would enjoy helping to educate senior citizens on fire-safety issues or install smoke detectors in their homes, let the interviewers know.

- **Why would we select you over other candidates?** A question like this can trip up a job candidate who was raised to be humble—this may be particularly true for female candidates. Think about your strengths and what they bring to the department. What about your goals and ambitions? How will your unique life experiences benefit your new firefighting family?

- **How do you handle conflict?** In many departments firefighters live together for 24-hour shifts. They sleep in common quarters and are called to emergencies while people may be in conflict with others. Something as simple as sitting down to watch a television show is complicated by the number of people who might disagree on the program. Think about a situation in which you had to employ diplomacy, particularly in a work setting, and were successful. Be sure to include the happy conclusion in your answer, particularly if the result was lasting.

- **What do you consider your greatest accomplishment in life?** This question presents an excellent opportunity to talk about perseverance. If your achievement is winning a competition, remember, it's the journey that counts.

- **Why did you leave your last job/what do you think of your last boss?** Whatever your answer, don't trash talk anyone. You didn't work for an ogre; you had a boss who kept you to tight deadlines. Because of him or her, you learned to work that much more efficiently. You did not work in hell—it was a demanding and fast-paced environment. You feel strongly, however, that it is time to apply the skills you learned there—list them!—to a career in firefighting. Keep your answer positive. Were you fired from your last job? The panel probably knows that, and likely knows the reason. So what have you learned from the experience?

- **What is your greatest failure? What did you learn from it?** This is similar to a question about a weakness. Again, the second part of that question, the learning experience, is crucial. Remember to include evidence of personal growth.

You may also be faced with scenario questions such as the following:

- **You must choose between rescuing your partner or an infant from a burning building. What do you do?** Your first priority is saving lives. If you make a judgment call based on triage, you will save the victim most likely to survive. Remember to explain your answers, because the panel is also evaluating your reasoning.

- **You see a firefighter taking something from another firefighter's locker; what do you do?** Do you approach him or her? Do you tell the owner of the locker what you saw? Do you report the other firefighter to your superior?

- **You are talking to a fellow firefighter in the station and smell alcohol on his or her breath; what do you do?** Do you look away? Go straight to the captain? Or talk with the other firefighter, diplomatically, to understand what is happening?

- **Male firefighters want you to help play a prank on a female firefighter; what do you do?** This could also be posed as a racial question. The panel won't condone sexual harassment or racism, so answer accordingly.

Though your answers are important, remember that firefighters work as a team. You need the right skills and abilities, but the panel also wants to find a job candidate who will work well within the department. Exhibit diplomacy, sensitivity, and honesty.

You may also be asked questions that deal with the hours or specific actions of firefighting. Consider the following questions as you prepare for your interview:

- How many hours of sleep do you need?
- How do you deal with panic? How do you help others who are panicking?
- How do you feel about working with a team? Do you prefer working alone?
- Are you afraid of heights?
- How do you feel about irregular work schedules?
- What would you do with your life if you became disabled?

No matter who poses the question or what the topic of the question is, you should always respond honestly during your oral interview. Don't just tell the oral board what they want to hear—tell them what you would *really* do in the situations presented to you and how you *actually* feel about the controversial issues or moral dilemmas they introduce into the conversation. The board comprises many respectable people who will be able to tell when you're being honest with them and true to yourself.

Prepare for the Oral Interview

Review all your answers on the application and anything else you have submitted for this job. Your interviewers will have this information and you don't want to contradict yourself in the oral interview.

> **Tip:** Think carefully about any trouble spots: The panel will also know about any brushes with the law, for example, and you should expect to be asked about them. This is not the time to become defensive. Were you fired from a previous job? Did you quit school due to financial troubles? How have you overcome these stumbles, and what have you learned from them?

Learn about the community, going beyond the geography of it to learn about the people. Is the area home to a high percentage of elderly residents, with possible medical and mobility problems? Are first responders likely to encounter drug abusers or other types of criminal activities on calls? Where might firefighters have to navigate neighborhoods of tightly packed apartments, sprawling subdivisions with few street signs, or areas without water lines? Is the community prone to brush fires, flooding, or tornadoes?

If you have served as a volunteer firefighter, you should have developed your firefighting skills and ability to work as a team. Even without firefighting experience, you can get a feel for the day-to-day responsibilities of firefighters by getting to know some, asking questions, and spending time at a fire station if it's permitted. Think about these subjects as you talk to firefighters:

- What's a typical day on the job?
- What motivated them to join the fire force?
- What challenges have they faced on the job?
- What advice do they have for firefighter candidates?
- What do they find most rewarding about their jobs?

If you don't have much experience working with others, consider volunteering. Firefighters often participate in public-safety programs or speak to students, youth groups, and civic groups. Community teamwork and mentoring children should be advantages: You want to serve the community, after all.

Public-speaking courses will also help you present yourself well in the interview and again later in public-outreach activities.

Ask someone you trust to conduct a practice interview. He or she can evaluate your body language and let you know if you speak too quickly or say "umm" or "like" when you're thinking. You can also practice speaking in front of a mirror. It may be unsettling, but you can focus on being still and calm.

> **Tip:** Take a calming breath before answering. It gives you a few seconds to think about what you want to say and will help you remember to speak clearly, without rushing. It also gives you time to be sure you have heard the entire question.

If you have access to a video camera (remember your cell phone may have this feature), sit down with a list of sample questions and answer them, and then review your answers, noting any fidgets or bad speaking habits.

Tip: In some departments, you may be called for a video-based test. These standardized tests are used to observe and assess judgment and interpersonal skills. Candidates may be alone in a room and videotaped as they respond to prerecorded scenarios. A panel reviews the responses later. Some agencies may even substitute the video-based testing for an oral panel interview. Prior practice recording answers may help calm the nerves that such a situation could trigger.

Take notes on the questions you had trouble answering, and think about how you can improve them.

Remember to answer open-ended questions completely. Don't ramble, however. When you have given a complete answer, stop talking. There is a limit to this interview, after all.

How to Present Yourself

Dress to impress and show up looking like the right man or woman for the job. Follow these grooming guidelines for a top-notch first impression:

- Get a good, conservative haircut. Men need not go super short.
- Shower.
- Shave (this is a firefighting safety issue, and though mustaches *may* be permitted on the job, it's better to go in smooth).
- Brush your teeth.
- Clean your nails and trim them neatly.
- Spit out chewing gum.
- Cover tattoos, if possible.
- Remove distracting piercings, if possible.
- Dress conservatively. This is not the time or place for an edgy tie or stiletto pumps. You want to join a structured, top-down organization: This is the time to show up in "uniform" and let the panel see you will fit right in. Here are some specific suggestions:
  - Men should choose a wool suit in dark blue or gray. Muted pinstripes are okay. Wear a solid or conservative striped tie and a long-sleeved starched shirt: white, off-white, or pale blue, but no patterns. Limit jewelry to a nice watch. Skip the cologne.
  - Women should also choose a tailored business suit or conservative dress with a jacket. Stick with solids: gray, navy, black, beige, or camel. Wool and linen are your best bets. Wear neutral stockings and carry a spare pair of hose. Shoes should have practical heels. Hair should be neatly styled and off the face, and jewelry should be minimal and conservative. Use fragrance lightly if at all.
  - Shine your shoes.

Look the interviewers in the eye and smile as you enter the room. Firmly shake hands. Greet everyone warmly and respectfully. Here are some suggestions for saying all the right things with body language:

- **Make eye contact.** If that makes you very uncomfortable, focus close to the person's eyes. Remember to blink, and glance at other interviewers as well, regardless of who asked the question.
- **Sit up straight.** Pay attention to your posture and face forward.
- **Lean forward.** Lean a little toward the interviewers; you will appear interested. Don't lean back.
- **Feet on the floor.** Don't tap your toes or swing your legs.
- **Don't create barriers.** If the chair has armrests, use them. If not, keep your arms outside your torso. You don't want to create a barrier between your body and your interviewers. Barriers such as crossed arms or legs can suggest defensiveness.
- **Don't fidget, change position frequently, or touch your hair.** These actions suggest, among other things, anxiety, boredom, dishonesty, or nervousness. None of that describes you, right?

After the Interview

The panel may ask if you have any questions. This is a signal that your interview is coming to an end. If you still have a question, ask it; otherwise, don't prolong the interview. You've made your best impression, don't ruin it or take up more than your allotted time. Don't ask them when you will learn the results of the interviews, either.

Remain calm as you finish that stellar interview. Thank the panel for meeting with you, and shake hands all around again. Thank the receptionist, tell the security guard to have a great afternoon, and leave with your head high and a smile on your face.

Once outside, resist the urge to high-five everyone you see. Save the celebration for home. Keep your game face on until you are far away from the interview site. Panel members could be looking out the window as you leave, and that is not the time to spit on the sidewalk and light up a cigarette, is it?

Send Thank-You Notes

Take a few minutes later to write a short note thanking the panel for considering you. This note displays professionalism and puts your name in front of them again. It also shows initiative, regardless of how the interview went.

If possible, write individual notes to each member of the panel. Some candidates learn who will be interviewing them before their appointments. If not, your friendly treatment of the receptionist could be repaid if you politely ask for the correct spellings of panel members' names following the interview.

Keep a friendly but formal tone, and don't try to "fix" any interview answer you think you fumbled—you don't want to remind them of anything negative.

Use a professional-looking card or standard paper. Mail the notes within 48 hours of your interview. Remember that faxes get misplaced and e-mail may end up in a spam folder, but mail makes a good impression. A handwritten note is also more likely to be remembered.

Take a look at the following thank-you note tips:

- Address the recipient respectfully: Mr. Jones, Ms. Smith.
- Express your thanks for the interview and the opportunity, stating the position you are seeking. You might mention something about the fire department that interests you, for example, increased medical training, a mentorship program, or specialized rescue teams ("It was a pleasure to discuss the department and in particular . . .").
- Remind them, briefly, of your qualifications ("As we discussed, I have doubled the number of new volunteers with my company, and recently received certification for . . .").
- Is there some critical information that didn't come up in the interview? Add a sentence or two about it and why it's relevant.
- State again that you appreciate the time this person took to interview you.
- Indicate that you are looking forward to hearing from them—you can't wait to hear about this job, right?
- Close with "sincerely" or "respectfully" and sign it legibly.

Proofread the thank-you note, have a trusted friend proofread the thank-you note, and mail it as soon as possible.

Analyze Your Performance

While the memories are fresh, jot down some notes about what you think went well and where you believe you fell short.

In many departments, candidates sit for a qualifying interview, and some will be invited to participate in a selection interview. Consider any questions you feel you did not answer well and think about a better way to express yourself on these subjects. You may face an entirely new set of questions in the next interview, but the process of answering them is much the same: Focus on character and personal growth.

If you, like many job candidates, are applying to multiple departments, evaluate each interview to improve your skills and better prepare for the next.

Appendix C

The Medical and Psychological Exams

The physical and mental demands of a career in firefighting are among the highest of any profession. Firefighters place themselves in perilous situations requiring both physical fitness and mental stability. Risking your own life to potentially save the lives of others is a serious challenge that often pushes you to your mental and physical limits—and sometimes beyond. For this reason, fire departments require job candidates to pass a number of different tests to ensure that they have what it takes to succeed on the job.

Firefighter candidates must complete a written exam, a physical test, and an oral interview. If you successfully complete all three of these requirements, a fire department may grant you a conditional offer of employment. Simply put, this means that you are guaranteed a position on the condition that you pass both a medical exam and a psychological exam.

The medical exam and psychological exam are designed to help the fire department ensure that you, as a potential firefighter, are physically and mentally healthy enough for the job. Specifically, they need to know whether you have any medical conditions or mental issues that might prevent you from doing your job properly and safely. To this end, you will be asked to undergo a series of medical and psychological exams. Once you pass these tests, you have cleared the final hurdle on your path to becoming a firefighter.

You should have discussed your health with your doctor before training for and taking the physical test (see Appendix A). If your doctor discovered any treatable conditions, such as high blood pressure, follow up after undergoing treatment to ensure that you're in fine form for the next step in the process.

In this section, we will guide you through the medical and psychological examinations. Although there is no way to study or otherwise prepare for these exams, it's helpful to know what to expect.

The Medical Exam

The medical exam used to screen firefighter candidates is similar to many other medical exams. Some departments may require a more in-depth physical, but here's a look at the basics.

The doctor will ask for a complete medical history, and you will likely be asked to fill out a form. This paperwork should request any information you have about known medical conditions, such as allergies. It will also ask you to list surgical procedures you have undergone and medications that you're taking. You will probably be asked to complete a family medical history, a reproductive history, and an occupational history as well.

The physician examining you will record statistics such as height, weight, blood pressure, and body temperature. He or she may check your eyes, ears, nose, and mouth as well as listen to your heart and lungs. The doctor is looking for signs of disease or infection, erratic heartbeats, and other irregularities that may be symptoms of problems.

All this information helps the doctor establish your Medical Base Line (MBL), which is a measure of how your body functions and appears when healthy. The MBL may also be used to determine future changes that you need to make if you wish to work as a firefighter.

Tip: Remember to allow the doctor to make his or her decision about your health. Don't be discouraged because you have a preexisting condition. Though you may be concerned about a health issue, many conditions, such as hypertension, may be controlled by medication or through a simple procedure. Doctors evaluate your health to determine whether any condition would prevent you from fulfilling your duties as a firefighter. They don't disqualify you for having a minor medical condition.

Because of the Americans with Disabilities Act (ADA), it is illegal for departments to screen candidates for medical conditions early in the hiring process. Once you receive a conditional offer of employment, however, any health issue that would hinder your ability to perform the work required of a firefighter could disqualify you. Some departments allow candidates to sign exclusionary forms for certain medical problems or disabilities. This means that the candidate could never collect a pension if the condition caused the firefighter to be medically retired. The candidate may be able to submit medical records showing he or she can work as a firefighter.

Medical exam results may not be available for several weeks. Blood and urine samples, for instance, will be sent to a lab for processing. You have to be patient.

The following sections provide more information about tests and examinations you may encounter in a medical exam.

Heart

A physician typically checks your pulse and listens to your heart using a stethoscope. He or she may also send you for a cardiac stress test or electrocardiogram (ECG) for a more complete picture of your heart health.

An ECG records the electrical activity of the heart. A technician attaches electrodes to your skin as you rest; the electrodes pick up information as your heart beats. The doctor looks at the recorded activity, which is usually a series of wavy lines on paper or on a screen, and interprets the results.

A cardiac stress test checks blood flow to the heart while you are active. Though you will have electrodes attached to your skin for this test as well, you will walk on a treadmill. As the intensity of your exercise increases, the doctor will check your blood pressure and pulse. After you stop walking, you will lie down until your cardiac activity returns to normal. You'll be unhooked from the sensors and a doctor will look at the results. Depending on the type of stress test your doctor wishes to administer, the experience may last anywhere from a half-hour to three and a half hours.

Lungs

Physicians use spirometry, or pulmonary function tests, to determine your lung function. The Occupational Safety and Health Administration (OSHA) requires spirometry testing for all employees who use respirators on the job. Firefighters use SCBAs, or self-contained breathing apparatuses, for their air supply while fighting fires and must have healthy lungs.

A doctor will have you inhale deeply and then exhale into a spirometer. You will probably be asked to exhale forcefully for as long as possible, and may be asked to breathe normally into the spirometer as well.

The tests measure your forced vital capacity (FVC), the volume of air your lungs can exhale, and other measures your doctor will use to determine your lung function.

Blood and Urine

You may have to submit a urine sample during your physical exam and have blood drawn. Some lab tests that may be ordered include cholesterol, blood glucose, anemia, HIV/AIDS, hepatitis, and cancer screenings.

Your samples may also be screened for illicit drug use. Your conditional offer of employment will probably be revoked if you test positive for illicit drugs—using such substances puts you, your comrades, and the public at risk.

Hernias

Doctors usually check a subject's organs and look for hernias during a physical exam. Hernias occur when an organ pushes through an opening or weak spot in a muscle, tissue, or membrane. Hernias are common in the abdomen and groin. The most common type is the inguinal hernia, located low in the abdomen.

In men, the inguinal canal is where the spermatic cord passes between the abdomen and scrotum. A man is usually instructed to turn his head and cough while a doctor checks for lumps above the scrotum.

In women, the inguinal canal is the opening through which the ligament that holds the uterus in place passes. A doctor checks for hernias by pressing on a woman's organs and looking for bumps.

Most hernias may be repaired through surgery and could result in a temporary disqualification from becoming a firefighter. A doctor may note a small hernia and recommend simply watching it for changes.

Reproductive and Urinary

In both male and female candidates, a doctor will check the kidneys, ureters, bladder, and urethra.

Doctors will probably check men for several conditions of the urinary system and reproductive organs:

- **Prostate gland problems:** Issues such as enlargement of the prostate
- **Testicular mass:** A lump on the testes
- **Epididymal mass:** A lump on the epididymis, the coiled tube that connects ducts on the testicle to the vas deferens

Doctors will likely check women for several conditions including gynecological issues:

- **Pregnancy:** Know the first day of your last period as well as your pregnancy history, including the number of pregnancies, live births, and miscarriages
- **Dysmenorrhea:** Severe pelvic pain during menstruation
- **Ovarian cysts:** Fluid-filled sacs within ovaries
- **Endometriosis:** Painful growths of endometrial tissue outside the uterus

Conditions such as pregnancy may result in temporary disqualification. Doctors may determine other conditions that are not severe enough to interfere with the duties of firefighting or may be corrected through various procedures such as surgery.

Vision

Vision exams usually include eye charts and other tests to determine whether you fit within the department's vision standards. Other tests will check for various conditions:

- **Eye conditions/disorders:** For example, cataracts, glaucoma, conjunctivitis, or retinal disorders or detachments.
- **Peripheral vision:** What you can see from the corners of your eyes when looking straight ahead.
- **Colorblindness:** The inability to distinguish between some colors is usually disqualifying. Firefighters must have color vision when using imaging devices, such as thermal image scanners.

Hearing

Doctors will check for ear infections and will probably conduct a hearing test using an audiometer. This device measures how well you hear tones.

For these tests you will wear headphones and indicate when you hear tones. These tones will test your hearing at various pitches.

Muscular and Skeletal

Physicians usually check for conditions such as arthritis, fractures, dislocations, and muscle strains. Conditions that heal over time, such as muscle strains, usually won't disqualify you for a job as a firefighter.

Recurring injuries, such as repeated dislocation of a bone, or conditions that will worsen over time, such as arthritis, may disqualify candidates. Again, doctors determine the severity of the condition and its potential to affect your ability to perform your duties.

Doctors also may look for signs of deformity and check your range of motion in your back, neck, skull, spine, limbs, and extremities.

Gastrointestinal and Glandular

The endocrine system regulates your body by releasing hormones. Glands including the thyroid and adrenal gland and organs such as the kidneys and liver are included in the endocrine system. A doctor will decide whether a condition such as hyperthyroidism or diabetes disqualifies a candidate.

The doctor will also check for some common gastrointestinal conditions and, if they are present, determine whether the severity merits disqualification:

- **Gastritis:** Inflammation of the stomach lining
- **Inflammatory bowel disease:** Inflammation of the colon and small intestine
- **Ulcers:** Open sores that can form inside and outside the body, caused by a puncture in the skin or mucous membrane that cannot heal
- **Obstructions:** Can occur within the small or large intestine or in the bowel when gastrointestinal secretions accumulate and mix with swallowed air

The Psychological Exam

For most of us, sitting down with a psychologist or psychiatrist or filling out a personality questionnaire may seem intimidating.

The psychological exam is not designed to uncover your deepest, darkest secrets. It's meant to determine if you have the right personality to join the department and if you're mentally prepared for the stress you will encounter as a firefighter.

Some departments require a more in-depth examination. Others are content with a basic personality test. You may meet with a psychologist or psychiatrist.

Whether in a written exam or a face-to-face meeting, be honest. Don't answer questions the way you think the department wants them answered. Mental-health professionals are trained to detect dishonesty.

The Personality Questionnaire

Questions on the personality test are designed to evaluate your attitude, interests, and motivations, among other aspects of your personality. Some include hundreds of questions and take hours to complete; if so, the test administrator will tell you how much time you have to take the test. Most departments will have you take a standardized test, such as the Minnesota Multiphasic Personality Inventory (MMPI).

One commonly used version of the MMPI scores on 10 clinical scales that measure such traits as disobedience, intelligence, self-concept, obsessions, and introversion. The test also scores on validity scales, which measure a person's attitude and approach to taking tests. The validity scales are often referred to as the lie scale; the faking scale; the defensiveness scale; and the "cannot say" scale, which refers to items not answered. There are also two consistency scales and a scale that may indicate questions were answered randomly, as though the test subject lost interest or didn't try. Though a computer usually scores the results, a psychologist with MMPI training interprets them.

Some tests ask you to rank your feelings about a topic or how you would react to situations. You may also encounter multiple-choice or true/false questions. Many tests check for consistency by asking the same question in different ways.

Don't try to analyze the question. It's usually best to read it through and go with your initial answer. The test is designed to compare your responses to those of successful firefighters to see if you have the personality traits needed to succeed in this career.

Consider some of the characteristics of successful firefighters:

- Flexible in thinking
- Self-motivated
- Empathetic and supportive of others
- Maintains pleasant and effective working relationships with peers and superiors
- Works well as part of a team
- Willing to accept constructive criticism

- Innovative
- Dependable
- Organized
- Sensible
- Calm in stressful situations and emergencies
- Able to work well with little or no supervision
- Follows the chain of command
- Makes safety a priority
- Treats all people with dignity and respect, regardless of race, gender, or any cultural differences

The Psychological Interview

If you are required to meet with a psychologist or psychiatrist, relax. He or she will probably ask questions about your family relationships and personal history, or ask you to talk more about specific answers you chose in the personality questionnaire. Your reasons for some of your answers will help the psychologist understand your personality and how you are likely to cope with stress.

You may also be asked about incidents that came up in your background check. Remember that it's best to be honest, accept responsibility for your actions, and show how you've learned from any past mistakes.

You may be asked only a few questions. If your answers are consistent with those on the personality questionnaire, the psychologist may have little need to go further. Following are a few examples of the types of questions you may be asked:

- What do you like to do in your spare time?
- How do you react to criticism?
- Why are you interested in a career in firefighting?
- How do you describe yourself?

You prepared for the oral interview by learning to listen to and answer questions (see Appendix B). This is another type of interview—without the added stress of facing a panel! If you are scheduled to sit down with a psychologist, draw upon the skills you developed earlier and keep a few thoughts in mind:

- **Be honest.** As mentioned earlier, your reasons are as important as the answers you give. The psychologist has seen the results of the personality questionnaire already and may be interested in your thinking.
- **Relax.** In any interview, take a deep breath and remain calm. You are interviewing for a high-stress career in firefighting; answering a few questions shouldn't tax your nerves much in comparison.
- **Answer the question.** First, remember to listen to the question. Then think before you speak. Ask for clarification if you aren't sure you understand the question. Stick to the question asked, answer it as well as you are able, and don't volunteer additional information.
- **Go with your gut.** It's pointless to second-guess the reason you are being asked a question.

NOTES

NOTES